MW01274396

I dedicate this book

May your generation be as fruitful as ours
... and even better.

And to my generation ... 'We did it, man!'

Enjoy the Read,

J. Htl

Night of The Sun

ISBN 978-1-304-62767-4

Mike McAndrew

Night of The Sun

"In war, truth is the first casualty."

Aeschylus   525 - 456 BC

Night of The Sun

ISBN 978-1-304-62767-4

Mike McAndrew

Night of The Sun

"In war, truth is the first casualty."

Aeschylus   525 - 456 BC

Night of The Sun

ISBN 978-1-304-62767-4

Mike McAndrew

Night of The Sun

"In war, truth is the first casualty."

Aeschylus   525 - 456 BC

Contents

Part 1

1	In the Beginning	1
2	Tiffin, Ohio	38
3	Charlie	49
4	A Day of Infamy	58
5	Winona	69

Part 2

1	Summer of 1966	83
2	The Road Trip	94
3	San Francisco	107
4	Mark	115
5	Winona	118
6	Protest and Acid	128
7	1967	135
8	Denver	163
9	Back to Winona	169
10	1969	185

Part 3

1	Drafted	187
2	Indicted ... Run You Bastard	199
3	Bum Fuck, Utah	203

4   San Francisco   208
5   The Monastery   214
6   Babylon Jungle   227
7   Chicago ... My Kinda Town   243
8   Madison   250
9   1970   263
10 May 1970   278
11 Madison   293
12 Oh! Canada   303
13 1971   316
14 Boston, New York, Maine,
    Nova Scotia?   355
15 Carol and San Francisco   374
16 Hiding Out in Amerika   383
17 1972   384
18 Ladysmith   400
19 Madison Redux   421
20 Where to Next   434
21 1973   438
22 Night of The Sun   443
23 The Long Way Home   460

Epilogue   472

Addendum   480

Acknowledgments   481

Prologue

To understand the 60's one must understand the 50's. To understand the 50's one needs to understand the 40's, and so on.

Both of my parents were born in the early 20's perhaps recalling some sense of economic stability.

Then the 30's came along. My parents were teenagers then and they vividly remembered going without.

The 40's ensued and the Big War. WWII. I recall my mom telling me that half the boys from her high school senior class never came back.

My parents formative years were years of struggle, pain, and great sacrifice.

Returning from the war the 'Greatest Generation' received the GI Bill, lived in a booming economy and rebuilt their lives. Homes were dirt cheap, interest rates low and my parents generation started having babies at a record rate.

My generation, the 'Baby Boomers' lived off the fat of the lamb. Some say we were spoiled and pampered, perhaps we were. We became the healthiest and best educated generation America had ever seen. We grew up in homes with all the major appliances and TV. We were the first TV generation, growing up watching *Leave it to Beaver*, *Lassie*, *Walt Disney*, and the like. But we also had a sense that these programs were false prophets. Life wasn't really like this. We began to question. We questioned authority.

We wanted our own music, our own fashions, our own identity. Movies like *Rebel without a Cause* and *The Wild One* and books like *Catcher in the Rye* and *On the Road* dusted the air of our group consciousness. Elvis cinched it! He broke the ice. He threatened every aspect of 'normal' life in the 50's. The older generation was scared shitless by him. "Turn that shit off," my father yelled when Elvis was on the *Ed Sullivan Show*. 'Turn that shit off' ... but we turned that shit on. The sexual undertones of swiveling hips, the long hair and sideburns. It was us. It belonged to us. The Baby Boomers had a hero and a 'look.'

The evil, hateful Senator McCarthy and his witch hunt for alleged Communists. They were hiding under our beds. Even us kids knew it was bullshit!

Eisenhower and his early warnings about 'The Industrial-Military Complex.' We were smart kids. Most of us got it, as they say.

The 'Be Bop Jazz' that played incessantly at my house, the books we read, ... somehow, we knew that half the stuff they were teaching us was bullshit. We sensed it in our very souls.

The Beatles blew the lid off!
All we really wanted was the truth.

This saga is all true. All of these events occurred. Let the reader know that; most of the events in Parts 1 and 2 are accurate as far as I remember and are written like a verbal scrapbook with little snippet stories.

Part 3 is different. For the sake of the story, some characters and situations are a compilation.

I've omitted several people or used false names because I didn't want to jeopardize their current status.

I did resist the draft, I did live under aliases, I did deliver packages for the underground, I never injured or physically harmed anyone, I was arraigned with a 42 count indictment, and I was pardoned by Jimmy Carter.

Our motto was, 'Don't trust anyone over 30.' I still don't and I'm 65 as of this printing.

and moved aside as Rad and I and walked away.

Boy, was I in for it now. But, when I got back to class it was as if nothing had happened. Don't know who the kid was but he wasn't in this class. Found out later he was a 7th grader and a bully. Noon recess came and I brought my own lunch so I could sit outside. A bunch of kids were tossing a football around and I asked if I could join in. "Sure." They all wanted to test the new kid anyway. They chose up sides and I was picked last. Didn't care. Within a minute I proved my salt by catching a touchdown pass from a lefty named Joe. We would become friends later on. Rad didn't play sports.

After school that afternoon the same kid that I beat up on the play ground was waiting for me down the street. He had two friends with him. I walked up to him and hit him five or six times and kicked the shit out of him. When I turned to see what his friends would do they had run down the street.

Guess I had a lot of rage in those days. He never bothered me again.

Before we'd left Rice Lake, in 1959, Dad and I had gone to the high school games. Football and Basketball. I remember a couple of Friday night football games and us kids just ran around. Didn't even watch the game. But it was great fun. But the basketball games were a different matter. Had to sit in your seat. It would have been pretty boring had it not been for a junior player named Pete Hugdahl. I saw him score over 40 points one night! He was amazing and my hero. We found out where he lived and watched from across the street as he shot hoops at his basket on his garage. Well, Rice Lake had a good team and almost made it to the State Tournament in Madison that year. Then, of course we moved to Ohio. The 1961 Rice Lake Warriors, led by Hugdahl and a kid named Freeze, we all called him 'Foster Freeze,' made it all the way to the championship game before losing to Milwaukee Lincoln in double overtime 77-75. It was their only loss of the season. My parents kept in contact with people in Rice Lake and we found out the score the next week. Mom received a copy of the *Rice Lake Chronotype* with all the pictures and stories.

I deeply regretted missing all of that.

Pete Hugdahl went on to the Air Force Academy and led that team in scoring for two years. He was the best high school player I ever saw.

The sixth grade drudged on. Mass every morning. Dough nuts and chocolate milk. 70 some boys crammed in a classroom. Every day was the same. One hour on each subject. As an elective I chose to sign up with the 'Little Singers.' A group of boys who sang at all the church functions and special events at the school. We wore altar boy garb and practiced two nights a week. All the popular boys were in the choir and we performed

with the men's choir. We learned all these difficult Latin hymns and Grego-
rian Chants. My voice was still a soprano and I could hit those high notes.
My mom said we sounded great in church. But, it was more of a way to
escape the house at night and hang out with my new friends. I made some
great new friendships in those days. Always being invited to birthday parties and after school pick-up games of basketball or football. As the winter
came on I began to shovel sidewalks for store owners downtown. We lived
a block away from downtown anyway, so I told the merchants I would
shovel their walk in the morning on my way to school and if need be, hit it
again on my way home after school. Many mornings after a flurry I would
bring a big scoop shovel with me on my way to school and shovel 6 or 7
different businesses. I could store the shovel in my locker. I made 50 cents
each time I shoveled a walk and before long was able to pay my mom back
the $20 I owed her plus invest another $20 into my coin collecting venture.
It snowed often that winter and was able to amass a small fortune. I had almost $100 in savings and always had money on me. Dad called me 'money
bags' and 'Moose' because I was growing like a weed.

Tim and I were out riding our bikes one day. We saw a mailbox with
the name 'Seagrits' on it. For some reason, we thought that was hysterical.
We decided to give my brother John a new nickname. He was 'Seagrits'
from now on.

John hated it, so the more he protested, the more we called him that.
The nickname stuck for years.

Mary was 'Irma,' Becky was 'Zuch,' Tim was 'Spitstavick,' and I was
'Moose.'

Dad wanted me to play Little League Baseball in the summer. I was so
scared I said I didn't want to but he insisted. One spring day in Tiffin they
had the try-outs and I showed up with all these people there and I was terrified! They called my name to bat and I hit one ball after another. I don't
think I ever hit one ball for an out because the crowd cheered me on until
they called up the next batter.

Then we had fielding. I wanted to play third base (my hero Eddie
Mathews played third) so they hit grounders to me. I didn't miss one ball
and was able to throw to first base okay. Then they had a sprint race and I
finished first in that.

They held a draft and I was chosen first by the Coca Cola team. Several kids gathered around me and congratulated me. We began practice
that week and it was apparent we weren't very good. We had a couple of
pitchers who couldn't throw strikes and a catcher who couldn't catch but
we had fun. It was great playing for the Coke team because we had plenty
of cokes to drink. We received our uniforms one day. Worn out wool suits

with red stockings and white pants and jerseys with the Coca Cola logo. The uniform made me itch and break out.

We played all of our games on Tuesday and Thursday nights at the Hedges-Boyer Park. I had never played a night game before and at first, I had difficulty seeing the ball. I struck out a couple of times. We lost badly. We won a couple of games and eventually my eyes adjusted.

The guy who obtained Dad's job for Essex, Jim Kress, and his family came to visit. Among the entourage was Grandma Kress. She was a hoot! Funny and profane. She insisted on watching one of my games. "I'll give you $1 for a single, $2 for a double, $3 for a triple, and $5 for a home run." Wouldn't you know it, I played my best game of the season hitting two singles and a triple. She was so excited I could hear her screaming and cheering when I hit the triple. She was so happy after the game, which we won, that she gave me $10! The highlight of their visit was Mrs. Kress. It was warm and balmy that July and everyone would sit in the back yard and the older folks drank and we had a barbecue. Mrs. Kress told us stories and sang songs to us. I still remember one of her songs sung in a Swedish accent:

"It was vinter
in the valley
and the vind
vistled around
the vindow sill,
and the vomen
in the vaudiville
philosphied around
the vestibule."

The baseball season ended and we won half our games. I continued to play sandlot ball every day with the neighborhood kids. We usually played a morning game and an afternoon game. Boy, was that fun. It was just a couple blocks away and I rode my bike. Tim started coming with me and they let him play. He was so funny. He kept everyone in stitches with his mimes and mimics. He created his own persona ... 'Spitstavick Knutsta-bak.' We all called him 'Spitz.' He would come to the plate and do this weird hilarious Austrian-German accent and call each pitch and play. Now, I was Tim's brother. Which was fine with me. He drew attention off me to him. He was just a crack up. I remained Tim's brother. I was content to fade into the background while Tim relished in the spotlight. I was always so proud of him and never felt envious.

The 7th grade came and went. Same old stuff. Did okay in class get-ting almost all A's. Continued mowing lawns, shoveling snow, building model airplanes, and building my coin collection. It didn't rival Rad's collection but I was getting there. One day I hit it big. It was a Saturday and I picked up $20 worth of dimes. Well, someone must have changed in their collection because I found every dime to fill the book and kept the rest as extras. Rad was jealous because he didn't get anything that day. Our friendship was never the same after that. I'm not sure what really happened. I had more friends than he did and participated in all the school events. I was even in the Boy Scouts for a short time. He only wanted to play board games and he was in fact, the Ohio State Junior Champion in checkers. I only beat him one time when he made a mistake and I was able to win. He was devastated! I wanted to play outside. Basketball and football and baseball. We were quite different.

I was in the Boy Scouts for a couple of months and hated it. The Scout leader was this gung-ho guy and his kid was a bully. We didn't really do anything except recite the Scout Pledge and then goof around. But, there was a camping trip coming up. It was in the fall and very cold and icy. We all drove to this lodge and slept inside. We made a fire and ate hot dogs and stayed up late. Everyone had a farting contest later that night. That was fun. The next morning we were to hike in pairs on different routes and meet at a designated spot. We would get our maps in the morning.

We rose to the smell of pancakes and eggs. Yum! We had a small meeting and drew names out of hat to pick our partner. My partner was one of the top athletes in the eighth grade and he just stared at me when I chose his name. He wanted to partner up with his buddy but he got me instead. Well, he was the boss and we set out on our route. The trails were marked so it wasn't hard to find it. It was to be a ten mile hike through the woods of Ohio. He wouldn't even talk to me at first but after a bit he warmed up and we talked about sports and girls. He was a really handsome Italian guy and must of had all the girls swooning. We were about halfway through our trek when he wanted to take a shortcut. I said okay. We started to cross a frozen marsh. I was right behind him when the ice cracked and he fell in over his head. He bobbed back up and I quickly grabbed a tree branch and laid down and he was able to grab it and pull himself out. We were only ten feet from the shore. It was cold out and he began to shiver. I said I should build a fire and he just nodded. Thank God I had matches on me and I was able to find kindling to start a fire. He was soaking wet. Soon, the fire was substantial and he began to warm but he was soaking wet. I suggested taking all his clothes off and he could wear my jacket. At first he resisted but the fire was warm now and he first took off his shoes and socks and I hung them near the fire. Then he took off his pants. He was turning blue and shivering really hard. I knew that by now we were late in our meet with the other scouts but I had to thaw this guy out first. His socks and shoes were warm but still wet and his pants had a long way to go. I put my coat over him and it seemed to help. The shirt had to come off next. He huddled in close to the fire. I scampered around adding more wood. It was ablaze and very warm. I just had a shirt and hat on but I was moving a lot so I was warm. I was hoping the others would come looking for us and that they would see the smoke from the fire. It was getting on in the afternoon and soon it would be dark. I thought of making a lean-to so I began gathering some timbers and propping then up. This kept the heat in and before long the socks were dry and his pants were warm and his shirt was steaming. He never took his underwear off though. Modesty.

It was now dark and we talked about finishing the hike. He was weak and still cold. His lips weren't as blue anymore and his clothes were almost dry. We had a flashlight but trying to hike at night is risky. I had continued enclosing the lean-to and it was quit cozy. Every fifteen minutes I had to gather more wood and it was becoming harder and harder to find more. I didn't think I could keep a fire going all night and I began to get scared that they wouldn't find us.

Well, we were talking now! "Let's walk out of here ... I'm okay now," he said. So off we trekked. He led the way and I followed. Every so often one of us would yell out. No response. After, what seemed like an hour, one of us yelled out and we got an answer. They had been looking for us but didn't know where we were because we had taken the shortcut! Back in safe hands and warming up in a car my new friend praised my actions. I got a pin for it.

But the scouts weren't for me. Too many rules and regulations.

At home there were five kids and Mom was pregnant. Paul was born in December and he was premature. Us kids couldn't even visit him in the hospital. Dad told us he probably wouldn't live long and that he had to stay in the hospital. He was there a long time but they eventually permitted me to view him in the 'Preemie' room. Looking at this baby through glass. He could fit in a shoebox and they had all these tubes stuck in him. It was surreal!

But, he did survive. Mom brought him home one day and all of us kids just fawned over him. He was so tiny. We had to wear masks over our faces when near him because his lungs weren't fully developed and he couldn't catch a cold. Mom set up a special section in their bedroom with a crib and a cloth draped over his crib and a ventilator. He coughed a lot. Poor little guy. He did start to grow and it was apparent that there was something wrong with him. He didn't react like the rest of us. He just sort of stared into space. He didn't laugh or cry or play with his toys hanging in the crib. I asked Mom and she just shook her head. Mom was sad. This is about the time I noticed Mom drinking a lot during the day. Dad was gone now almost every week day. Driving to Pennsylvania to Kentucky to Illinois.

He would call every other night. "I'm in Pittsburgh ... see you on Friday. How's school? Let me talk to your mom."

That meant I had to find Mom, and if she had been drinking all day, I had to wake her up and tell her Dad was on the phone. She was usually in pretty bad shape each evening in those days and I could hear Mom slurring her words and upset. The thing is, both my parents were drinking heavily in those days. The rest of the kids were running rampant in the neighborhood. Mom didn't cook anymore so our meals were helter-skelter. I kept busy with my coin collection and sports. The less I was home, the better. Dad would return home and find the house a mess, he would just go crazy and start beating us and make us clean the house.

Those were the days of *Mad Magazine* ... poking fun at and satirizing everything and everyone. The two spies ... making fun of the Cold War. Taking jibes at movies and actors and politicians. In a word, challenging everything that was 'sacred' and depicting middle class values with satire, humor, and horror.

Unconsciously, I suppose, kids started a rebellion against authority. I attribute much of this shift to *Mad Magazine*. The magazine questioned the shallowness and morality of the fifties and some of us took the message to heart ... which was, 'question authority.' Even the Pope and the President got it.

All in good fun though. But, for the first time in my life, it was okay to make fun of untouchable subjects. Looking back, a new permissiveness crept into society. There were mock spy shows, *I Spy* and *Secret Agent*, *The Beverly Hillbillies*, jabbing at the uptight rich, The *Tonight Show* hosted by Steve Allen who made Jazz and art acceptable.

And, with a new Liberal Catholic President who challenged us to "... ask what you can do for your country." Giving us a new hope and clear vision of peace and prosperity. I don't think I would be exaggerating too much to say that most of my friends, even in staunch Ohio, felt that the future was bright and promising.

But, things began falling apart at home. I was losing my religion while pulling straight A's in school. Both my parents were drunks. I look back now at this jumbled confusing time and wonder how I survived the chaos. I stopped going to Mass in the 8th grade and withstood some ugly stares and confrontational moments from other classmates. I can still remember my last Confession; "bless me Father for I have sinned ..." I told him I had 'touched myself' several times. "How many times?" "I don't know." The priest went on to tell me what a horrible sin that was and that I was cheating God. I was mortified! Did that mean that you only get so much sperm and that if you use up your allotment ... That's what did it for me! If I jack off, I'll go to Hell? Finally, the Monsignor called me into his office one day and grilled me about my beliefs. I told him I simply didn't and couldn't believe in the tall tales of the Catholic teachings. How could I believe in a religion that said a man walked on water? That was preposterous. I told him I believed in the Ten Commandments as a basic code of ethics and The Golden Rule but the rest of the dogma and bullshit ... The one true religion along with the hundreds of other one true religions ... baloney!

He was really pissed off and threatened to have me expelled. I didn't want that. So I made a deal. I would attend the mandatory morning Mass but would not accept the sacrament. I would cease being an altar boy but wanted to remain in the 'Little Singers' choir group. I was number one or two in my class with an A average so I had some leverage. He was a very intimidating man that demanded respect and was used to having his orders followed with no questions. I actually think he liked me and respected me. But, I would get him at the end of the 8th grade on graduation day in the church when my essay on 'What is Faith' was chosen as the winning entry. The Monsignor chose mine over all the others. He had only a number on the essay with no name, so he couldn't have known it was mine. When he drew my number I rose from my seat and walked up to the altar to accept the award and he smiled at me and shook my hand. The audience politely applauded and I took my seat. I had won my point!

More on that later.

Chapter 3

Charlie

Charlie Letterhos was my 8th grade teacher who somehow broke through my shell and respected me as a human. He insisted on being called 'Charlie,' and when he kept me after class a few times he told me I was the best student he'd ever had. Dumb as I was, I believed him. I don't think I was by a long shot, but he gave me some self-esteem ... something that had been stripped by my parents, especially my dad. I could never please him. (After a ball game one night he remarked, "I just drove 200 miles to see you go 1 for 4?" Another time, I showed Dad my report card with all 'A's and he just nodded and handed it back to me. Without a word or comment. No wonder I stuttered. I was traumatized.)

Up to this point, excepting Kindergarten, I had always been taught by a nun. Not only was he a man but he was a layperson; not a member of the clergy.

Charlie was on the surface an easy going laid back guy. But, somehow he knew how to get the most out of his students.

Always dressed in a tweed sports jacket with elbow patches, a dress shirt and tie, sort of a rumpled look, but in a neat appearance, loafers and dress pants, he fit the image of the 'Play Boy,' complete with an ever-going pipe wafting a sweet odor wherever he went.

"Now gentlemen ...," he would drawl in an almost southern accent, "please open your history books to page 167."

He taught every subject except religion which was, of course taught by a priest.

Sometimes Charlie would sit back at his desk and just start talking about something, anything really, suit coat off, tie loosened, pipe smoking away, and just talk to us. He engaged us in conversations about topical subjects; the bomb crisis, the missile crisis with the Russians in Cuba, our interests, "Do any of you have any hobbies?" And we would share and talk about our hobbies. It was his way of reaching us and for us students to really get to know our classmates.

That first week he gave us an assignment to write our autobiographies which would be due near the end of the school year.

He also informed us that our class would produce a play and that every one of us would be contributing to it from stage hands, to set builders, to actors.

He addressed each student as Mr. but he wanted to be addressed as Charlie. He was Charlie.

He put every one at ease. After seven torturous years of strict no-nonsense, no-fun nuns he was a gift. Charlie had a great sense of humor, finding laughs and even mocking some of the other teachers (nuns) and taking time to get the class excited about last night's *Tonight Show* or a book he was reading. It seemed that every day was a pure delight and you didn't want to miss a day because Charlie would come up with something exciting and new.

As I mentioned, he got the most out of us.

Personally, I almost stop stuttering and felt so relaxed in his class. I had made several good friends by now and could hold my own.

He demanded excellence. "Now, Mr. So and So, I know you can do better than that ..." But, he never made you feel bad. He made you want to do better. He would stop and explain things. "Did everyone understand that?" He made it okay to raise your hand and ask a question and say you really didn't understand this or that. He would often ask another student to explain the idea to the wondering student.

"Mr. McAndrew, what is so interesting out there?"

I had been day dreaming staring out the window thinking of I know not what.

"Nothing Charlie, sorry, I was day dreaming."

He stopped the instruction and we talked about day dreaming. When the brain just has to take a break and wander on it's own. I would have been chastised by the nuns for not paying attention. But, Charlie took the opportunity to embrace day dreaming. In an instant we were back to our lesson.

If one of us got in trouble with the Principal, Charlie would go to bat for us often times acting as an arbitrator.

Charlie had a very expressive face. Once I recall the Principal came into our classroom with some kind of proclamation. She was a very stern and angry looking person. Charlie stood behind her rolling his eyes as the nun drawled on. It was all we could do to keep from laughing.

I think that by the end of the school year Charlie had been to every student's house to meet the parents and see where we lived and how we lived.

Charlie Letterhos changed my life. I slowly came out of my shell. It was exciting to learn. For the first time in my life I was able to adequately express myself.

Shortly after the school year began, Charlie announced that we were to begin planning the class play. It was *The Absent Minded Professor*, not the Disney version but another one that had played on Broadway. It was a comedy. We had try-outs for the actors, some of the boys would play women's rolls. We started to spend one afternoon a week in the gym reading our roles with Charlie directing us. I was chosen to play the part of Biff, a college student. I had 70 or more lines to memorize. There were probably 15 acting parts which meant the rest of the class were stage hands, lighting people and prop people. We had several boys painting the sets. We practiced and rehearsed and learned our parts. By November we were meeting on Saturdays. Not all the boys were required to show up but the actors and stage people had to attend.

We had a couple of 'dress rehearsals' and everything went off without a hitch. We had boys standing off stage to feed us lines if we forgot. I was so nervous that I threw up. But, we got through it okay. Charlie made a couple of minor changes and we waited for opening night which was to be during Christmas vacation.

The local newspaper even did a blurb on the play with the cast's picture in the paper.

The big night came. I was scared to death but so was everyone else. The curtain rose and the first act began. I came on about ten minutes into the play. In one of the early scenes an actor playing an old man with a beard is supposed to light a lantern and walk on the set in the dark. He lit his beard on fire instead and ran around the stage yelping as he pulled the fake beard off and stomped on it. He calmly reattached what was left of the smoking thing and recited his next line. He brought down the house.

He was okay with just some minor burns and he had no eyebrows.

I entered with three other 'students' and we got an ovation. Don't know why but we did. Then I recited my first line and then my next line and I was just fine. The nerves were gone.

We had planned to have only three shows but as it turned out the play was a hit and we did seven nights. By the last show we were veterans now and I think our best performance was our last one.

The 'old man' didn't light his beard on fire again. We had to find him another one and it was too dangerous anyway so he used a flashlight.

This was Charlie for you. He brought the entire class on stage after each performance and let us take a bow. Proud parents and family friends and I dare say some theatre fans made us feel like men.

Personally, even my parents noted aloud a vast change in my demeanor. I was gaining my confidence and independence.

About this time my voice changed and I could no longer sing in 'The Little Singers.' I couldn't reach the high notes. I continued to attend morning Mass every school day because I had to but didn't receive Holy Communion. I just about caused a riot the first day I didn't join the line at the altar. I was the only person sitting in a pew. Everyone stared at me and I got some harsh words from other kids but no one could do anything about it. They all assumed, I'm sure, that I had committed some horrible unforgivable sin (a Mortal Sin, no doubt) that even God wouldn't forgive. After a few weeks no one even noticed when I remained in my seat.

If anyone cared to ask me, and several kids did, why I didn't receive Holy Communion, I would tell them that I didn't believe in it anymore. That shocked most of them but a lot of kids really didn't care. I didn't choose to be a rebel and at the same time I didn't like being force-fed ideals and '-isms' that I didn't sit with. ⁏

Spent the rest of Christmas vacation shoveling walks, building model planes and working on the coin collection. I began working on the autobiography that was due before the end of the year.

I asked my mom for help and she gathered old family pictures and I began to form a scrapbook of the images. We had an old typewriter and I started to write some things down. I asked Mom a lot of questions as she filled in the blanks of my early childhood. It was a monumental task but I made notes every day and then attempted to type them out. It was very difficult but I wanted to do the best job I could.

School started up again. I started to realize that I would be entering high school next year and that was intimidating. I didn't play on the 8th grade basketball team because I needed more time to study and work my little part time jobs. I was now cleaning an office downtown on Saturdays and that took all morning but I made a few bucks and could afford more model planes and add to my coin collection.

I had all A's the first semester and wanted to continue on that path. As long as I was near or at the top of my class no one could touch me.

And girls? Maybe because the sexes were separated ... even at recess ... I was afraid of them. I could talk to my mom and my sisters but girls of my own age seemed alien, like from another planet. They seemed more mature and sure of themselves. Some of the other boys had no trouble with girls. They could talk to them. Some of my classmates even walked them home. I would see classmates hanging out downtown talking to girls as I went about my business. I felt like an outcast!

I recall one night Mom had sent me to Marvin's Market to get some milk and I encountered two of the 8th grade girls outside the store. They were smoking cigarettes and they both said, 'Hi, Michael," as I entered the store. I nodded. I purchased the milk and as I left, both girls were still outside. They engaged me in conversation but I was unable to hardly speak. I told them abruptly that I had to get home and they both giggled.

I returned home frustrated and angry at myself.

I worked on the autobiography and the paper, 'What is Faith?' Since we had an endless library at home, I researched several books and found one by St. Thomas Aquinas. I skimmed the book and didn't really understand most of it but found some interesting passages on Faith. He was a philosopher and a great thinker. His insight gave me plenty to think about and plagiarize from. I also found some sources from the public library and the school library. I found that I greatly enjoyed digging up data and facts.

I relied on my mom for most of the research on the autobiography, embellishing here and there and filling in the gaps.

I wanted both papers to be masterpieces. I worked my butt off on both papers, often re-reading and re-writing them until I was at last satisfied. I showed both works to my mom and she made some suggestions. Both works were finished ahead of time.

Some kids hadn't even started on the projects.

I continued to do well in my studies and felt an inner determination to succeed.

At the beginning of the school year envelopes with our names on them were distributed to each student in the school. They were for the weekly donation to the Church. After the Sunday sermon, baskets were passed throughout the congregation and you were expected to donate what you could. A 'tithing' or ten percent of your income was expected. My dad had said he would take care of it so Tim and I never used the envelopes. And since I wasn't attending Sunday Mass anymore, I forgot about it.

The school published a list with all the kids names and amounts donated and of course, Tim and I, were at the bottom of the list with $0.

Charlie didn't say anything and I think he thought that was wrong to publish a list. But Tim was chastised in his class by the nun and several kids gave me shit.

Just another attempt at public humiliation by the Church.

The Catholic Church had a Blacklist of movies and books. I never paid much attention to it until I saw my mom, who was a avid reader, reading *Catcher in the Rye*. That book was on the 'list' and the only reason I noted it was because the priest in religion class had made a big deal about it. Saying it was sinful to read such literature because it had a Communistic and Paganistic view to it plus it glamorized sex outside of marriage.

I asked my mom if I could read it when she finished. "Of course."

By this time I had read lots of books and routinely pursued *Life Magazine, Look*, and *The Saturday Evening Post* plus read the newspapers. I loved to read. Since I was already going to Hell anyway, I figured one more sin wouldn't matter.

I read that book three times. It changed my life again. I could see why they didn't want anyone to read it. It told the truth. I was Holden Caufield. I understood everything in it. His search for meaning. My search for meaning. I aligned myself with Holden and became him. I had to keep it a secret, of course, because none of my friends could or would ever understand it. I was becoming more of an outsider because I was afraid to share my true feelings with anyone else. I just couldn't.

I became Holden. I observed. I watched and made mindful notes. I wanted to be invisible like Holden.

I was Tom Sawyer, Huck Finn, and Holden Caufield.

The school year ended with graduation and an awards ceremony held in the Church. We received our diplomas and some of us received special awards. I got one for perfect attendance and another for the 'What is Faith' paper. Charlie liked my autobiography and he gave me an A+. I came in second in the class academically.

Not good enough for my dad.

Got home and ripped my suit and tie off and hopped on my bike and rode off.

Summer vacation!

As mentioned before, Rad and I grew apart. My new best friend was Rick. We were more alike. He loved sports, was also a straight A student, and played golf! We began biking to the local municipal golf course in Tiffin and golfing. He showed me how to line the ball up and stroke it. I was still mowing lawns a couple days a week and he helped me get a part time job caddying at the Country Club. Plus, I was playing baseball in two leagues that summer playing four games a week. They were all night games. I lost interest in model planes and didn't work the coin collection very much.

Rick was a good golfer and he also caddied. He also played baseball in one of the summer leagues. He was a better golfer but I had it over him in baseball.

My favorite client when I caddied was a local doctor. He was the best golfer in town and he had a foursome every Wednesday morning. He often chose me to caddy for him. He was really nice and just took these guys to school. He consistently shot in the mid 70's. They played for ten bucks a hole. He would give me a ten dollar tip, which was so generous in those days.

One day however, I got this Dentist. I had been warned about him. He had a temper. The fourth hole was a dog leg par 5 with a lake on the right. My doctor would usually hit it safe, staying to the left of the lake. The Dentist lined up at the tee, he was already drunk. The other three guys and their caddies watched him drive the ball into the lake near the shoreline. "Fuck," said the Dentist.

We walked up to the ball and it was in about two feet of water and he told me to retrieve it. I was wearing his expensive watch. I never wore a watch and forgot to take it off before I walked into the water. I reached down and snatched his ball. I noticed, he did too, that the watch was full of water. It wasn't water-proof! He got really pissed off and called me some names. Then he lined up his second shot and drove it back into the lake. Way out there. Too far and deep to save the ball. He lost his mind and wrapped the club around a tree and was cussing a blue streak. He blamed it on me, I guess, because he called me every swear word in the book.

I put his clubs down. Dropped his watch on the ground and walked back to the caddy shack. I told the caddy master what had happened and told him I quit. I got on my bike and rode home. Partially angry, hurt, and laughing.

That ended my caddy resume.

I saw Rick a day later and told him what happened. "That guy's a prick."

Rick and I continued to golf in the mornings. I was using my mom's clubs which were too short so I started renting clubs from the Pro Shop. Those people were so nice to us that they just let me use a set without charging me. And, they sometimes let us do a round for free if we golfed before the course opened because we would tell them of any problems on the course. For example, if there were tree limbs on the greens etc.

We would bicycle back to my house and I sometimes had a lawn to mow. And, a baseball game at night. We were both going out for football in August for the freshman team at Calvert High School, so this would all end soon.

By this time we had moved to the big baseball diamond. I started to hit and hit and hit. I led one league in batting average, hitting mostly singles and an occasional double. Led both leagues in steals because I walked frequently and was on base a lot. I moved from third to second base because I didn't have the arm to throw from third. I even relieved as a pitcher once in awhile. I could throw the most wicked curve and slider that no one could hit. I was only good for about twenty pitches because, like I said, I didn't have the arm.

Baseball ended in the first week of August. Rick and I decided to get in shape for football. We met each morning and did exercises and ran wind sprints. He was a running back and he thought I should try out for halfback and receiver.

We considered ourselves in shape and ready.

Football camp started and after the first of two practices per day, I couldn't even move. This is Ohio and football was God. The coaches put us through the most grueling morning I have ever had. We had leg lifts, push-ups, wind sprints, and hitting. We didn't even have pads on. That afternoon was even worse. They issued pads and helmets and we had this one drill: two guys lined up about five yards apart and on the whistle you crashed head on into the other guy. I weighed about 115 lbs. then, skinny as a rail. I got punished. But, I hit as hard as I could. The big linemen loved this one because they had the upper hand.

After the first week even my hair hurt. It must have been in the nineties with high humidly. I've never sweated so much. After practice we took showers. This was the first time I ever took a shower with anyone else. I got used to it after a while and my modesty vanished. I was one of the boys. We had a swagger about us.

I did well in scrimmages. I was able to out run everyone. I played halfback and split end. I could see the varsity across the field as well as the junior varsity team. They were huge.

After a couple of weeks several guys quit. I made the freshman starting team. I returned punts and kickoffs too. I played some on defense. I had several little injuries but nothing serious. We played our first game and we clobbered this other team. I got loose on a pass play and out ran the defender into the end zone. My left knee popped and buckled. It hurt like hell.

It bothers me to this day. So, I was taken out of the game but I was okay after a couple of days.

There were several injuries on the varsity squad. So, they moved some guys up from the junior varsity squad. The kid who I saved in Boy Scouts was the starting quarterback on the varsity. God, was he good. He could throw a bullet pass right into a receiver's hands from 30 yards away.

One day coach called all three teams together and we all played. The first three teams on the varsity and the rest of us. I was put in to receive a punt and I made a couple of cuts and ran down the sideline and cut back inside and was smashed by a couple of guys. But, that run impressed the head coach with my speed.

So, I played on the freshman squad and the junior varsity squad.

Five or six of us from the freshman team dressed for the home varsity games. Our varsity team was great. They won their first three games. By the fourth game I got to play in my first varsity game. I was scared to death. There were people in the stands. I figured I might even letter if I got enough quarters in.

School, of course, had started. I was in high school. It was 1963. I worked my ass off. I think I worked as hard or harder than any of my other classmates.

Had classes in different class rooms. I was terrified of failure so I studied late every night at home and then woke up early to review. I received all A's that first quarter and was on the Honor Roll. I was so proud! My mom was pleased. I showed my report card to my dad and he just nodded and handed it back to me. I wanted to die!

Those were busy days and they passed in a blur.

Up at five. At school by eight. Football practice after school until 7. Home to eat. Study until 11. Asleep.

Day after day.

Let me digress.

President Kennedy had issued a challenge to the youth of America by declaring that we should be physically active. Schools throughout the nation implemented a vigorous physical education system. Calvert High did it's part. We were required to take four years of physical education ... gym class.

The varsity football coach was our instructor freshman year. I'll never forget the first class. It was the first period class. 8 a.m.

"Well, girls, (he always called us girls), let's do some exercises." I was in great shape so it was nothing. We went through the same series of exercises as football practise. Push-ups, leg lifts, jumping jacks, etc. "Let's see how many of you girls can touch your toes."

I was in the front row next to this kid with an amazing talent. He was double, no, triple jointed. He could pop his joints out of their sockets and do amazing human tricks, like touch his fingers and thumbs to his forearm. He could put his head behind and between his legs. Well, he put his elbows on the floor and bent his body in two. I couldn't believe my eyes. When Coach Miletti walked by and saw that he muttered a swear word under his breath and just stared at this kid. He still called us 'girls.'

The football season went on. I played a few plays in the last game against Lima Central Catholic. Both teams were undefeated. They had a linebacker named Jim Lynch who went on to play at Notre Dame and later the Kansas City Chiefs. Had the honor of being tackled by him. He knocked me into their bench. It was late in the game and coach put me in. I ran off tackle and cut to the outside. I had one guy to beat and all of a sudden I'm flying through the air into the Lima bench. I didn't even see him. We played to a 0-0 tie.

We had one more big game. The annual freshman-sophomore game. It was held on the practice field and I had no idea it was such a big deal until the game began. There were several hundred people in attendance and cheer leaders even.

We (freshman) beat the sophomore team for the first time in several years. I scored two touchdowns!

Chapter 4

A Day of Infamy

Football season ended a week before Thanksgiving.

The day was November 22, 1963.

It was a Friday. I was in Biology class. The last period of the day. An announcement came over the PA. It was the Principal. "We have a report that the President has been shot in Dallas."

The class was silent. The teacher told us to remain seated as she continued the class. A few minutes later the Principal informed us of the awful news that the President was dead!

Stunned and numbed, we just got up and left the classroom. Girls were screaming and crying in the hallways. Some kids had a blank stare on their faces, others just stood there looking lost.

I walked to my locker and grabbed the rest of my books and walked out of the school and scurried home passing through the downtown. A crowd had gathered outside a TV store on the sidewalk and silently stared at the TV screens. The audio portion barely heard over the street noise. Walter Cronkite sat at a desk confirming the President's death. I was only two blocks from home. I entered the house and my mom was hysterical. She had received the news and had the TV on. We sat watching. Stunned. Numb.

We spent the following two days glued to the set. A guy named Lee Harvey Oswald had been arrested and accused of the assassination.

My dad returned home that night and the entire family sat in front of the tube. The coverage went all night long. (The first time I recall TV running all night.)

By Sunday we were burned out from watching so much. The shock hadn't settled in yet. My dad said that we should all go out for a drive to get out of the house for a bit. I told my dad that they were bringing Oswald out and moving him. I watched in horror as someone shot Oswald on live TV!

I came running outside and told Dad that they just shot Oswald! He came running in and watched about two minutes of the chaos ensuing and turned the set off.

We all got in the station wagon and drove to a country park and had a picnic.

We were the only people there.

Basketball started up. I tried out for the freshman team and made it. Our coach had an interesting exercise. At the end of practice and wind sprints, he had us stand against the wall and jump as high as we could. An assistant coach marked how high you reached. First with each hand separately and then with both hands. We did this 25 times (75 total) until our legs ached and we couldn't jump anymore.

After a few weeks of this, each guy was jumping an inch or two higher. Just for laughs one day I ran at the rim and tried to touch it. I could! So could some of the other guys. We only played a few games before Christmas break and we always out-rebounded the other team. I was a lousy basketball player. But, I got rebounds and assists, didn't score much and fouled often. They started calling me 'Zelmo' after the St. Louis Hawks player, Zelmo Beaty, known for dirty play and fouling out of games.

I kept my grades up. Three or four of us were at the top of the class.

Mom wanted to go home (Rice Lake) for Christmas. Paul was so small but seemed to be holding his own. A few days before Christmas we all loaded into Dad's nine seat station wagon. Tim and I in the back seat facing the rear. Dad wanted to drive up through Michigan and pass through the Mackinac Island.

We hadn't been back to Rice Lake in a couple of years and we were pretty excited about seeing old friends and Grandma and Grandpa.

Paul started to get sick about half way through Michigan. A small fever at first and then a full blown cold. Mom held him in the front seat swaddled in blankets. The car heater was on full blast. We were so hot that we took off our coats just so Paul would stay warm.

We crossed the Mackinac Bridge and that was something. It was beautiful. A long bridge spanning the Lower Peninsula to the Upper Peninsula of Michigan.

Paul was turning blue and Mom was really concerned about him. We had crossed the bridge some time ago and the nearest town was Norway, Michigan. Mom wanted to take Paul to the hospital. He was blue and barely breathing.

Dad found the hospital. This was a very small town. We all got out as Mom and Dad rushed Paul into the emergency room. We waited in the waiting room.

I made a deal with God that if Paul made it through I would stop masturbating.

After what seemed like an eternity, a doctor came out and said that they couldn't revive Paul and that he had died.

I can't describe the shock and the heartbreak.

Not a moment later a nurse came out yelling for the doctor. Paul had come back and they had a heartbeat.

It was a miracle!

We stayed there for a few more hours and I assume that Mom had called Grandma about Paul. Dad decided to drive the rest of us to Rice Lake. So, we all piled, less Mom and Paul, into the car and drove the next four hours into Rice Lake.

Grandma was very emotional and somewhat angry because we took such a risk with Paul's condition.

Dad stayed the night and drove back to Norway the next morning.

It was a strange Christmas without Mom, Dad, and Paul.

Apparently, the story got out in Norway about the Paul being so sick and Mom and Dad at his bedside. The local Catholic Church sponsored a fund drive. Mom and Dad had a place to stay in someone's home. They alternated shifts at the hospital. They were fed home-cooked meals and the community of Norway paid all the hospital bills!

Paul, Mom, and Dad returned to Rice Lake just before New Year's and that's when we celebrated the most remarkable Christmas ever!

I broke my promise to God soon thereafter.

We drove back to Ohio via the turnpikes just in time to start school.

It was good to get back into the routine. I had several clients downtown who I shoveled walks for and the Saturday office cleaning job. They were all understanding that I took the break and I resumed doing my duties. Basketball practice took up a couple of hours after school and I usually returned home by 6 p.m.

Welcome to 1964. It had been such a dramatic last couple of months. Life wasn't the same.

The Kennedy assassination had changed us forever! Life would never be 'normal' again. It seemed all the hope and optimism we had for the future had been sucked out of us.

The country was trying to adjust to the horrible realization that Kennedy and the 'Camelot Era' were gone and Lyndon Johnson was the President.

We started to hear about this place called Vietnam, and Civil Rights, and some folk singer named Dylan.

One could sense a change in the air and it frightened most people. Especially in staid Ohio, where change was met with suspicion.

The draft was in place and several of the guys who had graduated from high school were being drafted by the Selective Service and sent to serve in the military. Boys were dying in Vietnam.

It was at this time that Tim created a personality named 'Jake Ogre.' Jake spoke in an Andy Devine like guttural, phlegmy voice. Jake always spoke the truth. Tim would contort his face and go into this alter-ego personality. I did it too. Tim and I spoke through Jake only to each other for years. We revealed our most sacred and deepest secrets to each other through Jake.

"Mike."

"Yes, Jake."

"Hi, Mike."

"What is it, Jake?"

"Am I ugly?"

"No Jake, you're the most handsome guy in the world."

"Thanks, Mike."

Sometimes I was Jake. We kept our sanity through our character.

Dad had bought this huge chemistry kit. We set it up in the basement. The kit came with everything: glass tubes and vials and even a Bunsen Burner. Dad showed us how we could produce distilled water for Mom's iron. We had vials of various chemicals to experiment with and a book of instructions showing different experiments. Tim took to it right away. He was the 'Mad Scientist.' We played with the kit until my interest waned. Tim, however, and his school chum, Mark Nevius, spent most of their time in the basement mixing up brews. They even figured out how to combine chemicals to make ammonium sulfide, a rotten egg smell, a 'stink bomb.' They cleared the house.

It was a cold winter with some snow. I continued the same routine. I really buckled down on my studies.

Basketball ended soon enough. I continued doing the jumping exercise I described before. I could now stand under the rim and grab hold of the rim with both hands, and I could dunk a softball, or anything I could palm, if I ran at the rim. Amazing!

That spring I tried out for the high school baseball team again but had little interest in playing for that coach. Rick and I began playing golf again as soon as the course opened.

Rick and I both got all A's again and felt we were entitled.

I signed up for summer baseball again and decided to try my hand at the American Legion team. These guys were good. Mostly high schoolers and some guys from Heidleberg College. I knew some of the guys. Most were from Columbia High School in town but a couple of the guys were from Calvert. Somehow, I made the team. Probably because of my speed and I could bunt.

We played a few games and won every game. I rarely played more than an inning or two but did manage to steal a few bases and sacrifice some runners.

We had a couple of pitchers who were un-hittable and a couple of home run hitters. I don't know why I was even on this team. They were really good. The Legion team made it through some play-off games and we were headed to State in Columbus.

We won our first game. The second game we faced a guy who should have been in the Major Leagues. I have never seen a guy throw that fast. He only had one pitch. A fast ball. Our guys just couldn't get around on it. We were down 1-0 in the 7th inning and we had a guy on first with two out. The coach had me pinch-hit for our pitcher and I figured they wanted me to bunt. But the coach said swing away because this guy threw so hard that it would have been tough to bunt for a hit.

I was a good contact hitter. I took the first pitch. I sort of heard it more than saw it but the guy was so consistent that I figured the next pitch would be in the same spot.

It was.

I swung and connected solidly and I watched in amazement as the ball sailed over the right center fence for a 2 run home run. I had never hit a ball out of the park before so I sprinted and almost over-took the lead runner. I got back to the dugout and all the guys jumped on me.

We won on that hit.

It was a lucky swing.

We lost the next two games and returned to Tiffin.

Football was around the corner. Rick and I were playing a lot of golf in the mornings and getting in shape in the afternoon by jogging and doing the exercises. No way were we going to be tortured like last year.

Football started and sure enough ... no matter how hard we tried to be ready when the real grind began I could hardly get out of bed the next morning. Two-a-day practices in hot humid Ohio just takes it out of you.

We had lost most of the starting team to graduation. Last year's juniors were now seniors and expected to carry the torch. We had lost so much talent that I didn't expect much out of this team.

After a week we began scrimmages and it was a train wreck. I was going out for a pass and I stepped in a gopher hole and broke my ankle. X-rays showed three small bones fractured in the mid-foot ankle area. My ankle was black, green, and purple and three times its normal size. I was told I would miss the season. They gave me a walking cast and a cane to walk with.

The pain was intense for a few days and I began a rigorous therapy campaign consisting of electric treatments and soaking my foot in a jacuzzi bath of hot water.

My dad had purchased a jacuzzi for his back. I would sit in there three or four times a day. I never missed a practice.

Meanwhile, things were unraveling at home. Dad was always gone and Mom was always drunk by the time I got home. The younger kids were fending for themselves. Mom stopped cooking dinner and we lived on do-it-yourself peanut butter sandwiches and crude burgers. When Dad did come home on the weekends he would throw a tantrum because the house was a mess. He would make us clean the place up usually resulting in him beating me.

I was so busy with sports and school that I didn't take the time to clean the house up each night and the younger ones couldn't help much anyway.

I kept going back to Kennedy's assassination as a turning point. It seemed like a permanent gloom and depression had settled, in a very subtle way, over the country, and even in my family.

I had lost my zeal for sports. My religion was hopeless. My home life was in peril. I only had a couple of close friends. Secretly, on the inside, I was scared of everything. I stuttered. My life was in pieces and I didn't have the words or where-with-all at the time to realize this but in looking back it is so clear to me now. I was in a state of depression with an unhealthy dose of stress.

My ankle healed and I got the okay from my doctor to start running again. He was amazed it healed so fast.

I started to run and exercise at practice but didn't participate in any of the drills or scrimmages. I had only missed four games. I insisted I was okay to play and they inserted me into a junior varsity game for a few plays. I was fine although the ankle ached all night. I played some in the varsity game on Friday night and made a couple of nice runs late in the game.

It seemed like I had lost a step though because I couldn't find the extra gear when I ran.

I finished the season strong playing both ways on the junior varsity team. We beat the freshman team soundly in the Big Game. I got loose a couple of times for TD's.

Basketball season started right away and somehow I made the junior varsity team. Rick and I being the last chosen. I didn't play much but was able to rebound and play defense. Even the coach called me 'Zelmo.'

School dragged on and soon it was Christmas again in this huge mansion. Dad bought a Christmas tree that touched the 16' ceiling and we decorated it with ornaments and lights. Paul was doing fine even though he was so small and fragile. No Christmas trip this year. We had a few ball games over Christmas break so I wanted to stay home anyway.

I got four 'A's and my first 'B' that semester. I'm slipping. I started going to the library and local bookstore and record store. I found some interesting reading and music. Dad always played his clarinet and played his jazz records at home and I needed something different. I began listening to folk music. Peter, Paul, and Mary and this guy Dylan I kept hearing about. I read some East Coast magazines about a student rebellion in music and attitudes. I didn't understand it but somehow knew that this was in my future and of great interest to me.

I went to a dance one Friday night after a basketball game. It was in the gym and they played records and we danced. I was so shy and had never danced. I stayed ten minutes and left in misery. I vowed to attend the next dance and stay longer.

There was this DJ at a Cleveland radio station that we used to listen too. He called himself 'Ghoulardi' and he played new music. His theme song was 'Papa-Oom-Mow-Mow' ... 'the birds' the word' ... and he had a huge influence on the teens of Northern Ohio. Tim and I listened to him every night on our transistor radio. I started buying '45's' and collecting some of the music. It was rock and roll and I liked it!

Started school again. Word started that this rock group was coming to the States from England. They were called the Beatles. Some of their songs were played on the radio and they caused quite a buzz. Ed Sullivan stated on one of his shows that he was going to have them on. We all marked our calendars.

The *Ed Sullivan Show* was a Sunday night program that everyone watched. It was a variety show featuring comedians and jugglers to magic acts and popular singers.

The big night came. All the kids in America were watching. The audience was full of screaming teenage girls. The show went on. No one wanted to watch the opening acts. It was torture. Sullivan would mention after each act that the Beatles were coming and the girls went nuts, drowning out Ed. He held his hands up trying to quite them down.

Finally, the show was half over and after endless commercial breaks he came back on and said, "The Beatles." The place went nuts. Couldn't hardly hear the music. There they were. George, Paul, John, and Ringo. The most influential band of the Century. They played two songs and that was it.

They had long hair and suits with no collar. They were cool!

The next day at school the Principal called a general assembly for the entire school in the gym. He asked us who had seen the Beatles last night and just about every hand went up. He then proceeded to tell us that Beatle boots, Beatle hair cuts, and Beatle music were forbidden on school grounds and you had to wear a shirt with a collar and that anyone breaking these rules would be expelled from school.

As that sank in during the day, I realized that this was the final straw. Most of my friends agreed. They had no right. Most of the boys, myself included, had 'butch' haircuts and I never heard any music played at school, and boots? Who wore boots?

That afternoon after basketball practice I bought the Beatles album. I was lucky they had any left.

Dad was on the road again so Tim and I listened to it over and over on the Hi-fi. We couldn't get enough.

The next day at school all the talk was still about the Beatles. Several kids had purchased the album and played it over the protests of their parents. Without realizing it, the counter culture and the protest era had added another facet; Rock and Roll. The Civil Rights Movement was already in full bloom in the South and schools that had been segregated were now integrated but that didn't affect us in the North ... not yet. And, we began to hear the first rumblings of war protests.

The Beatles created another turn in my life. I was loosing interest in sports although I still really wanted to play. I was torn between the changes coming in the future and what had been the past. All of this taking place in a three month span.

Tim had begun playing piano with Dad. I had no talent at music. I liked to listen to it but couldn't play a note. I felt myself drifting.

It was obvious from the beginning that Tim had talent. Dad would show him some blues chords and he played it right back. Amazing!

That spring Dad announced that we were going to move to Marion, Indiana. I wanted to die.

Dad said I shouldn't sign up for baseball in the summer because we would be moved by then.

Dad took me on one of his sales trips over Easter break. I took a few days off from school so I could go. First we drove to Marion and he showed me the high school I'd be attending. I shriveled in fear. He made a couple of calls then we headed for Cincinnati, Ohio. It was on this trip, (I had been on several other sojourns prior to this one), that he opened up to me for the first time. He told me of the trouble he and Mom were having and how much he depended on me to be 'the man of the house' when he was gone. He told me of his love of us kids and that we were the most important part of his life. He talked of his childhood and how he'd been raised by relatives because his parents were professional card players and were never around. He was an only child.

Then, he began telling me about being a Marine at Iwo Jima in WWII.

"It was supposed to be a three day operation. My platoon was to land on the third day and do the clean up. We had bombarded the Island for several days to soften it up and they figured that most of the Japs would be dead and the survivors would just surrender."

"We waited on the troop ship. Pretty nervous because we could hear the constant gun battle and the explosions. We really didn't know what was going on. This was to be my first engagement with the enemy."

"Finally, we loaded into the troop carrier and off we went. Half the guys were puking from nerves and sea sickness. We were packed in like sardines. As we neared the beach the first pings of bullets hit the craft. I knew we were near. Suddenly we stopped and the front gate dropped into the water and immediately three or four guys went down. The rest of us jumped into the water which was waist deep and ran as fast as we could to the shore. Everybody was yelling and I was numb."

"I hit the shore and dove behind a pile of Marines. I realized in a minute that they were all dead. Several of us used them like sandbags to make a shelter for us. We dug a hole and hunkered down. No one knew what to do. Several of my group had been shot and I could see them floating in the water."

"Night came and the tide came in. We were waist deep in water and couldn't move. It was pitch black so we couldn't smoke. No one slept that night."

"The first light came and the battle was ever constant. Never a lull in the gun shots. I hadn't fired a round because I couldn't see what I was shooting at."

"We got orders to move up the beach. So one by one we crawled out of this hole and moved about 100 hundred yards inland where we dug ourselves in again. The shots on the beach had stopped so we figured that the Japs were retreating."

"We could see more troops landing behind us. There were dead Marines everywhere. Some of the guys shit their pants because there was no place to go."

"That night it was pitch black again. There were about twenty of us in this foxhole. Someone crawled in. I was asleep but woke up hearing a commotion. A Jap had crawled into our hole. Must have been lost and somebody killed him. We lit a match to look at him."

"The next day, and I swear this is true, one of the guy's hair had turned white he was so scared."

"The noise of battle had moved inland and we got orders to move out."

"I was in a squad with about twenty guys and one of the guys had a flame thrower. We were ordered to burn out any caves that we found. That's how the Japs survived the shelling. They hid in caves. It was dangerous because there were snipers and we were being shot at. A couple of our guys got hit and one died right there. The other guy was wounded and we got him back to a medic. By this time the beach area was secure and we had reinforcements coming behind us. But, the job remained to clean this area."

"When we found a cave one of the guys would yell something in Japanese telling them to come out. We never heard a reply. Then the flame thrower would walk up to the entrance and burn them out. We could hear the screams from inside"

"While still on patrol we got surprised by some Japs. Several shots were fired and in the skirmish I stabbed one of the Japs with my bayonet and killed him. It was over in a minute and two more of our guys were dead. I reached into the dead Japs pockets and found his ID's and among them was a photograph of this guy with a woman and a small child. He was a father."

"I still have dreams about this."

"I never want you to go to war."

Dad was crying as he finished. I had never seen him cry before. It choked me up too. We sat in silence for a long time as we continued on to Cincinnati.

We arrived in Cincinnati and checked into a hotel room. Dad and I got some burgers and chowed down. Dad went to the bar downstairs and I stayed in the room and watched TV.

As I stared at the TV, I couldn't help but reflect on Dad's story about Iwo Jima. What that must have been like for him and the other guys. I even pondered about how the Japanese must have felt. I don't know if any of them survived. It must have been awful.

Cincinnati brought back some more memories. Every year the football team had an overnight trip to play a team on the road. Most towns were near enough to return home that night. Last fall we played a team in Covington, Kentucky, just over the river from Cincinnati. The team bus pulled up to the motel. We all exited the bus, stretching and yawning. The Coach checked us in. The manager of the motel ran out and told us that he couldn't have any Negroes in his motel. We had one black player. He had to stay on the bus. He couldn't eat in the restaurant or sleep in his room. We were really pissed off about that. The game was to be played the next afternoon and then we were to leave after the game. So, Carl stayed on the bus. He slept there and ate there and even had to use the bathroom on the bus. To a man, we were so pissed. Kentucky! We should have stayed in Cincinnati. Well, we played the game the next day, Carl was allowed to play, and we kicked their ass. We dedicated the game to Carl. He was one of us.

And I thought about the move to Marion. I didn't get a good feeling about that place. Leaving Ohio would be okay. I would miss Rick and the chance to play on a great football team my senior year. Our class was the most talented to come along in many years, so they told me. I thought of the good times I had in Ohio; seeing my first Major League Baseball game at Municipal Stadium in Cleveland. The New York Yankees vs. the Cleveland Indians. Seeing Mantle and Berra and Maris and Whitey Ford. Watching the zany Jimmy Piersall hit a home run and sprint around the bases and then slide into home plate. Attending an Ohio State football game in Columbus and watching Paul Warfield sprint down the side lines on a punt return. Seeing Jim Brown play for the Browns. Attending a Massillon-Canton high school football game and realizing I'd never play at this level. Half those guys later played at Ohio State. Huddling one night by the radio on a cold February night with my dad listening to the Cassius Clay-Sonny Liston fight and Clay beats Liston! So many great memories.

Woke up the next morning and Dad had returned. I must have fallen asleep before he came in. Didn't hear a thing. We both cleaned up and he had two quick calls to make and then we headed to Dayton where he was to have lunch with someone from Dayton Power and Light. I had to wear my suit and tie.

I came in with my dad on this call and he introduced me to this man. I used my best manners ... yes sir and no sir. We left his office and drove to a nearby restaurant and sat in a booth. They ordered beers and I ordered a coke. We ate burgers. Had desert. Dad had coached me on what to say. After lunch I patted my stomach, after eating a huge lunch and exclaimed, "That was good, ... what there was of it." And the man from Dayton Power and Light laughed and laughed. Dad got the contract.

Dad was pretty happy on the drive back to Tiffin. He said I did a good job. I still didn't want to move to Marion but was afraid to say anything.

We returned home. Finished up the school year.

Didn't sign up for summer baseball because we were moving in June. It was sad saying goodbye to a lot of friends ... again.

Dad came home one Friday afternoon in mid June and told us that the move to Marion was off and that we were going to move to Winona, Minnesota. Mom was happy because she would be close to Grandma and Grandpa. I looked on the map and found Winona. It was on the Mississippi River and had three colleges. Anything would be better than Marion.

But we wouldn't be moving until July. Dad was going to drive there and find a house and we still had to sell this one.

Tim and I didn't pull any tricks to sabotage the sale this time. We were both anxious to move and leave this town behind.

Mom and Dad hired a Real Estate agent and the house sold quickly. Dad called a couple of weeks later and said he had found a house.

We started packing everything up and waited for the Mayflower truck.

The movers showed up and it took them two days to pack everything. They had their largest truck and I couldn't believe everything fit.

Chapter 5

Winona

July, 1964.

We packed the rest of us and our stuff into the cars; Mom drove the red Cadillac convertible and Dad had the big station wagon. Both cars had cargo boxes atop loaded with stuff. I rode with Mom and Paul and Mary with the car packed to the ceiling. The rest of the family and Lulu Belle rode with Dad, likewise packed.

Mom followed Dad as we drove to the Ohio Turnpike. We drove several hours and Dad signaled that he was turning off at a Howard Johnson's for a pit stop. We were halfway across Indiana. We all piled out of the two cars and everyone headed for the rest rooms. Paul needed a diaper change and we sat in a booth and had a snack. After gassing up, we decided to change cars. Becky and John wanted to ride with Mom and I.

After the long stop, we loaded back into the cars having made the switch. Mom followed Dad back onto the Turnpike and off we went. Suddenly, Dad signaled and pulled off to the side of the road. Mom slowed and pulled in behind him. What's wrong! Dad got out and asked if we had Paul with us. No. We had left Paul back at the Howard Johnson's!

We had to get off at the next pay booth and turn around and go back ... go to the next pay booth and go back, again. You weren't allowed to turn around on the Turnpike. We got there and sure enough there was Paul being taken care of by the staff. What a relief!

So, off again. This time counting heads to make sure we were all present and accounted for.

Mom was a good driver but getting tired. We made it to the West side of Chicago. That was some hard driving going through Chicago. We lost sight of Dad several times and the traffic was very heavy. But we eventually caught up with him.

Somewhere in Wisconsin Dad pulled over again at a Holiday Inn and we stayed the night. We all jumped in the pool and Dad went to a Mc-

Donald's and brought back it seemed like, 100 burgers and fries and milk-shakes. Yum!

Rested, we took off in the morning and drove into Winona by the afternoon. We drove up the Mississippi River on the Minnesota side. It was beautiful! Bluffs hugged the river and trees and hills and I immediately liked it.

Winona was an old river town with bridges crossing the river to Wisconsin on the other side.

Dad took us to the house we were going to live in. It was half the size of the Tiffin house but newer and in good shape. A little back yard in a nice neighborhood. The Mayflower truck was already there and they had managed to unpack about half the stuff.

Tim, John, and I were to stay in the basement.

What a welcome we received. The previous owners, the Burmiesters, opened there new home to us and put us all up the first night. They had some kids about our age and we soon became friends.

The next day we finished moving all the stuff into the house. Our new neighbors came over and made dinner for us. Mom couldn't even find the dishes.

We made our beds as best we could. We three boys moved our stuff into the basement which was a mess. Dad told us he was going to fix up the basement for us and make the garage into a family room. All we did for the next two weeks was pound nails. Dad partitioned the basement so I had, for the first time in my life, my own room and John and Tim had a big room which they shared. Dad fixed up the basement bathroom and we had a shower and a sink and toilet. It was great.

We converted the attached garage into a family room, built a dog house for Lulu Belle, and painted it.

One day, two guys came over to the house and they introduced themselves as football players for Cotter High. They wanted me to join the team. I said I didn't want to play anymore. Eventually, Mom and Dad talked me into it. I really didn't have my heart in it.

I waited until school started before showing up for football. I attended the first game and they were terrible. The punt receiver fumbled every punt. They had no offense. So, I knew I could make the team. I told those two guys that I wanted to play so they told the head coach and I dressed in the locker room before a practice. They had me run some plays against the junior varsity team and I ran right through them then they moved me over to the varsity team and I did the same. There was a game on Friday night. A road game. I got on the bus not even knowing the plays.

They put me in at halfback and they gave me the ball. I got smeared on every play because there was no blocking. I ran out for a pass and was wide open but the quarterback threw the ball behind me. What am I doing here. This was a terrible team. We were beaten soundly.

Every muscle in my body ached. I was out of shape.

I got on the bus. I sat down. Apparently this was Darrell Holzier's seat and the guy told me I should move. "Fuck you," I mumbled under my breath, "I'm not moving." Just then Darrell came up and stated that this was his seat and that I had to move. "No." "I'll see you back in Winona," he said. The guy next to me informed me that Holzier was the toughest guy in town and that he was going to beat me up. I didn't care at all.

It was a short trip. I just wanted to go home. I didn't know anyone and was an outsider. We got back to Winona and we showered. No one even spoke to me. I had a couple of bruises and was stiff and tired and I waited for my dad to pick me up.

Just then Darrell showed up and I told him to just get it over with. "Go ahead, hit me, I don't give a shit," Darrell just stared at me and grinned. He put his arm around me and said I was all right. Apparently, not many stood up to him. He had some kind of respect for me. We became good friends.

The Murray family from Chicago came to visit. They were installing their son, Phil, at St. Mary's College in Winona. They stayed the weekend. Another drunken fest for the adults. Mr. Murray was an ass. He was authoritative and condescending. Tim and I hated him. After a night of drunkenness by the adults, we woke up and could hear Mr. Murray ranting and raving. Lulu Belle had chewed his shoes. Tim and I laughed our asses off. Serves him right. Dad, however, had to buy him a new pair of shoes. Mr. Murray was an asshole.

Classes began and I soon realized that I wasn't as smart as I thought I was. I was only an average student here. There were some smart people in this school. Probably because this was a college town. I had been a star in Ohio but not here. And I noticed that people here were much friendlier and kinder. I liked Winona from the start.

I started to go to dances and even had a girl friend. Mary Lou was her name but we had little in common and I was so shy (some thought I was conceited ... had to look that word up.) She soon started to date another guy much to my relief.

Football was a disaster. We had no offense. A quarterback who couldn't throw. We just ran the same plays over and over. We managed to win a couple of games but we were dismal. My heart just wasn't in it. Late in the season we travelled to Rochester to play Lourdes. They were ranked number one in the state. Two of our best players were being disciplined for attending a beer party and at the very last minute I was informed that I would be playing defense. I hadn't played defense all year. I was terrible.

Worst game of my life. Their quarterback (I forgot his name) went on to play in the NFL. He took us apart with passes. I got burned on a long TD pass to the guy I was covering. He made a perfect pass and the receiver got behind me. I felt like shit. I did make two nice returns on kickoffs. They kicked off a lot because they scored so often. They beat us 49-6. I wanted to die. Felt like I had let the whole team down. We were thoroughly trounced.

I had bruises all over my body the next morning and could hardly move.

That Monday, Pete Meier, myself and a couple others guys from the football team were called into the Principal's office. It concerned a party we had attended where there was drinking. Father McCauley was mean and didn't tolerate any variance from his principles.

It happened so quickly that I didn't even hear the exchange. When McCauley asked Pete if he was at the party Pete responded, "No," and Mc-Cauley hit him right in the face with his fist knocking Pete against the wall. (I was at the party for five minutes and left.) Pete was bleeding and hurt and the other three of us scurried from the office and waited outside.

Pete had been at the party and that is why he didn't play the Lourdes game.

Don't know if this really happened or not but we heard that Pete's dad found McCauley a day or two later and beat the living shit out of him. Ironically, McCauley later was transferred to Lourdes in Rochester.

Thankfully, football ended and basketball started. I tried out for the team. Cotter High had a legendary coach, John Nett, who had won several Catholic State Championships. He had a system which was taught at the grade schools too. After just one practice it was obvious that I wasn't going to make this team. I didn't understand the plays. All these guys had been running the same plays for years. It was all back door screens and picks usually resulting in a lay up. I was used to school yard style. They were really good. Coach told me I could stay on as a reserve. I did and learned a lot but never got the hang of it. I sat in the stands during the games. They didn't lose a game until the State final.

Before Christmas break we got our report cards. Two 'B's' and three 'C's.' Never had a 'C' before. These kids were smart. But, again, my heart wasn't in to it. I was losing self-confidence but as I look back, I was really losing my faith in the institutions. The Church, School, Government (the war in Vietnam was raging by now), the Civil Rights Movement in full fury, student protests here and in France, the new music of the British Invasion, the Beatles, Stones, and my favorite band, the Yardbirds. It was a most confusing time and yet a promising time.

Every institution, every corporation, every religion, system, '-ism,' my family, ... was a lie. I didn't believe in anything or anyone. Our government was murdering people in Vietnam and committing genocide on black people. The churches supported it. The majority of American citizens supported it. All my friends supported it. I feared to speak out.

Dad was gone sometimes for a month at a time and Mom was always drunk and she began having epileptic fits. One day I came home from school with a classmate of mine and as we walked into the living room there was Mom passed out, completely naked. I was mortified! My friend left and I grabbed a blanket and wrapped Mom up in it and carried her upstairs to her bed. She probably had a seizure and passed out. I witnessed several of these fits and each time Mom was rushed to the hospital until she regained consciousness. When Dad did return he was usually on a rampage about the house being a mess and he would beat Mom and I up. He broke my nose once. He beat the shit out of me in the kitchen because I 'smarted off' to him. He grabbed me by my neck and had a butcher's knife at my throat. Mom hit him over the head with a Dutch Oven and I ran out of the house. I never stayed in the house again when he was home. My friend Steve Price and his folks were really nice and they only lived a few blocks away. I ran over there several times. They knew the situation. They housed me.

About this time I was hired at McDonalds. $.90/hour flipping burgers and making shakes and fries. I supported myself with this job.

Spring arrived. 1965. It was the coldest of March's and the ground was frozen solid. The Mississippi River was frozen in large areas. Lake Pepin, north of Winona was frozen solid. Then, we had a blizzard. Lots of snow. Probably two feet or so. Then, just like that, warm weather and the rains came. It rained and rained. The ground was still frozen so the excess water had no place to go except to run off. The waters rose and rose. We were warned of flooding and man, did we get a flood. School was canceled and most of us kids were hired by the Army Core of Engineers to help construct a levee along the banks of Winona.

We filled sandbags and worked our asses off for two solid weeks. The water rose and rose until it was several feet over the banks and almost every home in Winona would have been flooded were it not for the levee. We saved our town!

For two more weeks I and a host of other guys patrolled the levee for leaks. Once in a while, a geyser would spout up behind the levee and we had to surround it with sandbags until the water reached its own level.

I realized how dangerous it was when we watched cattle float by and even, what we believed was, a human body. But couldn't be sure about that.

Rats the size of cats ran loose and some guys were hired to shoot them with .22's.

We were out of school for about four weeks and would have to make it up.

I made some new friends that month and felt that I had done something good.

School resumed and I went back to McDonald's.

One day I received a check in the mail. It was from the US Government for over $300. The check was for the time spent on the levee. Wow! I was rich.

I decided that enough was enough! It was time to lose my virginity. I took some of my earnings and hoped a bus to Minneapolis. I was in the right part of town. I ventured toward Hennepin Avenue and hung out. Several prostitutes checked me out but I was too afraid to say or do anything. Most of the women looked pretty ragged and rough. Finally, a young woman of an attractive sort approached me and asked if I wanted a date. Not sure what that entailed, I answered, "Yes." She took me to a nearby hotel and we got a room. It was a seedy place and the room only cost a few bucks. We got to the room and she rattled off a shopping list of sex acts and how much. I opted for straight sex. I was scared and nervous. She pulled my pants down and began giving me a blow job. I was soft and I think my hands were shaking. "Is this your first time?"

"Yeah."

"Relax, honey."

I laid down on the bed. Try as she may, there was no reaction downstairs. "Stay here. I'm going to get some beer. Be right back."

I felt ridiculous laying on a greasy mattress with my pants to my knees. I sat up and pulled my pants back up. She did return in a few minutes with two six packs of Hamm's. We each began drinking the beer and it did relax me. We didn't do a lot of talking. This time, after several beers, the magic worked and I lost my virginity. In fact, I lost my virginity several times that afternoon and night. She stayed until the next morning. She eventually left and I stayed in the room until mid morning.

I walked to the bus station and waited for the next bus to Winona.

Never did know her real name. Never saw her again.

That accomplished, I felt I could move on.

The school salvaged some of the track season after the flood and we had a few meets. I won every 100 yard dash and 180 low hurdle race.

I recall one meet where we traveled to some little town and they didn't have a real track, just a field with a string around an area that designated a 440. The 100 yard dash was uphill and facing a strong wind. I won in a time of 11.4. Ha! There were holes and pits in the ground and it wasn't safe to run on that surface. Another meet was held on a real track with compact cinders and a perfect surface. One guy had me in 9.9 seconds in the 100 but I took that as a 10.1. They averaged the times. The wind was at my back. If I hadn't broken my ankle ... I lost a step. I could still find that extra gear.

Summer came and I worked over 40 hours/week at McDonald's. Saved some money. One of the guys at work had some friends in St. Louis so we drove down there for a week. Took in a St. Louis Cardinal's game. They played the San Francisco Giants. Saw Mays play. And we attended a County Fair. My friend and I and his buddies snuck into a 'Girlie' tent. We saw a bare naked lady. This one gal could pick up a stack of silver dollars with her pooch. Amazing.

That was fun. Got home. Don't even think Mom knew I was gone.

Had a good buddy whose dad owned a boat house down in the Marina on the Wisconsin side. We used to hang out down there and drink beer. He had a speedboat and we would go out onto the river and ski and check out the sandbars for keggers and girls. Fun times.

Another buddy, Todd and I decided to borrow my mom's car one night for a joyride. We pushed the Falcon onto the street so as not to wake her up and off we went. Todd had a bottle of gin with him and as I drove and swigged he enjoyed the ride. I was uncertain as to where the headlights were so I was fumbling with switches when all of a sudden flashing red lights appeared in the rear view mirror. A cop pulled us over and since I couldn't produce a driver's license he arrested me. Todd had stashed the bottle under the seat. They brought me in and finger printed me. Called my mom. She had to take a cab to pick me up. We took another cab back to the Falcon and went home. It was 4 a.m. Todd must have walked home. The bottle was still there under the seat which I retrieved the next day.

Boy, was I in trouble! Had to attend juvenile hall court and was soundly balled out by some court appointed something or other jerk.

Todd and I 'stole' several more cars that summer!

Had another buddy named Tim Maloney!

He was a piece of work. The toughest, smartest person I've ever known. A dedicated 'D' student in school. He could recite and explain every major philosopher of the 20th Century, explain Einstein's Theory of Relativity, endless authors ... you name it, he knew it! Never self-righteous, just factual. We became fast friends.

He had this unusual talent though. He was a boxer. He was afraid of no one. I saw him do this on numerous occasions. He would walk up to the biggest guy in the bar and insult him and they would go outside and Tim would beat the shit out of the guy and then Tim would pick the guy up and buy him drinks. It was weird but he did this often. Twenty minutes later the two are the best of friends having a good time.

Tim and I would get blind drunk on his mother's home-made wine and talk philosophy.

He taught me a lot.

Later on Tim was boxing in the Golden Gloves program and I followed him to Minneapolis. He got all the way to the finals when this black kid beat him up. Tim wouldn't go down, he just stared at the kid and smiled. Three rounds later, and the decision made, his face a mess, Tim picked the kid up and hugged him!

Emil's best friend was Chris Grajczyk who was always around the house. Chris was a photographer and he took some iconic photos of the early Ferrais days; Emil's first band. He always had a camera and he made movies of Emil as well. He was part of the family having been annointed by my dad one day by hitting him. Dad came into Emil's bedroom and found the two of them lazing around in the squalor that was Emil's room and told them to clean the room. Then he hit both of them.

Yeah, Chris was part of the family after that.

Football started up again. This was my senior year and I expected this to be a great year. Our team was better this year because we had almost the entire starting team back.

We had a series of injuries right off the back losing one of our tackles and our tight end. But we were solid.

Our first game was with a powerhouse from Eau Claire, Wisconsin, St. Regis. I was running an end sweep when I got tackled by two guys and banged my left knee on a light tower. The damn thing was only two yards out of bounds. My knee really hurt. A play or two later I was split out as a flanker and as I laid a block on a guy my knee went 'pop.' It happened right in front of our bench. I limped to the bench and within minutes my knee was twice the size and purple. One of the dads was a doctor and he looked at it a few days later and told me and my dad that I would need surgery. I was hurting pretty bad and he gave me something for the pain.

My knee hurt all week so my dad made some phone calls and we drove to the Mayo Clinic in Rochester. The doctor I saw had treated several players on the Vikings so I was in good hands. He did some tests and looked at x-rays. He took me into a room and I knew I was in trouble when they strapped me to a table and put a rubber thing in my mouth to bite down on. He drew out the largest needle I'd ever seen and poked it into my knee and drew liquid out. I can't describe the pain. It was surreal. And then he did it again. After a few minutes the swelling had gone way down and the pain subsided. He gave me some exercises to do and wanted to see me in two weeks.

I was able to do some running on it and was able to walk fine. I missed a couple of games.

Our fourth game was coming up and the doctor said I could play some. I got a note from him. I ran full speed a couple of times and the knee hurt a little but I lied to the coach and said it was fine.

Game day. A Sunday afternoon home game. My grandparents, the Mally's, were in the stands. They had never seen me play. We were evenly matched and the game went back and forth. I didn't get in until there were about five minutes to go. The coach gave me a play. A halfback option with the halfback throwing to me. I split out. I faked inside like a 'look-in' pass and got behind the guy and Pete Meier threw a perfect spiral. I caught the ball and raced 62 yards for the winning play!

The whole team jumped on me in the end zone and we celebrated.

We kicked off and they marched up field. But one of our guys picked off a pass. Coach put me in to play halfback and I got the call. A sweep. I cut inside and then outside and ran for about twenty yards before being run out of bounds. I couldn't hardly run because my knee was swollen again. I would have easily out-ran them for a touchdown if I was healthy.

The game ended and when I got home I received a hero's welcome. Several people were at the house and I felt like a million bucks!

I was heartily received the next day at school. Girls came up to me and said they saw the play and I got lots of pats on the back.

At practice that afternoon I put that knee in the whirlpool and let it soak. Coach saw it and shook his head. I didn't scrimmage that week. By Friday night the swelling was down and I started the game against Austin Pacelli. Not two plays into the game I was split out and I put a block on a guy and I guess I got pushed into my runner because I was kicked in the side. I was in severe pain and couldn't breathe. They got me off the field and was brought into the locker room. They cut my jersey off. I was in agony. My dad and the basketball coach, John Nett brought me to the hospital in Austin. They x-rayed me. I had six broken ribs. As I was laying there they brought a guy in who had been in a motorcycle accident and laid him down next to my bed. He was obviously dead. Blood everywhere. I figured I was better off than him.

I was out for the season!

Watched the next few games from the sidelines. I was wrapped up but was going to all the practices. I had missed a week of school with the ribs. I was in so much pain that I had to sleep sitting up in a chair. Going to the bathroom was agonizing despite the pain pills I was taking.

I was doing terrible in school. I had to stay home and I hadn't worked at McDonald's in a week.

Dad was on the road again and Mom was drunk and I even snuck some of her gin to soothe the pain. It worked too!

That October the Twins met the Dodgers in the 1965 World Series. Grandpa had his season tickets and was able to obtain four seats down the first base line and the four seats in his box seat. I can recall watching the Twins on TV and I could see Grandma and Grandpa sitting in their seats from the center field camera. I told my friends at school that I was going to the World Series. They were jealous. Don Drysdale of the Dodgers pitched the first game and darn if the Twins didn't win. I got to watch a few innings from Grandpa's box and you could hear the infield chatter and the batters swearing when they struck out. Koufax pitched the next day and the Twins beat him too! Amazing. It was great. Before game 2 Grandpa took me upstairs to a private club. It was a bar really. I saw so many famous people. I couldn't believe it. Grandpa was getting tickets for the LA games. He and Grandma had seen every World Series game for years and years, sometimes travelling coast to coast. I guess Grandpa got his tickets and we left. As we stepped into the elevator, a voice called, "Hey Emil." It was Leo Durocher! He shook my hand. When I returned home and back to school all my friends said they saw me on TV sitting in Grandpa's box.

Eventually, I was able to run again. I could breathe without pain but my side was tender. The last game of the year was two weeks away and I wanted desperately to play that game. During that last week I scrimmaged some. The coach telling the guys not to hit me. I was out of game shape and needed some toughing up so I asked Bruce Olsen to do some blocking with me. We stood face to face and blocked each other. He was as tough as nails and he got under my face guard and knocked five teeth out. I was jinxed!

I rode my bike home and my mom screamed. I had blood all over me and she called a dentist. We rushed to his office. I had lost five teeth (the two front chipped teeth laying somewhere on the practice field) and had broken my upper jaw in two places. I had no teeth.

Oh yeah, my nose was broken again. I lost count by now how many broken noses I've had.

Came to school the next day and the principal sent me home. I was freaking everybody out. My face was swollen with two black eyes. I didn't even recognize myself in the mirror. The game was on Saturday afternoon. I was not going to miss that game. My very last game. I came to practice on Monday and coach informed me that I couldn't participate because I had missed school. Fair enough. I stood on the sidelines and watched. I think the team was inspired because nothing was going to keep me out of this game.

I had to stay home the next two days and I attended practice on the sidelines for the next two days.

I did manage to go to school that Thursday and Friday so I could dress for the game on Saturday.

Game Day. We played De La Salle at home. They were a good strong team and we played even for the entire game. I played about half the game. Didn't make any significant plays but at least I got to play. We lost in the final minutes. I cried on the bus back to the locker room. A season lost. No more football!

My dad had told me once that he wanted me to be on the cover of Time Magazine as the Heisman Trophy winner from Notre Dame. Didn't know if that was a wish or an expectation.

Tried out for basketball again and again didn't make the team. I was a better player by now but Coach Nett was a tough guy. I could out jump and out run the entire team. Intramural coming up.

I was still working at McDonald's. I was scheduled to work Christmas Eve. We always opened presents on Christmas Eve. I told Dad I should be home by 7 because we were closing early that night. But we ran late and I didn't get home until 8:30. I walked in the door and entered the living room and was met with a thrown package right in my face. I didn't see it coming and I threw it back at Dad. He lunged at me but I side-stepped him. He grabbed the collar of my shirt and tore it off as I ran out the front door and ran right through the screen door on the front porch.

There was a Lutheran Church down the street and since it was Christmas Eve many of the faithful were walking to church. I stood in the middle of the street, shirtless and bleeding from the screen door, cursing my dad. "You fuckin' son of a bitch, fuck you, you cocksucker." While the faithful, humming, 'Silent Night' and 'Oh, Come All Ye Faithful' silently trod to worship.

Must have been quite a sight.

It was cold and I was naked from the waist up. I ran to Steve Price's house and knocked on the door. Mrs. Price answered. "Oh my God, what happened?" I explained and they let me in and clothed me. They were having a quiet night at home but they understood. I stayed there for a few days until Dad left.

The package was a shirt.

We had the best team in the intramural basketball league but lost our only game in the championship game.

1966 came in like a lion. It seemed the entire world was falling apart and no one was paying attention. President Johnson was losing the war in Vietnam, student unrest and civil disobedience, and Martin Luther King and all the unrest disturbed my already unstable mind.

No one talked about this stuff in school. The teachers didn't bring it up. Everything was just 'peachy' as far as they were concerned.

I was becoming very cynical of life.

I always admired the satirist Mort Sahl and his sneer. That know-it-all and I-told-you-so sneer. That wonderful sneer. I practiced the 'sneer' in the bathroom mirror. A cockeyed, lip curled, teeth showing sneer.

Dad called it a smirk. He told me to "wipe that smirk of your face," and he did with a hard slap.

Some of my friends began calling me 'Slick Guy.' Must have been the smirk, er, sneer. Don't know which.

Emil (Tim) was playing in the Fabulous Ferrais by now and I was so proud of him. I bought his first guitar for him at Sears. Think I spent $35 for it. He learned to play it in ten minutes. I've never seen anything like it. Emil could pick up any instrument, sax, trumpet, guitar, and after some initial toots and strums, begin playing it. He basically mastered the guitar in a month and joined the band.

Emil was the class clown. He was and still is the funniest person I've ever known. He got his new name, a nickname, from his first day at Cotter High. The teacher asked him his name and he answered 'Emil.' It stuck. He did look just like my grandpa, Emil.

That St. Patrick's Day, Emil painted himself green from head to toe, and as the two of us walked to school, paint brush in hand, he painted the bottoms of his feet and left green footprints all the way to school. He was the hit of the school as green footprints were everywhere. Someone asked me if he was really my brother, "No," was my response, laughing. The Principal made him clean up the 'mess.' He had lots of help. All the kids were on his side.

So much was happening that spring. I had met a wonderful girl from the public high school. Her name was Vicky. She was the smartest person in her senior class. She really liked me and I suppose that's why I liked her. We went to movies and held hands and made out at the drive- in theater. Her parents were really nice and my mom actually liked her too.

She was beautiful and smart and was going to TCU in Fort Worth. I wanted to go to Notre Dame.

I was in love for the first time.

I was Captain of the track team. Emil and I were the stars of the team. I could out jump the high jumper, out run the 440 guy, jump further than the broad jumper, and so could Emil. I ran the 100, 220, 180 low hurdles, and the first leg of the 880 relay. Emil ran the 100, 220, the 880 relay, and the mile relay.

There was a new kid in school. His name was Mark Kennedy. His friends had been telling me how fast he was and he told them he could beat me in the 100. We began practice on the recently thawed yet muddy field at the Recreation Center. I led calisthenics because I was Captain. We stretched and did the usually routine and then we jogged for a couple of miles. I wanted to work on my starts so I put a starter block down and practiced. Mark came over and he was rather arrogant as he informed me that he was faster than I was. I sniggered and let it go at that. No use getting too excited about that.

After a few days I ran through my steps on the hurdles and wanted to run a couple of hundreds. I decided not to strain myself yet and only run at about 80%. I wasn't in shape yet and didn't want any pulled muscles.

Mark and Emil and myself lined up for the 100. Someone started us and off we went. Mark was fast. I didn't even run hard and either did Emil and Mark won easily.

The next day at school the talk was out that Kennedy had beaten me in the 100 and that he was now the fastest guy in school.

Our first track meet came up. I hadn't really busted one yet. We lined up for the 100 yard dash. I busted this one winning by 5 yards. Emil came in second and Mark was back in the pack. I just winked at him after the race.

We did have one of the better 880 relay teams in the State. I ran the first leg and Emil ran the last. Two other guys ran the second and third legs. Emil was amazing. It was a 220 leg and he was unbeatable.

Emil could never beat me in the 100 and I could never beat him in the 220.

In a later meet Emil tore his hamstring and never ran again.

There was a huge track meet in Rochester. About ten schools were invited. The meet lasted all day. I decided to compete in the 180 low hurdles only because the events required heats. There was no way I could run four 100's and four 880 relays.

I did fine in the heats for the hurdles winning two and coming in second on another. The idea being to run just fast enough to get to the final heat. I was the only one from our team to reach the finals in any event.

We lined up. Set the blocks. I busted it! I hit every hurdle in stride and took first. I set a new school record (beating my own) and was so proud. I think I could have taken the 100 too but it was a stretch to compete in two events.

A funny thing happened at the meet. Last year's Principal, Father McCauley was there and he walked up to Holzier and I, and said something. Darrell hit him right in the nose. "Fuckin' prick," Darrell said as he laid him down. McCauley got up and walked away. Served him right.

By the end of the season I had set the school record in the 180 low hurdles and the 100. Both of those records would stand for twenty years.

School ended. I graduated. Good riddance.

I had done well enough in the SAT's to be accepted at Marquette, The University of Wisconsin, and Notre Dame. Notre Dame was my first choice and Dad had always promised me that I could go there. But, it was not to be. Dad said he didn't have the money and he wanted me to stay in town to take care of the family and attend St. Mary's College in Winona.

This would be one of the biggest disappointments in my life.

I had always assumed I would go to Notre Dame.

Part Two

Chapter 1

Summer 1966

It was June 1966.

I had just graduated from Cotter High School in Winona, Minnesota. I had no real plans for the summer except to continue my job at McDonald's for $.95/hour ... I got a raise. After twelve years of Catholic School I was feeling pretty mixed up and confused. I no longer attended Mass and was feeling betrayed by doctrines that seemed to run contrary to my own beliefs. I had planned to go to college and was accepted at St. Mary's College in Winona. The idea of continuing a Catholic education didn't make any sense anymore but it was all that I knew. I had wanted to attend Notre Dame like my father but dashed hopes prevented that. I took the easy way out by accepting St. Mary's. Since I was a hometown boy they gave me a scholarship. Some of my friends were going to Marquette, the University of Wisconsin and other exotic places. I felt let down. My dad had always promised me Notre Dame if I kept my grades up but he didn't have the money. The thought of living at home was repulsive so I made plans to get my own place in town. My mom was constantly drunk and when my dad was around he also drank and beat Mom and myself up.

But I had to go to school. I was 17 and didn't have to register for the draft until I was 18, and I sure as hell didn't want to go to Vietnam. As long as I kept my student deferment I was okay.

One of my best friends Joe called me up and wanted to know if I wanted to go down to the river and hang out in his dad's boathouse. I said sure. He picked me up in his brand new red MG. His folks gave it to him for graduation.

"Hey, Mike, jump in man."

"Jeez, Joe, this is a great car!" I was envious.

I didn't have a car or a license but that was going to change.

"Mike, open the back window, it's hot in here."

"Ok," I replied.

And off we sped to the Marina.

We drove across the bridge which spanned the Mississippi River and drove down into the marina and parked by his dad's houseboat. We used to hang out a lot there. Sometimes we even took the boat out and rode to one of the dozens of sandbars that were known for wild keg parties. Joe unlocked the door.

The entire house boat floated. The boat was in the water in the middle of the houseboat. There was ample room with walk-ways on both sides. Two big doors swung open to launch the boat. The front had a kitchen with cupboards and stove and a fridge. The upstairs had a bedroom. There was always plenty of Hamm's. Joe turned on the stereo and I opened a couple of beers.

"Your car is cool. You're lucky your parents got that for you."

"Yeah, I know," asserted Joe, "they said if I stayed home and went to Winona State they'd get me a car. So, I guess I actually saved them money," he chuckled.

"Mike, what are you going to do this summer?"

"Work at McDonald's, I guess. Just like last summer."

I hated that job because I felt so self-conscious working inside this glass box where everybody could see me. And I made hardly any money.

"Not me, I'm going to work in a cannery and make some real money. I can make enough in two months to last all year!"

"Really?"

"Yep. Wanna work with me over there? My dad knows the owner and we can get a cushy job."

"Well, anything would be better than McDonald's. I hate that place. When can we start?"

"In a couple of days. They're harvesting the corn and the peas right now. I've already talked to them."

We settled back in and drank our beers. Joe could get more beer at the Marina because he told them it was for his dad. Joe's dad spent a lot of money at the Marina. We had it made. Joe called his girl friend up and she brought her friend along. We listened to the stereo and hung out. We had another case of beer and plenty of smokes, two willing girls and a chance to make some money. Boy, life is great.

The girls left and I asked Joe if I could sleep here.

"Sure."

He understood my predicament.

I slept like a rock. The boathouse gently rocked to the waves. I woke in the morning and dove into the backwater to wash myself. I found some coffee and smoked. Joe showed up about noon.

"I'd better tell McDonald's that I quit!"

"Be nice, Mike. Tell them you'll be back in the fall for school so you can still have a job."

"Yeah, that's a good idea. You're always thinking Joe."

I walked to the marina and called my manager and told him. He was really pissed off and told me I wouldn't have a job when I came back in September. I said okay and hung up. I did what Joe suggested but the guy was an asshole anyway. I didn't care. I'd find something else.

"Did'ja do it?"

"Yeah, he told me 'don't bother coming back.' That prick! They work your ass off and pay nothing and expect you to work the hours they give you....aw....fuck it!"

"You'll be all right. I've got a few bucks so we can party. Let's take the boat out and water ski and check out girls ... come on, Mike cheer up!"

We got the Evinrude fired up and got some more beer and Joe pulled out of the marina and we eventually reached the channel of the Mississippi. The sun beat down and we headed north to the sandbars. We found some other kids and partied. Joe wanted to ski so I pulled him around for a while. He was really a good skier. He never fell down. It was my turn so we switched. I had trouble getting up but after several attempts I made it. We had fun. Not a worry in my head. We trekked all the way back to Winona and went under the bridge. When we passed a barge, however, the waves caused me to lose my balance. I must have bounced two or three times before I bobbed up. I lost a ski and couldn't see it. Joe was laughing his ass off when he picked me up. I was exhausted but laughing too.

"Lets go back. Hey, how'd you do with Mary last night? She really likes you."

" I like her too. She's really intelligent and we just talked mostly."

Vicki had left for TCU a few weeks ago. She started school early. I knew I'd never see her again.

"Mostly?...what else did'ja do?"

I just giggled. Joe smiled that knowing smile.

We returned to the marina and moored the boat. I was a pretty good deckhand and hopped out to cushion the boat. That boat didn't have a ding on it and I knew Joe was particular about his boat.

Joe called the girls. This was like a going away party. We turned the lights down and listened to the Beatles over and over. Joe and his girl went upstairs. They were going at it pretty heavy.

"Want to go for a walk?"

"Sure," replied Mary.

The mosquitoes were thick and heavy so we brought a blanket along. We were both wearing shorts and were getting bitten alive. We found a nice spot under a tree on the bank of the river and looked at the lights of Winona.

"Mike, what are you studying in school?" asked Mary.

"Well, my dad wants me to be a dentist, So, I'll be taking Pre-Med classes. Lots of chemistry and math. How 'bout you, Mary?"

"Oh, I'm going to the U of M to be a school teacher. I love kids and want to teach grade school somewhere."

"Maybe I could visit sometime." I immediately felt embarrassed for saying that but Mary seemed pleased with that prospect.

She kissed me and this milky warm feeling surged through my entire body. My toes tingled.

The bugs were horrible and we laid under the blanket and kissed. I was floating. Mary moaned as I cupped her breast. A train rumbled in the distance. A barge slowly and silently passed as we made love on the banks of the Mississippi.

I told Mary I loved her.

"I love you too, Mike."

We didn't speak. We just nestled together. We made love again.

Joe and Alice were back downstairs when we returned.

"Oh, there you are ... I've got some gin I stole from my parents house ... want some?" cajoled Alice.

"Yeah," we all replied.

Alice also brought some 45's and we danced to 'Wild Thing' into the night.

The girls were too drunk to drive home. Joe and Alice went upstairs. Mary and I made a nest on the kitchen floor. We were both pretty smashed and Mary had the hiccups.

I felt like the happiest guy in the world. I had a girlfriend and was going to be a dentist.

Woke the next morning. "I feel like shit ... wanna go for a swim?" I whispered to Mary.

"K."

We just jumped in, in our underwear. No one was around. The cool water woke us right up.

"You okay? You look a little peeked."

"Yeah.....shit! I have to get home. My parents are gonna kill me."

We woke Joe and Alice. They were in bad shape as well. Alice didn't seem to care about what her parents thought but Mary was freaking out. They left right away.

Joe and I were supposed to be at the cannery already. So we threw our beaten bodies into the car and took off. Joe had packed some clothes but I didn't have a thing except the clothes on my back.

The plant was thirty miles away in Rushford, Minnesota. The place was pretty big. A few hundred cars were parked in the parking lot. Huge piles of corn and peas stood outside the plant. It smelled like rotting flesh. The place was so loud that you had to shout to be heard. The floor shook. I followed Joe into an office. A secretary sat at her desk.

"Hi Joe, welcome back. You want to see Mr. Henry? I'll get him for you."

Joe just winked at me.

Mr. Henry appeared momentarily and shook Joe's hand and said, "Come on in boys. Have a seat."

"Mr. Henry, this is my buddy Mike and he would like a summer job too. He wants to be a dentist and is going to St. Mary's this fall."

"Glad to meet you. Sure thing. Joe, I'll tell Steve. Mike, can you start right away?"

Steve was the plant foreman.

"Yes, sir!"

Well, true to his word, good old Joe came through for me. So, after filling out some forms and giving them my Social Security number, off we went. I met Steve and he was a nice guy. I followed him. Joe said he'd see me later. They gave me a card to punch in on a time clock. It must have been over 100 degrees in there and no air. It smelled so bad I thought I'd throw up. Steve led me to a ladder and we climbed up. We were standing on this 15 foot high steel mesh stand, several people, mostly Mexican, stood facing an assembly line of husks of corn. What you were supposed to do was grab the good husks and throw them into this open slot where it de-husked and chopped the corn. Simple enough. I took a slot and watched the guy next to me. We couldn't talk because it was so loud in there. He worked with alarming speed and dexterity. Doing ten husks to my one. I would get better.

After what seemed a lifetime, I began to get very dizzy. With the assembly line moving right to left and tossing the corn to the right I had to hold on with one hand. I was very hung over from last night. Oh, last night was so sweet. I missed Mary already. But, I had to work. If you stopped you would lose your balance and fall over. I don't know how these people did it! I can't see myself doing this job for long. Joe had a great job, he said, back in the warehouse where it was pretty quite and cooler. Maybe, he can get me back there.

Suddenly, with a jump, the whole mechanism stopped. It was break time. We had ten minutes. I couldn't even walk for a second. I guess I'd been working a couple of hours straight. I did manage to climb back down the ladder. I walked outside to get some air. God, this place stinks. The piles of corn looked higher than before. I smoked a cigarette.

Back to work. God, I'm hungry but this place is making my appetite go away. I just remembered I should have told my mom where I was. Oh well, she won't miss me anyway.

Within minutes that same sickening feeling returned.

Again, everything stopped. I lost my balance and hung on. Some shouting could be heard down the line. They were yelling in Spanish.

Something told me to go see what was happening. A man was lying on the grating and blood was spurting from his arm. He was rolling over and over and screaming. I tried to grab him but he kicked me and rolled over again. Then I saw why he was screaming. His hand was gone! He must have put his arm into the machine because it was jammed with corn. I finally managed to get him still. I told anyone to call for an ambulance. I tore my tee shirt off and used it to apply a tourniquet above his elbow. Steve showed up and he helped me with the guy. He was going into shock and we managed to raise his head. Someone else came with a towel to cover him. He was trembling. I couldn't understand a word he said but he was in severe pain and trauma. After what seemed like 30 minutes an ambulance showed up and they took him away. Everybody was shook up. There was blood everywhere. They found his mangled hand in the shucked corn vat. I don't know what they did with his hand or if they saved the corn. They shut the line down while everything got steam cleaned.

I decided to quit.

I told Steve and he seemed to understand but urged me to stay.

"Maybe we can find another job for you, Mike."

"I don't know."

"I'll talk to Mr. Henry and tell him what you just did to help that guy. That was quick thinking."

"Well, okay, my friend Joe works back in the warehouse. I'd like that."

"Stay here. Don't leave, Mike."

Steve promised to return. The sun was baking but it was still cooler outside. I waited under a tree by the edge of the parking lot. I felt sick. That was very upsetting to see. The poor guy. He wasn't very old and now he only had one hand. I hope he's okay. He's probably heavily sedated by now and out of pain. I was shirtless now, penniless, hungry, feeling pretty lost, and had blood all over me. Maybe I should just hitch-hike back to Winona. Fuck this, I mumbled to myself.

Steve did return.

"Mike," He yelled across the parking lot, "come with me."

I followed Steve back up to Mr. Henry's office. He looked upset.

"That poor bastard. Steve tells me you put a tourniquet on his arm. Good thinking. I'm going over to the hospital now to see him. They are going to transfer him to Mayo. We haven't had an accident like that here in several years. I feel terrible. We try to teach them safety but ... anyway, don't leave Mike. We have a job back in the warehouse taking inventory and storing the canned food before we ship it out. Steve will take you back there. Will you try it out?"

"Yes sir. Thank you, Mr. Henry."

"Steve, get him a clean shirt."

"Come on, Mike. I'm glad you're staying. We need smart people here."

I wiped myself down in the rest room, put a tee shirt on and Steve drove me downtown in his car. He bought me some new tee shirts and a pair of jeans and we stopped at an AW stand and chowed down a couple of burgers and a milkshake. It was nearly dark.

"I can't pay you back for all the clothes, Steve," I exclaimed.

"Don't worry, this is on the plant. You had a hard day and we really do want you to stay. Joe's dad is a close friend of Mr. Henry's and he would do anything for Joe. He's like a son to him."

I still had some blood on me so Steve took me to his house and let me take a shower. I put on the new clothes and we returned to the plant.

"Steve, I never punched out."

"Don't worry about that either."

"Steve, how long have you been here?" I inquired.

"My Uncle has grown peas and corn ever since I was born and I have always helped him out in the fields harvesting. Well, this plant came here when I was just starting high school and I've worked here ever since. We work year-round, you know. What we can this summer will be here for six or seven months before we ship it out someplace. The rest of the year we only need about ten people here but from spring to early fall we hire 500 or 600 extra people to help out. Without this cannery, Rushford would be nothing."

"Maybe I could work here during the school year. When I get a car, that is."

"Yeah, maybe."

"Where are you going to stay?"

"Dunno," I replied.

"I know this nice farm lady who has a Streamline Camper. I'll call her. Maybe you guys can rent it from her for the summer. It's too far to drive to Winona each day."

"Thanks, Steve."

What a first day on the job!

Joe and I hooked up again. We had a place to stay. I told him all about my weird day and he just laughed.

"Yeah, man, I know," the news had spread throughout the plant.

The camper was only a minute down the road. It was all arranged. Mrs. Kawaski was only going to charge us $15 a week for the two of us. The camper was small but it had an outhouse and outdoor shower and one bed and a pull out bed in the living room. We tossed a coin and Joe got the bedroom. I didn't care.

Mrs. Kawaski had two other campers on her property. I saw the neighbor lady smoking near her camper.

So there we were. It was late but we did think of getting a six pack before coming home. We sat and talked for a while but we were worn out so we hit the hay.

We both awoke at 6 a.m. We walked across a field to the cannery. I was supposed to begin my new job and walked with Joe to the warehouse.

The horrible stink. The noise. Thoughts of the horrors of yesterday filled me. Joe took off and I asked around for John, the warehouse foreman, where they stored inventory.

"You Mike?"

"Yes sir."

"I heard about your day yesterday ... bad way to start."

"Yeah, it made me sick. Have you heard if that guy is okay?"

"Dunno ... I heard they took him to the Mayo clinic. Poor bastard. Anyway, have you ever done inventory control before? It isn't hard. You just have to be good with numbers and pay attention. I'll train you myself."

John was a nice guy too. He looked so tired and worn out. I guess he had a lot to do. He showed me how to count the pallets of corn and peas as they were fork-lifted back into the warehouse. Each can had a set of numbers on it which designated what and when the product was produced. There were three or four guys that all they did was stack the pallets up with a forklift. As each pallet came in I was supposed to write it down with a time and date and then designate which row and stack they were in. It didn't look too hard but you couldn't miss a beat because they just kept coming in.

But, this was preferable to my first task. It was cooler and considerably quieter and cleaner and the floor didn't shake. I found out that they were paying me more per hour too! I was now making $1.78 an hour. Some quick math told me I could pay my tuition of $400 for the year and my rent when I found a place, and be able to eat and have money left over. I would just use books from the library. I could save enough money in two months of work. Because they let you work all you want and after 60 hours they paid time and a half. What a break. I would never be able to make that at McDonald's but I planned to work there during the school year just for pocket money. If they'd hire me back. Maybe I could even get a car!

I worked with fervor. Sometimes the line would break down and we wouldn't have any cans come in for hours. We would take a nap or play cards. John didn't seem to care. He just wanted to make sure that there was somebody here to keep track. The fork lift guys were all college guys from Winona State. They were cool. I wanted to learn how to drive one too. They made good money. They drove like maniacs and stacked the pallets 6 high. Probably 40 feet up. I don't know what held them up. The rows were straight and I was always nervous walking down in there because if a row would fall the entire warehouse would fall like dominos.

Days passed in a haze. I was working 18 hour days but it wasn't hard work so I was able to keep at it. Joe and I would hook up at the end of the day and swig beers. We were both filthy and a shower felt good. We made sure to pay Mrs. Kawaski the rent. She baked pies for us and even gave us sandwiches. She was really nice. We didn't see her much because it was midnight when we got home.

"I need a day off," I stated one night.

"Oh, here, takes a couple of these in the morning and some more during the day. You won't get tired."

"What are they?" I asked. "Bennies ... whites ... the truck drivers use 'em."

"Where'd you get these, Joe?"

"Some guy in the warehouse. I took a couple after the dinner break and I'm still awake."

"All right, I just want to keep working."

"That's the idea."

So, after only sleeping another 4 hours we awoke and trudged to the cannery.

"Take one now, Mike."

"Oh yeah. I forgot."

In twenty minutes I was zooming around the warehouse. The cans weren't coming yet. I walked into my little office and checked my log book. The guy who took my place for six hours was no where to be seen but he had logged for a couple of hours. I could hear the drone of machinery and felt part of it. I drank copious amounts of coffee and smoked a lot. I could feel the blood rushing in my ears. I felt great!

Joe and I continued working. We received our first pay checks and we were so proud and amazed. In three weeks I cleared almost $450. I'd never seen that much in my life. We took off at lunch and put some money in a savings account. I kept $50 in cash. I had my tuition paid for! I needed another check for rent and another check for living expenses. If we worked until late August we'd be rich. I was good at saving money. Joe cashed his check. We both bought cigarettes and some food. I paid Joe back the $20 I owed him.

"Let's party tonight," exclaimed Joe. "I know these two girls who might want to party with us."

"Great."

After our stretch Joe and I walked back to the camper. I noticed two shadows standing under a night light.

"Hey, they're already here," said Joe.

"Oh yeah, the girls."

Joe introduced me to Susan and Michele. Both were blonde haired girls from St. Charles. They both seemed pretty young. We turned the radio on and opened some beers. After some uncomfortable silences, we sort of relaxed and started a conversation. I was real quiet. I felt like anything I would say would be dumb. I was still feeling speedy and just wanted to sit back and enjoy. The music was blaring pretty loud so I turned it down a bit.

"What're doing?"

"Turning it down, man. Don't want to wake her up," referring to the landlady.

"All right," resigned Joe.

Joe had designs on Susan and asked her to dance. She didn't want to. Susan and Michele looked nervous so Joe backed down. I didn't want any trouble but maybe this was a bad idea. They looked so young. I just sat on the couch with Michele sitting across on a chair, Joe on the floor and Susan sitting near Michele.

I was missing Mary. I really didn't want to start anything with this girl.

"Are you guys working tomorrow?" I asked the girls.

"Yeah," answered Susan.

"Where do you guys work?" she asked.

"We work in the warehouse."

They worked in the warm part of the plant. They stacked the cans into these great round baskets which were lifted into huge vats of boiling water. The room was a sauna. Unbearable heat. I walked through there several times and immediately began sweating profusely. They had a hard job.

The hour was getting late and I could see that we were going no where with these girls. They were nice local girls who wanted to party with college boys.

We said good night to the girls.

Joe seemed disappointed that the evening hadn't gone better.

"I'm tired, but I don't think I can sleep," I stated.

"Me too!"

I put my head down and fell asleep in a second.

Six a.m. came too quick. We took fast showers outside, dressed, and walked across our field to work another 18 hour shift. It was sprinkling. Maybe, it wouldn't be so hot today.

"Here. Take this."

Joe handed me another benny.

"Thanks."

I eagerly swallowed the small pill.

"I need coffee."

"Yeah, me too."

We punched our time cards.

"See ya later, Joe."

We parted ways. I walked into my office and made a pot of coffee. After a couple of cups and smokes I felt awake again.

The cans began coming in. The forklift drivers brought in pallets as fast as I could log them in. One of the huge warehouses was beginning to fill up. Next week some of the food distributor semis would show up and we would load them up with peas and corn.

Steve came by to see how we were doing. He checked my book and seemed pleased. As long as I kept up with production he didn't care what I did.

I found Joe reading the paper atop his elevated post.

"Can I get another benny, Joe."

"Sure."

I was tired and didn't want to party tonight. I needed more than 3 hours of sleep.

I returned to my post. We had another production stoppage which lasted several hours. Me and the forklift guys hung out. I was making some good friends. I met Curtis and John and Terry from Dodge, Wisconsin. They were attending the University of Wisconsin in Madison. The guys from Winona State had quit. We exchanged addresses and phone numbers.

They were a good bunch of guys. They had long hair and I admired them. I thought maybe I would grow my hair out too. They talked against the war in Vietnam. They said they had marches on campus against the war and sometimes a riot would ensue. They described being tear gassed and running through the streets. It sounded pretty exciting to me.

The days passed and Joe and I received a couple more checks. I felt rich. The plant was catching up with the field production and started to close on Sundays. It was a welcomed break. Joe went back to Winona on the first Sunday and returned with a fresh supply of bennies and beer and food and some clothes. One Saturday night after work Joe and I decided to get good and drunk and stayed up all night drinking to the crickets and the moon.

"Joe, I've been thinking."

"Oh oh," Joe laughed.

"We should quit. I've got plenty of money for school and I'd like to have a summer vacation of what's left. Hell, we've got six weeks until school starts."

"Hmmm ...," Joe pondered. He was thinking. Scheming. He got like this, pensive and distant, when he was deep in thought. I must have hit a vein. He was quiet a long time.

"How 'bout a road trip?" he said.

"Yeah ... that would be cool. Where would we go?"

More silence.

"I got it!" Joe was animated. When he got like this it was best to go along with his whim.

"What ... what, tell me!"

"Yeah man, we'll take this great trip around the outside states of the country. You ever been to Oregon and California? To Alabama and Maine?

Yeah, we'll just circle the outside of the country. We won't stop, man. We'll just drive like madmen all the way. Like that guy you like ... who was that? That road book."

"Kerouac's, *On the Road*," I answered, even though I hadn't read it.

"Let's work another week and promise to come back next summer. This place is slowing down anyway."

"Okay."

We got very excited about this prospect. Joe's car, although small was in tip-top shape and would handle the voyage easily.

Chapter 2

The Road Trip

Well, needless to say, this is all we could talk about. Every break we discussed new ideas for the trip. I would need to return to Winona to tell my mom and get some clothes and stuff. I had a sleeping bag somewhere. I needed to go to the bank and put all my money in the bank in Winona. We figured that $400 in cash for each guy would be plenty.

We finished our stint at the cannery. We were both glad to get out of there but grateful for the work. We were all set.

My mom was none too happy about my trip. She wanted me to stay home. It was so depressing around her. She was drinking a lot and my younger siblings were out of control just coming and going, eating when they could scrounge food. My dad was gone somewhere. I didn't care anymore. I had to leave.

I called Joe. He was ready. He had maps and had changed the oil in his MG. We would leave first thing in the morning.

I could hardly sleep I was so excited. Visions of the great West and the East Coast danced in my head. I had been to most States but never to California or Texas or Florida.

Joe showed up at 6 a.m. We were so used to getting up early. My mom was still asleep. I didn't even say goodbye. We took off.

"This is great!" exclaimed Joe. "Here, have a benny."

"Don't mind if I do," I chuckled.

I had some coffee in the thermos and offered Joe a cup. I sipped mine. We left Winona on that humid August morning to fulfill our destinies. I felt so happy inside. So content knowing school was paid for and we had four plus weeks of road visions ahead.

We had only gone a few miles and we stopped in Red Wing to refill our thermos with coffee and buy some sweet rolls. I was logging every dime we spent. $1.49 so far. We would split expenses. I offered to pay for the bennies. Another $1.

We headed north on Highway 61 along the Mississippi River into the Twin Cities to catch Highway 94 West. I read the map and became the navigator. Joe had the top down on the MG. We had sunglasses on. We were cool. This was great.

"God, those things are cheap," I said, referring to the bennies.

"I know. This guy who works for my dad and drives the truck, gets them for me. They'll be great for school too."

"Yeah. I feel really good when I take one. I feel so focused and alert," I asserted.

Highway 61 Revisited. I was reminded of Dylan's song about this highway. We didn't have any killin' to get done, just drivin.' The road hugs the great Mississippi River with the bluffs touching the road on the left. Wisconsin is on the other side of the river. Bluffs over there too. The leaves hadn't started to turn yet. Green lush woods and sparkling blue water.

Suddenly the vista changes into farmland across gentle rolling hills. We are near the Twin Cities. Time to check the map. We need to find Highway 94 West. We got a little lost but managed to find it okay. It was mid-morning and there was heavy traffic. This was the big city to us. We both had to pee so we stopped at a service station and gassed up. One of us would always stay with the car. We had all our stuff just sitting there in the open. Joe went first. I paid for the gas and peed, got some more coffee. We hit 94 with a renewed gusto.

"This is great!"

"Sure is."

Joe was at the wheel. I only had a Learner's Permit but I didn't care. I could drive if I had to.

It wasn't long before the terrain flattened out. We could see forever, it seemed. The interstate wasn't completed yet and eventually the road turned into two lanes. That sure slowed us down. Tractors and trucks for an hour. We drove through every farm community at 35 miles per hour. We wanted to get well into North Dakota before nightfall but at this rate ... yikes. Somewhere east of Fargo the road turned back into four lanes again. We raced into the sun for hours. Visors down. Time for a pit stop. We had plenty of gas but filled up anyway. Peed. Checked the oil. Everything was a 'go.'

The sun was right in our eyes as we entered Fargo. We had travelled almost 350 miles in eight hours. We could go another four hours. Coffee was flowing. Bennies taken. Joe had stretched at the last stop and said he was fine. Nothing much on the radio. We basically sat in awed silence as the road unravelled new and wonderful sights.

"Two States down....um," I had to count, " hell, I don't know....23 to go."

We both laughed out loud.

"Joe, what's your major?" I inquired.

"Girls," he unabashedly answered.

"No, seriously."

"My dad wants me to get a degree in business so I can take over his business someday."

His father owned and operated a Food Distribution Company that catered to local restaurants. Joe and I had graduated together from Cotter High. We had chummed around for about a year or so. We had played football together. Had double-dated together. We did everything together. His parents were always nice to me. They also took me in after my dad had beaten me up. They said they would fix up an apartment for me over their garage with a kitchen and bathroom. Lots of people in Winona rented to students. They said I could rent it from them if I wanted to. I could now. I had some money. Joe's parents gave their blessing to our trip. Joe promised to write postcards along the route. He wanted to send one from each State. Cool idea. I didn't have anyone to send one to. I would remind him though.

Joe had dutifully mailed one at the last stop from Fargo. It had a picture of some guy sitting on a Buffalo. Joe had a wallet full of 3 cent stamps.

Joe had a clear future mapped out for him. I didn't have a clue. It'll come to me someday in a vision. A burning bush will appear and a voice will tell me to be a dentist, or something. Nothing career-wise interested me at all. I couldn't see being a travelling salesman like my dad. I liked to write but wasn't very good. I loved to read. Maybe I could teach. I liked literature ... but not that much. I don't know. It'll come to me.

Many more miles to Bismark. The sun was low in the sky and getting difficult to drive. Joe squinted his eyes.

"You all right?"

"Yup."

"Do you want to stop up ahead somewhere and eat?" I asked.

"Yeah, let's drive until dark and we'll stop at a truck stop. My dad says the food is always good and cheap there."

"My dad says the same thing."

We drove into the east side of Bismark, North Dakota and saw a truck stop looming ahead. Dozens of semi-trailers parked. Only a few cars. Must have been about nine o'clock. We had driven over 500 hundred miles. Wow!

Grim heads turned as we walked in. We sat in a booth. A waitress came over. She poured coffee without even asking. Joe and I both ordered fries and a burger. As we waited, we both kept an eye on the car. We had put the top up when we parked. A red MG seemed so out of place among giant trucks and a smattering of pick ups. I looked at Joe and just laughed.

"What's so funny?"

"We did it, man. Last night I slept in my own bed for the last time. I swear, I never want to go home again. I was reading a book by Margret Mead about these ancient tribes somewhere and she talks about the 'rites of passage' for boys and girls in the tribe. When the children ... like the boys are only 14 or 15 or something ... anyway, when they 'pass' the test ... like they circumcise the boys ... yikes! ... when they pass the test they are considered adults. You know, a Man or a Woman. Can't remember what they do to the girls but I'm sure it's gross. Anyway, maybe this is our 'rite of passage.' Do you feel any different?" I asked.

"Yeah," responded Joe, "I'm tired."

"No ... you know what I mean ..."

"Yeah, I do feel different. I feel like I'm free ... really free for the first time in my life. Away from my parents. I love my parents but they do everything for me. I envy you actually, Mike, because your parents don't care what you do. My mom just hovers over me all the time. I can't take a shit without her knowing about it. When I was little she wouldn't let me flush the turd down until she checked it out. God! And it's still the same. That's why I liked working in the cannery so much. My dad always wants me working in his warehouse. Fuck it."

After a pause, he said, "Yeah, I feel different all right."

The burgers came. Oh man.

"Our dads were right ... the food is great."

"Yumm," Joe chortled.

We ate in silence.

The waitress returned. "You boys want some desert? We got tapioca and home-made pie."

"Yes please ... I'd like a piece of apple pie," I said.

"Me too!" Joe responded, "Please."

"A la mode?"

"What's that?"

"With ice cream on it. You wanted it heated?"

"Sure. Yes!" we both answered.

"Classy place," I remarked.

Joe assented with a nod.

A trucker seated at a table across from us inquired where we were from.

"Winona, Minnesota," I answered.

"Where you boys headed?"

Joe told him the whole plan. We were going to drive around the outside states of the country.

"Why?" He had a troubled and puzzled look on his face. He drove because he had to. The thought of driving that far for kicks was foreign to him.

"Because we want to," I shrugged.

"Let me give you boys some advice," he offered, "don't drink a lot of coffee, don't eat nothing but apples and oranges and fruit, you know like bananas, no nuts, stop every four hours and get your mind right. Stretch your legs. Only drink water."

"Okay, Mister."

He got up and walked out.

He had been drinking a glass of water.

We watched the trucker pay for his dinner and walk out to his truck. Without saying it we both acknowledged him and gained our respect.

We both needed sleep. We had parked the car way back in between huge semi-trucks. We threw our sleeping bags on the ground out there and slept under the stars with the groans of diesel engines.

I slept like hell. The ground was hard. The truck noise incessant. The ground shook all night long. Had to piss like a racehorse. No one around so I pissed in the grass behind the truck stop. Joe moaned as he awoke.

"Sleep okay?"

"Fuck you," he responded.

We both laughed.

We were both so stiff and sore that we stretched and walked around to loosen up. My mouth tasted like something died in there. My right side was tingling as the blood re-flowed into starved veins.

"Look, a shower," we shouted in unison.

For a quarter you got about ten minutes of hot water. Man, that was the best shower I've ever had. Today was going to be hot again so I wetted all my clothes and put on the same stuff as yesterday.

Joe and I were dressed and packed by 7 a.m. and ready to go. After gassing up and buying some coffee and doughnuts we continued down the never ending road.

"I know that guy last night said 'no coffee,' but dammit, I want coffee."

"Me too," I agreed.

"We should hit the Montana border by this afternoon."

"Okay."

Joe focused on the road. Traffic was sparse and we made good time. The terrain had drastically changed from green rich cow pastures to barren hilly vistas. Some of it looked like a big gravel pit while off in the west we could vaguely make out the promise of the Rockies. Occasionally we would see herds of sheep and even spotted some bison in the far off. We had entered some kind of spooky empty huge vastness I had never seen before. It was scary at first because I felt so exposed. I had never experienced this kind of hugeness. It was as if the sky just grew and grew and we became smaller and smaller. The road opened before us becoming an eventual dot as the lines of the roads merged together.

We could see forever.

"I'd hate to break down out here," I stated.

"Yeah, who'd pick us up?"

"You know, I was thinking about what that trucker told us last night. You know, about eating just fresh fruit and no coffee or too much water. 'Cause I have to piss again and we lose a lot of time that way."

Joe nodded in agreement and said, "Let's stop at the next place we see and buy some apples."

"Okay."

Soon enough another truck stop appeared on the horizon. This one had a grocery store and a restaurant and even a place to wash clothes. So, we topped off the gas tank. I duly entered the figures in a notebook.

We walked to the grocery store next door and stocked up on apples and bananas and grapes. Couple of bucks worth.

"That'll hold us."

"Yep."

So far we'd spent under $40 and had travelled over 750 miles. It's hotter than hell today. Listening to the radio and nothing but cowboy music and religious programs. But a weatherman from Bismark tells us, before that station fades out, that highs of up to 95 degrees are expected. What water we have has to be for the car if it overheats. Joe is watching the temperature gauge closely but it never approaches the red line so I took a cup full of water and poured right over my head.

"What in the hell are you doing?" Joe protested.

"Coolin' off. Want some?"

"Yeah," Joe surrendered.

So I poured a cup over Joe's head.

"Whoooa!"

It cooled us off right away. We continued this method until the evening came as we entered the State of Montana. The Big Sky Country. Cowboys and horses and the biggest range I've ever seen.

"You getting tired? I'll drive, Joe."

"No, I'm okay."

The guy has been steady on the wheel. Except for gas and piss stops, he has driven steady. A true test of fortitude. I think he just wants to be able to say that he drove around the country and he can be honest about it.

No matter to me. I'm enjoying the ride. Day dreaming looking out the window. Watching a movie with no plot or story line. Just visions passing dreamlike in a relaxed state. Montana has no beginning or end. It just looms ahead, behind, all around and up. In all directions at once. The sky meets the earth in an unreal surreal sense. I feel insignificant and alarmingly small. I am lost and frightened. I don't feel important at all. But, I have an energy and I know Joe has it as well ... a push to keep going no matter what. This is the greatest day of my life. I've become a man. In the true sense. A man. Nothing sexual. Nothing more than a spiritual flow in my veins ... of being.

And I'm always thinking if I could live here. And I imagine I could. I could live here, among cowboys and sheep and horses on these magnificent plains.

We made the change from I-94 to I-90 somewhere near Billings and continued west. It is getting dark, about 10 p.m.

"Let's stop for the night," Joe resigned.

"Yeah, that's enough for one day. Jeez, Joe, if you want me to drive ..."

"No, I'm all right," he cut me off.

We found another huge truck stop. Neon lights glow in the distance. A dead man couldn't miss it. Hundreds of trucks with chortling engines. Dozens of gas pumps. Mostly diesel. Silhouetted figures dot the scene. Surreal. Against outlined Rocky mountain points. A melancholy fills me. This place was built for us. It doesn't really exist. But, it is here.

We parked way in back between the trucks. There was a little knoll which provided some privacy and security. We rolled out our sleeping bags and were gone.

Next morning ...

I vaguely recall pulling in here last night. We must have been that tired. It hurt to get up. I was so stiff and sore. The ground was hard and my body was not used to it.

"Fuck!" Joe groaned.

I stood and stretched and shook all over.

"I gotta piss!"

Found the showers again and put in two quarters and let the warm water bring me back to life. I didn't even towel off. It was already warm and the sun was up. I trod back to the car and Joe must have been in a shower too. I packed the car up and neatly rolled up the sleeping bags. Joe returned and we decided to eat and gas up before heading onward.

After two cups of coffee, both of us began to speak. Two days out and we were pretty shot.

"We should stay in a motel tonight," I said.

"That's a good idea. Maybe we can sleep in a bed every third night or something."

"You look like shit."

"You too!"

It was good to be here. We needed each other not only for company but for moral support.

"I feel like shit," I giggled.

We finished our breakfast and gassed up the MG. I cleaned out the car of garbage and wiped off the windshield. A million bugs had given their lives so far on our trip. Some of them were imbedded on the bumper. I hope they were enjoying the trip. Joe checked the oil and under the hood. The tires looked good.

We picked up a radio station from Missoula. At last, some rock and roll. 'Wild Thing' had just come out and they played it three times that afternoon. They played Beatle songs and Joe and I sang along. The Rocky Mountains dealt the perfect background. What a beautiful place. I can't believe people actually lived here. I was jealous coming from the flat plain states of Ohio and Minnesota.

We soon hit the Idaho border and were served the great pines and blue lake of Coeur d'Alene. The Washington border welcomed us as we headed into Spokane. I can't believe it. We are actually in Washington State.

Joe and I pulled over in a rest stop and gnawed on a couple of apples and drank some water. I bought a pack of Old Gold's that morning and we had a smoke. I didn't smoke that much yet but I figured it would be cool.

"Should we go all the way to Seattle? I'm looking here and we could cut through to Oregon and drive down the Columbia River. Look!" I passed the map to Joe.

"Hey, maybe that would work out. That highway goes all the way to Portland. Yeah, let's do that!"

Agreed!

We drove across the high desert plain of Washington.

"Look at that! What is that?"

We would see dozens of 'dust devils' that day. Strange surreal miniature tornados would suddenly appear and dance across the view. One even hit the car and moved us a couple of feet into the other lane. Luckily there was no traffic out here. This was such a deserted place.

Kinda scary and lonely.

Desolate-high-desert-mountain-eastern-Washington-State-blues. Miles of never ever-ending rolling hills with dancing surreal mini-tornados and black highway curling through these endless valleys and vistas like some giant unmade bed.

Little lonely farms.

A few cattle.

Horses.

Almost no traffic.

Driving 80 miles an hour south toward The Dalles and the Columbia River. Through Kennewick, Washington to get gas and a snack and a chance to look at people again. Pretty empty space out here.

I couldn't imagine living out here but I suppose the people who do live here couldn't possibly imagine living where I live.

"Wonder what people do out here."

"Dunno."

"Lets get goin'."

"Yeah."

Late afternoon. The sun was pouring in on my side of the car. I hung a tee shirt on the window. Hotter than hell!

"We'll be on the river in an hour Joe," I said after consulting the map.

"Hang a right at the water," I joked.

"Gotcha."

Soon enough we crossed over a bridge and were welcomed into Oregon. We headed due west for Portland. The historic Columbia River with tremendous dams, locks, and back waters much like the Mississippi River back home. Several small towns dot the river's edge. Quaint little places more to my liking. I've always liked the water.

Something biological about it.

Joe and I both really loved this part of the trip.

"Hey, we should find a place to stay along the river," I suggested.

"Yeah, maybe, hell, what's the hurry. I'm tired anyway."

So, we meandered down the road a bit and pulled off into this little town and found a safe place down by the river. Turns out that some other people about our age were down here too, camping. Somebody had some beer and before long we had a party going on. We made instant friends telling the other folks about our big trip.

A late night twilight glowed above as we watched and heard the soft constant roar of the Columbia. Had a great night's sleep in deep grass. Dreams of the road danced in my head and I felt afraid and free at the same time.

The roar of the river just knocked us out.

Got up gentle-like. Stretched and scratched. Walked into the cold rushing water and cleansed myself. It was like a Baptism.

"Get up buddy, it's a new day!" I shouted, waist deep in the river.

I felt renewed.

This must be the most beautiful place I've ever seen. We had pulled off the road last night and parked by the waters edge. Only a few feet from the churning water. What it must have been like for the Native peoples long ago living on giant salmon, fishing in waist deep water easily spearing fish into their nets. Today the wide waters were covered with boats, people fishing, and dams. The loud rude noises of outboard motors spoiled the peace.

But, somehow, it was beautiful.

Joe jumped in with a yelp.

"Fuck ... it's cold."

"Told you," I laughed.

My hands were blue and I couldn't feel my feet but the morning air was warm and soon the deep chill subsided. Joe looked like a shivering dog as he limped to shore and let out a loud "whooop!"

We dried ourselves, rolled up the sleeping bags, loaded the car and hit the road.

"Do you realize we will be in California tonight!" I joyfully exclaimed.

Joe just nodded with a satisfying grin on his face. We both knew this would be the highlight of the voyage. We had to see San Francisco and check out the hippie scene. I had only seen hippies on TV and I was at once attracted and appalled. I didn't know what to make of them. And LA was a must. Maybe we'll see a movie star. A friend of mine said he saw Johnny Carson driving down the freeway. Wow! That would be something.

Portland was an hour or two straight ahead and then due south through Oregon. What a beautiful place. Trees and water. The Dalles reminded me of Highway 61 in Minnesota against the great Mississippi River. Same kinda feeling.

Portland ... a maze of bridges and curling roads.

Now, we're headed on a freeway. Most traffic we have seen. Joe is a great driver though, and he's just drivin', man.

"I've got an idea," I said, "let's drive to the coast."

"Okay, I've never seen an ocean."

"Yeah man, lets go."

It was settled. I checked the atlas and found a turn off due west, all the way to the ocean. The Pacific Ocean. Imagine that. An ocean!

After a couple of hours we saw it. Neither of us spoke. A quietude.

Majestic. Huge. What words could describe. The sun was high. A ship on the horizon. It was the work of God.

Indeedy!

The beach was black! Not the sandy yellow tone we expected. Huh?

We parked. I got out. Nobody around. I took all my clothes off and ran like a banshee into the waves. Fuck. Ice Cold ....I was numb. I thought the Columbia was cold but this was a different cold. I lost my breath and just laughed.

"Come on in the water's fine."

Joe trusted me and did the same.

"Oh, fuck me!"

"HA!"

"You fucker!"

We both laughed so hard. I tasted the salt water and dreamed of sharks and other perils in this deep water. I swam out to the breaks and swam back. Joe had enough and ran to the safe shore. As I swam I warmed and felt like a fish. Lived long enough to swim in an ocean. I used to imagine myself in places like this, watching clouds that looked like dragons flowing across the sky on my back in northern Wisconsin, as far from any ocean imaginable, I knew that one day it would happen. I dove beneath the waves and opened my eyes to a scary endless blackness that excited me.

I was out about 100 yards and stiffening up. Decided it best to swim back. I rolled onto my back and let the waves carry me in.

"How can you stand it! You're blue."

"I know ... man, that is cold water. I've got an idea," I said, "let's build a fire and stay here tonight."

"Great idea."

It was settled. Joe and I gathered wood mostly from other fire sites and soon we had a bonfire going. The warmth was welcomed. There was plenty of driftwood available on the beach. Heaven. I'm in Heaven. We had tons of snacks and roasted some hot dogs and just watched the waves. It was late in the afternoon by now and figured California would still be there tomorrow.

We watched the sun slowly set across the water and huddled near the warm fire.

Sleep came easy. The rhythm of the waves rocked us to sleep.

Joe and I woke the next morning cold and shivering. The fire had gone out during the night and both of us must have been so tired that we neglected to add wood to the fire. So, we restarted the fire and within minutes we were warming ourselves near the flames. The sun was just breaking over the cliff tops. The air was bone chilling.

We nibbled on some chips and smoked several cigarettes.

"Coffee! I need coffee."

"Me too."

We gathered up our stuff and headed to the car. I checked the map. We were south of Newport. We headed down 101 and found a gas station. We filled up and I logged the mileage. Joe scraped bugs off the front of the car. Every known squashed insect of North America was plastered on the bumper, grill, and windshield! We gulped needed coffee and stocked up on smokes and bought a couple of gross looking cheese sandwiches and some pop.

"We gotta ways 'til California," I stated.

"Looks that way."

"Don't think we'll make San Francisco tonight..."

"Well," Joe thought a second, "we'll just see how far we can get."

It was early morning as we got back on 101. Hugging the coast all the way I sank into a day dream trance watching the ocean glitter and roll along. The engine just purred and Joe looked like a god. Hair waving in the wind. Top down. Smoking cigs and smiling.

Confidently driving with his right hand hung over the top of the steering wheel, one with his car, steering with his wrist. The sun peeking over cliffs moving from the east like she always does, casting long dark shadows across the road, touching and ending on sandy beaches ... everlasting beaches of black stones giving off a hiss as waves rolled and rolled lazy-like. No radio on. Just ocean sound. The smell of salt on my skin, in the air, on my clothes. The taste, man, the taste of salt. The air filled my lungs.

Making good time. Another 100 miles. We entered the town of Florence.

"Hey, that's my grandma's name."

"What? ..."

"Florence ... that's my grandma's name."

"Oh," Joe chuckled, "You'll have to tell her you were here."

"I think that is the most beautiful name in the world. Florence. Just rolls off the tongue. Like, Florence, Italy. Beautiful, man. Like a flower. Florence Nightingale ... Grandpa told me he fell for her because of her name. Imagine that!"

We decided to drive the coast all the way to San Francisco. Curiously, the beaches turned tan again and then black.

"Joe, how come the beaches are black?"

"Don't know."

"And then they turn back to tan again ... weird."

Patches of heavy fog hugged the mountains almost hiding them. The sea was a misty surreal scene of jetting rocks veiled in grey. It was beautiful.

"Never seen anything so beautiful."

"If we drive all day, I'll bet we can make San Francisco tonight. It's a long haul though," Joe said.

"We'll see."

Wasn't long before we drove into Coos Bay. Another gorgeous place. People actually live here. What have I been missing, I asked myself.

"Joe, I never want this trip to end. I went to St. Louis last summer. Remember? It was nothing like this; flat and boring and muggy as hell. This is ... I don't know ... paradise. I want to stay here. Don't want to go back home or go to St. Mary's. Shit man, this is beautiful."

Joe nodded and smiled. He drove on and on.

A couple of hours later we were at the California border.

'Welcome to California.' The sign said.

"We did it! We're in California!" I yelped.

They stopped us at the border and asked if we had any fruits or vegetables with us. We didn't. We drove on.

Somehow, I expected Hollywood lights and a Red Carpet and just kind of laughed when we passed through Fort Dick and continued south. The fog had burned off for the most part by now and I couldn't get over the 'bigness' of the ocean.

By mid-morning we needed gas so we stopped in Crescent City.

I was keeping a meticulous log of expenses and miles and it was my turn to pay. We bought sandwiches and more cigs and sodas. Joe mailed some more post cards. Off we go.

We were making good time. The long afternoon passed on and there were so many phenomenal sights that after a bit we didn't even respond anymore. People actually live here!

We were on Highway 1. "Joe, there is a Highway 1. Always wondered how they numbered them. And this is 1."

Joe drove and drove. I checked the map and said that we should head over to 101 at Bodega Bay and then head into San Francisco. "There's a park in San Francisco and this road goes right through it. Maybe we could spend the night there."

"Good idea."

We hit 101 at Santa Rosa. Another dreamy looking town, by far the largest we had encountered since Portland. The traffic really picked up. We were an hour from San Francisco and we gassed up.

"Looks like a hard drive from here, Joe. You okay?"

"Yeah, I'm okay."

We stretched our legs and peed and stocked up on snacks. The sun was just setting and we drove right into the sunset. Joe put the top up. We found a great radio station and drove into San Francisco.

"We're going to cross the Golden Gate Bridge in a few minutes."

And there it was. Magnificent. Lit up like a Christmas tree. A view of the City on the left and the eternal Pacific on the right.

We crossed the bridge and paid the toll. In a few minutes we were in the middle of the park.

"Joe, we should pull off somewhere and find a good spot to camp."

It was dark by now in the midst of this great city. We drove around for a while and found an isolated spot that even had a rest room nearby.

Parked the car and we nestled under some plants off the path. We could hear drums in the distance and wondered what that was all about.

"Hear that ... drums ... the natives are restless."

We had Joe's lantern and we ate sandwiches and drank our sodas. It was cool and a chill came over us. Couldn't make a fire but we had our sleeping bags. It was nearing midnight when we fell asleep.

Chapter 3

San Francisco

I was the first to wake. Had to pee and walked to the rest room. Washed my face and brushed my teeth. Joe was up when I returned.

"Up and at 'em. Sleep okay?"

"I guess," Joe stiffly rose and stretched and yawned.

"Those drums are still beating, we should check it out."

"Yeah, maybe we'll see some hippies," Joe added.

We had already spotted some hippies, with colorful shirts and long hair. Couldn't help but stare.

Joe cleaned up as well and we decided to check out the drums. "Sounds like it's coming from over there."

We packed up the car and drove towards the drumming. It was difficult to locate and the road curved round and round. Finally, we passed another curve and came into a clearing. There were hundreds of people sitting in this meadow and on the side of a hill. We parked and locked the car and walked over.

People were sitting in circles, some were dancing to the drum beat. Incessant. Sounded tribal. Colorful outfits. Long hair. We felt out of place. Two Mid-West hicks.

"Jeez Joe, what is this?"

"Dunno."

By now it was late morning and a grey mist hung over the meadow. The bright colors set off an interesting contrast.

"This must be that hippie thing that's been going on. The *Life Magazine* article ... remember," I stated.

"Oh yeah. Look at that guy's hair."

Joe and I walked nearer. We wanted to check this out for a bit and then hit the road again. We needed coffee and doughnuts.

Just then, a girl came up behind and between us and reached around our necks and put something in our mouths. She ran off giggling.

"Swallow it boys and have fun!" as she danced away in a sea of bubbles and colorful scarfs.

"What was that?"

We did swallow the tablets. Just like aspirin. We hadn't eaten yet and the drug started taking affect in only a few minutes.

"I don't feel so good. What did that girl give us?"

We couldn't find the girl. Then I spotted her. She did the same thing to other people. Putting a tablet in their mouth.

"I need to sit down," I explained.

So, Joe and I sat down and felt the waves of the drug come on and on and on. I was scared and didn't understand what was happening. A guy saw us and came over.

"You're first trip?"

"What are you talking about? You mean like we just drove out from Minnesota ... and ..." I couldn't even talk.

"No. Not that kind of trip. An acid trip man. That chick gave you acid, man, LSD. It's okay. You're tripping and the first hour is bumpy then you'll feel great."

He was comforting. In a way. But Joe and I were suspicious at this point.

"Name is Brian."

"This is Mike and I'm Joe."

"I'll stay with you guys for a while. You're going to be okay."

"Thanks, Brian."

"Here, have some water and eat these apples. You'll feel better."

Joe and I forced water down our throats and tentatively bit into an apple. An apple never tasted like that before. It was absolutely delicious! And our stomachs settled. I felt like I was blind drunk but this was different. I was totally aware and my senses were on fire. I looked at Joe and his pupils were the size of banjos.

Looking down I could see the grass grow. It was wiggling and stretching outwards. The sun was breaking through and it was a new day!

Colors. Vivid colors, swirled. People left trails of light behind them. Everything was distorted. I was scared. My heart was flying. I could see the veins in my hands. I looked at Joe. I'd never seen him before yet I had. What the fuck! I was loosing my mind. Sounds passed by in an amplified presence. I shook my head. It only intensified.

It was like looking through a piece of colorful stained glass that magnified and distorted everything.

At one end of the meadow I could see a flatbed truck with some guys hoisting speakers and amps. How nice, I thought. Music.

"The Dead are going to play. Ever heard them? Man, they are great. Captain Trips and Pig Pen ..." Brian was ecstatic.

"Who, no ... don't believe I have."

Brian was true to his word and stayed with us. Suppling us with water and more apples. He introduced us to a bunch of his friends. A wild assortment of hippie boys and girls. Didn't feel so out of place after a while.

Faces were distorted. Voices trailed off. Noticed music. The drums had stopped. The Grateful Dead were playing. A girl twirled by ... spinning in circles ... colors trailed in the air and hung there. I had lost my mind and was convinced I was crazy. I was scared but everyone else was having fun. Laughing and joking. Joe had a placid look on his face. He looked saintly.

He glowed. Radiant.

The music pounded on and on. What was this sound? The band was a motley looking crew. Two guys had the longest hair I'd ever seen and the lead guitar player wore pig tails. The keyboard player looked like a Hell's Angel and they had two drummers.

One song melted into the next. Indiscernible from one note to the next. Everything was melting as I moved through the crush of the crowd to the front of the stage. The ground was vibrating and I found myself tapping my thighs to the beat. People didn't dance in pairs but just danced en masse in one big pulsating heap. I had never heard music like this before. It seemed to come out of the air and was so natural and real. I looked around for Joe. He was somewhere. I couldn't stop moving and was dancing alone. Never danced alone before. And it all made sense. Perfect sense. My life up to now was the past. This was now. I understood everything ... even the things I couldn't understand ... I understood. I was full of love and hope and never wanted this instant to end. This music was perfect and this was the most amazing experience I'd ever had.

The guitar player played through the PA! (Have to tell Emil about that). His solos were several minutes long like in some great jam ... Monk and Miles like ... who are these guys?

There was Joe! A serene smile on his face. Brian and his friends were nearby dancing and smoking pot. I took a 'toke' and it brought on a whole new wave of colors. What a blast!

Waves of music and senses on fire. I wanted my hair long and face painted dancing naked to the Dead. Not so much rejecting the past but accepting a new future. What is this all about? Who are these people? A new freedom exploding in a psychedelic rainbow. A half naked pagan stomp. Flower children. Was this my new religion? A new religion based on the moment ... in a time freeze of honesty and equality where everyone is truly equal. Was this it?

The band took a break. How long did they play?

I wanted to tell the whole world about this.

Another band was setting up.

Brian said, "Man, you gotta hear this band. They're called 'The Jefferson Airplane,' man. They got this great chick singer. Grace Slick."

"Yeah, man, you gotta hear them," someone else chimed in.

Joe and I were too high to go anywhere anyway so we said yeah, why not.

"How are you doing?" I finally asked Joe.

"Okay, I guess. Guess we aren't going anywhere today. I should check on the car."

Brian said we could park in their driveway. Just a couple blocks away. So he and Joe left to move the car off the street.

I started to talk to a girl. She was really nice. All hippie garbed, bra-less, and me with short hair and a white tee shirt, jeans, and sneakers.

"I'm Mike, what's your name?"

"Linda."

She had flowers in her hair. She put one behind my ear. I was chris-tened!

I told Linda all about our trip and how we wanted to drive through all the border States.

"Why would you want to do that? But, that's far out, man."

"Yeah, I guess we're crazy. But it sure has been fun so far."

"You guys should come to our place ..."

"We are. My buddy Joe went with Brian to move the car into your driveway. You know, off the street."

"Cool, man."

The Airplane took the stage and roared into their set. The acid had worn off some but there still existed swirls of colors and trails whenever I moved my head. But, the paranoia was gone and I was feeling much better. My stomach was fine. I smoked some more pot and then some more and went into a dream. I could hardly stand up but once I did I moved to the music. Couldn't help it. It consumed me. They were a great band too!

I recall one song about "one pill makes you small and one pill makes you big."

Indeed!

Linda and I sort of danced. She kept eye contact with me and seemed to look right through me. I could see her soul. It was an amazing moment for this Midwestern hick.

God, this band was so good. Are all the San Francisco bands this great? Over the next months I would soon find out.

It was a tribal stomp. Dust rising in the air. Painted faces floating by in a surreal day dream. People smiling and hugging with flowers in their hair and peace in their hearts. I had found my people!

Brian and Joe returned. Don't know how they found us amidst thou-sands of twirling hippies. But they did.

"Let's all go to our pad and party!" Brian exclaimed in an enthusiastic burst.

"Yeah, Mike. Let's go," said Joe.

"I've got this magic mescaline."

What's that?

So off we trod. About ten of us. Brian grabbed a few other people and we glided a couple of blocks to their house. As I looked back at a scene I'll never forget. The Airplane playing to thousands of dancing prancing people. A cloud of dust hung over them like a magic cloud.

I was so high. Linda grabbed my hand and giggled.

The house was an old Victorian. A few blocks from the park. We could still hear the music, even inside. The place was a mess. It looked like a hundred people lived here and crashed here. No telling. Dishes piled and stacked all over the kitchen and the bathroom downstairs looked like Berlin after WWII.

But, no matter, we settled in. Throwing stuff around to find a comfortable spot on a couch. Linda and I nestled up. Jeez, how lucky can a guy get. Joe looked a little lost. He didn't have a girl. Somebody put an album on.

"Is that the first band we heard today ... The Dead?" I inquired.

"Yep, *Anthem of the Sun*."

"Jeez, they have a real album. Look Joe. I want to buy this when we get back home."

"Here, take this," Brian said.

"What is it?"

"Mescaline."

I dropped the tab on my tongue and swallowed. Somebody gave me a beer. Boy, did that hit the spot. Everyone took a hit of mescaline.

The music thumped on and I was brought back to earlier this afternoon. Was this the same day?

Waiting for the mescaline to come on, Linda suggested we go upstairs.

"Come on. I want to show you something."

I followed her up a grand bannister to the second level. Again, high ceilings. The second floor had several bedrooms all in a similar disarray. She led me to a bathroom. She told me to take my clothes off! She disrobed like it was nothing. My shyness sparked up and I couldn't even look at her. She started the shower and got in and I followed. The warm water brought surges of the mescaline on. I was swirling again in colors but without the paranoid sensation of acid. She hugged me and I got a boner. She soaped me up and down and I lathered her. It was magic. I was out of my body. I felt her breasts and hugged her close. She groaned and embraced me. The water felt distant and yet inside me. The sound of cascading water was mesmerizing and comforting. Her body warm.

"Come on. Let's get out."

We toweled ourselves and dressed. She led me up to the third floor. An attic of sorts with more bedrooms. She took me to her room.

A strong smell of incense greeted us as we entered. Several posters adorned the walls. A mattress on the floor. She had a stereo and she put on some music. We laid on the bed and soon were making love.

We tripped in each other's arms and talked. Smoked a cigarette. "Let's go back downstairs and see what everybody is up to."

We ventured back downstairs and the place was full of people and smoke and very loud music. I found Joe sitting in a corner talking with some people. He was having a great time. His eyes were so bloodshot that it was hard telling if he could even see.

Linda and I joined their little corner and sat close together looking into each others eyes. A new experience. Instead of shame and guilt I felt a new openness and acceptance.

"Guess we aren't going anywhere tonight, eh, Joe."

"Doesn't look like it."

We were both too high to move and besides, I wanted to be with Linda. Could feel a dilemma coming on; to leave with Joe and continue our adventure or stay here with Linda and the gang for more fun.

Didn't want to think about it right now, just wanted to have fun and party. The very thought of returning to Winona and attending St. Mary's made me sick to my stomach. But, I had to stay out of the draft. I even thought of attending school out here in California but out of state tuition was to high and I needed to take care of Mom when Dad was gone.

The music blared and I was getting an education. Brian was so exuberant with each new record or song that he played.

"You gotta hear this band ..."

I think at some point we took more acid and someone went out and purchased more beer and the pot just appeared. After so many hours the sun rose again and it was a new morning. Linda and I went back to her room and made love again and passed out sometime in this new age morning.

I awoke in a start and didn't know where I was for a moment. Having gathered my senses, I was very quiet not wanting to wake Linda and I walked downstairs to find Joe curled up on the floor in a pile of blankets. He was semi-awake and he sensed I was there.

"Mike, we should push off, man."

"I know, but, I don't want to leave just now. I want to stay here a couple of more days and check out the scene. I want to stay with Linda. Is that okay with you?"

"Well, I guess so."

"Sorry, man, I hope you understand. If it wasn't for Linda ... ," I trailed off.

"Yeah."

He was a bit perplexed and miffed but Joe was the kind of person who was accommodating and understanding.

So we stayed on. Finally, everyone else arose. It was the middle of the afternoon. Some of us decided to walk back to the park and see what was going on.

The drums were beating anew and a band was playing.

Brian informed us that this was Quicksilver Messenger Service, another San Francisco band. Is there no end to this great music?

"Joe, should we do some more acid?"

"Why not."

So off to the races we go once more. Linda and I danced and twirled and laughed and kissed and hugged people ... around and around we go. Where and when we stop ... no one knows.

I didn't want to talk to Linda about Joe and I continuing our voyage. Not just now. Part of me wanted to stay and part of me wanted to go. My guilt with Joe was weighing me down and my guilt for leaving Linda ... How do I get myself into these quandaries?

"Come on, I want to show you something," Linda said.

She grabbed my hand and we started to walk away from the crowd and across the park. We came to the edge of the park and crossed a busy street.

"This is the Haight-Ashbury District."

We walked up Haight Street. My mouth was agape. Thousands of hippies ... smells of incense and pot ... colorful shops with posters of bands ... smiling faces ... zoned out faces ... people selling dope of all kinds ... weed, LSD, Mescaline, etc. ... bright regalia ... a rainbow of colors ... a pleasant assault on the senses.

"This is amazing," I noted.

Wide open and free. No cops.

"This could never happen in Minnesota. The cops would arrest half the people here."

"I know, it's great," Linda concurred.

We walked several blocks until we came to the intersection of Haight and Ashbury.

"Where's the street sign?" I asked.

"People steal it so they don't even bother putting it up anymore."

"Wow."

We returned to the park strolling down the other side of the street. The music could be heard from a distance and we had no trouble finding it. Another band was playing and we decided to go back to the flat and find the others. They were there plus several new faces. Linda introduced me to people but I soon forgot their names. We took our place on the floor. The stereo was turned up so loud that I couldn't hear anything else. I found Joe in the kitchen having a discussion with some people. I nodded letting him know I was there. He grinned like a banshee, obviously high.

Had to talk to Joe about leaving or staying. But, that conversation had to wait.

Linda asked if I was hungry. How could I eat. I was floating in the heavens and just wasn't hungry. She grabbed my hand and led me to her room. We made love and slept.

Linda was gone when I awoke. Sleepy eyed and somewhat rested, I walked downstairs and found her. I was starving. We ate some toast and eggs found in the fridge. Had a couple of cups of coffee and almost felt human again.

"Where's everybody," I inquired.

"Must have gone out."

The house was empty. And quiet.

"Linda, what should I do? Joe and I planned this trip and now I don't want to leave. It's all your fault," I chided.

"What do you want to do? You should talk to Joe, he'll probably understand."

"He's such a good guy. A regular 'Joe,' an honest to goodness good guy and I hate to disappoint him but I'm falling for you and I want to be here with you and Brian and the rest of you guys. Shit, I've only known you for a few days ..." I trailed off.

"Yeah, you'll find your answer. Just wait and it will come to you."

"Okay.'

We kissed and stared into one another's eyes. Lost in another world. I picked her up and sat her on the kitchen counter and embraced and hugged her. I couldn't let go. It seemed that everything in the past was just that. The past. And this was now and the future. I was full of hope and optimism like I hadn't felt in a very long time, or never, for that matter. I didn't want this moment to ever end. She was so intense. My other girl friends seemed to look through me. Linda looked into me. I'd never let anyone in. This was new. I liked it.

Joe walked into the kitchen.

"What do you want to do?" I asked. "Should we stay here or go on?"

"What do you want to do?"

"I asked you first," I chuckled.

"I guess we could stay here for a couple of more days. We have plenty of time before school starts."

"Yeah, okay, man. That's cool. I didn't expect to meet Linda, ya' know and I kinda want to stay. In fact, I'm not really sure I want to go back to Winona. Fuck it, man, but ... I have to take care of my mom and shit. I don't know."

There was a pause.

I continued, "I feel like I'm letting you down, 'cause this was your idea and I agreed and it's so much fun. Everything's changed. I'm really confused."

"Mike, it's okay, man."

Joe always was the cool one.

We did stay a couple of more days. Linda took me over to Berkeley to meet some of her friends.

"This guy is intense. He won't allow any drugs or alcohol in his house. He's political. A revolutionary but really interesting."

We arrived at his place. Several people were gathered in the living room and they were in the middle of a discussion about politics, namely the Vietnam War. Linda introduced me to everyone and I shyly sat down. I was in way over my head. I had never heard such a discussion before. The outright hatred and mistrust of the US Government and the University of California and the cops etc.

Linda and I just sat passively and listened. And listened. I was like a sponge just soaking all of this in.

Chapter 4

Mark

Her friend's name was Mark and he was holding court.

"All the Man needs is an excuse to bust you, man. If you've got drugs on you they will bust you! Drugs just dull your senses and fuck you up. If you're stoned the Revolution fails. Don't you see that, man?"

It made sense to me. But, I was very skeptical about his politics. He was a 'radical' and I was a very ignorant Midwestern hick ingrained with very traditional values. Most of his concepts had never occurred to me. But, I was fascinated by him. He had a way with words and a strong personality. He attracted your attention and challenged your intellect. I liked him.

After a couple of hours Linda nudged me and said, "let's go." The discussion continued as we left. It probably never stopped.

We got back into her VW and we drove around the campus. "This is Telegraph Avenue. This is where all the riots start." I did recognize it from magazine articles I'd read. We picked up a copy of the *Berkeley Barb*, a local street paper. I leafed through it.

"Wow, they don't have anything like this back in Minnesota."

I was very excited. I didn't know it at the time but this day would burn an indelible mark in my psyche and meeting Mark would be a major turning point in my life.

Driving back to the City crossing the Bay Bridge ... a great vista of San Francisco. I felt in my heart that this is where I need to be but was guilt-tugged about Joe, Mom, and school. I knew that Linda and I wouldn't last but she was great for now. She was eons ahead of me in maturity and knowledge. I didn't deserve her in the sense that I had so much to learn and so much catching up to do. I was sad in this self-acknowledgement. But, it was the truth. Maybe I should continue on with Joe. But, I didn't really want to anymore. I had found a new awakening and challenges awaited me.

The house was full when we returned. Brian was there and it was reassuring to see him.

"Where's Joe?"

"Saw him earlier ... I think he's sleeping up stairs."

I needed to talk with him.

We hung out with the people in the living room. All new faces. The music blared and joints filled the air. I had been stoned for several days and it seemed like a dream. Someone passed me a pipe and I smoked hash for the first time blasting me into a new space. I was giggling at a joke Linda made and the smoke went into my lungs causing me to cough for a few minutes. It burned and with every cough I felt higher and higher until I fell off. I couldn't focus my eyes or even think and was just blotto. I remembered what that guy had said earlier in the day over in Berkeley ... or was that yesterday ... about drugs making you unable to fulfill the Revolution. I felt guilty, a bit, and realized he was right. What else was he 'right' about? His words floated through my memory. Yeah, his name was Mark.

Joe awoke from his nap. "Hey, man, how ya' doing?" I asked.

"Okay ... I guess. Hey Mike, I called my mom this afternoon, you know, just to let her know I was okay and stuff. Anyway, she wants me to come home. My dad needs help at the warehouse and I could use the money. I'm going to leave in a couple of days and drive back to Winona. Want to join me?"

"Shit, I can't decide. You know what? I'm going to stay here for a while."

Linda piped in, "Joe, I know a guy who needs a ride to Denver. He could help with gas. I'll call him. Is that okay?"

"Yeah."

"That would solve everything, man. I don't want to let you down. But, you see the fix I'm in," I said.

Linda returned. "He'll be right over. He's a nice guy and a friend of ours," she said swaying her arms.

Her friend showed up and he and Joe discussed specifics. He was a nice guy. A college student from Denver. He and Joe would leave in two days. I felt so much better.

Joe was cool with this plan.

Someone suggested that I could fly back, "The airlines have this thing called 'student-standby' ... you get a really cheap price and you wait and if there is an empty seat on the plane you get on. Simple as that."

I called the airport and found out that it was only $48 to fly to Minneapolis. What a deal. Even if I had to wait a day it would be worth it.

I still had almost three weeks until school started. I called my mom and told her I was staying on a couple of more weeks. She sounded pretty mushy and I wasn't sure she got the message. She told me she was pregnant again and expected the birth in September.

I had $175 left and I decided to buy 100 hits of acid and 100 hits of mescaline from this guy. I figured I could sell it back in Winona and as soon as they got a load of this I could sell it all for a profit and then buy some more. I sure wasn't a business man but if I paid $.50 a hit and sold it for $1, I'd double my investment. Turn $100 into $200.

In the meantime Linda and I spent our time either in sexual bliss or exploring the scene. Joe had already left. One day we walked over to Haight Street and the Grateful Dead were playing in the street. Thousands of dancing frolicking hippies filled the street. We dropped acid and Linda found some friends and we were seated on the pavement really digging the scene. Someone mentioned that they needed munchies. I said I would go. They gave me some money and I had a shopping list of sodas, various candy bars, gum, etc.

I walked through the crowd and as best as I could marked the spot where they were seated and swam up the street to a little market. The place was swamped. I gathered all the goodies. Double checked the list and when I was satisfied that I had everything walked up to the line to pay for everything. I was really high and the acid was surging through me. I finally got to the front and I poured everything out unto the counter. When I looked up the woman was this huge green monster who slurred her words in slow motion. I panicked but realized it was the acid. I fumbled with the change and the ogre counted out the right amount. I couldn't even fucking see. I somehow managed to make it back to the sidewalk. I had to sit down because I couldn't stand up. I started to crawl on my hands and knees clutching the bag of treats. The music was no help echoing in this cavern of people and buildings. All my senses were askew. I did have the where-with-all to stay on the sidewalk as I inched down the street. I was lost. Had to stop. Everything was swirling in a kaleidoscope of colors and sounds. Above the din and the colors I could hear my mind crackling like broken glass. I was panicking. The shopping bag was heavy due to the several cans of sodas. I had to crawl ... move one hand ... then the other ... move one knee ... and the other ...while dragging the bag. I had made a mental picture of where everyone was in the crowd. I remembered a store front with a 'Help Wanted' sign in the window. I kept searching for the sign sneaking peeks between the legs and feet. There it was. I glanced to my left and spotted the group. I made it!

"That didn't take long," someone said.

"You have no idea," I retorted.

I was so glad to be back.

We snacked on Snickers and M&M's and cokes and chips. Boy, did that taste good.

I did manage to buy 100 hits of acid for 35 cents a hit from a friend of

Brian's. He called it 'Purple Haze.'

I wanted to stay longer but I had to get back home. Linda and I promised to write every day. I planned to return at Thanksgiving or over Christmas break. I thanked Brian for taking us in and all the other people.

It was the first week of August and Linda drove me to the airport. She couldn't park anywhere so we made a hasty goodbye with a lingering kiss.

I walked up to the Northwest Airline ticket counter and purchased a one way student-standby ticket to Minneapolis. $48.

The plane left in an hour. I had my stuff in a ruck sack and checked in. The guy told me to sit over there and wait. He said the flight wasn't sold out so I had a good chance to board.

They called the booked passengers to the gate and they all boarded. They called my name. There was a seat left. I got on. What luck!

It was the second time flying and this was in a real jet with food and several cokes.

We arrived at the Minneapolis Airport and I had some difficulty finding a bus downtown to the Greyhound Bus Terminal. Eventually I found the right bus and it dropped me off two blocks away. It was pretty seedy around here and I quickly walked into the terminal and bought a ticket for Winona. The bus didn't leave until tomorrow morning. I spent the night with derelicts and cops. Safer than the street though.

Seemed like an eon waiting for the bus so I wrote several rambling love letters to Linda and one to Brian promising to return.

I half slept and kept one eye open all night.

At last I boarded the bus for Winona.

Chapter 5

Winona

I walked home and found the house in total disarray. Apparently, Dad hadn't been home in weeks. Mom was very pregnant and the kids were fending for themselves. I hadn't been around all summer and so I hadn't noticed Mom's belly before now.

There was so much to do. I had been gone for over a month. I called all my friends, including Joe who was home also, and made plans to get together. My brother Emil was in his room and I began to tell him all about San Francisco. I also showed him the acid I had with me and told him he had to try this stuff. "Just make sure you're in a safe place." I gave him a couple of hits and told him of my plans to sell it off. I had some mescaline too.

I got together with Joe and some other buddies and I sold several hits to them. I told them that the acid was strong but the mescaline was easier to handle.

A few days later my mom came to my room and asked me to drive her to the hospital. "The baby's coming." I panicked and dressed as quickly as I could. It was 5 a.m. I drove the Falcon to the hospital and got Mom into the Emergency Room. We waited and waited. The doctors ran some tests on her. After several hours they concluded that it was a false alarm so we drove back home.

I told Mom to wake me up if she needed to.

Dad was nowhere in sight and we didn't know where he was.

School was to start in the second week of September. I got a rush realizing that I was going to be a freshman in college. I was only seventeen but had a birthday coming up on August 25.

A few days later the phone rang. It was very early in the morning. I had a phone in my room. "Mr. McAndrew?" a voice said.

"Yes."

"You're the father of a baby boy!"

"What!"

"You're wife just had a baby."

"Oh no ... I'm her son."

The baby was premature by several weeks. I ran upstairs and sure enough, as the rest of the household slept, my mom's bed was empty and the Falcon was gone. She had driven herself to the hospital! I had to get to the hospital so I called a cab.

I arrived at the hospital and soon found my mom's room. She was holding Patrick Casey McAndrew. He was perfect. Mom and Casey had to stay in the hospital for a couple of days so I drove the Falcon back home. Everyone except Emil was up and wondering where Mom was. I told them about Casey and they all wanted to see him. Visiting hours were this afternoon so we planned to go then.

Casey was the most perfect baby I'd ever seen. Completely healthy.

Dad finally called and I informed him that Mom had the baby. He said he'd be home in a few days. I gathered the kids and told them that we had to clean the house. They all really chipped in and Mary and I must have done ten loads of laundry. We cleaned the fridge and stove and made up Mom's room. Even Emil helped!

I mowed the lawn and made sure the house was in order for Mom and especially for Dad.

We got Mom home and a few days later Dad came home ... to a clean home ... and a new son. Dad went grocery shopping and stocked us up again. He stayed drunk for a week but was in a pleasant mood.

With life sort of back to normal, I pursued my new life. I wrote a letter to Linda expressing my undying love for her and received the same. Emil managed to sell most of the acid and mescaline, having been the new rage in Winona, word soon spread and I was a much sought out guy. Could I get more? Yes! So I called Brian and sent him $100 and soon received another shipment. I was making more money doing this than ever working at McDonald's.

Emil and I had this secret. He loved the stuff and so did the band. Unbeknownst to their flock, the Fabulous Ferrais were stoned on their asses playing cover songs. Their music slowly evolved into long interludes, much like the Dead, with some protests from the 'Joe College' types, but most people really dug them. They were probably the most important band outside of Minneapolis and Chicago. They played five nights a week in various clubs in the area. They had a huge following. Emil was the star. He was amazing. Funny beyond words and the best bass player in the Midwest.

The band would eventually release a single, *Can't Explain*, by the Who and *I'm Not talkin'* by the Yardbirds. The record got some airplay on WGN in Chicago.

My hair was short and I wanted to grow it long. No one in Winona had long hair except a couple guys in the Ferrais. Jim's hair was over his ears. I saw guys in San Francisco who had pony tails down to their butts!

At the same time I read and re-read the *Berkeley Barb*. I sent off for a subscription. I noticed one article in their about SDS. What in the hell was that. There was an ad in the back for membership in SDS. Students for a Democratic Society. Also, there was an ad to join the American Communist Party. I sent off for that, too. Why not!

I was just curious. I wanted to belong to something I could believe in. After all the let-downs from the Church and the family ... I had to do something for myself. I was so ignorant of what was going on. Oh, sure, I knew about the Civil Rights Movement but that seemed so distant from the lily white world of Minnesota.

I turned 18 on August 25 and had to register with the Selective Service (SS) for the draft. Since I was a student I received a 1-S deferment, meaning that as long as I stayed in school I would stay out of the draft. Some of my buddies who didn't attend college were registered as 1-A, meaning that they were eligible for immediate call-up. I knew some guys who were already in Vietnam and watching the evening news was scary because of the number of casualties.

I started my freshman year with courses in biology, chemistry, algebra, English Literature, and religion, plus labs for biology and chemistry. I was over-whelmed from the first day. I decided to return to McDonald's for some extra cash. I also rented an apartment from some friends of Dad's. (Joe's parents hadn't fixed up their garage yet.) They had converted a two car garage into an apartment. They added a second floor and it was one big room. It had a kitchen area, a bathroom, and a laundry downstairs in the garage. The place was warm and I could play my stereo. The people were really nice. It was great and they only charged me $35/month for rent. I now stayed there whenever Dad was home.

At first, I worked my ass off at school. Trying to keep up was a losing battle. I was behind after one month. Working at McDonald's, (they rehired me) trying to hold the house together when Dad was gone, getting high on weekends, staying out of the Army, writing letters to Linda, etc. Was too much! I woke one night and had a terrific stomach ache. I went to the bathroom and sat on the toilet. I looked in the toilet and it was black. I was bleeding. I did nothing about it because it didn't happen again for a long time.

Thanksgiving break was approaching and I made plans to fly to San Francisco. I had sold out the latest supply of drugs and I had to see Linda and Brian.

I worked the night shift at McDonald's. I had a test in my Shakespeare class the next morning. I opened the book and placed it above the grill as I made burgers. The owner's son was managing that night. We called him 'Ronald McDonald.' His first name was actually Ronald. He was a complete incompetent ass. He ordered people around and treated us badly. He gave me shit because I was studying for the test.

"Hey, McAndrew, you can't study on our time."

"Fuck you."

The other managers always let me study as long as I got my work done. I could fry burgers with my eyes closed.

"If you don't put that book away I'm going to fire you."

I had had enough of the little prick. I picked him up and locked him in the walk-in freezer. I opened one of the smaller doors where we kept the cheese and burgers and such and handed him a coat and a cup of coffee. I turned on the light for him. The other guys were laughing and going 'right on, Mike.' Nobody liked him anyway.

After a couple of hours I let him out and never worked at McDonald's again.

I skipped classes on Wednesday and Thursday, a week prior to Thanksgiving, and headed for the airport on Friday afternoon. Purchased a student stand by ticket and waited at the gate. Sure enough, I got on the flight to San Francisco. I had called Brian ahead of time to let him know I was coming. I couldn't get a hold of Linda on the phone but did write her a letter.

Took the Airporter to Union Square and hopped a bus up Geary Street to the Pan Handle and walked over to Brian's place. Brian was there.

After hugs and greetings Brian told me that Linda was going with another guy. That shook me up pretty hard but I got over it.

I wanted to hang out for the rest of the night because I was tired from the flight. Some people came over and partied until late. Linda wasn't staying there any longer and someone else had taken her room. I crashed on the couch in the living room.

I awoke the next morning to crashes in the kitchen. Brian and his girl friend were making breakfast and they invited me to join them.

"Morning," I mumbled.

"How'd you sleep?"

"Okay, I guess. Hi, I'm Mike from Minnesota."

"I'm Gale."

"Oh, I'm sorry. Gale, this is Mike. The guy I was telling you about. He's cool."

We had some coffee and eggs and toast. That got the engine going again.

"Hey man, sorry about Linda. She moved out a few weeks ago. I guess she didn't tell you. That's cold," Brian said.

"I'll be all right. Happens."

I didn't really let on my disappointment and broken heart. Just stuffed it away with all the other junk.

"Hey, Brian ... do you know that guy in Berkeley. His name is Mark. I wanted to see him too. I've been reading the *Berkeley Barb* trying to keep up with stuff. Do you know him?"

"I met him a couple of times. I'll try and get his phone number for you."

"Thanks, man."

After breakfast, Brian and Gale took off. I walked down to the Haight just to walk around. It wasn't the same. I noticed lots of spare-changers and street people hanging out. Gone was the positive energy from the summer. It didn't have the same happy feeling at all. In fact, it seemed slightly dangerous and creepy.

After a few hours I returned to Brian's place. We had a chance to talk. I wanted to buy some more acid and mescaline. He said he could arrange that. I told him that several people in Winona were getting stoned and listening to the San Francisco bands, particularly, the Dead.

"Oh yeah, before I forget, here's Mark's phone number."

"Thanks. I'll call him later."

Brian said I could stay here as long as I wanted. I invited him to check out Winona sometime. I told him about the music scene there and the birthing of a hippie movement. He seemed interested and said he would some-day. I told him he would always have a place to stay. I don't know what he did for money but he always seemed to have it.

Brian was a walking encyclopedia of music. He had every album it seemed and he instructed me. We played music for the rest of the day and night. There was so much new and fresh music. I made a mental note at first and then decided it best to write down the names of the groups.

"This guy Zappa is interesting ... and I like the Airplane and Quick-silver ... the Doors from LA ... Jimi Hendrix, Janis ..." I told him that the Yardbirds were my favorite group and of course, he had their albums.

Eventually, I called Mark. He answered the phone.
"Hey Mark, this is Mike. I met you this summer and I was with Linda."
"I remember you."
"I'm back in San Francisco over Thanksgiving and I was wondering if I could stop by tomorrow to see you."
"Yeah, make it in the afternoon around three."
"Cool, see you then."
Brian told me which buses to take and we dropped some mescaline and drank beer until the wee hours and listened to the exquisite sounds of the sixties. I particularly like the Dead's album *Anthem of the Sun*. We must have played that one ten times!

Daylight.
I awoke in the late morning to rustling in the kitchen. The other room-mates were making breakfast and invited me to join. Such a nice group of caring souls. It was 11 a.m. I showered and grabbed the bus schedule and a rough map of Berkeley and headed out to see Mark.

I was confused and lost but I made it to Berkeley okay. I had an hour to kill so I wandered down Telegraph Avenue and into the campus. Must have been Sproul Plaza when I stopped to listen to a speaker. I had missed the 'Free Speech Movement.' A woman, quite passionately, spoke of 'equal rights' for women ... not just the right to vote, but, equal pay, sexism, the role of women as mother's and patriarchs, the end of women as sex sym-bols, etc. It was as if a light bulb went off in my head. Of course! It was an epiphany for me. I would never forget that speech and she changed my outlook, my attitude, and my life!

I arrived at Mark's house, sans drugs, of course. He greeted me.
"Mike, come in, brother."
He asked me all sorts of questions. I told him in reply that I was attend-ing a small Catholic college in Minnesota and some of my family history, although I was always reluctant to provide too much detail, and that I had subscribed to the *Berkeley Barb* and had joined SDS and the American

Communist Party. He seemed pleased with these revelations. He asked me about how I felt about the draft and I told him I felt it was illegal and that I felt that there was no way I could kill innocent people fighting for their homeland and that WWII was a whole different scenario. But, I was still an ignorant Midwest boy who had everything to learn.

"But, you're heart is in the right place."

We were drinking tea. We were alone. He again warned me of the dangers of drugs and said that the police were watching his place because he was a rabble-rouser.

"If you're high all the time, you can't revolt. The Man wants you high so you are at their mercy!"

I knew in my heart that he was right.

"Acid has opened doors for me, Mark. I have a fresh way of looking at things."

"True. But, after the first trip, which can be a spiritual awakening, after that it becomes a source of entertainment and recreation and that is useless."

A pause as I digested that.

"You need to find your inner light. But, you are on the right path," he added.

"Can I stay in touch with you after I return to school."

"I wish you would."

It was getting late and I had to return to the City. He hugged me and wished me luck. I did the same.

My head was whirling as I walked to a bus stop and began the reverse trip.

I arrived at Brian's place an hour or so later. I was transfixed by Mark's words and thoughts all the way back. I knew he was right. I just knew it but I still wanted to get high and party. I was at a fork in the road. A crossroads. I told myself not to make any rash decisions right off but to wait and let everything settle in.

I walked into Brian's house and stuck a joint in my mouth.

So much for that. For now.

"We're all going over to some friend's house for Thanksgiving to-morrow. It's just a couple of blocks from here. We need to pick up some potatoes."

"I'll get 'em. How much should I get?" I offered.

"Ten pounds should do."

I walked down Haight to Stanyan Street and walked into a market and picked up the potatoes. I also got some onions and butter. It was the least I could do.

"Should I peel these now or wait?"

"She said to wait until we got there."

"Okay."

Brian and I talked and listened to music. I didn't want to trip tonight. I told him what Mark had said and we had a good discussion about the pros and cons of drugs. Mostly pros. Brian was a few years older than I was and I trusted his wisdom. He was a few credits short of graduating from Berkeley with an English major. He wanted to teach. He knew a great deal about American literature especially the recent work of the Beats. I had heard of Kerouac and Ginsberg but he actually had their books. All of them. I grabbed *On the Road* before I went to bed and read until very late. I damn near finished it in one reading. It blew my mind. I had never felt prose like that and was at once sucked into the magical world of Sal Paradise and his crazy sidekick. I wanted to be him. Now I was Tom Sawyer, Huck Finn, Holden Caufield, and Sal Paradise. I wanted to read everything by Kerouac. Everything.

"Up and at 'em."

"Urgh...."

"What time is it?"

"It's Thanksgiving you bastard ... get up."

I quickly showered and we gathered up the spuds and another bag of food and headed out the door. It was 10 a.m. We walked not three blocks and entered another Victorian. We introduced ourselves and I asked where the kitchen was and was directed to it. Several women were preparing food. The kitchen was huge with lots of counters and big sinks. I asked someone (didn't know who was in charge, if anyone) where to put the potatoes and asked if I could begin peeling them. "Sure ... here's a pan and a potato peeler."

I sat on a chair and began peeling. Ten pounds is a lot of potatoes but I really enjoy chores like that. Must be the Irish in me. The women were talking away and I just peeled and listened. I'm shy anyway and it's better if I have something to do. I filled one pan and asked for another.

More and more people began arriving. People brought tons of food into the kitchen until there was no place to put it. Beer was everywhere so I was sipping on one. The sweet smell of pot filled the air. Music drifted in from someplace. A joint appeared. I continued to peel.

I was content.

Two hands covered my eyes from behind. It startled me. "Hi, guess who?"

"Linda?"

She gave me a big hug. I stood up then sat right down.

"I'm so sorry I didn't tell you about Greg."

"Who's Greg."

"The new guy I met. It just happened. I still have feelings for you ... but ... he was here ... and ... you were there ... I don't know ..." she trailed off.

"I'm sorry," I said.

"Yeah, so am I."

I told her that she looked nice and I was happy to see her. I felt embarrassed when she introduced me to Greg. He seemed like a nice guy.

"See ya."

I continued peeling. I wish there were more potatoes. I wanted to hide in potato peels.

I popped another beer and asked one of the women if there was anything else to do.

"Yeah, there is. Could you help us set the tables. We need to move some furniture around to make room. Set up these tables. This one's for food and we need a table cloth. Sue, where are the table cloths?"

We unfolded card tables and moved stuff around. Which, was a challenge because by now there were at least fifty people. So many happy people. This is how it should be!

The aroma. Oh my! Turkey, or should I say turkeys and a ham baking. Pumpkin pies. The potatoes. My mouth was watering. Some of these people looked as if they hadn't eaten in days. And a grand feast was before us!

A 'Beggar's Banquet'!

The food was placed on tables and people helped themselves. I've never seen so much food! A couple of hams, a couple of turkeys, vegetables galore, potatoes mashed and sweet, gravy by the bucket, cranberry sauce, etc.

Someone put on some classical music. People were seated everywhere, on couches, at the tables, on the floor. It seemed every space was taken up.

Linda was seated across the room from me engaged in a conversation with some people. I averted her eye contact and ate like Henry VIII.

I had seconds and thirds. There was enough food for an army. No shortage of anything. But, we made a dent in it. As people finished eating they brought the dishes into the kitchen and left them on the counters and in the sinks. What a mess! I began washing dishes and soon had the help of two other souls. It was a losing battle at first but we made headway. I washed, another stacked and dried and the last person dried and put dishes away in the cupboard. Two other women were busy wrapping up the left overs, which were plentiful. No one left hungry.

It took us two hours but eventually the house was clean again.

God, that was fun.

Brian and I were too stuffed to think. Gale, Brian, and myself struggled back to Brian's place.

During the feast, Brian's friend had brought another order of acid and some mescaline to the party. I hadn't witnessed the transaction but, I had given Brian $100 and he returned with a bag of stuff. I put it safely in my pocket and said not a word. I now felt my pocket to make sure it was still there. It was.

"I'm heading back tomorrow. I called my friend Joe, You remember Joe, right? Anyway, he said he could pick me up at the airport tomorrow night before heading back to Winona. I told him if I didn't catch the flight that I would call him. He was at some relatives over Thanksgiving. Anyway, man, I've got to head back. I've got homework due on Monday and I haven't even opened a book."

"They gave you homework over the break?"

"Yep ... fucking Jesuits and Christian Brothers are tough, man."

We were pretty worn out from the long day. One of the roommates was gone for the weekend so I crashed in her room. Told Brian I would say goodbye in the morning before I left and I had already planned to come out over Christmas break.

Got up early, took a quick shower, and said goodbye and thanked Brian. I don't think he heard me though, as he slept.

Took a bus downtown to Union Square and caught an Airporter to the airport. I had several hours before the flight. Bought my standby ticket and waited. This was a good day to fly because most people were flying on Saturday and Sunday.

I did get on the flight.

Arrived in Minneapolis and Joe was there to pick me up. We drove directly to Winona. Good old Joe!

I filled Joe in on the weekend and laid a few hits on him.

Got to Winona early Saturday morning. Walked to the house. Dad was in town. The house was a mess. Dad was at the bar. Emil told me that Thanksgiving was hell. Dad got mad at Emil and dumped a bowl of potatoes on his head and then proceeded to beat the shit out of him.

Mom was passed out upstairs. I grabbed my books and some clothes and food and headed for my apartment. There was no way I was staying here.

Even this place wasn't safe from Dad. He could just barge in at anytime. I locked the door anyway.

I hit the books and wrote two papers. I walked downstairs to the cooler in the garage and took a couple of beers back to my room. I would tell Mr. Kukos, my landlord, about it later. He let me have beer in my room. He was cool. He knew my dad and somehow would protect me from him.

I took a hit of mescaline and later that night walked down to the lake to think. I had to think.

I was depressed about Linda, I wasn't doing well in school, my stomach ached all the time, I was worried about the draft, Mark had given me much to think about. It seemed there were two counter cultures; the hippies and the politicos. Couldn't be both. I had to make a choice. It seemed unjust that rich white guys, like me, could avoid the draft by going to school. Hell, I couldn't even vote yet or buy a beer but I could kill Viet Cong.

The starry sky spread over the lake in swirls of light. I liked this magical world. I wanted to stay here.

I knew I was the only SDS member at St. Mary's. And for sure the only member of the American Communist party. The *Berkeley Barb* was delivered to my apartment and I read it cover to cover. I decided to show my colors. I made a placard from cardboard that simply stated 'Stop War.' I had seen that in the *Barb* and thought it appropriate. I brought it to school that Monday and stood on the steps of the library. Most students looked at me askance or acted like I wasn't even there, and one guy spit in my face. The news of my protest travelled all over campus and I was not the most popular man on campus.

I repeated the protest the next day and one of the Brothers came out and made me take it down. Stating that I had no right to protest.

It was then I knew I was on the right track.

Chapter 6

Protest and Acid

I didn't hold the sign up again. Eventually, a couple of guys approached me on the sly and said they agreed with me.

I managed to sell all of the acid and mescaline. I had enough money for a return trip to San Francisco over Christmas.

Dad had taken off again for his job and when it was safe I ventured back home. Mom was doing poorly. She was having epileptic fits again. My little sister Mary had taken over kitchen duties and was cooking every night. Everyone watched over young Casey and Paul. There was plenty of food in the fridge. Emil was playing in the band nearly every night. The rest of the brood was seemingly doing okay. One of the neighbor ladies was checking on them every day. Which helped.

Mr. Kukos worked at a local manufacturing company named Fibrite. They used fiber glass to manufacture all sorts of plastic products. He said I could work there part time in the evenings if I wanted. I said I would after the first of the year. I had to get my grades up first.

I had made a couple of friends at school. Nearly every guy was from Chicago. I started to hang out in the dorms and a few times during B.S. sessions the Vietnam War came up. By far, most supported it but there were a couple, like myself who opposed it. I was getting educated. I would drop terms like Imperialism and Colonialism into the conversation as if I knew what they actually entailed. I didn't stutter when I engaged in these rap sessions. I stuttered in the classroom.

My hair was getting longer. I was gaining confidence. Some long hairs and even a couple of hippies appeared on the Winona State campus but not here at St. Mary's. I was the only one. And, I had a nice little business going; selling drugs. Several guys asked me to get more and I said I would in a few weeks. I planned to purchase a larger stash next time I visited San Francisco.

In the meantime, I focused hard on school. I decided to drop the sciences and math in the second semester and take more English classes and an art history class. We were required to take a physical education class (gym) too so the second semester would be easier.

I managed to pull down a 2.5 GPA the first mid-term. Biology and chemistry being my downfall. I didn't get science or math that well. I was strong in English and history.

Joe and I were still hanging out. We drove to La Crosse several times to hear bands play where we could drink 3.2 beer.

We caught the Ferraris several times and Emil was becoming a star. I even 'roadied' for them sometimes to gain free entrance and all the beer I could drink. I recall one evening in La Crosse. The band was taking a break. After fifteen minutes or so one of the guys asked where Emil was. He was nowhere to be seen. We checked the rest rooms and the band room. Finally, I ventured out back where their station wagon was parked. I saw Emil's ass humping some girl.

"Emil," I shouted, "You're on!"

"Be there in a minute."

Walked back inside and told the others he'd be right back.

I still had enough money in the bank for school and travel. Life was good. My draft exemption was solid.

Slowly and surely I was drifting to the political side of the room. The rock and roll life was fun but young American men, especially blacks, were dying in Vietnam at an alarming rate and this had to stop!

Life at home was hell. I left every time Dad came home. Mom was doing poorly. It was falling apart.

My stomach hurt all the time. But, at least I wasn't shitting blood. I didn't know about stress in those days. I must have been at the breaking point. I wanted a girl friend but the pickings were slim. St Theresa's, the girls college down the hill, was a bastion of Catholic virtue. Hardly the place for me to find an adequate mate.

I couldn't wait to return to the Bay Area. I had written several letters to Mark and he had responded with missives of great intellect. His thought-provoking letters sent my head into a spin. I needed more and understood little. It dawned on me how ridiculous it was attending a college where I wasn't learning anything. I hungered for a real education. A pragmatic and real approach to life and ideals.

I finished up the first semester and headed for San Francisco.

It was frigid in Minneapolis and warm in San Francisco. I should transfer out here.

Arrived at Brian's and partied. Met some new people but the vibe had changed. The free-for-all 'Free Love' attitude of last summer was gone and a more sedate feeling prevailed. I still liked it.

I got a hold of Mark. Had to see him. Made plans to visit in a couple of days.

Brian and I were becoming good friends. I invited him to come to Minnesota in the summer. "Not in the winter, man, it's too cold." We cruised Haight Street and found it full of young homeless run-aways and strays and hard core dope peddlers. I didn't like the scene at all so we ventured downtown and then over to North Beach. He showed me Vesuvio's and where the old 'beat scene' had happened. To City Lights the coolest bookstore. And the topless bars where Carol Doda was performing. A huge neon sign with her nipples blinking. This is the greatest city, I thought. I wanted so bad to live here and every time that thought came up I felt guilt and shame because I should be home taking care of the family and studying hard for school and working at a job to make money and serving my country and praising God. Oh God! It was all too much!

I called Mark and we met at a cafe in Berkeley.

"I can't talk at home. I think the place is bugged."

"Really?"

"Yeah, really!"

"What I wanted to talk to you about is pretty sensitive and it can't go any further."

"Understand?"

"Yep."

"Okay. Good. You seem pretty sharp, Mike, and are eager to learn and healthy. I need a reliable contact in the Midwest to keep me up on the latest.

You've been to Madison and Ann Arbor?"

"Not Ann Arbor but Madison, yeah, lots of times. I even applied for school at the University of Wisconsin."

"Oh great, that gives me an idea. Would you be willing to enroll at Madison for a summer class?"

"Yeah sure ... why?"

"I'll fill you in later. First, I have to test you to see if I can trust you."

Mark then proceeded to tell me that there were some people he wanted to keep tabs on. Specifically a couple of guys in Madison who he had previously met but wasn't sure which side they were on. Apparently, according to Mark the New Left had been infiltrated by the FBI and he needed to verify their allegiance. And mine!

I was so naive. It was all new and like some weird James Bond spy thriller. Except this was real and I needed guidance. I told Mark that this was all new to me. But, I was against the war with every grain in my soul and was not only willing but proud to fight against it. I was just beginning to realize the other factors involved. I knew a little about Martin Luther King and the Civil Rights movement, I knew practically nothing about the Women's Movement, I was getting more knowledge, thanks to the *Berkeley Barb*, on the Anti-War Movement.

Mark said he liked me from the start because I was a fresh face and not depressed like so many of the old leftist movements from the '30's through the '50's. He like Midwesterners because they seemed kind and honest, unlike the East and West Coasters who were cynical. I listened. The afternoon passed into evening and we parted.

"Mike, one more thing. Stop selling drugs in Winona."

How he knew that ...

Okay. This would be the last time. I made up excuses in my head on the way back to the City. I needed the money. It was fun. People thought I was cool. I knew he was right. It would compromise me.

My head was ablaze. What test? Why did he want me? I was a hick. He was sophisticated in these matters. Mark was a mystery to me. Who was he? Should I trust him? Yes, I should trust him. Maybe ... I don't know. No, he was a good guy. I could trust him.

The Bay Bridge loomed from the window on the bus. The City, oh, what a City, danced in the lights. Calling me, I thought. The City.

"Brian, you home."

No answer. A couple of his new roommates were in the kitchen.

"Hey, how are you doing? Seen Brian?"

"He said he'd be back in a while."

I waited in the living room. The stereo was blasting. I smoked a joint. Guilt shadowed me. Stoned. Adrift. Turmoil-ed about the future. My stomach sank as I thought of my family. School. Money. Another drug deal in my pocket. Christmas. Fuck! Christmas. I almost forgot. I'll get presents when I get back to Winona. My stomach ached. I needed food.

Went out to get a burger on Haight Street. Fucking depressing scene. Spaced out zoned out hippies. Got a burger and some fries. Felt better. Brian was home when I returned.

"Hey man, I gotta get back. Want to be home for Christmas. You have to come out sometime Brian. You've got a place to stay."

"I will, man."

I gathered up my things and the latest stash of drugs. This time I had some white crosses too. Speed. The 'truckers helper.'

I could sell everything in Winona and make a couple of hundred bucks. I could afford Christmas presents. I had enough money for the second semester. I was set.

Brian and I partied late. A few people came over but I was lost in space and didn't engage. Too much on my mind.

I left the next morning for the airport. They told me at the ticket counter that the next flight to Minneapolis was sold out but I decided to take my chances and bought a student standby ticket. I waited at the gate and as the passengers were loading they called my name. Someone in First-Class had not shown up and low and behold I got the very last seat. In First- Class!

I dined on steak and salad with a piece of pie for desert and the stewardess even let me have some champagne!

It was a great flight.

Same routine to Winona. Waited all night for the next bus.

It was two days before Christmas and when I arrived at the house I was immediately assaulted with 'where have you been' and 'your dad is looking for you' and the rest. I told Mom that I wanted a truce for Christmas and that I was going shopping. I got something for every member of the family and it felt good. I even bought some wrapping paper and cards. I did the best I could at wrapping.

I made some phone calls at my apartment and soon moved all the merchandise, except for several white crosses, which I kept for personal consumption. Those little devils came in handy for studying all night. Better than coffee.

I called Joe and he came over. He had two six packs of Hamm's. We listened to music and I told him all about my adventures. The drugs and about Mark. Everything. We smoked some pot and I gave him a couple of hits of acid and some speed.

"Should we do it now?"

"Why not."

Off we flew into 'never, never land.'

Joe had brought over a couple of Dylan albums. It was the first time I had really listened to him. It was intense and I realized the sounds and words of fury and truth in his voice. I knew then at that moment that I would walk on the political side of the street!

Joe and I talked and jived all night long. He was a trusted friend.

I wandered over to the house, weighed down with Christmas presents, on Christmas Eve. The house smelled nice. A decorated Christmas tree was in the living room. A turkey was cooking in the oven. The whole family was in the den watching TV. Dad was even cordial.

I helped Mom set the table. She asked me how everything was. "Fine." God, if they only knew. Dad said I needed a haircut. Even Emil was home. They weren't playing on Christmas Eve.

We all sat down to eat and Dad said grace. We dug in. There was so much food.

I helped clean up and load the dishwasher. The family settled in the living room and we passed out gifts. All in all it was a pleasant evening. It would be the last Christmas Eve we would ever have together.

Dad and Mom were both nice and the younger ones played with their new toys. We each received a check from Grandma. I got $100 which was a fortune. Grandma also sent us a huge box of Christmas cookies which were mostly powdered crumbs because of the shipping and handling. We sprinkled the crumbs over ice cream. Yumm!

I grabbed my new sweater and shirts and headed to my apartment. Home sweet home.

1967 was only a week from now!

On the day after Christmas, after cashing Grandma's check, just on a whim, I walked to the bus station and purchased a ticket to Madison. I'd been there with my dad a couple of years prior. "Look at the Beatniks, Mike," is all that I remember. It wasn't a long trip, a couple of hours. I found the campus and walked around. It was cold and bitter. I found the Student Union building. It was open.

A large noisy place. Found the cafeteria in the Student Union and got some coffee and doughnuts. Checked my watch. Plenty of time to catch the bus back to Winona. I didn't pack any clothes so I was unburdened. Music blared over the PA. So different from staid St. Mary's where music was forbidden in the Student Union. Found a table to sit. The place was packed. Mostly long haired hippies. I was surprised actually. But, I had heard that Madison was a happening place. Mark had asked me to check out the scene. No time like the present. I made mental notes. "Never write anything down."

I struck up a conversation with a couple of guys sitting at the next table. They both had long hair and they looked familiar. It was Curtis and John.

"Did you guys work at a cannery in Minnesota last Summer?"

"Yeah, we did ... hey, man, I remember you. Did you guys ever take that trip?" one of them said.

"What a coincidence! I was hoping to run into you guys. Jeez! Yeah, Joe and I made it as far as San Francisco. We met some great people there and ended up staying for awhile. We never made it any further!"

"And, you guys go to school here. Right?" I continued.

"Yep, were both freshmen."

I told them I was going to St. Mary's in Winona and that I was just taking a look around and was going to return home tonight. They invited me to stay.

We walked to their place on Mifflin Street. The neighborhood reminded me of San Francisco only with larger houses and yards. It was the student living section. Even though it was cold and the windows were shut, music filtered out into the street. Their house was in the middle of the block. After a few minutes it was apparent that theses guys were very political and liked to get high too! Perfect. Between joints we discussed the war and rallies and I told them about Haight Street and Berkeley. They said I could stay as long as I wanted. I had some money on me and I said I could chip in for food. One of the older guys in the house went out and got a case of beer and the party was on. The house was a mess. Don't know how many people lived here. Most were home for Christmas so I could sleep in a bed upstairs. We sat in a circle, soon joined by several other people. They talked and I listened. They spoke of 'actions' ... taking over the Administrative building, trashing the ROTC building ... and other possibilities.

I would have much to relate to Mark. This place was a "Berkeley' in the Midwest. It wasn't just luck that I met these guys. It was destiny.

I told them about conservative St. Mary's and how I had turned about twenty people on to acid and mescaline and about my adventures in the Bay Area. But, not a word about Mark.

We all seemed to hit it off and were soon giggling and laughing from the beer and pot.

Little did I know then that this group would play a large role in this saga.

I arrived back in Winona on New Year's Eve. Emil's band was playing at Winona State and I wanted to be there.

What a night! The whole town was there. It was freezing outside but it sizzled inside. The Ferrais' played three sets. I helped them set up in the gym and tear down after the gig. I was so buzzed that I didn't even feel the chill in the night air. At midnight the band came out with horns and streamers that they threw into the crowd. The place went nuts. I danced my ass off with a girl I knew and we had fun. I invited her and her friends to the party after the gig but I think they got scared off by the drugs. I staggered to my apartment at 5 a.m.

It was 1967.

Chapter 7

1967

Still had a week before school started. Mr. Kukos took me to work one day and I applied for a part time job working in the lab at Fiberite. I would test product and write up a report to give to the chemist. Different companies would want a plastic product that would have so much tensile strength, withstand so much heat, etc. and our chemist would make a formula to meet their specifications. My job was to mix the formula up and test it out. I started in a couple of days. I worked two nights a week from 3:30 until midnight with a half hour lunch. The pay was great and I worked with two other guys both from Winona State.

I worked around my new school schedule. It would be easier this semester; English, history, a philosophy class, religion, of course, and phys-ed. No math or science. Jeez, I had to keep the grades up to stay out of the draft.

School started up again. I had phys-ed first class three days a week. Got to the gym and dressed for class. This will be a breeze. The instructor was a hard assed jock. Mr. Mollock. He was the baseball coach. He was old and mean. He lined us up and took roll call. He looked at me and said, "I don't want any girls in this class," a few snickers. My hair was getting long. I had no intention of cutting it.

We had some basic tests to take. He wanted to see where we were at physically. The first test involved climbing a rope that had been tied to the ceiling of the field house. It was about 50 feet to the ceiling I would guess. Their was a ribbon tied to the rope about ten feet up. The idea was to climb the rope and touch the ribbon and then descend. Half the guys couldn't climb it at all but several did succeed. It came my turn, "Let's see what Susie can do." I was pissed off by now so I climbed all the way to the ceiling, not using my legs, mind you, just my arms, with my legs stuck straight out. I came down. Didn't say a word. Some of the guys were grinning at me. Mollock looked stunned.

The next event involved a sprint. I kicked everybody's ass in that too!

Then came a mile run. Won going away.

He wanted to see how high we could jump. I ran to the basketball rim and hung on to it! No one else could even touch it.

We did push-ups and leg lifts and I held my own. Mollock realized I was the best athlete in the class and he never said another word to me about my hair. He continued, however, to affectionately call me 'Susie.'

After that first class we mostly played basketball games. It was too cold to go outside.

Our hockey team was the talk of the school. They hadn't lost a match. Our rink was outside and the fans sat on snowbanks. It was something. The University of Minnesota was coming down to play us and the whole school was there. We won 6-0.

We were actually considered a national power. Several of the players were from Canada. This one guy had one eyebrow and was as dumb as a post. But could he skate. Forgot the guys name but he later played in the NHL.

But, more pressing matters. I had written Mark a letter, sent to a different address than his home and told him about the visit to Madison. He wrote back asking me to make more visits and dig around and try to find out about a couple of individuals. He told me not to be obvious about it and to let things come to me. I understood.

I could go back to Madison over some weekend. John and Curtis were cool and it would be fun.

January in Minnesota is not for the weak. It was below 0 for the entire month. Best to stay inside and hibernate. I really buckled down on my studies and my job. I had to get my grades up.

I kept in touch with Mark and Brian and my new friends in Madison.

I dabbled with intramural basketball and volunteered to help on the school paper. I'd always been interested in journalism. They gave me a Nikon one night to photograph the basketball team. I knew some basic photography. I came back with a decent shot of the game. They said I could cover more games. Which I did. Had always liked photography.

I noticed that my stuttering was disappearing and I wasn't afraid to speak up in class. Another fella was selling dope on campus and that was fine with me. I didn't want to do that any more. I was busy, busy, busy.

I stayed half the time at Mom's and the other half at my apartment. Mom's place was chaos. Dad was gone most of the time and Emil was rarely home leaving the youngsters to basically fend for themselves. My sister Mary was amazing as she took charge of the place and learned to cook and made sure the others cleaned their rooms and helped out. I was torn between the two homes.

TV news of Vietnam made me sick to my stomach. Blacks were beaten up down South. There was rioting everywhere it seemed that police beatings were occurring on a daily basis. The Black Panthers stalking and being stalked by the Oakland police. Student protesters beaten and tear gassed. Young men being slaughtered in Vietnam. The Vietnamese people being bombed and napalmed. I needed to do more; to become more involved. Studying inane college courses. It was all too much!

New terms like 'counter culture,' and the 'anti-war movement,' the 'Women's movement,' etc. began entering the conversation. Maybe there was hope after all!

I kept up a steady line of correspondence with Mark. He said I was his eyes and ears in the Midwest. I was getting an education from Mark and the *Berkeley Barb*. Both contended that we were being misinformed about the war.

Some things that once mattered; school and grades, having a neat appearance, lost their relevancy.

Made a quick trip to Madison over Easter break and saw the gang there. Met some new people. Everyone I knew in Madison was political and seemed hell-bent on ending the war. Peace marches seemed to be an everyday event in Madison, usually ending in some crazy rock throwing tear gassed fiasco.

I made a discreet inquiry about the people Mark had wanted me to tail. No one I knew, knew them. I asked Mark if he had a photo. He didn't.

While Winona was staid and peaceful. I decided to organize a peace march in Winona. I had no idea what I was doing so I enlisted all the people I knew who were supportive of the Peace Movement. About twenty of us. We made posters and placed them on the three campuses in Winona announcing the event. We knew nothing about permits or anything of that nature. When the big day arrived we assembled at one end of downtown and started marching. We were amazed how many people joined us. Onlookers stood at the curb as if watching a parade. It was pretty funny. We chanted and had drums beating and it was cool. The police showed up at the end of downtown and told us to disperse. We stopped but no one moved. Three cops looking pretty helpless and ineffectual.

After a twenty minute standoff the crowd, now having swelled to a few hundred, began to break up.

The newspaper had a photograph the next day.

The guy who had spit in my face months earlier for holding up a 'Stop War' sign marched with us. That irony wasn't lost on me. Several members of the local clergy took part and I was pleased that no one was hurt and that no one was arrested.

We had made our point!

That night several of us, riding the high from the march, got together and planned for more marches and a sit in.

I wrote Mark about the march. He was very supportive.

I kept my grades up and was still working nights. Several of the guys at work heard about the march and gave me a hard time about it calling me names. It got so bad I wanted to quit. Mr. Kukos was concerned because he rented to me so I told him I would move out but he wanted me to stay. He felt bad about the 'morons' at work, as he put it, "They're just simple guys who feel threatened by long hair and the peace thing, don't worry about it. I can take care of them. I'm management and they have to do what I say. Are you sure you don't want to stay because you were doing good work. But, I understand."

I decided to eventually quit Fiberite and took a 'leave of abscence' but stayed at Mr. Kukos'.

Summer break was coming up and I decided to work in a cannery near Madison. John and Curtis could get me a job there.

Things were unbearable at home. Mom was having frequent fits and the kids were not doing well. Mary held it together as best she could and when Dad left I would go over to the house and try to put things back in order.

Life was chaos!

I had a continuous stomach ache. One day I noticed blood in the toilet again after a bm. It got worse and worse. Finally, I made a doctors appointment and after a barrage of tests it was determined that I had a bleeding ulcer. I told the doctor of the stress I was under at home and school and the draft. He told me to stop drinking coffee and gave me medicine to take. After a few weeks the symptoms went away and my stomach stopped aching.

I did have a couple of interesting classes in school. One was in comparative religion. I was amazed how similar all of the major religions were not only in structure but in dogmas as well. The other class was an English Lit class. I loved to read and I changed my major to English Lit. I wrote a long paper on *Moby Dick* and the professor liked it so much he asked if he could keep it!

But, I was getting tired of school and felt guilty getting a draft deferment just because I could afford college. Life didn't seem fair. Watching the news each night was depressing and scary. It was the inner city kids, mostly blacks, who were being killed. And no mention of the Vietnamese people killed each day. We were supposedly 'winning' the war as it escalated and escalated.

The school year ended. I had a 2.8 average. I could have done so much better but I just didn't care anymore.

Joe decided to work for his dad all summer.

I headed for Madison and found John and Curtis. On their word I got a job at a cannery outside Madison. I worked in the warehouse cataloging the thousands of cans of peas and corn. Similar to last years' job. It was daunting at first but I soon learned the tricks which made it easier. About one third of the workers were Mexican. They lived on site in little wooden shacks with no water or bathrooms. They had no kitchen or electricity and had to shower and cook in a separate building. The living conditions were very poor. Most of the Mexican workers had their entire families with them and some of them held eight or more people in these very small shacks. We also found out that they were paid less and were given the worst jobs. Shifts generally ran twelve hours a day seven days a week with no over-time pay. The hardest jobs included the sorting of the crops and palletizing the cans as they came down the conveyer belts. Both jobs were incredibly monotonous and noisy in extremely hot conditions. The college kids didn't do this work for the most part.

I stayed at John and Curtis' place in Madison. It was only a ten minute drive to the cannery.

Some of us were talking one night and someone came up with the idea of organizing a union for the cannery workers. We even contacted attorneys and labor dispute experts. I knew nothing about organizing a union. I listened and learned a great deal. We gathered facts; wages, living conditions, working conditions, dangerous equipment in the plant, etc. We even enrolled one of the Mexicans to be a spokesman for them. He spoke English and he told us the Mexican's were afraid of such talk because it would jeopardize their jobs. After several of these 'meetings' we presented the company with our proposals and were told we were all fired unless we backed off. It seemed that the only people who wanted fair wages and working conditions were a hand full of white students from Madison; the Mexicans were too afraid, the management was against us, and the major-ity of the other workers were against our proposals too!

It was a loosing battle. We had heard of Cesar Chavez in California but his people were spread too thin in California to spare any help for our cause. The United Farm Workers Union were up against it. Only the under-ground press seemed to support their cause and the main media basically shunned them. We had no press coverage at all except one little article in one of the Madison underground papers.

It was my first experience trying to organize a union and I was begin-ning to see how things really work in this country; namely, the rich control the politics, police, courts, public opinion, etc.

Each day I saw workers stagger out of the plant after working in sweltering conditions. If it was 100 degrees outside it had to be 120 inside with noisy (so loud you had to cup your ear as a person shouted) conditions, limited ten minute breaks and bathroom breaks. The floor shook and rocked because of the machines. People passed out every day. And then back to their little unventilated boxes.

If the working conditions were bad at the plant I can only imagine what they were like in the fields with no shelter from the beating sun.

But, there was no way we could defeat the management. They weren't bad people as most of my compatriots would have you believe, they were following orders and things had always run this way.

Trucks would pull up with the corn or the peas and the smell was overwhelming. When they harvested these crops various rodents and snakes and such were included in the cut.

Meanwhile, back in the air conditioned warehouse I continued to do my job inventorying a few thousand pallets a shift. I had enough money for school next year and only wanted to work a couple of more weeks then head back to California to see Mark and Brian.

I said good byes to John and Curtis and several new friends from Madison. I hadn't collected any information on those people for Mark because all I did for two months was work and sleep, but, I did make some new friendships and I'm sure that at a later date they could be useful.

I returned to Winona to take care of some business and told Mom I'd be back in two weeks. Off again I flew to San Francisco. Brian had moved to the Mission District in the City, an area full of cheap flats and great cheap food. It was my introduction to Mexican and Latin American cuisine.

Brian was the same. The Haight had gotten too dangerous and expensive to live so he found this great flat on Capp Street that he shared with four other people. Great neighborhood full of music and the smell of food.

"Hey man, let me show you around."

We walked up and down several streets, checking out the shops and bars and restaurants. It was really safe over here and it had the sense of a community.

I had to see Mark too.

Mark was doing well, entertaining a constant flow of politicos. He gave me a reading list, among them *The Port Huron Statement*, which would influence me the rest of my life. I found a copy at a bookstore in Berkeley along with several other interesting looking journals, a book about Marx, the *Little Red Book*; quotations from Mao, and an article about Che, a copy of *On the Road*, because I hadn't finished it, and *Howl*. That should keep me busy for awhile.

We caught up on things and I told him I was transferring to Winona State next semester because it was cheaper and way easier than St. Mary's.

I had become worn out by the Catholic thing by then and needed a break from working so hard on my studies. I would have more time to devote to the movement, which was beginning to flourish in Winona. Anti-war sentiment was abundant on the Winona State campus and hippies ruled the day.

"Sorry I haven't found out about those guys, Mark. I haven't met anyone who knows them and I didn't hang out in Madison this time."

"I have to be discreet ... you know," I added.

"That's cool."

I stayed in the Bay Area for two weeks and then flew back to Minnesota.

Dad came home one day. He told me to come to the house. Mom was hysterical, screaming and crying. Dad told me he was taking her to the Mayo Clinic in Rochester and that he wanted me to come along to watch Mom so he could drive. We got in the car. I noticed a fresh black eye on Mom. She was crying and moaning and begging Dad not to take her there.

"You need to dry out, Pat."

Mom had been having fits again and the local doctors hadn't a clue why. She was taking several prescription drugs and drinking constantly.

I figured that was the reason for the fits. We made the half hour trip and Dad and I guided Mom into the hospital to register her. This took a long time, even though they were expecting her, and we got her up to her room in St. Mary's Hospital adjacent to the Mayo Clinic.

She was pleading and sobbing.

Dad and I actually had a nice talk on the way back.

"Your mother is an alcoholic and she needs help."

"Is she going to be all right?"

"Hope so."

When we got home Dad gathered all the kids in the living room and told us that Mom would be gone for a few weeks and that they were supposed to obey me when he was gone. He left me some money for food and hit the road.

"I'll call."

A neighbor lady helped us out. She said she would take care of Casey and Paul. School didn't start for several weeks yet.

Things went okay for the first week. Mary was a champ and the rest of the kids really did their part. I told Mary I wanted to see Mom and that I would take a bus to Rochester and stay the night there. I rose early and walked to the Greyhound Station and caught the bus to Rochester. I checked into a hotel next to St. Mary's and paid for the night.

As soon as I had my room I walked over to the hospital and asked to see my mom. They said she had been moved to the Psychiatric Wing.

When I found that section I walked through the doors and there was a large room with several people watching TV or staring out the windows. One man was naked standing in the middle of the room. I walked to the desk and asked to see my mom and they gave me a room number. I walked in and there was Mom lying in bed drooling and staring with vacant eyes. She didn't even acknowledge my presence. I freaked out and ran down the hall and asked to see the doctor. He came out in a couple of minutes and I attacked him. Yelling and screaming ... "What did you do to my mom?" I was hysterical. Two big black guys grabbed me and restrained me. I calmed down in a couple of minutes.

The doctor then proceeded to explain what they had done to my mom. She had an operation called a hysterectomy. He explained that to me. Then they started giving her electric shock treatments to cure her of her alcoholism.

"Your mom is going to be fine," he assured me. I apologized for my outburst and we left it at that. Dad never mentioned an operation to me or the shock treatments. Mom was never the same again.

A nurse caught my attention as I was leaving. "Do you have a place to stay?"

"I'm staying at the hotel across the street."

"What's your room number?" I told her and walked back to my room. Nothing to do so I walked around Rochester for a long time. Mom looked like a zombie. I was scared and very, very angry. I was mad at Dad and at the doctors. I was just mad.

I grabbed a few burgers and walked back to my room. I ate and watched TV for awhile.

There was a knock at my door. It was the nurse from this afternoon.

"Wanna go to a party?"

"Sure."

She came in and I put on a fresh shirt and off we went. She was kinda cute and didn't look like a nurse in jeans. She had a car. We drove a few blocks to an apartment building.

"If you don't like it we can leave."

Room to room people and the smell of pot hung in the air, some music playing in the background. Did see a girl from Winona across the room. She didn't notice me. Jean grabbed my hand and she introduced me to some people and we found a cozy corner with a chair and an end table. Jean found some beers and we had a pleasant time. Most people were connected to the clinic and they talked doctor talk and I just listened.

After an hour or so Jean said, "let's go."

Jean bought some more beer and we headed back to the motel. We watched TV and talked. Jean was a nursing student and was very serious about her profession. She was a few years older than I and wasn't interested in a sexual thing at all. I wasn't either. All I could think about was my mom.

"She'll be okay in a few days," Jean assured me.

"I don't know. She looked like a zombie."

I thanked her for taking me to the party. It got my mind off things.

"If you want, I'll check on your mom for you and let you know how she is doing."

"Would you, that would be great."

I told Jean about the situation at home and that Dad was gone and how I was taking care of the rest of the kids. We exchanged addresses and phone numbers. She was a real friend.

It was getting late and Jean took off. I watched some crap on TV and fell asleep.

I felt desolate.

Caught the morning bus back to Winona. Walked home and gathered the kids up and explained to them that Mom was going to be in the hospital a bit longer. I only shared the real horror with Emil.

We had run out of money and Dad hadn't called recently. I called Dad's boss in Fort Wayne and explained the situation to him. He was really nice and wired a couple hundred bucks to me via Western Union. I called Western Union and they had it in a few hours. Mary and I went to the grocery store and stocked up.

I was driving the Falcon for errands. Still had no license. Just didn't care.

Had a birthday coming up but didn't much feel like celebrating.

I was turning 20.

It was my 20th birthday. August 25, 1968. I came home to blow out candles and open a couple presents and eat a much needed dinner. Dad was home and the atmosphere was pleasant.

After dinner and cake and receiving a couple of shirts, Dad and I adjourned to the den and began watching the Democratic Convention from Chicago.

These were troubled days. Martin Luther King had been assassinated as had Robert Kennedy. Johnson had stated he wasn't running again amid the turmoil of the Vietnam War. Nixon was the Republican nominee. Therefore, the Convention was open to contenders like Eugene McCarthy and George McGovern but our Minnesota boy, Hubert Humphrey seemed to have an edge. I was for McCarthy and so wanted him to win. He had the intellect and compassion that touched so many young people.

Dad and I sat back watching the horror unfold. Demonstrators were being tear gassed and beaten senseless by the Chicago police while inside the Convention everything seemed rosy.

I called Joe.

"Are you watching this?"

"Hey man, let's go to Chicago!" Joe asked.

"When do you want to leave?"

"Right now."

Joe arrived in an hour. We packed sleeping bags and some sandwiches. Off we went. With my dad's blessing.

"Oh yeah, happy birthday."

"Thanks man. This is history, man," I stated.

And I went on. "Did you see the cops beating people up. Women, little kids ... anybody in the way. I'm done standing around watching this bullshit. I want to fight back. The real war is here. Even my dad was pissed off at the cops. Even my dad! I thought the Democrats were against the war. I guess not. You know I worked for McCarthy's people for a couple of days in Madison canvassing to get votes. I'd knock on a door and introduce myself and most people would shut the door in my face but some people let me in and some confessed they supported Gene but were afraid to say so in public. What kind of country is this, man? When people are afraid to publicly express themselves. This country is so divided I sometimes think there may be another Civil War." I was ranting now but Joe let me continue. "It's split between young and old. Shit, I would have fought in World War Two but not this piece of shit. A generation split. Kids against their parents. I was always taught to respect my elders with 'yes ma'ams and yes sirs' but I've lost that respect because I don't like being lied too. We are being lied to everyday by our own government and it seems only the young realize that!"

"Fuck the pigs," Joe piped in, "and Happy Birthday!"

"Ha, ha. Thanks, man. Twenty years old. Can't vote but I can kill Viet Cong. Is that irony?"

"Sure is."

It was an eight hour drive to Chicago. I had a map and found out where the Convention was. We drove all night and were tired when we arrived in the outskirts of Chicago.

"Maybe we should find a park and take a nap before heading over there," I suggested.

By first light we drove into a city park and unfurled our sleeping bags for a nap.

We didn't sleep long if at all. The city noise. I consulted the map and we drove toward the International Amphitheater on Halsted Street. We were actually several blocks away when it was apparent we were close. Joe wanted to find a safe place to park the car and we lucked out finding a parking garage within ten blocks. I said I would pay. We had only planned to be around for a few hours and then split back to Winona.

We got out and began walking toward the noise and commotion. There were protestors everywhere and it wasn't hard to find. Tear gas filled the air and our eyes began to sting. Some kids ran by and we followed them. We ran and walked for several blocks joining a mass of people marching. Soon we were on Michigan Avenue with thousands of protestors.

This was to be my first real protest march. The crowd was chanting anti-war slogans and adrenaline raced through my veins. Many people had signs. Joe and I marched along. Lost wasn't the word. Where are we? I had the map in my hip pocket along with the address of the parking garage. We were suddenly met by National Guardsmen as well as Chicago cops. A menacing looking group. Mostly fat white guys in contrast to the very boyish looking Guardsmen.

There was a commotion way up front and the next thing we knew we were tear gassed and crazy cops lurched into the crowd from everywhere swinging batons and clubbing people. Joe and I ran for it. Most of the marchers, having nowhere else to go, ran down side streets only to be met by more cops and Guardsmen and tear gas.

The gas burns your lungs and eyes. I know why it was named tear gas. People were screaming and running for safety. Joe and I, both being athletes, were finally able to reach a relatively safe spot some two blocks away and up wind. I saw people running out of office buildings because they had been gassed. The tall buildings trapped the gas.

We were back near the Convention Center. I saw TV lights and camera crews and trucks with network emblems. Thousands of people congregated near the hall and tension was in the air. Everything seemed chaotic. Cops on horses, Guardsmen lining up, megaphones from both sides yelling and screaming orders and epithets, pushing and shoving and again an explosion of nightsticks and tear gas ... people screaming and shrieking in absolute terror. I saw a cop on a horse beat the shit out of a demonstrator as he tried to cover up and protect himself. Blood splattered the wall behind him as he lay motionless on the sidewalk. 'Chickenshit fucking coward pig!' I could see that some of them were enjoying this. Beating up unarmed peaceniks. What bravery and dashing in battle.

Joe and I jogged for an hour staying one step ahead of the massacre and the gas. The trick was to keep moving and don't get slowed by a mass of people. That's when the pigs attacked. I saw a cameraman trying to photograph this melee when a cop on a horse rode up behind him and dropped him with one swing. The camera came crashing to the ground.

"Hey, Joe we're all the way back to Grant Park."

I had seen football games at nearby Soldier's Field. It wasn't the same now. Cops were everywhere swinging batons and hitting anything that moved. They hit helpless people already wounded and bleeding from a previous attack. People screaming in pain.

It was getting late in the afternoon and long shadows appeared. I told Joe maybe we should think about heading out. He agreed.

Now, how to get back to the car without getting gassed and beaten.

I read the map and we decided to walk around the riot. We strode off like two college boys on an afternoon stroll. We probably walked twenty blocks out of our way but made it safely back to the garage.

The guys at the garage acted like nothing was going on.

Wow!

Back in the car we headed home. We both had jobs and had to get back. I didn't work until tomorrow afternoon at 3 giving us plenty of time to get home.

"As one of my professors would say at the end of a lecture, What did we learn today?"

"I learned, never to go to a riot wearing loafers." I answered.

We both laughed pretty hard at that one.

"Seriously man, what the fuck was that! Kids just getting pounded and gassed. I thought this was a free country. Remember, I was telling you about this guy in Berkeley, Mario Savio? He stood on the steps at Cal Berkeley speaking about freedom of speech. It seems if you are an anti- war protestor that you must be anti-American. I think just the opposite ... to question authority is American. And you shouldn't be beaten with nightsticks and tear gassed just because you don't agree with the Establishment!"

Joe and I drove through the night landscape of Wisconsin crossing the Mississippi River at La Crosse and a short sprint into Winona.

"Drop me off at my apartment would 'ya?"

I wanted to be alone for the day before I worked tonight. The last 24 hours would probably take years to sink in. I had trouble taking a nap but managed a couple of hours before I trod to Fiberite for the night shift. I would eventually find out that Fiberite manufactured the fiberglass plastic material made for the gun butt for the M-16 rifle. I quit shortly thereafter.

Dad called me the next day. He wanted me to come along with him to pick up Mom from the Mayo Clinic. He picked me up and asked me about Chicago. He mostly smiled and nodded his head. Didn't comment much on it but was happy Joe and I were safe.

About half way to Rochester Dad informed me that the company was moving him and the family to the Pittsburgh area and that Emil and I would stay behind to finish school.

"When are you moving?"

"In two weeks."

"What!!"

"I want you boys to help with the move."

"Yes, sir."

Dad had already purchased a house in some little town called Irwin, just outside of Pittsburgh.

We arrived at the Mayo and collected Mom. She looked like a ghost. Pale and drawn. She didn't say much.

Dad told her about the move and she showed no reaction. She would never be the same.

We returned home in time for the night shift. A night of mixing and testing fiberglass products. The fiberglass made me itch and soon I developed a major rash on my forearms. They sent me to doctor who prescribed an ointment and told me to protect my arms with plastic bags tied off at the wrist. A few workers made fun of me but the rash eventually subsided. Meanwhile, one night I was in the warehouse looking for some samples when I heard some moaning from behind the shelves. I thought someone was injured so I ran to where the noises were and walked upon two people screwing on a pallet. They saw me and stopped. Their respective spouses worked the day shift. Just then their supervisor appeared looking for them and he saw them conjoined! What a fracas! Word soon got around the plant. It was all people could talk about. I'm not really sure what happened to them. If they kept their jobs and if they kept their marriages because I quit. Jeez!

I spent the next several days packing boxes for the move. We still had hundreds of books and tons of clothes. The Mayflower people had dropped off a load of different sized boxes. What a chore!

The Mayflower crew showed up with their largest van and for the next two days managed to fit everything into it. It was crammed with stuff tied to the back gate and towing the Ford Falcon behind.

The rest of the family piled into the car and we said our good byes. And that was that! Off they drove to Pennsylvania.

I was to follow them on the Greyhound the next day. Dad gave me money to travel with. I would help on the other end unloading. Emil could stay with me in the meantime. He was starting Winona State too!

It was really sad watching them drive away. Mom was in shock, I think, she didn't know what was going on. This whole move had come on so sudden.

Emil and I went back to my apartment. We had moved all of our stuff over there and the place was cluttered. Emil went and got some beer. He always looked older anyway and the bartenders on the east-end didn't care. We got both got drunk and smoked some pot. He had to play that night. I called it an early night because tomorrow was a long travel day.

I got up to catch the bus to Chicago where I had to transfer to another bus to Detroit and yet another bus to Pittsburgh. The trip would take a couple of days. I brought sandwiches and plenty of smokes.

We got into Chicago that evening. It was already dark. The Greyhound station was a dank and seedy place with scary people hanging out. I found a bench to sit on in the bright light. I was relieved to see two cops walk by every half hour. The same cops who had chased me a week earlier? Probably not. The bus for Detroit finally arrived and I picked the last seat by the window in the rear. This seat sat three people. I sat next to a white woman who was with a black man. We didn't talk. The bus pulled out and I must have been tired because I soon fell asleep. I was roused some time later by moans. I opened my tired eyes to espy this woman giving the black guy a blow job. I was so embarrassed and yet aroused. I had to pee so I made noises like I was waking up and they stopped. I crawled over them and went to the rest room, which was near by. I crawled back over them excusing myself and lit a cigarette.

They didn't resume.

We pulled into Detroit and I only had to wait an hour for the bus to Pittsburgh. By now it was getting light and I felt more secure.

Down into Ohio on the turnpike. All too familiar ... into Cleveland. I stayed on the bus while some passengers departed and others boarded. Some Amish folks got on. A curious bunch.

In a few hours we arrived in Pittsburgh. I had to catch a bus to Irwin. It didn't leave for another four hours. I had no way to get a hold of my folks because they had no phone. I had to wait it out.

I decided to go for a walk and check out Pittsburgh. I remember being here with my dad several years ago and it was snowing big snow flakes. I put my hand out and when the snow melted there remained a chunk of black soot. The air was bad and it smelled like a foundry. People looked sullen and sad.

The bus to Irwin took three fucking hours. Stopping at least twenty five times. When I got to this god forsaken place all I could do was ask people where the address for my parents was. No one really knew so I called a cab. Another wait but finally at ten p.m. I arrived at their house. There was the Mayflower truck. Half unloaded. My dad was loaded. I helped unload box after box.

It was a much smaller house than the one in Winona. It was in the suburbs with boxy yards and steel fences and each house looked the same. Some neighbors helped us.

I don't remember going to sleep. I was so exhausted.

Awoke the next morning on the floor in the basement. What a mess. Dad and Mom were already up and we had coffee and cigarettes for breakfast. A kindly neighbor lady brought over a tray of donuts. That was really nice of her.

Dad's plan was to do the bedrooms first. We put the girl's room together and then the boy's rooms. Mary and Becky had their room and Paul and Casey their own room. John was to have a basement room. The master bedroom was of course, for Mom and Dad.

Poor Mom, she looked lost. I felt bad for her. I think this move was way too much for her.

By the end of the day the house was sorta put together. All the books were in the basement and so was the piano. John had a little covey down there. The kitchen was a task. We still couldn't cook because nothing was put away so Dad went out and bought a ton of McDonald's burgers and fries and shakes.

We all were tired and worn out. Dad and I found a grocery store and stocked up on groceries. We filled three shopping carts!

Mary and Mom were putting the kitchen together and the girls had found some neighborhood kids to make friends with so it was all working out.

I didn't like this place. No soul.

I told my dad of the troubles of the bus trip and he said he would fly me back home.

I had to be back to start school and Emil and I had to find a place to live. My place was too small.

Dad drove me to the airport and I flew to O'Hare in Chicago where I was able to catch a commuter flight to Winona.

I was so glad to get home. I started walking from the airport and a friend of mine picked me up and drove me back into town.

School started in a couple of days. I hadn't any books. I got back to the apartment and found it full of people. Emil holding court as they drank and got stoned. I related the bizarre story of the bus trip and everyone got a laugh.

Later on Emil and I discussed the idea of finding another apartment. We needed something larger with at least two bedrooms. I looked in the paper and found an ad for a place downtown on Third Street. Emil and I called the landlord and he showed us the place. It was on the top floor, the third story, overlooking downtown. It had two huge bedrooms and an even larger living room with sixteen foot ceilings and access to the roof next door. It was perfect. The rent was $135 a month. We needed roommates so Emil called Mudcat from the band and he knew two other guys, Snipe and Twig, (we all had nicknames except myself) and we began moving in that night. I even found another friend of mine who wanted my old place. Smooth as pie.

Emil and I had a bedroom and Snipe and Mudcat the other. The living room was so huge that we partitioned off a corner of the room for Twig. We were all Winona State students. I had transferred.

From the moment we moved in the place, it was known as 'Third

Street,' and became Party Central for Winona.

There always seemed to be people hanging out playing music and getting high. Going to classes became obsolete. After missing several days of class and after being up for three days on speed, acid, dope, beer, mescaline, and sex, it was apparent that I would be classified 1-A on my next draft notice.

Girls passed through here like a revolving door. Third Street was the center of the Universe and it would be next spring at the earliest before I had to worry about the draft. An eternity!

One night this guy dropped by and told us of this amazing drug dubbed 'The Love Drug.' It was named that because apparently it made you love everyone. Emil and I were given a free dose and yes indeedy, it made us really horny with an intense feeling of well being.

Emil and I conferred and decided we could make a fortune on this stuff. The price was right ... 50 cents a dose. It came in little glass tinctures. And if you mixed it with orange juice it cut the bitter taste.

We called the guy up and met with him a couple of days later. I had money so I gave the guy $50 and we purchased 100 vials.

Word soon got around that we had this stuff and the party was on. I sold a few vials at first but was so high I just started giving it away. The fridge was full of MDA (the Love Drug), beer, and orange juice.

An immense feeling of ecstasy and rapture filled your body and mind with boundless energy. For some people the urge to strip was overwhelming. For others sitting and staring out the window sufficed.

The Grateful Dead's *Anthem of the Sun* pounded our senses.

More people arrived. The place was packed.

I ended up in the shower with several people. This is how I met Linda (another Linda). Five or six people groaning and groping one another.

Linda and I squeezed out of the shower and jumped on my bed and made love. Emil was with a girl on his bed. It was a free-for-all. People helping themselves to more MDA and by the time I walked back into the kitchen, only ten vials remained. I grabbed them and stashed them in my room.

The living room was full of people in and out of varying degrees of dress. All sense of shame and ego and vanity and pride had vanished.

Once the 'rush' wore off one was left with an alert sense of calm and focus.

I had met Ralph that night and a group of us sat in a circle and talked. It was a high level rap session. Ralph was an intellectual and we hit it off on all levels.

I spoke mostly of the anti-war movement and my experiences from Chicago. Joe chipped in with his assessment. We spoke of the War Resistance Movement and the Civil Rights Movement, The Port Huron Statement, SDS and the such. I shared my experiences on the West Coast and Haight-Asbury.

Linda understood. Ralph understood and perhaps a few others.

For most, I believe, it was their first taste of the counter culture.

All the men were concerned about the draft. I told Ralph that I planned to resist. Not go to Canada but to fight against the war in America. To be as much of a thorn in their side as possible. To challenge their conscience. Linda thought that was cool. Most of the people listening were scratching their heads. This had never occurred to them before

I stopped myself short of divulging any real information. I had to be careful. I was stoned and I had the tendency to brag and embellish. I'm Irish. These guys just wanted to get and stay high. They didn't want to hear this.

I didn't tell anyone this at the time, but Mark had given me a list of contacts from Ann Arbor to Chicago to Madison to Berkeley and even some people in Chicago who could provide fake ID's. I had carefully hidden the list and knew I couldn't tell anyone about this.

I had been entrusted. I couldn't fail!

The party seemed to ebb and flow for a week or so. We tried in vain to get more MDA but were unable to. Bummer.

I wasn't attending school at all. The other four roommates were though. They were also terrified of being drafted. Winona had already lost two of her sons in Vietnam. One kid I knew. Not well, but I knew him. 18 years old and dead. How many more?

What a party that was. In a week or so, when the dust had settled, we all had girl friends. Linda moved in with me. Since Emil was never home anyway, it didn't seem to matter. She was the center of my life. I had never lived with a woman before and this was all new to me. I had no privacy but I didn't want any either. We stayed stoned all the time and held hands when we went out. Some of my old friends from high school and St. Mary's called me a 'hippie' and didn't want anything to do with me. I was an outcast again but accepted by the 'new wave' in Winona.

But, business first. I had to take care of several things. I knew I would be drafted by this spring so I went to the Draft Board in Winona. It was ironic that Mrs. Price worked there. I asked her for a form to fill out. It was for a 'Conscientious Objector' status.

"Hi Mrs. Price, how are you?"

She looked surprised to see me.

"I'm fine Mike. Boy, your hair sure got long. Is it better now that your folks moved?"

"Oh yeah. Say, I need a CO form."

"What's that?"

"It's a form called 'Conscientious Objector.' Do you have it?"

"I don't know."

She was alone in the office. File cabinets behind her made a formable background. I presumed this is where all the names and data were kept for the draft eligible men.

After several minutes of looking through a drawer in one of the file cabinets she turned and said she'd have to get back to me.

"Okay Mrs. Price, say hi to Steve."

"I'll do that. Come back in a few days and I should have the form by then."

"Okey dokey."

Mark had given me the name and phone number of a guy in Chicago who could get me a set of fake ID's. I called him and said I would be in town next week. He said okay. He told me to bring a photo of myself. I still had high school graduation wallet sized photos.

Good to her word, Mrs. Price had the CO form for me in a couple of days.

"For Heaven's sake. They were right here all along. I just didn't know where. Sorry Mike."

"That's okay. I'll fill this out and return it."

It was a long form. Several pages. It asked several questions pertaining to faith and beliefs. It asked if I was against the war, if I was a Communist or affiliated with the Communist Party and other silly questions. I simply stated that 'Jesus said we shall not kill.'

I returned the form to Mrs. Price and thanked her again. She was a kind person. I never held it against her for working there. She had taken me in more than once after Dad had beaten me.

I couldn't tell Linda about my doings in the resistance. I couldn't tell anyone. Mark had drilled that into my head. I told everyone I was going home (Pittsburgh) for a few days and that I would return.

Instead I traveled to Chicago.

I called the guy up and he gave me directions to his office. I took a cab to save time. His office was in a seedy part of South Side Chicago in a warehouse district. I knocked on his door and I heard, "come in."

I didn't know much about the Mafia but this guy had to be Mafia.

"35 bucks for a set. That includes a student ID, a drivers license, a social security card, and most importantly, a student deferment card for the draft. For an extra $25 I'll include two gas credit cards. What'll it be?"

"I want two sets of cards with two separate names plus the credit cards. Here's $120 and six wallet photos. When can you have 'em done?"

"Two days. Call me."

The guy scared me. The building scared me. Bums and trash littered the street. It wasn't safe during the day. One could only wonder about the night.

I called a friend from Loyola. He happened to be home and I went to the safe North Side to stay with him for a few days.

I had a couple of other contacts as well and the next day got a hold of one of them. Paul.

"That fucking Convention, Man. That radicalized more people. The whole City is pissed. Fucking Daley and his thugs. And then they arrested a bunch of guys charging them with Conspiracy to Riot. What a joke!"

"I heard about that. Seven or eight guys, right?" I asked.

"Something like that. Abbie Hoffman and Jerry Rubin and Bobby Seal of the Panthers. Jesus!"

"Hey Paul, I trust you. I'll need a place to stay when I'm in town. Can I stay here if I need a place."

"Yeah man, what's up?"

"I can't tell you everything but I'm going to get drafted this spring and I'm resisting. I'll need safe places and cool people. You can't ever tell anyone this. Okay?"

Paul and I had a lot in common. He was also a student and a member of SDS. He told me about a faction of SDS that wanted a violent overthrow of the government. Pipe bombing government buildings and even kidnapping. Robbing banks.

I sat and listened intently. I don't know. I just don't know.

I had always wanted peace. I had studied Ghandi and Martin Luther King and believed real change could come through active, peaceful, resistance. But after seeing just one night of the Democratic Convention I had serious doubts about that too!

I just don't know.

I stayed at Paul's for a couple of days. Meeting his friends and hanging out. I called my ID man and he said he had everything ready.

I said goodbye to Paul and thanked him. "See you again, my friend."

I took a cab to the office building. Seemed like the same bums were hanging out. Scary faces. Menacing. I ran up the stairs to the third floor and knocked.

"Come in!"

"Oh it's you. Yeah, got them cards done. One set youse Mark Cole from Wisconsin and the other Mark Heddington from Stout State. Plus four credit cards for gas. If youse use these", he said pointing to the gas cards, "throw 'em away after youse use 'em. Got it?" I nodded.

"And don't tell nobody," he added.

That went without saying.

The cards were perfect!

I arrived at the bus station and only had to wait an hour. I caught the first leg to Madison and waited to transfer to Winona. I just knew Madison was in my future.

I returned home and immediately hid the ID's. They would come into play later.

My head was spinning. Too much to contemplate.

I arrived back at 3rd Street and the party was still in progress. Someone was sleeping in my bed so I hopped in Emil's to get some rest. The place was a mess and the noise was intolerable. Linda came over and crawled into bed with me. Frankly, sex was the last thing I wanted. My head was spinning. I couldn't tell her of my 'new' identities although I wanted to. I had to think. I was sure I'd be drafted by this spring. I hadn't attended a class in weeks. I was a drop-out. Other questions surfaced; should I support and partake in a violent overthrow or maintain a passive resistance? Some members of the SDS had broken off the main body and proclaimed that they would through terrorist acts, overthrow the government. They called themselves the 'Weathermen.' I felt in my heart that violence would just beget more violence and turn off most of the American citizens. And yet, protests seemed to accomplish nothing but a police riot. I hadn't heard a word from the Draft Board concerning my CO appeal. I thought of going to Canada but I wanted to fight injustice here. The thought of prison terrified me. I heard that draft resisters were getting five year sentences. Two local guys had already been killed in Vietnam. My ulcer was bleeding again. I felt lost and alone with no one except my sympathetic friends to turn to. I had to see Mark.

Mudcat came into my room.

"Mike, your dad is in town and he's looking for you."

"What!?"

"He called Sam's dad and Sam passed it on to Emil. Your dad is staying at Sam's dad's place."

"What the fuck does he want?"

"Dunno, man."

Sam was the drummer in the Ferrais. My dad had no idea that Emil and I lived in this dump. He'd go nuts if he found us here. I decided I should call him right away.

"Hey, Dad. It's me Mike."

"Where are you?"

"Downtown."

"I'll pick you up at the library in fifteen minutes."

No 'hi, how are you' or small talk. He sounded drunk and pissed.

I walked to the library and waited. He drove up.

"Get in," He demanded. "you look like shit. You're getting a haircut and some decent clothes."

"Why?"

"Shut the fuck up."

He was in a rage. No use trying to reason with him. We drove to a barber shop. I got a close trim and a shave. Next we went to Penney's and he bought me some slacks, new shoes, and a sports jacket.

I felt like an idiot. He didn't say a word.

"Where are we going?"

"To Duluth. You're signing up for the Merchant Marines. That'll keep you out of the draft."

What the fuck. He was crazy.

We drove up Highway 61 through the Cities all the way to Duluth. It was getting late so we stayed in a motel. He was in a better mood after a while. We checked into our room and we walked to a tavern and ordered some burgers and beer. I was underage but I drank beer anyway.

"I don't want you going to Vietnam. If you get into the Merchant Marines you can stay out of the draft. Besides, you'll see the world and make some money. Don't you want to do that?"

The idea did appeal to me.

The next few hours were some of the most pleasant time I had ever spent with my dad. He was really nice to me and listened and paid attention to me the rest of the night.

The next morning Dad drove me to what looked like a Coast Guard facility. We met with this Coast Guard officer. He was very nice. He explained the procedure to me. First, I was to have a written test, then an oral test, and finally a physical. This would require three days or so. If I passed everything I could stay in the barracks and wait for a ship. If they were hiring I could go on as a cook's helper.

Dad and I chatted some and he said he had to leave. He gave me a couple of hundred bucks.

"The room is paid up for a week and I'll fill the fridge with food and beer and cigs."

I said goodbye to Dad.

I took the written exam.

"Come back tomorrow at ten for the oral exam."

I walked several blocks back to the motel. Sure enough. Dad had stocked the place with food and beer and a carton of Old Golds. I made a burger and sat back and watched TV and drank one of several beers. Life is good.

I was back at the office at nine forty five.

"Mike, come on in. You did very well on the exam yesterday. Most recruits can barely read."

We took the oral part. He asked me lots of questions about history, some math and asked me questions about my mental health. This took about two hours and I was finished with that.

"Tomorrow the physical."

"Okay, see you at ten."

I walked around Duluth for a while. I liked it. Steep hills leading to great views of Lake Superior. Reminded me of San Francisco. I ventured back to the motel. I needed food and beer.

The third day a doctor poked and prodded me and made me walk and lift things.

When we were finished the Coast Guard guy told me to wait at the motel and that he would contact me when the results of the tests were known.

"Should know in a day or two."

Two days later the manager of the motel informed me of a phone message. The Coast Guard wanted to see me.

"You did quite well on all the tests, Mike. All you need now is a passport and you'll be ready to board a ship."

They gave me a photo ID as a Merchant Marine.

I filled out the forms for a passport. It would take a month to get my passport so I decided to return to Winona and wait. Once I had the passport I could go anywhere that a ship was docked and try to get on it.

This gave me a great option.

I thanked the Coast Guard officer. He was really nice.

I returned to Winona the next day by hitch hiking. It was faster than the bus. It took five rides.

I received a letter from the local Navy recruiter. He wanted to see me. I called him a couple of days later and we met at Winona State in the cafeteria. He handed me a pack of papers.

"All you need to do is sign these..."

"What are these?"

"You're dad met with me last week and he signed you up for the Navy. Six years and a guarantee of no combat!"

"What the fuck ... fuck you, man ... I'm not signing anything."

My dad. Brother! He just couldn't let me live my life. I was so pissed off at the Navy guy. I went back the next day and told him I was sorry for yelling at him. It wasn't his fault. My fucking dad!

I was bushed and it was late when I returned to the apartment. Linda was in Emil's bed. Asleep. Someone else was asleep in my bed.

I woke Linda.

Linda was so sweet but I just couldn't maintain a relationship.

I told her that and she cried. Fuck it ... I can't do anything right.

We joined the others and got very high. The person in my bed slept on.

Several hours later, high and drunk, we moved the party downstairs to Charlie's Bar. All the college kids hung out here and Charlie never seemed to card anyone. We drank 3.2 beer and played the jukebox like everything was okay.

Linda and I made love that tonight and I finally slept in my own bed. Emil got home very late or early from a gig.

By three o'clock that afternoon the apartment was filling up with people and it started all over. After another week of this nonsense I decided to call Mark. By this time I was calling a third party. Mark's phone was most likely tapped. I left a message. "Tell Mark I'm coming out in a few days. This is Mike." How any more times would I call myself Mike. Soon I would be Mark. Ironic that I was given the name Mark on both ID's.

I had quit my job at Fiberite so money was short but I had a few hundred bucks saved up. I was always good with money.

The day came to leave. Linda and I were on shaky ground but she understood. I think. I didn't know when I'd return. I had to set up a network of people who I could trust. I only trusted Emil in Winona. I loved all the other people but they couldn't be trusted to keep their mouths shut.

I found Mark and told him of the ID's. He seemed pleased. We walked to a cafe in Berkeley. He said that things were really crazy in Berkeley.

He gave me a crash course on the underground.

"First, never tell anyone where you've been or where you are going. For example, say you are in Chicago and you find the safe house. If someone asks you where you came from say Minneapolis if you came from St. Louis. When you leave you'll tell them you are leaving but if someone asks you where you are going tell them anywhere but where you are really going. Secondly, never use your real name, use your alias. Thirdly, no drugs or alcohol when you travel and that goes for everyone else in the car too! Just gives the pigs an excuse. Fourth, you don't know me. And you don't know me. Fifth, if you think you are being tailed, which is a distinct possibility, stop and look in a shop window, cross the street, see if that guy does the same. Try to lose them by walking into a store and walk right through the place and find a back exit or hold your ground and don't go to where you were going. I'll educate you more on this later. How to lose a tail. Sixth, except for pay phones, never say anything of consequence on a phone. You have to assume it is tapped."

"Now, I have an assignment for you. Here are your boarding passes for a flight from San Francisco Airport to JFK in New York. Use your Mark Cole ID's. You'll get on the plane to New York and return on the next flight." He handed me a three inch thick package heavily bundled in tape. "When you arrive at JFK walk to your left and enter the men's room immediately on your right. Walk to the very last urinal and take a pee. A man will walk to the next urinal and ask if you had a pleasant flight. You'll answer 'yes' and hand the package to him. Don't look at him and don't engage him in conversation. You will go the gate and await the return flight. When you arrive in San Francisco take the Airporter to Union Square. Someone will contact you there and drive you back here. I'll see you then."

"Oh, I almost forgot. Here's $200."

I did make the flight to New York on time. I put the bundle in the inside pocket of my jean jacket. I had my ruck sack with a change of clothes which I took with me on board.

What was inside this package? I never asked Mark and part of me didn't want to know. I was a little nervous as we flew away. Looking down on the Bay and the Golden Gate Bridge. Such a beauty!

I settled in for the long flight east. They served lunch and I smoked and stared out the window most of the way. I closed my eyes but didn't sleep. The guy next to me slept. He looked like a businessman. I had the window seat. America is so big and vast. From the great Pacific to the grey Atlantic. How could one not love this country.

The flight had departed early in the morning so we arrived in New York around three. Looking down at Manhattan and the Statue of Liberty brought chills of excitement.

Well, here goes. I followed Mark's instructions to a tee. I found the men's room and walked to the last latrine. I put my ruck sack down and a man walked to the next latrine and asked, "Have a pleasant flight?"

"Yes," I quickly handed him the bundle and finished peeing. I never saw his face.

I walked back to wait for the return flight. I had a couple of hours to kill so I walked around the terminal and found a bookstore. I bought a *New York Times* and waited.

That was very weird and scary. What was in that package ... cash, letters, documents, dope, all of the above. I would never know and wouldn't ask. If Mark chose to tell me he would. 'Forgetaboutit!' As they say in New York.

The return flight was equally as long and boring. This time I still had a window seat and the guy next to me wanted to talk. He showed me pictures of his wife and kids and my hair had grown some, he wanted to know everything about the 'counter culture.' I was reluctant to share anything of substance with him. I told him I was a student at Wisconsin and even got to test my new identity. This was going to take some getting used to.

Initially, when I got on this flight, I was concerned that the stewardess would notice me and think it odd that I was on the next flight, but to my relief, they had changed flight crews.

I did manage to sleep some of way back to San Francisco. I caught the Airporter to Union Square just as Mark had instructed. I heard my name called out.

"Hey Mark, my name is Steve. I'll give you a ride to Mark's. He wants to see you."

"How was your flight?"

"Long, man. I managed to sleep some. I've been on an airplane 12 of the last sixteen hours. I've got a buzz in my head."

"I bet."

Steve was a pleasant guy and we made small talk on the way to Mark's.

It wasn't long before Steve dropped me off. I knocked on Mark's door. I lost track of time. It was dark. Late at night or early morning.

"Hey, Mike, or should I call you Mark? Come in."

We sat in the living room. We were alone. He grabbed some coffee and we smoked cigarettes. He turned on the radio.

"Good job today. I got a call shortly after you dropped off the package." What was in that, I wondered but would not ask. If Mark chose to tell me ...

"Thanks."

"You must be tired. You can stay here a couple of days and get rested. I have another chore for you. You're my mailman," he laughed, "I want you to go to Denver with another package and then you can return to Winona. Don't tell anyone about this. Too many people could get hurt."

He wanted to know every detail of my trip and I told him. I told him I wondered what was in the package but never tried to peak inside. It was like a Christmas box wrapped up and so tempting to tear off a corner to see what it was. Like when I was a kid peeking at the gifts at Grandma's house under her Christmas tree. But, I never did and would not because I really didn't want to know. I ruled out drugs because I knew how Mark felt about that. Fuck it! Just let it go.

Mark had rides arranged for me to Denver and Winona.

First, I needed sleep and food. I spent most of the next day lazing around Mark's house. I cleaned his kitchen for him. The least I could do.

I was leaving tomorrow morning.

"Here's another $200 for you. This will cover gas and keep the rest. When you get to Denver call this number and ask for Jack. Leave this at the house. These people will know what to do with it. Tell Jack who you are. You are Mark, remember. Get used to that. Jack will drive you to Winona. Call me when you arrive. Ok? I won't be here tomorrow when you leave. Larry will be here at 8 a.m. There's an alarm clock by your bed. Later, man."

We hugged and I slept.

Got up at 6 and showered, ate toast and coffee and was waiting when Larry drove up.

"You must be Mark. I'm Larry. Let's go to Denver, man!"

Larry had a long bushy pony tail and a red beard. I carried my package and ruck sack and climbed in the red VW bug. I noticed Colorado plates.

"You from Denver, Larry."

"Born and raised."

He was a few years older than I. I soon discovered he was a good driver. He was built like a line backer. Over six feet and around 225 pounds.

"We're gonna book all the way there, man. Just stop for gas and piss. I've got some cokes and chips in the back seat if we get hungry."

He turned the stereo up and we listened to KSAN until the station gently faded away. Heading East on 80 toward the Nevada State Line through the Sierras.

Larry gave me a history and geography lesson.

"This is where the Donner Party spent that winter. They got snowed in from a huge blizzard and legend has it that they ate the dead bodies. Fucking gruesome, man. But I guess I would too ... to stay alive."

"Couldn't they hunt any animals?"

"Guess not."

"Coming into Lake Tahoe. Ever been here before?"

"No, never. It's beautiful. I've heard that the skiing is great in the winter."

"It is. We're really lucky the weather is good because it can snow over fifty feet a year up here."

"Really!"

We roared through the night making a couple of pit stops. Larry and I raced through the cool Nevada night at 80 mph. No speed limit here. Gambling and prostitution are legal and just about anything goes. But, cowboys and red necks scare me. We stopped at a truck stop and got out. Larry gassed up the car and I went to pee. A trucker wearing a cowboy hat called me a 'faggot hippie.'

"I oughta teach you a lesson you little faggot."

He thought twice when he saw Larry walking towards us.

"Gotta problem, Mac?"

"Fuck you," he mumbled as he shied away. Larry was about 6'2" and didn't take shit from anyone. Larry just smiled at him as he walked off, thinking better of tangling with a big long hair.

"Fuck him, man."

Larry had a grin on his face and walked into the restaurant. I sheepishly followed. All eyes were on us. We sat in a booth and ordered coffee and apple pie. After a few minutes the staring stopped. We paid our bill and thanked the waitress leaving a nice tip for her. I think she liked Larry.

"Don't take shit off anybody, man. Just smile at 'em and walk away if you can. If you can't ... we'll do a little dance."

"Jesus, Larry, I'm gonna hire you as my body guard." I joked of course, but was half serious.

"I grew up around those types. Most of 'em are all talk."

"Thanks, man. I don't want to fight anymore. Our own people are divided over this fuckin' war. It's really scary sometimes because we're fighting our government and most of the other Americans. I just don't get it. The southern whites are murdering Civil Rights Workers and marchers. The cops are beating up students and cowboys threaten us at a truck stop. For Christ's sakes!"

We were somewhere near Elko. A God forsaken place. The sun was rising from the east. Pretty flat and barren looking. High desert.

"It's pretty flat from here to Salt Lake City. Home of the Mormons. You know about the Mormons don't you? Kinda of a weird religion sect. Founded Salt Lake City as some kind of a haven for 'em because nobody would put up with them. Some guy named Smith or something like that, moved a whole bunch of 'em out there to get away from being persecuted by Christians. Really interesting story but I think they're strange. Don't smoke or drink and some of them have multiple wives. And they built this huge temple in the middle of town. Ain't my cup of tea but people does what people does. No skin off my teeth."

"Yeah, to each their own. That's what my grandma says."

Hours passed. The day lightened by the sun now warming the air. Larry was right. Very flat and desolate out here. An occasional sign of civilization like a farm house broke up the monotony. 'Welcome to Utah!' I wasn't so sure after listening to Larry ramble on about the Mormons. It struck fear in my heart.

Salt Lake City was larger than I expected. It smelled really bad, like a huge fart.

"That's the Salt Lake. It's the brine. Billions of dead shrimp. Stinks huh?" Larry laughed.

The lake was like an inland sea, extending to the horizon. We soon passed through the one mile high city and trekked upwards towards the Wasatch Mountain Range. I really liked the mountains. Snow capped mountains hugging green valleys. The day was ending again and we needed gas and a desperate pee stop.

"The people are a bit friendlier as we head east. No sweat."

A truck stop loomed ahead and we did our routine. I gave Larry some money for gas.

"No, no ... it's my treat. I've given several people rides for Mark and he takes care of all that."

"Jeez, can I buy you a piece of pie and some coffee?"

"That you can do my friend."

No one paid any attention to us at this stop. Early evening and the place was almost vacant. We ordered our pie and coffee and in a few minutes felt sleepy but we needed to push on.

"Ain't stoppin' 'til Denver. Come on Mark. Let's hi-ball it!"

We filled our thermos with coffee and hi-balled it east.

The Wyoming Rockies are most impressive. Peaks that rise above the horizon. Snow capped. Deep valleys hidden from sight. Sharp rocked cliffs that hug the highway with frequent warnings about falling rocks. It's like flying.

We hit Cheyenne and headed south into Denver. Larry can drive, man. Eyes on the road. Blazing!

"Let's make one more pit stop. Gotta piss like a horse. We'll be home in a couple hours."

That we did. No pie or coffee this stop. Just gas.

The skyline of Denver appeared. Looming large like The Emerald City of Oz ... a Shangr-La like Xanadu. A hidden city among these royal Rockies. Such a sight!

Larry drove into the city. Among neighborhoods familiar to him, he pointed out places of interest, immediately forgotten by me, too many to remember.

"We used to hang out there in high school," pointing to a park as we roared along.

"That's a great bar. I'll take you there sometime. Great music"

And so on.

We arrived at a house. Lights on and music playing.

"I'll take you in and introduce you to everybody."

A room full of people. I shyly followed Larry into the house. I noticed he didn't even knock. He just walked in.

"Hey everybody, this is Mark."

"This is everybody."

I just laughed.

Everyone seemed pleased to see Larry. He was a popular guy. Amidst 'how was your trip' to 'great to see you, man' Larry glided through this throng giving and getting hugs and kisses.

I waited by the doorway.

"Mark, this is Jack."

"Hey, man."

"I've got a package for you." I whispered.

"Great. Come in here," as he lead to a bedroom, "let's see."

I opened my ruck sack and produced the envelope.

"Far out, man. Good job. Thank you."

He put the package aside and led me back to the party. I met another ten people and caught some of the names. I sat next to Jack. They passed a joint around and someone handed me a beer. Ah!

"You must be tired and hungry. I know how Larry drives without stopping. Want anything?" Jack asked.

"No, man. I'm fine. Just nice to stop moving and have a beer. No thanks ... really, I'm fine."

"Ok."

"We'll leave in a couple of days. I've got some business to take care of first and then we'll leave for Minnesota. I'm supposed to be in Chicago in a week. I'll drop you off on the way."

"Sounds good, Jack."

Looking around the room. Lit by candles and a soft light. Heavy incense and pot. Plenty of beer and laughter. Mellow music by Donovan. Larry was in his element again as he pranced around the room with his friends. After a bit I was relaxed and the constant feeling of motion ceased. For now.

An hour or two passed. Jack showed me a room with a mattress on the floor. I curled up and dreamed.

Click ... clack ... falling through the crack. Going too fast. Out of control. Spinning falling. Crashing into a tree.

Awaken in a sweat. Alone. Scared. Don't know where I am. Who am I? Mark Cole or Mark Heddington.

Chapter 8

Denver

Up and at 'em. A new house. New people. Can't remember their names. Remind myself to be Mark. I'm Mark.

Had some toast and eggs. A cigarette. Coffee.

Sit in the living room. Wait for Jack. Eventually, Jack saunters in. Sleepy. Grumpy. He doses himself with coffee.

I take a needed shower upstairs. Careful to clean up afterwards. Find the kitchen in a complete mess. I began washing dishes. Stacked on a table ... on the stove. Find more about the house. Drying dishes piled high defying any architectural design. Can't find a clean towel to dry them with so I left them. A girl comes in looking for coffee and seems pleased that the dishes are clean. She can't find her cup.

"Have you seen a cup with flowers on it?" she enquired.

"Probably in there somewhere," I laughed.

She laughed too and grabbed the nearest cup without toppling the stack of dishes.

One thing Mark had told me was that since I was a guest in someone's house that I should help out with chores. Like washing dishes etc. It was the least I could do. After all, they fed me, got me high, and provided me a place to rest.

Jack told me he had business to attend to today, I presumed that had something to do with the package I delivered, and that he would return later. That was fine with me. I needed a day to catch up.

Found a book to read and hung out on the front porch. After awhile I took a walk around the block. Denver had a nice feel. I rounded the final corner and saw Larry's VW parked in front.

"Hey man, there you are. Come on, I'll show you Denver."

Off we flew. Larry was amped up after a nights sleep in his own bed. He showed me his old high school and the home he grew up in. A near by park where the local kids hung out.

"Check it out, man. This is where I first good laid and smoked pot, took acid ... the whole bit."

"Later on let's go out to this bar. They have music every night and cheap beer."

"Cool. I'm not twenty one yet, Larry."

"No problem."

We drove through downtown. As expected, suits and tall buildings. We continued into a seedy part near the railroads. I think this is where Kerouac was writing about when he and Neal invaded Denver. Dive bars and liquor stores. Pawn shops. People hanging out looking mean and drunk. Every city has a Bowery.

Larry was hungry so we stopped at a restaurant.

"Hey, Larry," someone shouted.

Seemed everybody knew Larry. He was the friendliest guy. This was his town. I made a mental note to keep in touch with him.

"This is my friend, Mark. He's from Minnesota."

The waitress brought coffee and we were soon joined by a couple of fellows. They both had long hair too.

We ordered burgers.

"What brings you to Denver, Mark?" asked one.

"Just passing through. Larry is showing me the sights. Must say I like Denver. It's my first time here."

"I grew up with these two guys," Larry noted.

I didn't feel like divulging any more personal information. Larry and his friends talked away with promises of getting together soon. I was content in my own little world.

We soon left. Paid our bill. It was on me.

"Wish we had more time. I'd show you Boulder. Way up in the mountains and just about the prettiest place you've ever seen."

"I'll be back. Maybe next time."

Larry punished this VW. Climbing hills and showing me the city.

Ever present mountain peaks framed the city. It was beautiful indeed. We smoked a bowl and I just sat back and enjoyed the scenery.

"I'll tell you something, Mark. If Mark from Berkeley says you're okay then you are gold!"

"I'm just a schmuck from Minnesota who hates the war and racism and sexism and bullies and all the rest of the bad shit. I'm not alone."

"Cool, but any time you are near Denver, call me and I'll make sure you have a place to stay. The same goes for Jack. Things are going to get heavy and I can't tell you much except to say that a lot of people are in deep with the law and we intend on keeping them safe and out of jail. I figure if enough people fuck the system they will cave. I don't want to know about you really except that you seem cool," he said.

"I gotta tell ya. I'm new at this. I just need to be involved. I want to help. Mark is nine times smarter than I am. I'm a novice. But, my heart is in the right place."

"Cool, man. Let's party!"

We drove to a neighborhood bar. Bar stools at the bar, a few tables, a pool table, and booths against the walls. A small stage in one corner. A couple of guys were setting up a PA.

Larry ordered a couple of beers and we headed for one of the booths.

"This is Coors beer. Ever had one? The best beer in the world. They got it on draft here. Don't worry about being carded here. Nobody gives a shit."

It was good beer. Really hit the spot. Seemed like wherever we went everybody knew Larry. A few people came over and greeted him.

"This is my bud, Mark."

"Their gonna have a band tonight. Dunno who. But, who cares. Music is music. Right?" Larry said, animated and grinning.

"Let's play some pool," he added.

We stuck our quarters on the table and waited our turn. After several games Larry got up and set the balls for the next game. The guy broke and sank two balls. Then he missed. Larry had solids and damn near ran the table. The guy took his turn. Sank one and then scratched sinking the eight ball.

"Well, Mark. Guess its you and me."

I grabbed the triangle and racked the balls, making sure it was nice and tight. We were playing for beers. The guy brought a beer for Larry and set it at the booth.

Larry broke and didn't make any balls. I was a better than average player and I ran the table on him. Mostly luck really. Larry had to buy me a beer. I beat the next five players until someone beat me. We had a table full of beers and Larry was loving it.

"I can't drink all these. Here, have a beer," I chortled.

"Jeez, you're pretty good at pool. Where'd you learn to shoot like that?"

"We had a pool table when I was a kid. Played all the time."

The music started. The place was packed. Someone came around to collect a dollar for the band. They played cover songs. Some Stones and Beatles, Kinks etc. They were pretty good. Larry was dancing and I soon joined him having asked a girl to dance. It was fun.

It was getting late. Jack and I were leaving in the morning. I should get some sleep.

"All right, man, let's go," Larry said.

He dropped me off at Jack's place.

"Goodbye, my friend."

Larry reached across the seat and gave me a big hug.

"Next time I'm in town I'll definitely call you, Larry. Thanks for everything."

I walked in the house and a few people were hanging out in the living room. Jack was in the kitchen.

"There you are. I was hoping you'd show up," he seemed a little pissed but he laughed, "we'll leave around nine or ten tomorrow morning."

"Okay, Jack. I was out with Larry and he wanted to show me a good time. We ended up at some bar listening to music."

"Larry's cool. See you in the morning."

I was tired. I curled into a sleeping bag and was gone.

Next morning.

"Get up sleepy head."

Jack was up and ready. I brushed my teeth, packed my ruck sack and hopped into his Dodge Dart.

Off we go. He to Chicago and me back home to Winona.

Within minutes we were in the plains of Nebraska. Flat and forever. The road straight. Blue skies into the horizon. What a contrast from the Rockies to this. America is so vast and ever changing.

"I've got bread for gas and snacks," I boasted.

"Great. Me too!"

Jack had a different personality than Larry. More reserved and quiet. We didn't talk much for an hour or so and then Jack opened up.

"I think what Mark is doing is setting up a network across the States. He wants key people in key areas. We need money for transportation and food and safe places for people to hide out. I'm going to Chicago to meet some people to set up some shit to go down. The Democratic Convention has really pissed some people off and we want to stir up some shit there to let the pigs know that this shit doesn't sit with us. We need to fight back."

"I need to know how to contact you if I need to get a hold of you. And vice versa," he continued, "also, I know you're planning to resist the draft. What are your plans for that?"

"I haven't gotten that far yet. I'm definitely not going to Canada. I want to be as much of a thorn in the FBI's ass as I can."

"Right on!"

"I figure the more man power and resources they waste on me and the thousands of other resisters the better. Just the wasted money alone. Think of it. Millions of dollars of tax payers money blown on us, not to mention what the fucking war must be costing. Eventually they'll be broke. I hope, anyway."

"Good thinking. You're right. Eventually the American people will come to their senses."

We looked at each other and giggled a hopeful laugh.

The flatness. Little farm houses. Endless wheat fields. I'd go crazy living here. Nebraska was the perfect metaphor of what America is. Flat with no imagination. Bland. Calm and pleasant on the outside yet holding the promise of an anxious brutality.

The land, having been ripped open and permanently scarred to feed America and the world. Native peoples massacred and butchered in the name of the 'American Dream.' No sense of history or responsibility. Conscience free, morally justified 'land owners' furrowed neat rows of corn and wheat over bloodied fields of empty promises and treaties. Imagine how this land must have been. Endless prairies, grazing bison, clean water and sky. No Interstate Highway. No Shell stations. And, I am as guilty as can be. I brought this on.

Am I really making a difference. Maybe I should just go and kill until I am finally killed in the unending cycle of madness. I would be like these neat furrowed fields. Stalks of corn standing at attention like good little soldiers until they are harvested and die. Sheets of wheat sway in the breeze like the unquestioning masses. "Because it's always been this way."

"North Platte comin' up."

Jack brought me out of my day dream.

"Let's stop and gas up," he stated.

Jack pulled into a service station. A guy ran out and 'filled it up' and checked the oil. This little Dart just hummed. I bought some cigarettes and chips and some cokes, ignoring the advice of a trucker who once told me to not drink anything but water, but, never mind, I wanted a coke and some potato chips.

"Oh, thanks, man. This should get us to Iowa. At least there are some hills and curves."

Jack loudly crunched chips and slurped a coke as we slowly progressed across the landscape.

"Jack, I'm just curious. How did you meet Mark?"

"Oh, let me think. It was over a year ago in Boulder. Larry and I and a bunch of other people attended a meeting one night for SDS. It was a gathering of folks from the East Coast and the West Coast. Mark Rudd was there. You know who he is, right? One of the founders of the SDS. Anyway, we sat through a speech by this guy and a woman. I've forgotten their names. Anyway, we all mingled in the hall and met one another. The purpose of the night, it seemed, was to enroll more students, raise some money, and organize. Organize, organize, organize. That's all we heard. I was a student at Boulder then and lived in a house with a bunch of other students and most of the people there needed a place to stay. Somehow Mark from Berkeley ended up at our place and we spent a few days with him. He was against drugs and beer, but on the whole he had a lot to say and he made sense. He was really into the Free Speech thing and the anti-war movement and he convinced me to become more earnest in fighting against the war and the draft."

"So, in answer to your question ... I've known him for nearly two years," he concluded.

"I don't know why he picked me. I feel like I was recruited. I'm an okay learner and stuff and my heart is in the right place and all, but for the life of me I don't know why. Why me?"

"Don't worry about that, Mark. You'll do just fine. If it's any consolation to you ... I would have chosen you too. Don't underestimate yourself. I feel unsure myself sometimes."

"You do?"

"Yep."

We neared the Iowa border. It was getting dark and the terrain gradually changed into rolling hills as the road wound its' way to Minnesota.

Winter can be treacherous in Iowa. Known for black ice. I mentioned this to Jack and he slowed down. The roads seemed fine although winding. Couldn't really make good time through here.

We had a long drive ahead.

"Let's stop for a bit. I need coffee and a good stretch," Jack stated.

We pulled into Iowa after passing through Omaha. Jack spotted a truck stop ahead and we pulled in. We filled up with gas and peed. Parked the car and walked into the restaurant. Truckers filled the place but we were able to find a booth way in the back. Which was fine with me. Didn't need any more evil stares or confrontations. I needed to eat so I ordered some soup and a burger. Jack was hungry as well and ordered a burger.

"I'll get this, man," I volunteered.

"Des Moines comin' up."

We were just a couple of hours from Winona. Jack was so different from Larry. Larry reminded me of a big happy Sheep Dog. Friendly and out going. Jack was much more reserved. Short black hair, wire rimmed glasses, and sparse on conversation.

I wondered what Jack was up to in Chicago but I felt if he wanted to tell me he would. Eventually I would learn many secrets myself. It was better to keep some things to myself.

Chapter 9

Back to Winona

We had driven through the night. First daylight as we drove through Rochester. Too many bad memories left here. Jack still had a long drive ahead of him and I offered to put him up for the night but he declined, opting instead to drive all the way to Chicago.

"Thanks, man, I'll be in Chicago by tonight."

"Okay, but you have a place to stay anytime you're in the area."

Jack drove right to my door. We had exchanged phone numbers and addresses. We said our farewells and he drove off.

What a weird trip this had been.

I was Mike again.

The place was a mess. I walked into my room and was pleasantly surprised to find my bed empty. Several letters were scattered on my bed and I noticed a letter from the Selective Service and another from Winona State. I nervously opened both. Winona State had dropped me and sent my grades, or lack of, to the Selective Service. The Selective Service letter informed me that I had been reclassified as 1-A. I never had my Conscientious Objector hearing!

I collapsed in my bed and slept the day away.

I awoke in a start. Emil came home. We talked and talked. I told him everything. He swore not to tell anyone. I had to tell him. I trusted him totally.

Meanwhile, a few people came over. Everyone was glad to see me. I asked about Linda and got a couple of weird looks. Seems that she was going with this other guy. Just as well. I couldn't possibly have a girl friend and do all this other stuff. Someone asked if I had any acid to sell. I told them I wasn't doing that any more. They'd have to find another source. That wouldn't be hard.

I was concerned, to say the least, about the draft. I thought it would take them at least until the spring before I would get called up. I needed to check with Mrs. Price at the Winona Draft Board to ask about my CO hearing.

I had a buddy going to the University of Minnesota. He was in law school. I needed some advice on this. I had many questions. To my knowledge, I was only the third guy in Minnesota to resist the draft. Would they arrest me right away? Or would they indict me first. This could take months. I just didn't know.

Mark would know. I could call him too.

The night passed pleasantly with friends and dope.

The Minnesota winter was upon us. We had one radiator for this huge place. There was ice on the inside of our bedroom windows. We still had hot water. There was steam on our breaths the next morning. Snow was falling. And falling. Soon a blizzard was on us. It snowed so hard you couldn't see across the street. We hardly had any food. Charlie's bar was open downstairs and we all congregated there to eat and stay warm. We stayed there most of the night. You couldn't go anywhere anyway. It must have snowed three feet with huge drifts. I remember laying down in a booth and falling asleep. I was so worn out from everything.

Riding my trike as fast as I could. Someone was chasing me. I couldn't go fast enough. I rode as hard as I could across a big field. I came to the edge of the field and drove off the cliff. I was falling and falling. Falling.

I awoke in the booth. It was early in the morning. People were still here at Charlie's. The snow had stopped. I looked out to see a winter wonderland. Someone handed me a cup of coffee. I held the cup in my hands and touched my cheek with it. It warmed me. I felt safe here huddled at Charlie's Bar.

I hope Jack made it to Chicago safely.

We spent the next three days cowering in the apartment. Nothing much to do. I wrote several letters to my parents and grandma, and my future-lawyer friend in Minneapolis.

After a few more days and the snow had cleared, I decided to call Jeff, the future-lawyer, because I was so anxious to find out how all this would go down.

"Hi ,Jeff?"

"Yeah."

"This is Mike McAndrew in Winona. How are you?"

"Fine. What's up?"

"Well, did you get my letter?"

"Yup.'

"I need to see you about this. Do you know anything about the procedures and what I can expect and all that?"

"Not everything yet but I've begun to look into it. All I know so far is that they won't arrest you at the Induction Center. It may take months for an indictment to come down and then and only then will they arrest you. But, yeah, in the meantime, come on up. I've got a place for you to stay and I have some people I want you to meet."

"Cool. Hey Jeff, call me Mark when you introduce me. I'll explain later."

"Whatever you say ... Mark."

"I'll leave tomorrow on the bus. See you tomorrow night."

Jeff gave me his address and instructions on which buses to take.

Told Emil I would be gone again for a few days. We talked some about the apartment and that I had noticed things were missing and that we never got any peace and quiet.

"Maybe we should find a place for just the two of us."

"I'll ask around."

Arose early the next morning and only had to walk two blocks to catch the bus to Minneapolis. Nice ride along the Mississippi River stopping in each little town on the way ... Wabasha, Red Wing, etc. These towns were so peaceful and far removed from the war images and Civil Rights unrest and mayhem seen every night on TV. Why in God's earth would I want to go to a place like that (Vietnam). Unless you were somehow trapped in it; born there and couldn't escape. That would be just bad luck.

Nearing the Cities. Stopped in Hastings before crossing the river over a great bridge. Farmlands appear with long stretches of snow covered fields. An occasional fence post popping through. Bright sunlight and sparkling fields. Beautiful beyond words.

The Twin Cities aren't especially beautiful cities. They are surrounded by beauty but man's touch has desecrated the landscape with tall buildings built without regard to beauty. Buses and cars and noise rule downtown. Pedestrians climb over snow mounds, now a filthy grey, to cross streets. Everyone in a hurry to leave one place to get to the next. Living in the future without knowing the present.

Caught a couple of buses to get to Dinky Town, a student section on the campus of the University of Minnesota. Bob Dylan had played here and honed his craft a few years ago in the local bars and cafes, which were numerous.

I found Jeff's house as per his directions. Another group home. Jeff greeted me at the door. I had met him at St. Mary's a year or so ago. He was older than I and attending law school.

"Mark you made it!"

"You remembered," I whispered off to the side.

He nodded.

"Come in. Everybody this is Mark. He'll be staying a few days."

I shyly nodded to everyone. A dozen people littered the living room. Some on the floor, others draped over couches and old chairs. I settled in and listened as the conversation took up again. These were all law school students, I presumed, because the topic was some obscure (at least to me) court case about what, I wasn't sure.

Jeff could tell I wasn't following the rap so he pulled me aside and showed me where I would be sleeping. It was a huge hallway closet that would be private.

"Oh, neat. Thanks, man. Jeff, let me ask you something."

"Okay."

"If I was to hire you as my attorney that would mean you would have 'client attorney privileges,' right?"

"Yeah, why."

"Because I want you to help me out on the legal side of what I am about to do. I'm going to resist the draft and then go underground. I don't want to go to Canada. I hate hockey," I joked. "But, seriously, I want to fight against this injustice here and help other guys resist. Can you help me in this?"

"Yes," after a pause he went on.

"The people you met briefly downstairs are all law students. We are working with various groups in town to help the needy, the poor, the American Natives, the blacks, and guys like yourself. I gotta tell you, a lot of this is new ground and we are figuring this out ourselves. Most of the laws are against us and we need to get cases into the courts to over-turn some of these laws. Oh yeah, I'll be your attorney and I can give you advice when I get my certificate, which at the soonest will be in two years. In the meantime, I can always get advice from other attorneys who are with us in the cause."

"Cool, man. Listen. I have to let you in on some of the stuff I do. I have a couple of aliases. Both with the first name of Mark, by the way. Easier to remember. Only a few people know this. You met my brother Emil. He knows. And a guy in Berkeley knows. And you. You can't ever tell anyone because of what I do could really hurt some people. I'm kind of a mailman. I deliver packages and messages to people. I never want to know to whom but that's what I've been doing. I have a network of people and places to stay on the West Coast, here, Chicago, Madison, and am working on setting up the East Coast. But before I go on, I have to deal with the Winona Draft Board. It's a coincidence that one of my best friend's mom works there. I applied for a CO a few months ago but haven't heard back and I was recently informed that I was reclassified as a 1-A. This means that I will have to take the physical at some point and presumably take the oath. My question is this. How do I proceed?"

"You should take the physical and go through with that. But don't take the oath. My understanding is this: if you don't show up for the physical they can harass the shit out of you but if you go through all that and then refuse to raise your hand they can't do shit to you until you get indicted, which could take several months. The trouble is, there aren't any cases like this in Minnesota but there are several in California. I'll check those out for you. It is a Federal issue so it would apply in all States. In the matter of applying for a CO; they have to give you a hearing on that. I do know that for a fact. So, in the meantime, I'll check up on this stuff and you sit tight."

I decided to return to Winona. What was I doing? I had so many doubts. I felt inferior whenever a group conversation turned to politics. I knew nothing. I couldn't talk that talk. Everyone was smarter than me, better looking, and normal. That was it. I wasn't normal. I was a square peg trying to fit into a round hole. It was no use. I was scared to my very soul and sometimes I felt I should just give up and join the Army or kill myself. Either of those options seemed unreasonable though. I wanted to get drunk and stoned and just escape.

I got home. I was bored with the apartment and the incessant comings and goings of people, some I'd never seen before. The drugs flowed.
One morning we were awakened by sirens and lots of noise. I looked outside and saw two fire trucks in the street and people looking up at our apartment. A loud knock on the door announced the arrival of several firemen dashing through our apartment. They opened the kitchen window which opened to the roof. Smoke billowed in. The greasy spoon downstairs had caught on fire. One of our overnight guests, Larry, calmly got dressed and followed the firemen out onto the roof. A moment later he returned with two pounds of pot tucked under his arm. I couldn't believe it. The firemen hadn't even noticed him! He was invisible.

Turns out he was dealing out of our apartment. I didn't like that. Enough! It was too risky for me to stay here. I knew some people who lived on a farm near the St. Mary's campus.

I would be safe there. Two couples and myself. I moved into a small room in the back of the house. I noticed when I moved that I had several things missing. My bike for one. And records and books. I still had all my clothes.

I even informed Mrs. Price at the Draft Board of my new address.
Winter had hit and we stayed warm huddled around a wood stove in the kitchen. The land owner had a small barn and some chickens and he visited each day to feed them. We fed the chickens when another blizzard came. The old road was closed for a week. It gave me time to gather my thoughts and collect myself. I took some acid and stared out my window. Was I a coward or a hero? Was I scared or brave? Can I do this? Should I do this?

Took a long walk under a full moon in the deep snow. The snow was blue and the shadows played tricks. I saw figures dashing from tree to tree.

The wind blew drifts of deep banks. It was very cold but I was warm. I climbed a fence and walked among cows. They must have thought me strange, walking alone at night in the snow. I was numb and feeling everything at once. I counted stars twinkling above. The moon smiled and I smiled back.

Christmas was upon us again. The other couples went home for Christmas and I had the house to myself. I had some money left and drove my buddy's car into town and loaded up on food and cigarettes. I wanted some beer so I called one of my older friends and he got some beer for me. Emil came over and we had a nice day together. I made burgers and we got drunk. It was nice.

I was lonely in that house alone so I traveled with the band for a few gigs. I helped them unload and load equipment and for this was entitled to free beer. They were really good by this time and they packed every bar and club they played in. I could dance with the girls and get high. After the gigs the equipment stayed there because they were playing all week. We only packed the guitars when we drove back to Winona. It would be three in the morning when I got home. We were all tired. Mudcat dropped me off at the farm. I climbed into bed. Same thing tomorrow night. Christmas week. The band played at 'Your Uncles Place' in La Crosse. It was the place to be. The New Year's show was great. Horns and streamers announced the New year. 1969!

What was ahead?

The couples returned and I decided to take a trip to Madison. John and those guys there knew me as Mike. How could I tell them to call me Mark. I should just tell them the truth; that I was in trouble with the FBI over the draft etc. I figured if I straightened this out now it would be easier than later.

I called Mark in Berkeley. He asked me to go to Milwaukee first and check on the Milwaukee 14. Back in September several members of the clergy had broken into the Draft Board and taken the 1-A files out onto the street and burned them. Evidently, some of them were out on bail and Mark wanted me to see if they needed help. This had been national news and I was really getting my feet wet. I wasn't sure how to do this. It shouldn't be difficult to find them. I'd ask at Marquette, the local University, and check the underground newspaper. Also, Mark gave me a name and number of a person in Milwaukee to contact. His name was Tom. Maybe Tom knew how to reach these people.

The best way to get to Milwaukee was to travel to Minneapolis and then onto Milwaukee. Or hitch hike. It was winter but I might luck out. The colleges were still on Christmas break and students would be travelling.

So, I made a sign that said Milwaukee and stuck my thumb out.

Wouldn't you know it. A friend of mine from Cotter High, who attended Marquette, picked me up and we drove all the way there. What luck!

Of course, I couldn't tell him anything. But, we chatted all the way there. I told him I was jealous of him because his parents were helping him through school and that he was attending Marquette. He appreciated that.

"Jeez, I heard you turned into a crazy hippie and that you were selling drugs."

"Where'd you hear that!"

"It's all over town."

"It's funny how things get twisted up like that."

"Do you have a place to stay."

"I think so."

"If you need a place let me know. Write my phone number down."

Soon enough we entered Milwaukee and he dropped me off on campus. I liked this town. Four beer taverns on every corner. You could drink at eighteen. I would have loved it here.

I found a phone booth and called Tom.

"Hello."

"Hello, this is Mark. Hopefully you are expecting me."

"Oh yeah. I am. Where are you? I'll come pick you up. What are you wearing."

I told him where and what. He said he would be here in half an hour.

"Are you Mark?"

"Yeah, you Tom?"

He was a thin guy with glasses. He drove an old chevy through the neighborhoods of Milwaukee.

"First time here?"

"No, I've seen the Packers play in County Stadium."

"Fuckin' Packers are the greatest!" he blurted.

"This is my place up ahead. Listen, I can only put you up for one night but I found another place for you. We'll meet some of the '14' tonight. They have been holding meetings trying to raise money and consciousness about their action. Come on in I'll get you settled."

Tom lived in a closet in a house. Don't know how many people actually lived here. Some were students but most were street people it seemed. Tom said I could sleep on the couch. Now I could understand why I couldn't stay there long. I didn't care about that now.

Tom seemed like a nice guy. Easy going. I braced myself for tonight.

"Tom, could I lay down for awhile and take a nap. I'm pooped."

"Sure, you can use my room."

It was a closet, like I said. But, it had a mattress. I stretched out and fell asleep.

"Hey, Mark, wake up man."

"Ooooh."

"How long did I sleep?"

"A couple of hours. Come on. We have to make the meeting."

"Yeah, right."

I was ready in five minutes. God, that felt good. I needed that.

"Can I bother you for a quick coffee?"

I grabbed a cup and gulped it down. Smoked a cig and was ready.

"Where are we going?" I asked.

"Across town to a church basement. You know that all these people are clergy. That's why they meet at this church. It's their defense team."

Several minutes later we arrived at St. Matthew's, a Catholic parish. We walked to the basement where seventy five or so souls had gathered. Tom introduced me to some people. The meeting began, I guess, with several people talking at once. I didn't know who was who or even if there were any of the original '14' present.

"Yeah, there's four or five of them here. That guy and him..."

Tom pointed out a few of the '14.' They all weren't present.

I listened for a bit. I didn't understand anything until an attorney really called the meeting to order. He spoke in an animated way punctuating key words and waving his fist. Preaching aside, he made some good points about challenging the courts concerning the rights of draftees. He claimed that many had been drafted out of high school as soon as they turned eighteen. An eighteen year old couldn't even vote or drink in most states. He also claimed that the draft was racist because by far the majority of kids drafted were minorities from the ghetto who couldn't afford college.

Then he arrived at the point of this meeting. Money.

"We need money folks! Lots of it. We need money not only for legal fees but for housing and food. We expect that all of the '14' will be expelled from his or her parishes and they will need shelter awaiting the trial. So many good people have stepped forward and offered help in one form or another but we need money. The court was generous with the bail but we can't count on their generosity."

And on and on he spoke. Mark had sent me here specifically to probe and find out if any or all of the '14' wanted to run or stay and face prison sentences. Mark had told me that he knew some people that could hide them if necessary.

Meanwhile, I sat and listened and watched. One guy caught my eye. A very dark haired heavy bearded man who stood on the side and paced back and forth.

"Who's that, Tom?"

"That's Father Pete ... or at least I think he used to be a priest. He's a really intense guy. You'd like him. He isn't part of the '14.' "

"Introduce me afterwards."

The meeting ended. Tom introduced me to several people. I met some of the '14' and was deeply impressed with their commitment and passion.

Pete was outside smoking. Tom called Pete over. They talked a bit and I just listened. Pete said he was going to St. Louis in a couple of days. He wanted to know if I wanted a ride and could share expenses. To this day I don't know why I consented.

"Sure, man. Should be fun."

"I'll let Tom know when I'm leaving. See you then."

"Cool."

"I guess you're going to St. Louis," Tom said as we walked to his car.

"Guess so."

In the next couple of days I had a chance to learn all I could about the '14.'

On September 24, 1968, a group of fourteen men, all members of the clergy, broke into the Selective Service offices in Milwaukee, grabbing nearly 10,000 1-A classification records, took the boxes out front, doused them with homemade napalm and burned them. They were consequently arrested, later released on bail. The trial was scheduled for later this year. Their action had gained national notice and Mark wanted me to be his eyes and ears.

The group desperately needed money for their defense fund. I relayed all that to Mark the next morning. I told him I was going to catch a ride with an ex-priest to St. Louis. He gave me a name and a phone number in St. Louis.

In the meantime, Mark wanted me to talk to a couple of them if I could to find out their plans i.e. would they stay for the trial or did they want to go underground?

Brother Basil O'Leary was one of the '14' and Tom knew him. Tom took me over to where he was staying and we chatted a while. It was clear that this group was willing and wanting to go to prison. It was a message that they wanted the American people to know that some people were willing to sacrifice their freedom for justice. He was a very nice gentile soul. 'Wouldn't hurt a fly' kind a guy. If people like him were in prison ... yikes!

In fact everyone surrounding this group were solid people. I had to become smarter and become a better person myself. I felt so inferior most of the time. I didn't deserve to breathe the same air as Brother Basil.

Tom and I left. When we got into the car Tom asked me if I could deliver some letters to an address in St. Louis since I was going there anyway with Pete. I said sure.

"I need a beer. How 'bout you?" Tom inquired.

"At last, a brilliant decision."

We went to a college hang out and drank 3.2 swill. The place was packed. Tom found a booth in the back. Students played pool and listened to the jukebox. This was fine.

"Mark, it's none of my business, but, why are you here?"

"Mark wanted me to see what this group was like and stuff."

"What are you going to tell him?"

"That you were very helpful and that the group and their supporters seem strong and together. You know, stuff like that."

I felt uncomfortable talking about this with Tom or anybody for that matter.

"Let's play pool. Do you play pool?" I asked.

"Sure."

We played several games. The bar provided four tables. Plenty of room and the beer flowed.

I felt Tom wanted to grill me some more. I really didn't feel at liberty to discuss much with him. And, it was hard to carry on a serious conversation in a noisy bar playing pool.

It was late and I told Tom I was tired. We left the bar and drove to his place. He said I might as well stay here.

"That was fun."

"Yeah, it was. Good to take a break from all the legal stuff."

"Know what you mean."

"I guess Pete is going to pick me up tomorrow, so I should get some sleep."

It was past midnight. I crawled behind a couch and slept in the living room. I wanted to make sure I didn't miss Pete. I thought about the last couple of days and had a surreal feeling about it. I felt like an outsider, which I was, but I felt like these people didn't want to let anyone in. I couldn't put my finger on it exactly. Oh well, live and learn.

"Hey, Mike, you still want to tag along?"

It was Pete.

"Yeah ... what time is it?"

"It's time to go, man."

It was 7 a.m. My whole body cringed. I was slightly hung over and very sore from sleeping on the hard wood floor. I stretched and shook. I needed to pee and I brushed my teeth. I was ready in ten minutes.

"I'm ready, Freddy!"

Pete laughed. This was going to be fun. Pete was the loosest of the entire group and he struck me as a kind of a joker. Ready to have fun at any moment ... at any cost. He was shorter than I with thick glasses and a thick mane of black hair that hung in his eyes. I guessed he was at least thirty five or so. I just couldn't picture him as a priest.

We tore out in his Chrysler. Pete had the radio on tuned to a jazz station out of Chicago.

"You dig jazz?"

"Yeah, I do. My dad was a jazz clarinet player. Grew up on the stuff."

"Cool, man."

I had some letters from Tom to deliver. Mark had told me to get in touch with a guy named Steve in St. Louis. I was just along for the ride. And, what a ride it was. Pete never stopped talking and he drove fast and furious. What had I gotten into?

It wasn't long and Milwaukee vanished. We were headed into Chicago. Pete was a heroic driver. Nothing fazed him. Winding through thick traffic never slowing down. Weaving and dodging the whole time.

"Where'd you learn to drive like that. Wow. Man, you can fucking drive!"

"Thanks."

It seemed like Pete was making up for lost time.

"Why did you become a priest?"

"I had the 'calling', you know, I wanted to be a priest since I was a little kid. I liked the ceremony, the wardrobe, the respect a priest demanded ... all that stuff. I went through the seminary and took my vows. They sent me to this little parish in Indiana. It was okay but I'm a city guy. Grew up in Brooklyn, you know. I need the action. So I asked to transfer. They sent me here to Milwaukee. I really liked it. I was a campus priest at Marquette. Great basketball and a great school. Well, the war came along and for the first time in my life I began to question and to doubt. I felt guilty at first and tried to talk to other priests and nuns about it but no one would listen. I became interested in the anti-war movement both here and in Chicago. They made sense to me. My own church backed the war. How could they? Eventually, I was so torn that one day, after months of personal torment, believe me, I resigned. The monsignor couldn't believe it. He had never known anyone that quit before. Since I was doomed to hell anyway, I've been catching up on fucking and getting stoned!"

Pete paused and took a deep breath. He looked askance at me and chuckled. Then he continued.

"Seriously though, this fuckin' war has to end. The draft has to end. No more killing in the name of democracy! I'm headed to St. Louis to see an old buddy of mine, a priest, to see if he can raise some bread for the '14.' "

"You're welcome to tag along as long as you want. I just wanted some company on this trip."

"What's your story Mark?"

I gave him a brief synopsis.

Pete nodded and continued to drive.

Through Chicago and into Illinois we raced.

"Be there early tomorrow morning."

Pete and I smoked and jabbered all night. Traffic was light. The roads clear. It was a good night to travel. We stopped a couple of times to gas up and pee. We must have been an odd sight. The hippie and the thug. Pete had a menacing look to him even though he was a caring person inside. However, if provoked what rage resided in him?

I hoped that the people in St. Louis were expecting me, if not Pete said he had a place for me to stay. It was too cold out to crash in a park.

I hadn't been to St. Louis in a couple of years and they were still working on the 'Arch.' As we pulled in St. Louis in the early morning I noticed that the gap had been closed.

"Is the 'Arch' open to the public?"

"I don't know. It's really something isn't it?"

"Indeed. If man has the imagination and ability to engineer such a feat how hard could it be to end war. No money in peace I guess. Commerce needs conflict," I observed.

"Wise words, my friend."

"Pete, could you take me to where you're staying and in a couple of hours I'll call this number to see if they are expecting me."

"Yeah, okay."

We drove through some neighborhoods until we came to a Catholic Church. "I'm staying here with my friend Father Perry. We were in the seminary together and have remained friends."

I didn't expect this. An elderly woman answered the door.

"Pete, you made it!"

"This is my friend Mark ... Mark this is Mrs. Greer."

"Pleased to meet you."

"Hey, Pete. Welcome!"

It was Pete's friend Father Perry.

After introductions Pete and I joined Father Perry in his study. We had coffee and sweet rolls. I could tell that they wanted to talk so I asked if there was a place where I could clean up and take a nap. Mrs. Greer showed me a spare bedroom that had a bathroom and shower and even a phone. I was all set. I needed a shower and wanted to lie down for an hour or so. I asked Mrs. Greer if she could wake my by 11. She was really nice.

I could call Steve then.

"Mark, you asked me to wake you at 11."

"Oh ... yeah ... thank you Mrs. Greer."

Where am I? In St. Louis. Right. Had to get my bearings. Staying in a rectory for Christ's sake. Had to laugh at the irony of it all.

Reached for the phone and called my contact, Steve. He wasn't home. A roommate answered.

"This is Mark calling. When will he be back?"

"Tonight at 5:30 when he gets off work."

"Okay, Thanks. I'll call then."

Walked downstairs. Pete was having breakfast. The table was set with eggs, toast, jelly.

"Help yourself ... there's plenty."

I did. The food tasted good. Maybe I should have become a priest after all.

"How do you plan to get money for the '14?' "

"I don't really know yet. I'll knock some ideas off of Father Perry. He's an old friend and I trust him. We think alike."

"I called my friend but he wasn't home. Can I hang out here for the day?"

"Yeah, sure."

I had the letters to mail out so I found a letter box and dropped them off.

I walked around the neighborhood. I liked St. Louis. My family had visited this area in my youth. I had fond memories of the zoo and Stan Musial. The winters were mild but the summers were brutal. Wherever I visited it always occurred to me if I could live there. At this moment in my life I was so scattered I didn't know if I'd ever be able to live anywhere for any amount of time.

I needed a walk.

A small boy rode his trike down the side walk. It was me as a child. I prayed he didn't have to experience the horrors that I did as a child. I prayed he wouldn't fall off his trike. He appeared to watching ants. I used to watch ants. Busy little bastards endlessly climbing into and out of their sand mound. What's down there, anyway? Obviously not concerned with our issues, the war, racism and all the rest. I envied them. I envied the little boy. Oblivious to me as he concentrated on his ants.

And I wish sometimes for a more simpler life. Reduced to watching ant hills. With no concerns about the world situation. No cares. Maybe I should just resign myself to go in the Army and get it over with. The fear of dying is foremost, I must admit, but the idea of killing innocents is abhorrent to me. There can be no excuse for that. 'Just following orders' does not hang true with me. It's an excuse. Like Harry Truman once said, "The buck stops here."

Maybe I could become a priest or a brother. If I was a brother I could always change my vows. But, that would be a cop out too. Or go to Canada. I've heard a lot of guys are doing that. Or, just watch an ant hill.

I called Steve again when I returned to the rectory. He had expected me. I told him where I was. He hesitated.

"You're at a Catholic Church? Okay. I know where it is. I'll be there in twenty minutes."

Steve showed up at the curb. I thanked everyone and said good bye to Pete.

"I'm Steve. You must be Mark."

"Yeah. Thanks for picking me up."

"What are you doing staying in a church?"

"I got a ride from an ex-priest. It's a long story ..."

"Well, that's a first."

We drove through town. I told him that I had a connection with St. Louis. Some of my dad's relatives lived in the area and so forth.

We arrived at a house in a black neighborhood. It was a very old house with a falling down porch and a patchy yard. Stuff littered the yard. Didn't look very inviting.

We seemed to be the only ones here. Steve showed me a spare room where I could sleep and put my ruck sack.

"Mark called me and he wants you to take this package to Minneapolis."

Again, it was about letter size. Sealed and taped shut with an address and name and phone number attached.

"Yeah, I can do that."

"I've even arranged a ride for you. Can you leave tomorrow?"

"Sure."

Steve had a class that night. He said he'd be back by nine. I found a book to read downstairs and curled up in a chair and read. Someone walked in the front door. It gave me a start. It was one of the roommates.

"You must be Mark. I'm John. Steve said you be here. Make yourself at home. Hungry?"

"Hi, John. Pleased to meet you. Yeah, I could eat something."

He offered me a beer and we made ourselves a ham and cheese sandwich. Hit the spot.

A few minutes later Steve came in.

"Oh, good. I see you met John. John's cool. He knows Mark in Berkeley too!"

"Cool. So tell me. What's going on in St. Louis these days?"

"Not much really," answered Steve.

"We've had a couple of protest marches downtown. They have been peaceful so far. The newspaper is in favor of the war as are by far most people in this area but you can feel more and more people coming out against the war. The area is still deeply divided over racial issues. There were riots in East St. Louis a couple of years ago but we haven't heard much noise from them in awhile."

"What I'm hoping for is that I can count on you guys to stay in touch with Mark. I'm going to be moving through here once in awhile and will need a place to stay ..."

"Oh yeah ... of course. You can count on us."

"Great."

"Hey, I've got a great idea, let's go have a beer."

We walked around the block to a corner bar. A mixture of working class and students. We sat at the bar. The jukebox played. A pool table in the back.

"Three Bud's."

"Here's to peace, man," I exclaimed. We clinked our glasses and drank heartily.

It was good to know you could still get a $.35 glass of beer. We had several rounds.

"Steve, do you know what time my ride is coming?"

"Yeah, Bill should pick you up around 10 a.m. One more round and let's get going."

I was up at 8. Showered and shaved. Was ready when Bill arrived. I thanked John and Steve.

"I'll see you soon."

Bill drove a beat Ford Falcon.

"Hope the roads are clear. Never know this time of year."

"This has been a rather mild winter so far. I always worry about Iowa. It gets icy there."

"Yeah, I know. Well, let's go. With any luck we can be in the Twin Cities early tomorrow morning."

I had to thank my lucky stars. It seemed wherever I travelled Mark had arranged a place for me to stay and a ride. I looked over at Bill as he drove. Another kind, intelligent person.

We hugged the Mississippi all the way to Davenport, Iowa. Always chuckled at the name of this town. A cozy, river town. Much like Winona. We crawled through the main drag. Gassed up and peed. I wished I was only going to Winona but I had this package to deliver.

"Won't be long before we're in Minnesota."

Bill didn't talk much. He lived in Minneapolis, he said, with his girlfriend and attended classes at the U of M. Nice guy. Just shy, I guess.

We passed by Winona. Thinking of all my friends and problems and history here in Winona. I'd soon return though.

We hit the Cities at first light. I told him where he could drop me off. I walked a few blocks to the address. It was off Lake Street. A seedy part of town inhabited by Native Americans and poor white students. I knocked on the door.

"Who is it?"

"Mark."

"Mark, who?"

"Is Thomas here?"

"This is Thomas."

"I have a package here from St. Louis."

"Why didn't you say so! Come on in."

I could hear several locks unlocking and the rattle of chains.

Tom was a big guy. Burly.

"I just got in from St. Louis. Mark from Berkeley asked me to deliver this to you."

"Oh, Thanks, man."

He opened it in front of me. A couple of letters tumbled out and an envelope containing a couple hundred bucks, I guessed.

"Well, I guess I'll be going."

"Yeah, thanks a lot, man."

I let myself out. It was pretty cold out and early so I started to make the long trek to the bus station when just for laughs I stuck my thumb out on Lake street.

"Where to?"

"Winona."

"Hop in, man. I'm going there too."

"You're kidding me."

"No man. I go to Winona State."

"Shit, so do I."

"Never seen you before."

"Me neither."

"Hi, my names Mark."

"Name's Cliff."

"You haven't seen me because I don't go to classes," I laughed.

"That explains it.'

We jabbered all the way to Winona. He knew my brother's band, 'The Ferrais', and we had some of the same friends.

"We gotta get high together sometime."

"And we shall."

He produced a joint and we merrily puffed away.

Oh, the luck!

Cliff dropped me off on Highway 61 and I hitched/walked out to the farm.

"Hey, Mike. How was your trip."

Oh yeah, I thought to myself, I was Mike again.

"Fine. How are things around here?"

Jim and Molly were the mainstays here at the farm. All the others seemed to drift through like the wind, staying a month or two and then moving on. I was in this group.

I had some mail. Grandma sent me $100 for Christmas. I gave some money to Jim for rent and food. I was beat. I crawled under my blankets in the cold room and fell asleep.

I awoke. It was dark. I wanted to see Emil. They must be playing to-night. He had mentioned that he may try to go to Pennsylvania for Christmas. I really didn't want to go.

The next couple of weeks passed in a blur. I was sitting tight waiting for a letter from the Draft Board informing me of my CO hearing. I checked the mail every day. No luck. I talked to Mark and Jeff, my lawyer, frequently. Jeff reiterated that the Draft Board had to give me a CO hearing before they could draft me. That was good to know. Mark didn't have anything for me just now. He told me to stay put.

Chapter 10

1969

1968 had been a year, an historic year, fraught with assassinations, more war dead, a country in turmoil and unrest and riots. The country seemed to turn against itself. People were so divided and torn ... polarized. Civil war seemed a real prospect. Parents against their own kids and vice versa. The old against the young. A generational gap. This country was torn in two.

'Humpty Dumpty had a great fall ... they couldn't put Humpty together again.'

Bobby, Martin Luther, killed. The despised Nixon was President-elect. Things weren't looking very good.

I vowed to fight against the injustice and hatred with my whole soul. I felt so strongly that I was right. I'm only one guy and a man. Lord knows I have faults. Lust, greed, ego. I'm guilty! I had to change my ways.

I walked into town and visited the library. I wanted to catch up on the news. I was reading one of the papers when I saw an article that astounded me. Father Pete, the guy who I had ridden with to St. Louis a month ago had been arrested in some bizarre shoot out with police. Apparently, he had attempted to rob the church of their Sunday collections and had been caught by the parish priest. The priest called the cops and Pete had an arsenal of weapons and they were involved in a shoot out in the church.

No injuries.

He had mentioned to me on the trip that he wanted to do some fund raising for the Milwaukee 14. A rather unorthodox method of fund raising.

But, fund raising none the less!

Holy shit! My mind raced. My finger prints were all over that car. The article mentioned that Pete had crossed State lines with illegal weapons. Was I an accomplice? I never looked in the trunk. Maybe he got the weapons in St. Louis. Christ, I knew nothing about this. Father Perry and Mrs. Greer would tell the cops about me. Shit man, I was just hitching a ride. Besides, they only knew me as Mark, no last name. I never mentioned where I was from or going to. Maybe I lucked out. I decided to hang tight and low.

I should stay clear of the Milwaukee 14.

Wow. Fucking Pete.

I was torn between two schools of thought. Those of us who believed in peaceful resistance and those of us who believed in a violent over- throw of the government. Like Trotsky and Lenin. Two opposites on the same side of the coin. Was burning 1-A draft records a violent act? Robbing a church? Shooting at police ... definitely. And where did getting high and enjoying music and girls and dancing come in?

Reading the news papers in the Winona Library. People whispering and softly moving about. I wanted to shout at the top of my lungs.

"STOP THE WAR."

But, I didn't. What would it take to wake these people up. How many more dead boys, killed politicians and civic leaders.

The violent angle definitely had it's points. But, in my heart I leaned more toward the non-violent resistance angle.

I don't know. I just don't know.

The whole world was crazy.

Part 3

Chapter 1

Drafted

1969 came in with a heavy snow fall. We stayed hunkered down in the farm house. We had plenty of milk and eggs from the cows and chickens. We baked bread in a wood stove. I chopped wood and kept the fire stoked. We hardly knew there was an outside world. January and February passed and March howled in. Windy and cold.

I checked the mail every day. I had to walk out to the main road, about half a mile, to check the mail box. The mail came late in the day.

It was the middle of March with the promise of spring around the corner when I received a letter from the Selective Service. I tore it open. I was to report at the bus station in two weeks for a physical in Minneapolis. I was to bring only a tooth brush and the clothes on my back. That meant, I guess, that if I passed the physical I was to be shipped out that same day.

What about my CO hearing?

I called my friend, Jeff, in Minneapolis. He told me that they had screwed up. The next day I went into town and spoke with Mrs. Price. They had no record of my appeal.

Figures.

It was my word against theirs. Who do you think would win that one?

And ... it seemed awful quick for my name to come up. A friend of mine had dropped out the same time I did and he hadn't been called up yet. I wondered, as did Jeff, if they hadn't put my name on top because I was a rabble-rouser. That was against their rules as well. But, I couldn't fight them. They would just lie anyway.

I talked with Jeff several times. He advised me to actually go ahead with the physical but not take the oath. He said that at the very end of the ordeal they made you stand on a red line and take the oath. If I didn't take the oath there wasn't a thing they could do to me and I could walk out of the place.

I also called Mark and informed him. He told me that they wouldn't do anything to me and that they would probably send me several notices to return and take the oath with no hard feelings. Mark and Jeff both felt that it would take a Grand Jury several months to indite me and then at that time if I ran I would become a fugitive. If captured I faced at least five years in a Federal Penitentiary. I had no intention of ever being caught.

I had everything set up. I had a network of good people and places to stay. But, more importantly, I would stay very active fighting against the war and racism. I could easily go to Canada but I wanted to stay here and fight. I figured that was the patriotic thing to do. In my way of thinking I was acting as a patriot. I wanted to change the course of this country away from Colonialism. I wanted people in other countries to admire us, not fear and distrust us. I wanted a better world. And if my little act contributed to the betterment then I was doing the right thing. I had to listen to my heart and my conscience. I wasn't going to kill for the rich and powerful. I wasn't doing their bidding!

Well, here we go. All the planning and deciding. It was as if my whole life had come to this moment. It was surreal.

Early in a cold fog waiting to board a military bus to eternity. Some of the guys looked scared to death. Some were all gung-ho. Wanting to kill. Maybe they were too violent to get in the Army. We boarded and a guy in fatigues called out our names. Everyone accounted for.

We left Winona on that cold morning. How many of these guys would never return. Or in a box. Or with missing limbs. Or with missing sanity. Life long stains from the war. "Out damn spot, out!" But the stain would never vanish. Never.

How many times had I passed this way before. Highway 61 Revisited. Indeed.

God, I was scared. I had doubts, no doubt. Was I doing the right thing? I couldn't turn back now. All my friends in Winona had given me a big send off. The Ferrais played at the farm and lots of people showed up. Even got laid. We had food and fun. I told everyone there that I'd be back that night or the next day. Word even got out to the *Winona Daily News* and I reluctantly gave them an interview. I think I came across as arrogant and self-righteous. I just couldn't turn back now. This is how a parachutist must feel like. I have to jump. I have too.

And jump I did!

They unloaded us and marched us into this huge building. Hundreds of other poor saps stood in line. I didn't know Minnesota had so many young men. I was one of only a few long hairs and was immediately mocked and jeered by the jocks. I could have taken half theses guys apart in a second but I just acted like I didn't hear them.

Army guys yelled at us and told us to line up and shut the fuck up. "No talking, assholes," we were all assholes. 'All men are created assholes.' Equal, but assholes. This wasn't real. I was truly intimidated.

This was worse than I imagined!

Line after line. They poked and prodded and asked questions and sent us on and on to the next line.

Standing in a large room with a hundred other guys holding our clothes in one arm. Garbed in our underwear. Two guys walked behind each one of us and told us to drop our underwear and one guy looked up my asshole. I thought of several jokes at the time but kept them to myself. "Find what you're looking for?"

Simultaneously, a fake doctor walked in front of us and told me to turn my head to the side and cough as he held my balls.

I was starring out a window and watched a crow gracefully alight on the very top branch of a tree while a flashlight probed my inner regions. I wanted to be that crow. I would have landed on that very branch myself. I wanted to be that bird right now.

More lines. More waiting. I saw a shrink. He asked the most inane questions and stamped my bundle of papers, which was by now substantial.

A long wait. We had to stand the entire time. Menacing Army freaks paced along our line growling and snarling like badgers. "Fuck you," I thought to myself. I told him!

My turn came up. This guy looked through my stack of papers. He never once looked up or acknowledged me. He put his stamp on top of the others. "Next."

Finally, we were allowed to put our clothes back on. We were led to a cafeteria. They gave us a lunch of some sliced meat and mashed potatoes drowned in gravy. I wasn't very hungry and just nibbled.

After an hour or so we were led into another large room and made to stand in rows on a yellow line. A Marine animal shouted and barked at us threatening all kind of violence and doom if we didn't stand still.

We had to get in line according to our number. I wasn't even human. I was #237. An Army guy read the rote. He told a couple of guys to step out. They had been turned down by the Army. Nobody wanted them. In this arena it was a disgrace to be rejected. Hell, I figured it was a good luck omen. Maybe, just maybe, they didn't want me either. I sure as hell didn't want them.

They called my number. "Here." No such luck.

Well, here goes.

He finished the rote. A Marine walked in and told us that we were all being drafted into the United States Marine Corps. He told us to step up to the red line and raise our right hands.

My body was trembling. I was sure everyone in the room was staring at me. I didn't move. I remained on the yellow line.

"You ... what's your name?"

"McAndrew."

"Step up to the red line and take your oath."

"No sir, I can't do that."

"You are a piece of shit, Mister. You've disgraced these other brave men." His face was an inch from mine. His face was reddened by his rage. He had bad breath.

The Marine read the oath anyway. He just went ahead with it. It was a moment when these guys no longer belonged to their parents or friends. They were Marines. They belonged to the Marine Corps!

As the Marine read the oath and all the men in the room recited the oath, I walked out of the room clutching my papers. They couldn't stop me. A Marine stepped in front of me.

"Get out of my way."

He did!

It was obvious that these guys had never seen anyone just walk out. Their startled looks gave them away. Their heads swiveled looking at each other for guidance. Not one of them had the balls to make a decision. 'What! They didn't tell us about this ... what the fuck are we supposed to do if a guy walks out? You can't walk out! Walk out? What the fuck.'

Yeah, I walked out. I just walked out! The adrenaline in my body was soaring. I eventually found my way out of the building. There was the front door. I could see the street outside. I crossed the huge marble floor and reached the door. No one was trying to stop me. No one was yelling. No one seemed to even notice me in the daily hubbub.

I pushed through the lobby and the front doors. I was outside. I noticed a camera crew standing off to the side on the steps. I spotted a trash can on the front sidewalk at the bottom of the stairs. I walked directly to the trash can and threw all my papers into it.

"That's him!"

At first, I believed I was being arrested or something but soon realized that a TV film crew surrounded me asking questions all at once.

"Did you not take the oath ... How does it feel to be a 'draft resister' ... What are going to do next? ... Are you going to Canada?"

Just then Jeff, my attorney, pushed and shoved some reporters out of the way. He stepped in front of the cameras. "No more questions. My client seeks justice and what is right. His crime, if indeed he has committed a crime, is one of conscience. We ask that you respect his privacy at this time. Thank you. No more questions."

I was stunned. Jeff grabbed my arm and led me to a car parked at the curb. Some people were in the car. Jeff shoved me into the back seat and we drove away.

"Thanks for saving me! How did the press find out about this. I don't want all this publicity."

"I'm guilty. I told *WCCO* and the *Tribune* and the *Pioneer Press*," confessed Jeff.

"Why?"

"To protect you. They won't do anything to you with the cameras on you."

I resigned myself to Jeff's judgment.

"I tried to get a hold of you, but you weren't home."

He was right. I stayed in town the day before so I could get to the bus on time.

Jeff took me to his house. Several people were there. It was a party. A true surprise party! I hadn't thought much of what I was going to do after this. I was really moved by this display. I started to cry after receiving hugs and congrats. I never expected a reaction like this. Evidently, this put me in an elite group. Up to this point other guys had resisted the draft, of course, but I was certainly one of the first to resist the Vietnam War in Minnesota. Someone had mentioned that a guy had resisted the draft in World War Two and spent five years in prison.

Before I knew it a beer was in my hand and the sweet scent of pot wafted throughout.

I've never wanted fame. But, I guess, for one day it was okay. I met all these new people from the Cities.

We partied on and on. Jeff said I could stay here with him.

We watched the evening news and sure enough there I was, walking out of the building and throwing my papers into a garbage can and then surrounded by the press and Jeff coming to my rescue. A reporter spoke about me like he knew me and he explained to the viewers what I had done.

I better stay low. A large group of people watched the news. Several pats on the back followed.

I was exhausted from the long day. Jeff showed me to a room upstairs where I could sleep.

I'd call Mark tomorrow.

I awoke in a start. I was so tired from last night. Everybody wanted to talk to me. I just collapsed.

Jeff said I could use his phone but I chose to walk to a corner market and call Mark from a phone booth.

He picked up.

"I did it!"

"Who's this? Oh Mark, jeez ... great. I'll call you back in ten minutes."

I gave Mark the number of the phone and waited.

"Wow, man. Let me be the first to congratulate you. I'm proud of you.

What are you going to do?"

"Jeff, my attorney, advised me I could return to Winona and basically wait until the indictment comes down. He said that they couldn't touch me until then. He thought it would take a couple of months at least before that happened. In the meantime I'm gonna take off in a couple of weeks. I want to say goodbye to my grandparents and stuff. Jesus, I was on TV and in the papers."

"Really."

"Yeah. I don't like that. I don't want all the attention."

"Don't worry. They'll forget you by tomorrow."

"I hope you're right."

"Stay in touch and be cool!"

I hung up.

Jeff had gone to class and I was left alone. Finally, alone with my own thoughts. I called my mom and told her. She wasn't impressed or concerned. I don't think she really cared.

I called my grandma. She invited me to visit them in Rice Lake. I said I could catch a bus tomorrow and she said that would be fine.

I called Emil in Winona.

"Hey, we saw you on TV last night! When are you coming back?"

"I'm going to see Grandma and Grandpa first and then I'll come back to Winona."

"We'll have a big party for you."

"Love you, Emil. I'll see you soon."

I had never told Emil that I loved him. I guess I was sensing my own mortality and vulnerability.

I hung out at Jeff's. He came home and was surprised to see me.

"Is it okay if I stay here tonight?"

"Oh yeah ... yeah. Of course. I thought that maybe you would have split. But, yeah, man ... of course. Anytime, man."

"Hey, I've got some money. Let's go out."

We found his neighborhood bar.

We settled into a booth and he ordered beers.

"I'm so fucking scared. I've got a question, though. Since you are my attorney, but you aren't a lawyer yet, and aren't privy to attorney-client privileges ... in other words, are you like a priest in a confessional ... you know, like you don't have to reveal anything to the cops.?"

"Not yet. Once I pass the bar I can claims those rights."

"So, if I told you stuff now would you be bound to talk."

"Yes."

"Okay. I can tell you some of it. I'm going underground and will be using fake names. I'm probably going to need to talk to you from time to time. I'll never tell you where I am or what I'm up to but I will need advice from time to time, namely, what's going on with my case, you know, stuff like, are the Feds looking for me and what do you hear. You know, stuff like that. I've got to have some other eyes and ears. I don't want you to jeopardize yourself, so be cool, man."

"Right on, man."

"Let's drink some beer and relax."

"Fuck, yeah!"

We clinked beer mugs in a toast to 'The Revolution.'

To the revolution. I didn't know the first thing about a revolution. Castro and Che knew about a revolution. Mao knew about a revolution. Who the fuck am I kidding?

Got up late the next morning. Hung over and groggy. No one was home. I took a long shower and made coffee. I called Greyhound. I could catch a bus to Rice Lake later this afternoon.

Called Grandma. I'd be in Rice Lake at 8 p.m.

My hair was still short; an inch over my ears, and I had some decent clothes to wear. I wanted to see Grandma and Grandpa before going back to Winona, and before slipping underground.

I left a note for Jeff and caught a bus downtown. I wanted to hang out for a while. I needed to clear my head. People bustling and hustling along Hennepin Avenue. Same old hustle, man. Second hand shops, and cool dudes slinking ... liquor stores with token winos and paper bags, ladies on the make. Dangerous at 2 p.m. and even more so at 2 a.m. The intricacies of the world seemingly have escaped these people. People lost in their booze and survival instincts. I'm going to another world. A world where lawn care is vitally important. Appearance is everything.

How many times I've traveled this road on the way to Grandma's house. Would this be the last time?

Grandpa was waiting for me.

"We saw you on the news!"

"Oh yeah. I wasn't ready for that."

Grandpa and I had always restricted our conversations to baseball. It was hard for him to talk with kids. I used to listen to him talk to customers at the shop and at Kohler's Bar. He could talk to his friends. He was a self-made millionaire, I was sure, he was 'The Man' in Rice Lake, but he yielded for Grandma. She was the 'Boss.' They had the most loving relationship I've ever known.

Before going to the house Grandpa wanted to show me the completed high school and some property that he owned. I don't know why he wanted to show me this but he did. That was Grandpa. He really just wanted to talk to me. He rambled on about the dangers of drugs and 'those crazy hippies.'

Then just like that he hands me some money and tells me not to tell Grandma. I thanked him and promised not to tell.

" ... and stay away from homo sapiens ..."

He meant homosexuals. "Okay, Grandpa, I will."

"Mother (Grandma) made dinner for you."

He always addressed her as 'Mother!'

Grandma's house always had this smell. This great smell of cleanliness and baked brownies. She greeted me with a big kiss on the cheek and a long hug. She held my forearms and stared into my eyes. A look of pride and fear stared back at me.

"We saw you on the news!"

"Yeah, Grandpa told me. I didn't know they were there. My attorney set that up. He thinks it'll be better for me if everyone knows."

"I s'pose."

As promised, Grandma had dinner ready for me. A hot dish. I had coffee and brownies for desert.

"Thanks, Grandma, that was great."

Grandpa retired to the living room and turned on TV. Grandma and I remained in the kitchen and talked.

"You know it's going to break your mother's heart."

"Would she prefer I come back in a box," I retorted.

"Grandma," I continued, "I've thought about this for a long time. You know I was going to do this. I told Mom and Dad too. The only person in my family who agrees with me is Emil. My brother Tim. He's the only one. Not Mom, not Dad, not anyone. This has been the hardest decision in my life. You and the Church raised me to love and respect people, to tell the truth, to treat people with respect. What did you expect?"

"Michael, I agree with what you did. I'm just so worried what will happen to you."

"What ... you agree with me ... oh Grandma."

I hugged her and began crying. Deep sobs. Grandpa came running in. I couldn't control myself. All the energy of the past seemed to gush out of me. I broke down.

After several minutes I was able to speak.

"I'm so scared, Grandma. I don't know if I'm doing the right thing. I may end up in prison for five years. I'm going underground. Do you know what that is?" she shook her head, "It means that I'm not going to turn myself in. I'm going to run and run and do everything I can to end this war. People are dying. It has to stop. If my resistance wakes up one person ... it'll be worth it."

"You see," I continued, "you and Grandpa are sitting here listening to me and you must be wondering about this war. World War One and Two were different."

I could tell I was getting through. We had never talked about anything as heavy as this. It was always baseball with Grandpa and helping Grandma around the house. I knew they had faced tough times in their lives. Grandpa had served in World War One in Paris and Grandma was the youngest of twelve motherless kids raised on a farm in Northern Wisconsin. I knew that they had gone through some tough patches also.

"It means everything to me that you support me on this."

We made the mandatory visit to Aunt Ginny and Uncle Rich's house. They were both very critical of my decision, as expected. There was no use arguing with them as they both grilled me making me feel very guilty and wrong. But, I knew that was coming.

Not soon enough we returned to Grandma's house. I just wanted to be alone.

I slept dreamless. I could smell breakfast downstairs. Grandma had already gone to Mass and Grandpa was working.

"Good morning, Grandma."

"Eat your breakfast and then you're getting a haircut."

"What ... I don't need a haircut."

"Yes, you do."

"I'll do it for $100," I joked.

"Okay."

"You mean it?"

"Yes. I'll give you $100 if you cut your hair."

"Let's go."

Grandma and I drove downtown to Grandpa's barber.

"Mrs. Mally ... how are you? Haven't seen you in a while."

"Hi Floyd. This is my grandson, Michael. He needs a haircut."

I sat in the chair. I hadn't had a hair cut from a barber in a long time. He put the cloth over me and swung me around. I faced myself. I'm thinking that this would be a good disguise. Short hair and clean shaven. I'd be going against the grain. Again. Always the fish swimming up stream.

His skilled hands clipped and buzzed away. He only knew one hair style. Short.

"Thanks Floyd."

Anything to make Grandma happy. I stepped out of the chair feeling a breeze around my ears. I didn't even want to look at myself. It was basically a butch with a small tuft of hair in the front. 1955 haircut. For a mere $1.75 I looked like a moron.

But, true to her word; Grandma reached into her purse and produced five twenties. Nice.

"Grandma, I was only kidding ..."

"No, take it. I was going to give you some money anyway. You'll need it. What are you going to do and where are you going? I'm so worried about you ... oh, and don't tell your Grandpa I gave you money," she trailed off.

I thought she might cry but she didn't.

We drove to Grandpa's shop and I said farewell.

I caught the early bus back to the Cities.

I was sad. Would I ever see my grandparents again? They were getting on in years. I needed to get back to Winona but I wanted to tidy things up with Jeff in Minneapolis.

I walked all the way to Jeff's.

"What the fuck happened to you?"

"It'll grow back ... my grandma offered me $100 if I'd cut my hair. She didn't raise a fool."

Jeff laughed.

"You look like a moron."

"Thanks, man. Do you have a hat I could wear?"

"Listen, we have to talk. We have to set up a system where I can contact you. Mark and I have a cool thing set up. I can reach him in a couple of hours and he says it's safe from prying ears and eyes. We should do the same. For example, this place wouldn't be cool at all. We'd have to assume that this place is wired. So, I could call a friend who would get a hold of you and you could call the number I leave. It would be phone booth to phone booth. I think that's the safest way. And, as far as mail goes. I could always pick it up if I had any, but, I'm not going to worry about that. I'll mail letters from here and there," Jeff listened intently.

"Sounds good. Remember my friend Greg? He'd be the perfect one to contact. He knows your case and he's in some of my classes. I trust him."

"Ok. Let's talk to him at some point and set that up. In the meantime, I need to go to Winona and settle things there. But, first. Let's get drunk. My grandma gave me $100. It's burning a hole in my pocket."

"I did some digging into your case. You say that you applied for a CO hearing, right?"

"Yeah."

"Well, they never gave you a hearing and they were required to. The other issue that concerns me is that they have an order that they call up the names and it looks like they put you on top of the pile. If we can prove this maybe, just maybe, we can null the case."

"Too much to think about. Let's have a beer"

I scrunched up in the corner of the booth and drew my knees to my chin. Jeff knew some of the people in the bar and a few joined us. No one recognized me. Must have been the haircut or no one really cared. Probably both.

"I'm gonna scoot in the morning, Jeff. I want to test our communication method in a couple of days. I'll call Greg and then wait for your call. It's probably best if I set up a day and time. I know you're busy, So, let's say I call Greg on a Wednesday, okay? I'll say something like ... tell Jeff to call me at, I'll leave the number, on Thursday at 8 p.m. I'll always use your time. If you don't call in ten minutes at the prescribed time then we'll have to set up another time."

"It's crude but it should work. US Mail won't be safe. You'll be a target in a few months."

"Fuck it! More beer."

I decided to hitch hike to Winona. I needed to save money and with my new clean looks I had no trouble catching a few rides to Winona. I found Emil.

"What the fuck happened to you?"

"It's the new me. I'm going Republican!" I joked.

"No shit, man. We saw you on TV."

"Oh, I know. Jeff set that up. Even Grandma and Grandpa saw me. Aunt Ginny and Uncle Rich gave me shit for it but I expected that from them. Thought I'd stained the family name and all. Grandma was the only one to support me. In fact, Emil, you and Grandma are the only two family members that are behind me."

"Everybody wants to see you. Let's go to Charlie's Bar. Word will get out in no time."

We had hot dogs and endless beers. Everybody laughed at my hair cut. I did too. I pulled a stocking cap down to my eyes.

"We saw you on TV." A hundred times. I hate this. I wanted to crawl under the table.

I saw the hat first. Then the uniform. It was Ralph. He had been drafted several months prior and was home on leave from Boot Camp.

"Ralph!"

"Hey, man"

We both had short hair cuts.

"I heard you walked out of the draft in Minneapolis."

"Yeah."

"Wish I'd done that."

"How long are you home?"

"Three more weeks."

Ralph was one of the first hippies in Winona and was a close friend of Emil's. It turns out that Ralph had impregnated his girl friend and there was talk that they might get married. Ralph was on his way to Vietnam, he said. I saw fear and resignation in his eyes.

More and more people stopped by. Most supported me, some were skeptical, some critical, all seemed impressed mostly that I had been on TV.

Linda showed up. We hung out for a couple of days. I think she wanted to come with me. I had to do this alone. It was very difficult for us because

I was in love with her.

I returned to the farm. I wanted to stay here as long as I could. It was quiet here.

A few weeks passed. Linda and I hitched into town. Naturally, we gravitated to Charlie's Bar. The talk of the town was that Ralph had disappeared. Conjecture was that he freaked out about his girl friend and future kid and the fact that he was supposed to go to Vietnam. No one had seen him in about ten days.

Emil told me he had been really depressed. He had had a fight with his girl friend and he really didn't want to go to Vietnam. I thought that I could help him to safely hide out.

The pressure was on. That morning when Linda and I were hitching a car drove by and I heard, 'Coward," screamed at me from a passing car. I didn't know who it was.

The *Winona Daily News* wanted to interview me. I said okay. They sent a reporter and a photographer, my old friend, 'One Shot' Kelley. It was great to see him again.

She asked the most expected questions and I gave expected answers. Mr. Kelley took a nice shot of me and they ran the article the next day.

I was a celebrity in Winona. I did this not only in an attempt to affect my case but to reach other young guys and let them know that they didn't necessarily have to lie down and die for a corrupt war.

I guess a couple of more weeks went by. I got a phone call at the farm. It was Emil.

"They found Ralph."

"What do you mean."

"They found him in his car over in Wisconsin. He shot himself."

Emil was sobbing.

What the fuck. A strong shot of adrenaline pierced my heart. I had to sit down. Ralph! Not Ralph.

Linda and I arrived at Charlie's. The place was packed. Every one was upset about Ralph. People were crying. We had thought that maybe he just took off because he couldn't deal with the pressure. Everyone had questions. No one had any answers.

All we knew was that Ralph was dead.

Another victim of Vietnam.

His distraught parents arranged the funeral. We all attended the service. It was horrible. As I entered and sat down Ralph's mother approached me and began yelling at me saying, "It's all your fault ... you and you're smart ass attitude and drugs and anti-war shit ... it's all your fault ..."

I was shocked and embarrassed. Someone grabbed her. It was her husband. He pressed his face into mine. "Get the fuck outta here, or I'll kill you."

I was numb. To this day I've never made any sense of that episode.

Linda and I walked out onto the sidewalk. I couldn't even speak. What did I do? I felt like shit. I sat down and put my hands into my face and cried. I cried all the tears I could find until I could cry no more.

God! What the fuck was I doing?

We found out later that Ralph's parents had targeted most of Ralph's friends. They even insulted Ralph's girlfriend. They'd never married but I heard that she had the child.

I was in constant contact with Jeff and Mark. I was ready to hit the road. One thing for certain: I wasn't going to wait around to be indicted. Once indicted the Feds would pick me up.

Chapter 2

Indicted ... Run You Bastard, Run

I said my good byes. Emil threw a monster party for me that lasted a couple of days. The band played. We took over Charlie's Bar.

In Winona I was either a hero or a traitor. No in between. It was very difficult to say goodbye to Linda and Emil and several other good friends. I knew that things would never be the same.'You can never go back home.' I just knew that Winona and my friends would never be the same.

Jeff had told me that the Grand Jury was meeting. The Draft Board had sent me two warnings in the mail informing me I could still enlist in the Army. No hard feelings. Not a chance!

I had a good plan to escape. I assumed they were watching me, knowing I would run. After the parties and fun I returned to the farm. I made myself visible for a couple days. I went to the library and hung out at Charlie's.

I only told Emil. No one else. Not even Linda.

One night I walked out. It was very late. I made sure that no one was following me. It was 3 a.m. I left the farm and walked through the woods all the way to the railroad tracks in Winona. I waited and hid. A slow moving freight train rolled along the tracks. I had taken this one before. I would be in Davenport in several hours. I had carefully packed all my gear and ID's. I had prepared for this. I hopped the train and climbed into a car. It was early spring and cold. No one else was on this car. I was gone!

I didn't even tell Emil where I was going. I told no one.

I was Mark Heddington and Mark Cole.

Michael McAndrew was dead.

The night chill caused me to huddle in a corner looking out at the passing scene. The Mississippi on one side and a near by cliff on the other. I noticed La Crosse and knew that soon I would be in Iowa. A good place to hide.

I was in survival mode and had no time for sentimentality or emotion.

Next. What's next. Okay, I made it to Davenport. Took a bus to Des Moines. I had about $300 on me. I would take another bus to Denver. That bus leaves in an hour.

I read too many spy books but I plied the tricks. I watched for anyone watching me. No one seemed to notice. I took an inventory of the sad faces in the Des Moines bus station. A voice called my bus. Only six people got on. I had to be so careful in this stage of escape. I felt like the Feds were everywhere.

I sat in a rear seat and lit a cigarette, I was alone. I watched out the window I noticed nothing out of the ordinary.

I felt safe!

Westward ho! First stop. I stayed on the bus. A few people got on. Mostly black people who sat in the rear with me. I was deep into a book and pretended not to notice.

We reached Omaha and I had to change buses. I waited in the lobby for a couple of hours. I bought some smokes and hung in the recesses. They called the bus to Denver. I was pondering the possibility of seeing my friends or passing through. I guess I'd decide when I got there. Watching the great flatness of Nebraska. Endless farms of wheat, corn and such. The bread basket of America.

The sun was setting in the west. Great golden streaks lit huge tumbling clouds. What a great country, I thought. Filled with a weird patriotism all of a sudden. I was a child again. I was so scared I trembled in insecurity. Alone. Really alone now. I imagined the family in that farmhouse. Gathered around the dinner table. Heads bowed in a thanksgiving grace. Worn out tired in a good way from the daily toils. The scent of home made bread and soft conversation. Peaceful.

Maybe I was a coward. Maybe everything they said about me was true. I was a traitor. No I wasn't. I was a believer in justice. Equality. All the tenets of the Catholic Church, my grandma, my country. The Constitution. 'All men are created equal.' 'Thou shalt not kill.' These mantras reinforced me. Gave me a position I could defend.

Could the other passengers hear my thoughts? I had to look cool on the outside. But inside. Oh God. My stomach growled and cried out for calm.

I lit another cig. It seemed to relax me, some. It didn't end the torture.

Denver. Denver will always remind me of OZ. A city of lights rising from the mountains. A gateway. Like a keyhole to another room.

We arrived in Denver. I got off the bus with no intention of getting on another. Downtown was fairly seedy and menacing. I'd been here before. I walked several blocks. I spotted a freeway entrance. Highway 70 heading West. It was late but why not.

I walked up the ramp and stuck my thumb out. A car stopped almost immediately.

"Where you headed?" I asked.

"Grand Junction."

"Cool."

I got in.

He looked like a salesman.

"You a student."

"Yes ... yes I am."

"I usually don't pick up hitch hikers but you look like a clean cut young man."

"Thank you, sir.'

I applied my best 'young republican' front. I just wanted to get to a safe place. I didn't need to rile the good citizens of Colorado.

"I'm a salesman. Lonely job."

"Hey, my dad is a salesman. Back east. Works for Essex Wire. Heard of 'em."

"Power cable ... right?"

"Yep."

Common ground established he drove me to Grand Junction. It was day break.

"Thank you, sir."

"Good luck to you."

I was bushed tired. I walked off the free way and found a little park. I unrolled my sleeping bag and crawled deep into some bushes and slept for a few hours.

I awoke. I needed something to eat. There was a restaurant down the road. I packed my gear and set out. I washed up in the bathroom. I ordered coffee and eggs and toast. No one gave me a second glance.

Back to the freeway. Hopefully, I could catch a nice long ride. I must have stood there for three hours. God, I was being punished. Even the hippies drove by. I looked too straight to pick up, I guess.

Finally, a young Mormon couple took mercy on me and gave me a ride to Price, Utah.

They were very shy but very nice.

"Kind of you."

"It's the Christian thing to do."

"Name's Jeb and this here is my bride Martha."

"Mark. On my way to California for school. Thanks for the ride."

"Martha's mom is sick so we're going to her dad's ranch to help out her dad."

"You guys are Mormon's? Right!"

"That's right."

"Never met a Mormon before. I'm Catholic."

"Well, we're all God's children."

"I agree."

Nothing like a little diplomacy to settle the air. They seemed like nice people however removed from the outside world. They seemed to either not care or be interested and surely did not know much of the outside world. The outside world being things like Civil Rights and the Anti-War movement. Didn't want to bring it up. Just wanted a ride.

We stopped several times because Martha was sick.

"She's due any day now."

My God, she couldn't be 16 years old. Jeb was much older. Probably mid 20's.

Well, he was exempt from the draft wasn't he!

In a way I envied them. Completely oblivious to all the turmoil and upset in the world. But, they had their own problems.

It was getting dark by the time we reached Price. We must have stopped ten times for Martha. She smelled like vomit and kept apologizing.

"Gotta let you out here Mark. The ranch is up this road. Gotta get Martha inside."

I understood.

"Thanks for the ride and God bless both of you."

I meant it too!

I could see the twinkling lights of Price, Utah ahead. I had eaten and had water with me. The night was clear and the first stars blinked in the mountainous sky. Just beautiful here. It was chilly but not too cold. I stuck my thumb out for a while. Only two cars passed by. I decided to spend the night right here. I climbed off the road and hunkered down in the high weeds safely off the road and out of sight.

I must have been tired. I counted the stars. They were dancing and huge. I could feel the thin mountain air. The cold seeped through my sleeping bag, and I slept like an angel.

Chapter 3

Bum Fuck, Utah

There was frost on the grass. I was shivering. I pissed a steamy pee. I was cold to my bones. I noticed a herd of sheep grazing in a meadow. It was a beautiful place. But, I gotta go.

I climbed down the embankment onto the road. Price looked about three miles up the road. I need to move to warm up anyway.

I stuck out my thumb. I used my left hand with my back to any traffic. None came. I walked in silence except the morning chirps of birds.

I neared the eastern edge of town. It was long and narrow. I figured I could find a restaurant to clean up and get some coffee.

I was walking due west with the morning sun warming my back. Thumb out, just in case. This town was pretty dead. Like a ghost town in a movie. Nothing stirred.

Just then a police car pulled next to me on the road. A big fat cop wearing a cowboy hat and sun shades like 'Cool Hand Luke.'

"Now, son, you know you can't do that in my town."

"Do what sir?" in my most polite affection.

"You can't hitch hike in my town."

"Sorry sir. I won't."

"You better not. I'll bring you in."

"I'll give you five minutes to get out of my town."

I looked ahead. Unless I had a ride or was an Olympic sprinter, it would take me longer than that. The town looked to be five miles long. Three blocks wide but five miles long.

"Yes sir. I'll get a move on then."

This is all I need. Some podunk idiot cop harassing me. Arresting me. And getting some swelled head because he single handed captured one of them 'radicals.'

'HIS TOWN?' What the fuck? Where am I. It dawned on me like all the jokes about Egypt too. I'm in BUM FUCK UTAH. I nearly laughed out loud but managed to restrain myself. I'm sure it was against the law to laugh in Price, Utah.

"Your Honor, I arrested this man for smiling. For smiling in Utah."

"Thirty days."

The jackass circled me every block. He was trolling at 2 mph then he would speed up and circle again. He must have done this ten times until I was mercilessly at the outskirts of HIS TOWN.

He circled once more and I nodded to him. He nodded back.

I walked and walked. I was tired from carrying all my gear but I trod on. I was afraid that I might infringe on his outskirts too! Didn't want to do that.

My back was aching so I dropped everything and stretched. I soon picked everything up again. Shit! I needed water and was getting hungry. Fucking asshole.

I walked until Price disappeared. I took my gear off and sat on the side of the road thumbing. An occasional vehicle passed. The afternoon was warming up. I spotted some trees ahead. I had to get out of the sun. I took a nap hidden under the trees.

God. Would I ever get out of here?

I walked down to the road again and just sat there. I got plenty of dirty looks from passing motorists but no takers. It dawned on me that I would have to spend the night here!

Nightfall came as it always does. I had travelled ten miles today. It's a long walk to San Francisco from here!

Thankfully, I was able to sleep. It seemed warmer under these trees. Their branches hugged me as I nestled on the soft ground. An owl in the distance hooted. Peaceful.

I decided that tomorrow I would try to find a farm house where I could at least get some water.

Morning came. I sucked water drops from the morning dew. It momentarily quenched my thirst. I had to fill my canteen. That was a priority. I shivered as I rolled up my sleeping bag and gathered my stuff. I attached the sleeping bag to the top of my rucksack. It covered my entire back side and my head. I had to walk to get warm. I walked to the road and began walking and hitching. After a few moments I heard a car approaching. I turned just in time to see what looked like a carload of teenagers coming fast. I saw one of them unroll the passenger side window and I turned my back on them as they flew by.

I was pummeled by Bic pens! A couple dozen of them hit me and the ground around me. One of them even stuck in my rucksack. Well, I had enough pens for a while.

As they passed I heard them yell, "Fuckin' hippie!"

This is not a very friendly place.

Now my senses were on high alert. I was very scared and wary of anyone that did stop to pick me up. How the hell I ended up out here ... I need to be more careful in the future and only accept rides that will take me to popular spots.

Anyway, after I had fetched the Bic pens I continued walking down the road. I was very hungry and thirsty. I desperately searched for a farm house. None in sight. I had sucked as much moisture from the grass but the sun was up and evaporating the drops.

I must have walked a few more miles when I heard a semi-truck coming. This was the first truck that passed. I stopped and turned toward the truck and it began to slow down. Yes! He slowed. It took him a bit to stop. He was 100 yards down the road. I walked to the side of the truck. It was a ways up and I couldn't see anyone in the cab. The door opened. I stepped up. A long haired rough necked fellow sat behind the wheel. He had a cowboy hat on and hair past his shoulders.

"Hop in."

And I did. My gear fit easily behind the seats.

"You look the worse for wear my friend."

I tried to talk but couldn't. I hadn't spoken in a couple of days and I guess I was so thirsty that my vocals cords just closed up.

"Jesus man, have some water."

He handed me his canteen and I gulped.

"Slow down. Just wet your lips."

I nodded.

He was an angel who came to save me.

Eventually I was able to speak.

"Thank you for picking me up. I thought I was going to die out there."

"And those people would have let you die too. Not too friendly out here."

I told him of my entire ordeal. About the cop and the pens and evil stares from the locals.

He just nodded.

"Name's Charlie."

"I'm Mark."

"I'm headed to Salt Lake City and then all the way to San Francisco. You're welcome to come with, man. First thing we gotta do is get you cleaned up and some food in you. There's a big truck stop outside of Provo. We'll stop there. You can shower up and do a load of laundry while I fill the truck up and get the oil changed. Take most of the afternoon. Too fuckin' hot to drive anyway."

"Charlie, I think you saved my life!"

"Think nothing of it. I'm a good judge of character and I could tell you are a good person and were in deep shit. Fuckin' Mormon's sometimes. They take care of their own but don't care for anyone else. Doesn't seem like the Christian thing to do. Oh well, let's get you fixed up, Mark."

"Hey, Charlie, need a pen?"

We both laughed. I gave him about five pens, I guess.

"You weren't shittin', we're you?"

"Nope."

I drank some more water. I was feeling human again.

We pulled into this huge truck stop near Provo. Dozens of trucks were parked here and there. Some being refueled. Some just parked. Some engines running, the deep rumble of diesel engines. Loud. In unison.

Charlie pulled into a bay and talked to a guy. Charlie was built like a middle linebacker. No one in their right mind would give him shit because he had long hair. The truckers respected one another. It was a strong bond of brotherhood. They stuck together.

"Mark, here's twenty bucks. Go inside get some change. The showers are over there. See 'em. Costs a quarter for fifteen minutes. Buy a pair of shorts and wear those while your clothes dry. Here are my clothes. Throw all the shit together. We're going to be here for a few hours. I really need an oil change. Then we'll eat. Got it?"

I stood in the shower. It was the greatest shower of my life. I must have drank most of the water before it hit my body. I put another quarter in. It felt so good. Our clothes were in the washer. I already had a pair of shorts, and a clean tee shirt so, I put those on. I didn't even bother drying myself. It was so hot that I dried in minutes anyway. Charlie was off doing some business with the mechanics.

I waited in a grassy shaded area that provided some protection from the sun. Charlie popped up out of no where.

"You got the clothes?"

"Yep. Right here."

I had folded them in two neat piles.

"I'm gonna take a shower then we eat."

Charlie seemed to know everyone in here. The waitress winked at him as we ordered.

"Hey, Doll Face. Miss me?"

"You know it."

I ordered a burger. " You're gonna have a New York steak."

Okay. Steaks and beer were ordered. "It's on me Mark. You've had it rough the last couple of days. This'll make up for it."

"Thank you, Charlie."

My guardian Angel. His name is Charlie. He had long hair and everyone waved at him and said hi. Who is this guy?

"Jeez, I'm stuffed!"

"Hey, Doll, we'll have two apple pies a la mode and more beer."

"She's an old flame. Got one in each port, ya know," he continued.

I just smiled at him. We finished up. He paid his bill.

"Man, I can't thank you enough."

"Forget about it. Let's roll."

We settled into the cab. "Here, take a couple of these."

Two little white tablets rolled into my hands.

"What are these?" playing it dumb.

"Whites. The truckers helper. It's speed, Mark. Keeps you alert and awake. We all use 'em. Some guys doing the long hauls drive all the way across the country without sleeping for two days. They can make more money the faster they reach their destination. Dig?"

"Cool, man. Right on."

We left Provo and headed North to Salt Lake City and then due West. We'd be in San Francisco by tomorrow night.

Charlie and I gabbed all the way. He pointed out places of interest. Each place had a story. And each story was more interesting than the last. I now knew my roll in this. I knew why he picked me up. Charlie was lonely and wanted someone to talk to. I was along to listen. And listen I did. He was a travelogue of knowledge. He'd been everywhere in the lower forty eight states. When I mentioned I was born and raised in northern Wisconsin and in particular Rice Lake, he knew that area as well. He spoke with authority about runs to Duluth and back to Chicago naming each town on the way!

Across the great salt flats of western Utah. Flatter than a pancake as they say.

"This is where they have those super fast cars. Craig Breedlove drove a car like 300 mph. Imagine that! If I could drive that fast ..." he trailed off laughing.

Within a few hours we entered Nevada. Northern Nevada being very different than the lower half. Appeared to be more suitable to human habitation. More mountainous and I even spotted some green here and there. It was pretty. The sun had long since set but a twilight lingered into the evening.

I watched Charlie expertly grind through the gears as we rose and sank through this landscape. He was a man in his element. I envied him.

"There's a great truck stop outside of Reno. We'll stop there and gas up and eat."

So much of me wanted to confess to Charlie who and what I really was. I knew he'd understand. But, I just couldn't do that. I was Mark Cole on this trip. I was a student at Stout State in Wisconsin. Or was in the University of Wisconsin?

We talked and talked. I soon learned Charlie's life philosophy and he mine. The whites enabled us the energy and strength to keep going.

Charlie told me to help myself. He had a thousand of them in a jar. I emptied a pack of smokes and grabbed a hand full. I put them in the empty pack and stashed it in my pocket.

"They're cheap as hell. I get them for less than a penny a piece. All the truckers use 'em. Couldn't do my job without 'em."

"Thanks, man."

This guy was my savior.

We pulled into the truck stop. This place was huge. Must have been 100 trucks parked. The roar was deafening. It took a long time to fill up both tanks with diesel. I went to the bathroom and cleaned up some. Charlie met me at the front door of the restaurant. Charlie nodded to a couple of guys he knew. Friendly place. No one hardly noticed me. I looked like 'Joe College' and no one was going to mess with Charlie.

We found a booth. A waitress appeared.

"Hey, Doll Face. Miss me?"

"Charlie, you snake. Yes, I did miss you. Where have you been?"

"Here and there. I've got a quick run to Frisco and then LA. I'll catch you on the rebound."

"This is my friend Mark on his way to college."

We ordered steaks again and beers.

"Charlie, I never asked you and it's none of my business but, where do you live and do you have a family?"

"Ha, I live in my truck and the whole world is my family."

He had a bed in his rig. I had seen his 'room' when I stashed my stuff back there. I noticed loads of books. Charlie was smart and strong. He dressed with panache. I had a lot to learn. I wanted to be like Charlie. Not a truck driver but the kind of person who demanded and gave respect. He was honest and he never said a bad word about anyone. I need to be like him.

"Let's grab another beer and hi-tail it to Frisco."

Chapter 4

San Francisco

The traffic and energy picked up immediately as we crossed the state line into California. Charlie was an amazing driver. He talked to me and on his radio constantly. The man could perform several tasks simultaneously with artistry.

We flew through Sacramento and joined the pilgrimage of red lights into the City. Crossing the Bay Bridge viewing this gorgeous place filled me with melancholy. Charlie dropped me off near the waterfront. I grabbed my ruck sack. I looked at Charlie. He was smiling as usual.

"Thank you Charlie. You saved my life."

"Good luck to you Mark. Peace."

And that was that. I stepped out to the sidewalk and with a sadness watched Charlie drive off.

I called Brian and was relieved to find him home.

"Mark! Where are you?"

"On the corner of 2nd and Bryant. There's a bar on the corner. I'll wait outside."

"I'll be there in ten minutes."

"Brian! Am I glad to see you."

I had told Brian about my draft stuff and filled him in on my alias and the fact that I would be indicted soon. Since the first day I met Brian I knew I had a trusting friend.

"I moved to a new pad. I'm in the Mission District now. You'll love it."

Brian and several other people were renting a huge flat on Capp Street, a few blocks off Mission Street. There was plenty of room and two bathrooms.

"You're secret is safe with me."

"I know."

"I had to get out of Dodge. The heat was on. My attorney told me that I better split or I'd get picked up. They wanted to make an example out of me."

"Fuck, you have an attorney?"

"Yeah, sort of ... he's a friend of mine. He's still in law school."

"I was on TV and in all the local papers. I never wanted this much attention. But ..."

"You can hide out here. No one here will know. As far as they are concerned you're just a buddy from Minnesota. Which is what you are."

"Thanks man. Sorry 'bout not buying more dope but it just got too hot for me."

"Oh yeah, I know. Don't worry about that. Speaking of which ..."

Brian produced a joint and we slipped into a dream.

The whites had worn off after a few beers and smoke. I gratefully crashed in a back room.

Morning. Sun streaked through the stained windows. A neighborhood dog barked. I heard Spanish.

People in the kitchen.

"Hi, I'm Mark."

"There's toast and eggs. Coffee's on the stove," a voice stated.

"Thanks.'

"Brian's asleep. Help yourself."

"Thank you.'

Slow to wake up. Hung over from the long trip and last night. I checked my pocket. The cigarette pack intact. I dropped a white. I chewed on a piece of toast and drank the coffee. The eggs made me retch. I smoked my first cig and walked out to the back porch. An enclosed backyard pushed

against three story wooden buildings. The morning noise rising from behind walls. The distant roar of the City.

Senses becoming gradually acute. I had to call Mark. Wondering about
the mess back in Minnesota. Had I been indicted yet?

I walked around the neighborhood. Mexican music and food and Spanish. Several good and cheap restaurants. A wonderful place to hide out.

Found a phone booth and called Mark. I went through the usual procedures. I waited at a phone booth. The phone rang.

"What's going on."

"I'm in San Francisco. Things got too hot in Minnesota. I'll be indicted soon. Don't know when. What should I do?"

"Hang tight, Mark. Let's see how bad the Feds want you and then
we'll go from there. In the meantime give your lawyer a phone number
where he can call you. Okay?"

"Okay. Thanks man. Right on."

I needed to make sure it was okay to stay at Brian's. I hated to suddenly just drop in like this but he understood.

I walked downtown. There was a demonstration at the Civic center.
Country Joe and the Fish were playing on the back of a flat bed truck. It
was an anti-war demonstration. This one was pretty mellow. Several speakers got up and spoke. Then the band played;

> *"One ... two ... three ... four*
> *what are we fightin' for ..."*
> And.
> *"Give me an F*
> *give me a U*
> *give me a C*
> *give me a K*
> *what does that spell*
> *FUCK!"*

The word shouted out in public felt so liberating. The word fuck had
been compromised by Norman Mailer to 'fug' in one of his books. It was
the forbidden word. Saying it out loud or for that matter even thinking
about the word probably meant a sure sentence to Hell, at least. And here I
was shouting 'fuck' as loud as I could. It was therapeutic!

The crowd was chanting FUCK and laughing. Even the cops were
laughing. It was all in good fun. San Francisco was such a different scene
than Berkeley and Madison. The demonstrations there usually ended up
in violent riots with tear gas and crazed cops clubbing everybody in sight.
Burning cop cars.

It was a beautiful day. I walked to Market Street. I started to walk

toward the Bay. I made it all the way to Montgomery Street and then headed to North Beach. Got to Columbus and Broadway. Looked around City
Lights bookstore. Bought a couple of Kerouac books, *Satori in Paris* and
Desolate Angels, and *Naked Lunch* by William Burroughs. Walked across
the alley to Vesuvio's and had a beer. This was the life. I began to read but
found myself people watching more than I could concentrate.

I was learning certain areas of the City. I felt confident that I could
walk back to Brian's on Capp Street.

Brian was home from work.

"Hey, Brian. Can we talk a sec?"

"Yeah, sure. What's up?"

"I was wondering if I could stay here for a couple of weeks. I can pay
some rent and chip in for food and stuff. If it isn't cool just say so. It's
cool."

"Of course you can stay. My roomies are cool. We all work during the
day so you won't be bothering anybody. I'll fix up that back closet so you
can sleep there. Don't worry about the rent. This whole place only costs
$75 a month. That's why we live here. The landlord is totally cool. He gave
us a deal because we're in the process of fixing up the building. In fact, can
you paint? He needs a painter. You could work here, Mark. I'll call him
tonight."

"That would be perfect. The last thing I want is to be in the way. You
know."

"Let's go out and eat. I know a cheap Mexican place that's really
good."

"Sounds good to me."

We walked to 19th and Mission. We snacked on salsa and chips while
we waited for our order. Mexican torch songs serenaded us from the jukebox.

"This neighborhood is a mix of South American and Mexican people.
Most are Mexican and probably illegals. I've met people from Argentina
and Peru. And Central America. You know the politics down there are really fucked up. Dictators and such. This must seem like the promised land
to them. So, most of these people walk on the safe side and don't want any
trouble."

"This could be a great place to hide. But, I've got a lot to do. You
remember Mark from Berkeley, right? Well, He's got stuff for me to do.
Now, Brian. I know that you know, but I just have to say it. You've got to
be cool with me. You know that my real name isn't Mark but you have to
always call me Mark. And please don't ever tell anyone, not anyone, that
I'm a draft resister and am underground and shit. I don't want to jeopardize
you so when I just show up like this. Well, that's the way it has to be. I hate
to sound paranoid but, fuck it, man, I am!"

"Don't worry man. You're secret is good with me."

"Let's get some more beer and go to my place and smoke some shit!"

"Good idea, Ollie!" in my best Laurel and Hardy impersonation.

The next day I met Brian's landlord.

"I hear you can paint."

"Yeah, a little."

"I want to start on the outside of the building. I've got scaffolding and all the equipment. We have to scrape the old paint off first and then it has to be sanded and prepped and then primed and finally the top coat. Are you up to that, Mark?"

"Sure."

"I can pay $3.50 an hour. Is that all right?"

"Sure is."

There were six of us scraping the two story structure. It was slow going. The six of us didn't even finish the back of the building on the first day. At this rate it would take us two weeks just to scrape it. A sand blaster would be faster but there were neighbors close by. There was maybe two feet of space on the sides of the building. Too close for sand blasting anyway.

Since I 'lived' here I figured I could easily put in ten hour days. My arms and shoulders ached and I was covered with dust. I wore a bandana over my face to keep the dust out of my lungs.

The sides of the building weren't too hard to scrape because the sun never hit here. A couple of guys used sanders to finish the rear of the house. It was surprising how in only a few days we were ready to prime the house. Mr. Eddy (the landlord) wanted to paint the building in one day, if possible.

We used these large brushes. Again, spraying was out of the question. A slight breeze would cover the neighbor's house as well. Mr. Eddy made a bunch of small repairs. He fixed the eaves and replaced a couple of windows. We used a grey primer and the six of us did finish in one long 12 hour day.

This was really going to help. I had already accumulated over $200 and counting. I could give Brian some dough and pay my own way.

Brian got home from work and admired our work.

"Looks great! Suppose now you're going to raise the rent," he chided Mr. Eddy.

"Hey, that's a good idea," he retorted.

The front porch was wet so we used a rarely used side door to get in. The other tenants upstairs had to come through our place to get upstairs. It was pretty funny for a couple of days.

Mr. Eddy wanted to clean up and paint the inside as well.

"Any ideas on how we'd do this?" I asked.

"One room at a time. We move a tenant out for a day and we do all the repairs, scrape the walls, prime it, and do the finish the next day. I want to do the floors too."

"Oh. I know, the upstairs people can move all their shit to the basement and sleep wherever. We could finish it in five days!" Brian suggested.

"It takes at least that long to do the floors. But, let's hold a house meeting and work this out," said Mr. Eddy.

And that's what we did. Everyone cooperated in the project. We had a crew that cleaned out the basement. We put plastic sheets down there to protect everyone's stuff. The house was a hubbub for the next three weeks.

The outside of the house was gorgeous. Done in a grey with magenta trim. All the windows worked again. The front stairs sturdy and safe. A sense of pride overtook all of us.

Even the neighbors commented.

Mr. Eddy showed me how to refinish hardwood floors. First, you apply a very caustic varnish/paint remover. Second, you use a putty knife to peel up the varnish. Third, you sand the floor with a big floor sander and do the corners by hand. Fourth, you apply a sealer. And lastly, you paint several coats of varnish, lightly sanding after each coat. Three coats should do it.

It took us a month to finish the project. It looked like a new house! Mr. Eddy paid us. I had almost $500 now. That should keep me going for the next several months.

Word finally came down that I had been indicted in Minnesota. Apparently, the FBI and local cops hassled all my friends and Emil as well as my grandparents and parents back in Pittsburgh. They didn't know where I was.

I got a hold of Mark. He wanted to see me.

The next day I trekked over to Berkeley to see Mark.

"Man, are you hot!"

"What do you mean?"

"Half the cops in Minnesota are looking for you. You're name and picture have been in the paper and on TV. I think you should hide out for a while. I can put you in Northern California in a monastery, of all places, or New Mexico."

"A monastery?"

"Yep."

"Hmmm. What's in New Mexico?"

"Some friends of mine live on a commune. A hippie commune."

"That doesn't sound too good to me."

"I'll take the monastery."

"OK. Go back to San Francisco. Tell Brian you're hot and are leaving. He'll understand. Grab your stuff and I'll be in touch. I'll fill you in later. But, I think you'll like it up there. A bunch of World War Two nuns from

Belgium run the place. The older ones actually worked in the Resistance against the Nazis. I've met a couple of them and they are really cool and you'll be safe. They don't like the war either and are on our side."

Mark and I hugged.

I didn't want to leave the City.

"Hey Brian. I'm buying. Let's go eat and have some beers. I've got to talk to you."

"Yeah sure. Let me clean up first."

We settled into a booth at a pizza joint.

"I saw Mark today. I've gotta leave. Seems that I was indicted and the heat is on. Mark's going to let me know when I leave. I can't tell you where I'm going but it's some place in Arizona. That's all I know," I had to lie to him but it was for the best.

"That's a drag, man. Don't worry. I won't tell anyone."

"I know you won't."

Chapter 5

The Monastery

I hated to leave the sanctuary of Capp Street. I headed over to meet with Mark in Berkeley.

"Barry is going to drive you up to the monastery. He should be here in a while. In the meantime, here is an address that you can communicate with me. I'll send you letters if needed."

Barry showed up.

"Hey, man. How are ya' doin'?"

"Nice to meet you."

"We're in luck. My dad bought me a brand new VW. So, we'll have to walk over to the dealership and pick it up."

I hugged Mark goodbye. Barry and I walked several blocks and crossed the freeway to the VW dealership. I had my ruck sack slung over my shoulders. It seemed heavy. Soon enough we approached the lot. Barry shook hands with a guy. The car was ready. A brand new yellow bug. It was beautiful! It had 4 miles on the odometer.

"Hop in, Mark."

The car had this 'new' smell to it. Barry fiddled with the mirror and moved his seat to fit his large torso. He put sun glasses on and pulled his hair back in a pony tail.

"Jeez, I've never been in a new car before. This is great," I declared.

"Me either. Ready?"

"Ready!"

"You know where this place is?"

"Oh yeah. But first we're going to stop at my friends place up in Mendocino County for the night."

The car performed perfectly. We both smoked so we dutifully broke in the new ash tray. The radio worked. Everything worked!

"My dad promised to get me a new VW if I graduated. I graduated from Cal and am now trying to get into grad school. I'm interested in English Lit."

"Oh yeah! That was my major. I didn't graduate though."

We talked literature and great writings. We had a lot in common. We both agreed that the Beats were very interesting as a literary movement. Especially Kerouac and Ginsberg. I told him all the stories about my family having all these books and how I'd read *Catcher in the Rye* and others even though the Catholic Church had banned them. Barry nodded and laughed knowingly. He was from Berkeley and both his parents taught at Cal. He was blessed. Born into an academic liberal family, he possessed an automatic 'pass, go to the top,' skip the draft and become an academic.

Nonetheless, Barry's heart was in the right place. We talked about Mario Savio and the Free Speech Movement and about the student that had been shot and killed by the Berkeley police, about the Black Panthers and Huey and Bobby and the fledgling Women's Movement and of course the ongoing Anti-War and Peace Movements. Barry really knew his stuff. I guess it helped by being in Berkeley, the hub of the student protest movements.

Northern California is one of the most beautiful areas in the world. Even from the manicured landscape of the freeway, one is amidst the Redwoods and Sequoia's and the rolling hills. It takes your breath away.

Barry drove his new car with care. Eventually, he had a few hundred miles accumulated. He mentioned that he'd have to change the oil at 3,000 miles but he thought he should do it sooner. He truly loved this car. I was extra cautious not to scratch or otherwise mar his trophy.

He had some friends in Mendocino County. He wanted to show off his new car. We pulled off the freeway and drove deep into the forest. It was gorgeous. I've never seen trees like this before. They touched the sky.

We came to a dirt road. I don't think the sun ever reached the ground here. The dampness found your bones. I was feeling claustrophobic. We reached our destination and were greeted by a goat and two barking dogs. John and Samantha stepped out. They warmly hugged Barry and I was introduced. They marveled at Barry's new car. The bright yellow in stark contrast to the deep green forest.

John and Samantha were part of an exodus from the Haight-Asbury to the country. A back-to-nature hippie fad. They had a garden, carefully fenced in to protect the crop from deer. They also had the strongest pot I'd ever smoked. It was too strong. After a few puffs I couldn't hardly move or talk. John played some music on his stereo.

We ate some 'organic' food which tasted like dirt. I craved a Snickers and some beer. They didn't smoke either so I stepped outside to smoke a cig. I knew I had to be more tolerant but I was scared to death and lonely and so unsure of my future. I wondered about what was going on back in Winona. Was Emil being hassled? I'm sure he was. My parents and siblings and grandparents. I wanted my own life. I wasn't comfortable being in the hands of strangers, even though I trusted them implicitly, I wanted my own freedom to make my own decisions.

I could hear the wind ruffle the tree tops. So high. Must be hundreds of feet. I wanted to sit on top of that tree like when I was a kid and be in my own little world.

After we'd eaten and smoked more pot, John showed me a space where I could sleep. I was tired. All the travel and worrying had worn on me.

I was awakened to loud yelling and shouting. It was light. Early morning. I put my pants on and ran to the noise. I stood on the front porch. What I saw shocked me.

Barry's brand new VW was demolished ... the roof was caved in, the doors and all the paneling dented. The car looked like it had been rolled over several times.

John was screaming at his billy goat and hitting it in the head with a baseball bat. The goat stubbornly holding his ground. 'Whack.' The goat didn't budge an inch.

Barry looked forlorn. His new VW smashed up like that.

Apparently, the goat didn't like the new yellow object in his territory and attacked it. It looked like the dumb animal had stood on top of the car and jumped up and down. The roof was severely caved in. I didn't even know if he could drive it like that. The inside of the car was undamaged. I have no doubt that if the goat could have opened the door he would have eaten the seats.

Well, that sure put a damper on things. John was apologizing to Barry and Barry was in shock. The car didn't have 300 miles on it.

I thought John was going to shoot the goat. Finally, he stopped hitting it with the bat and the goat walked away. I didn't realize how hard their heads were.

I told Barry not to worry about me. I'd find a way to the monastery somehow.

"No man, I'll get you there. The car is drivable. Just looks like shit. Fuckin' goat."

Samantha looked forlorn as she prepared some breakfast for us even though I don't think anyone was hungry.

We smoked some dope and sat on the front porch. Finally, Barry started to giggle. Then we all did. After all, it was pretty funny.

Barry and I had planned to leave first thing today. We pounded out some of the roof so that we could at least sit up without hitting our heads.

"Fuckin' goat."

Eventually Barry and I were ready to roll. John and Samantha looked despondent but Barry cheered them up.

"Don't worry, I've got insurance!"

"My dad is gonna shit," Barry said as we drove out the dirt road.

We had a few hours before we reached the monastery. Barry and I just shook our heads. It was a miracle that the windows were not broken. The car drove just fine. We got a couple of looks from other cars as they passed us.

We drove into the small town of Garberville. "Just a few more miles, you're gonna love this place Mark. The people are super nice and you'll be comfortable."

We were deep in Redwood country. The trees. It was beautiful and scary. It made me feel small and insignificant. How could trees grow to such heights?

"Barry, you've been a saint. How can I ever repay you? I'm so sorry about your car ..."

"It's only a car, man. It can be fixed ..."

"I mean it, man. Thank you."

We approached the monastery. I had envisioned an ancient castle like structure high in the mountains like a Tibetan retreat but this was different. Modern squared shaped cottages with a main building and something that must have been the chapel.

We got out of the car. A woman walked out.

"Hello Barry," in a thick French accent.

"Sister Ambrose. So good to see you."

"What happened to the car?"

"Long story, Sister. Sister Ambrose, this is Mark."

"Pleased to meet you."

"Well, I've heard about you. Seems that you caused quite a commotion! Ha ha. Welcome, my son."

"This is Sister Ann and Father Roger. Please come into my office. Would you care for coffee or tea. Have a seat everyone. Barry, I know you have to leave, can you stay for a while?"

"Of course."

"I am Sister Ambrose. I survived World War Two working in the Belgium underground fighting the Nazis. Our order is against all wars and we consider you a hero for resisting the draft and refusing to fight in this unjust war. You will be safe here. The only people who will know your true identity are in this room."

"We have some rules which must be followed. We have taken a vow of silence. We do not speak unless necessary except at dinner and daily Mass. You are welcome to attend Mass if you choose. We do not force our beliefs on visitors. You will be required to work for your food and lodging. Brother John will show you."

"For now Sister Ann will show you your quarters. I know you must have questions and they will be answered. We welcome you Mark."

Sister Ambrose was a short woman with sharp black eyes. She wore a work shirt and jeans. None of the clergy wore any of the robes associated with being in the clergy.

The grounds were immense. A larger area, probably several acres, had been cleared for buildings, many still under construction. Sister Ann led me to a small cottage. It was sparse but very clean and smelled of fresh wood. There was a living room, a small kitchen with a fridge and a bathroom. It had two bedrooms. A dresser and small bed filled each. It was home. I was living alone.

Sister Ann told me that dinner was at 6. She seemed really nice. Barry came in and sat with me.

"I gotta go, dude."

"Thanks for everything, man, Sorry about your car."

"Oh yeah, ha, what a mess. I'll get it repaired in no time. Don't worry about it. Take care, Mark. See ya."

We hugged.

And with that Barry drove off. I unpacked my things. I noticed no ash trays so I smoked outside. The vastness. The soaring redwoods. There was a swish sound from the wind. I heard a stream nearby and walked to it. I noticed salmon by the dozens in the stream. Some of the fish had their flesh dripping off them. Several of the fish were laying on their side, dead.
I watched in wonder as one fish would wiggle and release a white cloud among some stones. These salmon had somehow returned to the place they were first born and returned from the sea to spawn. The wonders of nature. Thankfully, I had studied and learned their behavior in biology class at St. Mary's a few years ago. And now I was witnessing this with my own eyes. How fortunate!

I had no watch to tell time. No TV to watch the news.

I walked around the grounds. Quite spacious. I heard someone chopping wood in the distance. The sound echoing.

I felt so alone!

We had dinner at 6 p.m. sharp. Most of the food was grown at the monastery. They had a greenhouse built to grow vegetables. They baked all their own bread and cakes. A local farmer supplied milk and eggs.

I met the rest of the people here. I was introduced as Mark. I counted fifteen nuns and two men plus three guests. We were allowed to talk at dinner. After grace we passed the food around. It was vegetarian except for the diary products.

After dinner I met Brother John who I would be working with. He was built like a Marine. Strong and reserved. He was deeply tanned. It was his wood chopping I had heard this afternoon. I was to meet him tomorrow morning at 8. I was required to do chores. That was fine with me. I needed something to do. One of the nuns showed me the chapel. There was a morning Mass at 6 a.m. every day. She also showed me a well-stocked library. I noticed several newspapers. I would have reading material.

After dinner I walked to the library and borrowed a few books.

I retired to my cottage. I was going to inquire about having coffee and a coffee maker. I didn't think I could have beer but It would be nice to have cokes and snacks. I remembered a small town about three miles from here. I thought maybe I could buy smokes and snacks there.

The night sounds were impressive. Owls hooted and coyotes howled. I didn't sleep real well. I was afraid to go outside but I did as I smoked and thought of my predicament.

Morning came too soon. I met Brother John as planned. I started to speak and he shushed me. Oops. Sorry. I forgot.

We walked to an area covered with brush and small trees. He gave me a pair of clippers and showed me how he wanted the brush cut. I presumed that he wanted to clear the area. It was very strange to work without speaking.

He was very strong and persistent. I needed to stop frequently to catch my breath. Brother John brought water with him and offered me some.

We worked for a couple of hours then took a break. Not a word spoken.

Back to work until we broke for lunch. We walked back to the main area and had sandwiches and milk and juice. I had missed breakfast. Again, no one spoke.

After eating we trekked back to our work area and worked until 5.

Dinner was at 6 so I went to my cottage and showered. I found out that a washing machine and dryer were in the main building and I could wash my clothes there.

I had everything I needed but was afraid of going crazy without real human contact. I didn't have to work on weekends and found out that we were only three miles from the ocean.

After dinner I walked to the stream, it was the Mattole River, and watched the salmon. It was so sad. The males dumping sperm over the eggs and burying it with their tails. Exhausted and near death, mouths slowly opening and closing, gulping their last breaths, having fulfilled their destiny, dying.

Summer was upon us and the sun was setting later. Huge shadows cast by the towering redwoods. I planned to explore the area this weekend.

I tried to make friendships with the other guests but they were here on a religious pilgrimage and I sensed didn't want to be bothered. I was pretty much alone. The other sisters knew not to ask me too many questions. I wasn't too keen on telling my life story over dinner with twenty strangers.

I watched the fish and listened to the sweet sound of the brook. I walked back to the cottage and read. I wanted a beer. Oh well. I would need smokes in a couple of days too.

Slowly and gradually the cultural shock wore off and I adapted to the silence and the regimen. I even attended a couple of Masses. More for the company and to hear voices.

Brother John and I worked together every day. Every day was the same, except the pile of brush and tree stumps changed. I noticed that my appetite was increasing and that I was developing a physique again. I stopped smoking and began jogging. I was in shape. Two months of this and I felt strong.

I also immersed myself into the writings of Thomas Merton, a Trappist monk who wrote about pacifism and social justice. He was a mystic and difficult, at first, to understand. The library had several of his books. Since I was a bit of a monk myself I felt a kinship.

I still had this inner rage. I could sense it. I wanted so much to purge myself of hate and anger. Sitting by the brook often calmed me. The quiet gurgling soothed me. The fish put on a show.

Over the ensuing few weeks several visitors came and left. Sister Ambrose informed me one night at dinner that in a week or so they were expecting several guests and that I would be sharing my room. I was actually happy to hear that. Someone to talk too.

Once a month visitors were allowed to visit the monastery. The vow of silence was exempted for the day. A few of the sisters were American and their parents came to see them. Since I was a 'permanent' resident I was included in the festivities. We were allowed to have beer! Boy, did that taste good. Hadn't had one in a couple of months. I was envious in a way. I wondered how my parents and grandparents must be doing. They must be worried about me. Somehow I had to get a letter to them and let them know I was okay.

Sure enough, the next week a load of people showed up.

I watched the people pile in and unload their luggage. I wondered which one would be my roommate. As I watched, it was just like a busy hotel. A limousine pulled up. A driver scurried to the back door and opened it. Out stepped a dark skinned man dressed in black and red. Was he a Bishop? He acted holy. He looked no one in the eye. He waited for people to escort him into the main building. The limo drove off.

The show was over. I walked back to my cottage and read. A knock at the door. One of the sisters was at my door with the limo man. I let them in.

"Excuse me, Mark. This is your roommate for two weeks. Cardinal, I'm sorry I can't pronounce your name, please forgive me."

"I am Cardinal, shall I say my name, no, it is too long, I'm from Bombay."

"Please come in."

I had been used to being alone. I looked forward to having a roomie. But a fucking Cardinal! Holy Shit.

"How do I address you, Cardinal? Okay? I'm Mark. Just plain old Mark," I laughed.

"You may call me 'Your Eminence'."

I showed the Cardinal his room and the bathroom. He was still dressed in his amazing attire. Little red shoes and a red cap and the most elegant robes, black and scarlet or I guess the color cardinal. He went to his room, shut the door and all was quiet.

I felt invaded. I went for a walk. Luckily tomorrow was a work day. I could keep myself busy with silent John.

I walked to the library and curled up with a book.

I considered leaving. I wasn't sure how long 'His Fucking Eminence' would stay. Maybe he would move when most of the other visitors left. Some of the people were to leave in a week. In the meantime ...

When I returned 'His Eminence' was sitting in the living room. He had removed his robes and was garbed in jeans and a tee shirt.

"Mark, I'm afraid I made a poor impression on you. Call me Val. I'm so used to being treated like a king. I'm supposed to be a servant of Christ and humble. You seem like a decent chap."

He spoke in an English accent.

"Oh, that's okay Val. I was quite taken when you arrived. Most of the visitors here seem like pilgrims, you know, very humble and stuff. What brings you here Val?"

"I needed a vacation and a friend of mine mentioned the Redwoods Monastery as a perfect retreat."

"What brings you here?" Val asked.

What could I say.

"A religious retreat," I lied.

"I've fallen out of faith and I wanted to get back in touch with the doctrines of the Church," I better stop while I'm ahead.

"Is this your first visit to the States." I changed the subject.

"Yes, it is. I spent some time in LA and then I travelled up here. It's a vast country but not as large as India."

Our cultures were so different.

Val walked with me around the grounds and I told him about the salmon stream. I thought he might enjoy that. He seemed like a nice guy after all.

We joined the others for dinner. Our little group had grown to about fifty people. It was nice to hear the chatter of happy people. Tomorrow was Sunday and the chapel would be overflowing!

I stayed on to help clean up. I enjoyed washing dishes. We didn't have a dishwasher. So we did it by hand. Because of the extra dishes, instead of fifteen minutes of clean-up it took us half an hour. With the kitchen cleaned up and shiny again, I walked back to the cottage.

"Hi, Mark."

"Hey, Val. Did you enjoy your meal? We don't eat very elaborate meals but the food is great and there always seems to be plenty to go around. We bake all our own bread and cakes and pies and we eat healthy ... are you saying Mass tomorrow?"

"Yes, I am."

"I'd like to attend."

Val continued reading and writing at the desk and I went for a long walk. The sun had gone down and night descended. I brought a flash light with me. As I shined the light across the open field I could see yellow eyes staring back. Probably deer, I thought. Maybe coyotes. No, it was a mountain lion!

When I returned Val had gone to sleep. I read for a while and slept as well.

I sat in the back of the chapel. The visitors filled the small room. The Cardinal gave Mass. It was a good show. Lots of pomp.

I headed for breakfast. Pancakes and juice and coffee. I ate and waited for the guests to finish. I helped clean the cafeteria.

I took a long walk. Watched the fish and read Merton. I was still torn between either a violent or non-violent reaction to the war. On one hand it seemed practical to resist the war machine with violence simply because that was how the cops reacted. But, non-violence spoke volumes. The cops looked ridiculous stomping non-violent people. In the long run perhaps this would sway public opinion to our way of thinking. I was for the best and quickest solution to ending the war. I didn't really care how it was achieved.

Merton, Ghandi, and Martin Luther King were pacifists. The Weathermen weren't. Mark had told me about them on my last visit. It seems that a faction of the SDS had broken off from the main body and formed this group. They believed in the violent overthrow of the government. It seemed so idealistic to me. Like the tee shirts with Che printed on them. Far removed from getting your ass shot or spending your days in jail.

I had attempted to read Marx and Stalin and Mao and Trotsky. Trotsky seemed to make the most sense because, it seemed to me, he pulled for the common man and wasn't an elitist. I, frankly, didn't understand Marx or Mao.

I don't know shit. I'll just make up my own mind.

Merton did interest me, however.

Most of the guests would be leaving tonight and tomorrow. There was hope that I would have the cottage to myself. Val wasn't back from chapel when I returned. I laid down to read and took a nap.

Since it was Sunday the vows of silence were relaxed. I walked into the cafeteria and made some coffee. Brother John was there. He said we had some heavy work tomorrow.

I walked to the brook and watched the fish. So sad and beautiful. The cycle of life played out.

I was bored today. I wanted to get back to Berkeley. I'd been here several months but it seemed much longer than that. The people here were saintly and kind. I didn't deserve them. I wanted to get high and laid. I desperately wanted a cigarette.

I wrote a long rambling letter to my parents expressing my love for them and trying to explain why I did what I did. I wasn't even sure how I'd mail it but I wrote it anyway. I used to write to my grandma every month. She must be worried sick. I wrote a letter to her also. I'd mail them as soon as I left here. I was certain the FBI was watching their mail. Fuckers. A guy goes and kills people and he's a hero while they want to put me in jail. Doesn't make a lick of sense.

Back at the cottage. Val was there. We talked briefly. He said he was going to move to his own cottage in the morning. He was a very nice man. But it would be nice to have the place to myself again.

I was restless. I walked into the redwoods. It was very easy to walk among these giants. Because the sun didn't reach the ground, nothing much grew. I wandered deeper and deeper. I found a tree with Russian carved into the trunk. The Russians had been here in the 1880's. They left some Russian Boar behind. I followed a path for an hour and lo and behold there was the ocean! I walked down to the coast. Stacks of washed up drift wood in a random majestic array!

Storm clouds gathered to the west. I should get back. I didn't tell a soul where I was going. I climbed the steep cliff. I saw where the Mattole met the ocean. I didn't notice any salmon. How in the hell do they get up that river? Amazing!

It was getting very cold and dark. I reentered the forest. It was like night in here. I knew I could find my way back. And I did. The temperature must have dropped twenty degrees and it started to rain. And rain. Snow flakes appeared. Suddenly, we were in a blizzard. I made it back to the cottage just in time. It was a wet snow. Couldn't hardly see across the field. Val was pretty excited because he had never seen snow before. I showed him how to make a snowball. If more snow fell I'd show him how to make a snowman. Luckily, we had heat and safety. Man, that storm came out of nowhere. Without a TV or radio I had no idea what was going on in the outside world, much less the weather.

I fell asleep reading. I awoke in the middle of the night. Loud 'cracks' pierced the night. It was still snowing. By now, several inches had fallen. The sounds of breaking limbs were frequent. The redwood trees could not hold the weight of the heavy snow. Huge limbs broke off and fell to earth. Some of them twenty feet long and stuck deep into the ground. The locals called these broken off branches 'widow makers.'

Val woke up too. The noise was very loud and eerie.

"You'll have some good stories to tell when you return to India."

"Indeed."

The snow continued to fall and so did the redwood branches.

Brother John had told me that only two things can kill a redwood; snow, if enough limbs broke off. And cutting a deep ring around the trunk which would cut off the nutrients and water. He said the underbrush was too damp to burn. I believed him.

Well, no one could leave until the snow melted. Brother John and I shoveled the sidewalks. It was a heavy moist snow. This snow would melt in a day or two and then things would return to normal. I liked how the snow muffled the sounds.

"Hey Val, come on outside. We're going to make a snowman."

I waited until he appeared in the doorway. I threw a snow ball at him. He cowered in fear. I threw another one. When he realized it was me he laughed and attempted to make one too. He had never been in snow before. I had him on the run. He was laughing really hard.

"Here man, you have to grab the snow in your hands and then bunch it up like this."

"Like this?" as he hurled one at me.

"Yup."

This place needed some fun.

"We're going to make a snowman. First you roll up a ball like this. Here, help me. The bottom one has to be the biggest ball."

We rolled a big ball.

"Leave it here. Now, we're going to roll another ball, but not as large as the bottom one. Then, you're going to help me, we lift the second ball onto the bottom one. Finally, we're going to roll the head. I'll show you."

Val was mesmerized.

"If God created man, then we are creating 'Frosty the Snowman'," I joked.

He looked at me like I'd blasphemed but immediately broke out in laughter.

"Or maybe we'll make him a priest," I chuckled.

We finished rolling the final two balls. Now, the snowman had a base and a body and a head.

I showed Val how to use branches for arms and two stones for eyes and little stones to make a smiling mouth. We needed a hat so I grabbed one of mine. Val said "No, no" and he put his Cardinal's cap on it.

Perfecto!

"Cardinal Frosty," I exclaimed.

We had to show the others.

They approved. They made their own snow men too but 'Cardinal Frosty' took the prize.

Val and I settled into our cottage and we began a most interesting conversation on what was prayer and what it meant. Val had really opened up in the last couple of days and especially after building the snowman.

I asked what he prayed for and to whom. He said he prayed to the 'Heavenly Father' each day for forgiveness.

"Who is the 'Heavenly Father'?"

"God."

"And forgiveness for what? You're a Cardinal, you don't sin!"

"Yes, I do."

"Val, I don't know if there is a God like we think him or even her to be. I just don't know. I do believe that there is a Supreme Being or Entity or something. All of this," waving my hands, "couldn't just be an accident or some random coincidence or maybe it is. I just don't know. Does that make me a bad person? I pray for peace. I pray for my friends. I was raised on guilt and shame and I feel bad about myself all the time but at least I realize that and I'm praying that I can grow beyond that. I pray for love in the world."

"I pray for my people. As you know, India is a very complex land. Very many societies within one. My flock represents only one faction of this huge land. Poverty and disease are prevalent. My religion can only hope to raise the spiritual souls of the believers. It is a most difficult area in this world. God has chosen me to lead these people. I am at once humbled and challenged. I ask God that I can fulfill my responsibilities."

Listening to Val pour his heart out, I gained a new respect for him. I realized that he really believed. That was more than I could say. I was full of doubts.

The snow melted over the following days. 'Cardinal Frosty' drooped and sagged. Eventually most of the visitors left and sadly Val moved to his own cottage.

I had my privacy back again. I missed the company but did enjoy my privacy.

Life returned to normal. I worked with Brother John most days. Long silent grueling days. We worked really hard. I chopped wood most days. My body was responding. I had muscles and my strength returned to full power.

Another month or so passed. I hadn't heard a word from Mark or from anyone from the outside world in several months. I hadn't forgotten my role though. I immersed myself in the readings of Thomas Merton. I bought into his theory of pacifism in an ideal world but we didn't live in a perfect world. We lived in a very violent world full of deceptive, greedy, and hateful people.

Another month passed. Time seemed to stand still here at the monastery. I hadn't received any outside news of any relevance in some time. Eventually, curiosity would get the best of me. There was no TV nor any current newspapers and no radio. The sisters were so kind and understanding I think they sensed my edginess and frustration. I needed to get a hold of Mark.

I would need to walk to Garberville some several miles away and phone him. I didn't want to call him from the monastery. Too risky.

Another 'family' weekend was coming up. Val had since left. There were a couple of visitors but I paid no attention to them. I continued to work with Brother John most days. I was a model of fitness and health.

Family members for some of the sisters began arriving Friday evening. The American sisters could invite their families a few times a year for a weekend visit. All vows of silence were suspended.

I was in the dining room that night and one of the sisters introduced me to her parents. "This is Mark, he's a 'draft resister!'"

Just like that! I thought no one except the three knew about me. Evidently they all knew. I was as gracious as I could be hiding my shock and alarm like some great actor.

After dinner I walked over to Sister Ambrose.

"I have to see you immediately," I said in a hushed tone.

We walked to her office. "Sister Katherine introduced me to her parents and told them I was a draft resister. Sister, I thought no one else knew. I have to leave," I was agitated.

"Oh, it's my fault. I told a couple of the other sisters and they must have ... oh, I'm so sorry."

"I have to leave immediately. Tonight if I can. Can someone drive me to Garberville so I can hitch hike?"

"Oh, Mark, I'm so sorry," she began to sob.

"Please don't cry. It isn't your fault. You have been so kind and generous to me. I shall never forget."

"I'm going to pack my things."

I was ready in a few minutes. Sister Ambrose knocked on my door.

"I'll make it up to you. Sister Mary will drive you to Berkeley. It's the least we can do."

"Oh, thank you."

I wanted to say goodbye to everyone. Hugs all around. I'll miss Brother John and Sister Ambrose and those wonderful moments with the Cardinal. I'll miss the salmon and the walks through the majestic redwoods. I'll miss seeing a mountain lion one night. I'll miss this holy place that gave me shelter.

Chapter 6

Babylon Jungle

Sister Mary, dressed in jeans and long blonde hair pulled back in a pony tail, was a beautiful woman. We had time to talk as she drove to Berkeley.

"If you don't mind me asking. You are so pretty. Why are you a nun?"

"That's okay. You're not the first to ask. I had a calling as they say. I wanted more out of life than to be a housewife and stuff. I wanted some spirituality in my life. I was raised in a strict Catholic family in Boston. A large Irish family. The boys were always bothering me in high school. I went to college, a private girl's school, St. Catherine's in St. Paul ..."

"No ... that's where my mom went. What a coincidence. Did you really. No kidding. Wow!"

"She did? When?"

"I think she graduated in 1945 or so. Not sure what year."

"Wow is right. Small world. Anyway, I had such a great experience there. I found my calling. Maybe someday I'll change my vows. I don't know. For now it seems right. I want to teach. So, I'm planning on leaving the monastery so I can teach. I only need a couple of credits to get my credential."

"Wow, I'm blown away. The same school as my mom ..." I trailed off. "And I went to St. Mary's in Winona. You must have heard of that school."

"Oh, yes. Of course. What are you doing now?"

"I'm a draft resister running from the FBI and the justice system. I sort of took to heart all the teachings of the Catholic Church but I must say that I've dropped out of the Church. I just can't be a part of their hypocrisy. I have to fight against this war and racism and sexism. I'm a dreamer, I guess, can't help it. I've probably ruined the rest of my life but I have to do this. I'm not a great person or anything like that, in fact, I'm a giant screw-up and a looser most of the time. Everybody in my family, except my grandma and my brother are against me. I feel so alone and scared but I'm stubborn, you know. Must be the Irish in me."

"Yeah," she laughed, "must be."

Sister Mary drove right into Berkeley and dropped me off on Telegraph Avenue.

I thanked her and wished her good luck.

Back in civilization. What a shock! The hustle and bustle the noise the traffic. First thing I did was buy a pack of smokes. Boy, did that taste good. The cigarette settled me down a bit. I had decided to call Brian in the City first.

I called his number from a phone booth. No answer. I thought it best to take a bus to the City. I didn't know if it was cool to get a hold of Mark yet.

I eventually arrived at Mission and 22nd streets and walked to Brian's place. I hoped he still lived here. I knocked on the door and a woman opened the door.

"Is Brian here?"

"He's still at work."

"When will he be back? I'm a friend of his."

"He should be back soon, I guess."

"Cool. I'll check back later."

I walked to a nearby park and waited. I bought a newspaper on the way. I had a lot of catching up to do. The war was still raging and the Giants still sucked. I read Herb Caen and had a laugh. The City still hummed. I had to call Mark. I called his number and left the number of this pay phone. I waited. The phone rang.

"I'm back in the City."

"Why? What happened?"

I told him everything. He filled me in on my status. The Feds had hassled my parents and family members as expected and had put the fear of God in my friends in Winona, but it seemed that I was safe here and in Berkeley.

We made plans to meet in a couple of days.

"I've got something for you."

That could only mean one thing. I had a delivery to make. It felt good to be back in action again.

Brian was home when I returned.

"Dude, Marsha said that some guy had come by looking for me. I guessed it was you. What the fuck are you doing here? It's great to see you again, man. I've been concerned, you know."

"No, man. I've been fine. I had to leave where I was hiding. Have the Feds been here?"

"Nope."

"Cool."

"You know what I need? Beer, weed, and ass."

"Ha ha ... no problem with the first two. Let me get cleaned up and we'll go out."

I told Brian all about the monastery and the Cardinal and Brother John and the mountain lion and the snow ... everything.

We had smoked a joint on the way over and that with a couple of beers put us in a mellow mood.

"I'm going to meet with Mark tomorrow. He said he had something for me. I'm not sure what that means but it probably entails some travel."

"You look really healthy."

"I chopped wood and worked almost every day up there. I even quit smoking! But, here's the deal ... I have to find out if I can return to the Midwest again. I want to hear what happened in Winona and with my parents and grandparents. I'll get a hold of my lawyer in Minneapolis. He'll know. In the meantime, it seems that the Feds don't know about you or Mark and that's great. Let's keep it this way. You are a trusted friend Brian. You know the rules ... you can't tell anyone about me. It'll just get you in trouble and we don't want that."

"Hey, man. The Dead are playing at Winterland tonight. Let's go!"

"Now you're talking."

The line reached up the block and around the corner and then some. Joints and wine passed freely from person to person. Panhandlers looking for free ticket money. People singing their favorite Dead song. The doors finally opened and the line slowly moves. Most people are so stoned as they shuffle into the vast hall. Frisbies fly through the air. Bill Graham greets us at the door. Tickets cost $3.50. Brian and I wander in and walk around. What a great people watch! Seems that the entire youth movement is here. The strong scent of pot fills the auditorium. 'It's a Beautiful Day' takes the stage and plays a stirring set. Their hit song 'White Bird' demands an encore. 'Dan Hicks and His Hot Licks' follows. "How Can I miss You When You Won't Go away?' 'Quicksilver Messenger Service' kicks off the third set. They are a great San Francisco band lead by guitar play John Cipollina. They played until 11 p.m. A long break in between sets as the roadies set up the Dead's vast equipment.

Most people in here are tripping. Brian and I are drunk and stoned and having a blast. We moved up front so we could see the band. The Dead finally took the stage and immediately blew the roof off the place. They were the best 'live' band ever. Many other groups had better records but the Dead could flat out play! Watching and listening to Garcia I realized I had indeed returned to the Babylon Jungle and all of her entrapments. In the midst of a hippie stomp. Dancing, moving, feeling the energy of my people. All fear had evaporated in the din of Garcia's solos.

A naked Allen Ginsberg hugged and gyrated on Garcia's amp and danced suggestively. Members of the San Francisco Mime troupe transcended reality.

The line between audience and performers vanished. We became one, in unison in this great stomp.

Realizing that there was always this side of the youth movement; the dopers and hedonism which was a great escape from the realities of war and racism. Trying to weigh the two seemed an impossible task. On one hand they seemed like opposites, one selfish and the other selfless, one full of frolic and fun, the other full of danger and peril, one sober the other not, one side a polar opposite of the other, and yet joined at the hip somehow.

But, this sure was fun and I needed to blow off some steam after spending several months at the monastery.

Brian and I staggered out of Winterland with a couple of thousand other souls at 4 a.m. We began walking up Post Street and soon enough cut over to the Mission. We were at his house in half an hour. Too wired to sleep, we sat up and talked. He had a few beers in the fridge and they helped soothe our spirits.

What a great night!

"I fuckin' love the Dead, man. They're the greatest!" I said.

"Here's to the Dead.," we clinked beer bottles in a toast.

"You can sleep in your old closet, man."

I found a blanket and rolled up a towel for a pillow and was soon asleep. With St. Stephen rocking in my head.

Tortured by nightmares. *'Click ... clack ... clack... a sidewalk crack ... don't fall in ... don't fall in ... a tree ... a broken face ... screaming ... pain ... in pain ... darkness.'*

Woke late in the afternoon. What a night. I was hung over and felt pretty shitty. I managed a shower and that helped some. I was supposed to get in touch with Mark. I walked to Mission Street and found a phone booth and made the call and waited.

"Can I see you tomorrow?"

"No, make it the day after. I'll meet you at that cafe at 1 p.m. See you then. Are you okay?" he wondered.

"Yeah. Thanks, Mark. See you then."

I felt guilty for getting so fucked up last night. Fuck it! Mental health.

I needed that.

I walked around the Mission. I loved this place. Always smelling food. Burritos and tacos. My mouth watered. Latino colors. Bright reds and greens. Lovely dark friendly faces. Affordable clothes. Artwork. Salsa music. I know this place and I don't. Earthy scents and stores selling Mexican and South American wares. Not like Woolworth's in Rice Lake with expected goods. Unexpected items. Little artifacts of Mexican children and dogs, statues of Jesus and Mary and gauche colors and scents.

Discovering a new world.

Woke the next morning and made it to Berkeley. Mark was waiting for me in a corner booth.

"Hey Bro, how's it going?"

"I need some coffee," I said.

"What happened up there?"

"Once a month or so they had family day which meant that families could come to the monastery and visit with their daughters. There were several young American nuns at the monastery. Anyway, I was under the impression that only Sister Ambrose and Father Roger knew I was a draft resister."

"Well, a bunch of people were hanging out after Sunday Mass and I was introduced to one of the Sister's mom and dad and she mentioned to them that I was a draft resister. I tried to suppress my shock. I excused myself and went to Sister Ambrose who admitted to telling some of the other nuns about me and I guess they must have told the others."

"So, I made the decision to leave immediately. I thought it would be best, you know, like, I wouldn't have to worry if word got out and the somebody doing their civic duty would tell the cops. So, here I am."

"Wow. I'm bummed that they would talk like that. I thought I could trust them. Guess not. Anyhow, you look really healthy."

"Yeah, man, I worked hard every day ... chopping wood, cleaning out the cottages, painting. And I read a lot. Mostly Thomas Merton, of what I could understand. You know who he is. I feel really strong!"

"Good. That's good because I've got something for you. I want you to go to Tucson and then on to Austin, Texas. I've got a couple hundred bucks for you. Then, and here's the big one, I want you to go to Chicago. Remember the convention last year? Well, it seems that a bunch of SDS folks are organizing something called 'The Days of Rage.' Now, here's the deal, the FBI has infiltrated the SDS. I want you to find out who they are. You'll have to be cool, man, because everybody is paranoid so they all suspect newcomers to be FEDs. You're going to have help. You're going to meet Carol, she's a beautiful smart woman. You two are going to be lovers, at least to the outside world. I'll explain later. Two heads are better than one! And that trial is going on, The Chicago Eight. It' a zoo. You'll be snooping around that too but not too close because the FEDs are all over that thing. Carol will tell you everything when you get there. Paul in Chicago is expecting you and he'll handle your arrangements. Here is a new phone number to call me at. Only use it when you need too. Your ID's are good so continue to use them. Stay away from Winona and your family."

"I picked you Mike," he said, "because you are an honest, open-eyed wonderer, like me, who only wants peace and truth."

"Jeez, Mark, I hope I can live up to your expectations. All I got is common sense," I chuckled.

"I know. That's exactly what I'm talking about."

That was the gist of our conversation. Who was this guy, I often wondered. I put all my trust and faith in him. He was like a zephyr traveling unseen through an unseen American night landscape. A Spirit. A feeling. An entity. A mystery.

I'd be leaving in a couple of days for Tucson and then on to Texas. Mark had given me two neatly wrapped packages. One for each destination and the names and addresses for each. He had rides set up for me. This was like spy shit. I felt like 007 but was too much of a nerd to pull that off, besides, I never wanted to hurt anyone.

Brian and I had a long talk over several beers. We had become soul brothers. Joined at the hip by our love and faith in life and freedom.

"Hey, I got some bread. I want you to have a few bucks," I said.

"No, man, you need it. Keep it. I don't want it. I know you, man."

"Fuck you. Let's go out. I'm payin.' "

"Ok," Brian laughed and patted me on the back.

"Fuckin' Mick."

We both laughed.

After a few beers and bullshit we headed home. I had a long day tomorrow. I was supposed to meet a guy at the corner of Valencia and 24th at 10 a.m. He was driving a blue VW bug. Not another VW I thought.

"Hey, man get in. Name's Cliff. You're Mark, right?"

"Right. Glad to me you."

We shook on the awkward hippie revolutionary handshake. Not the straight forward kind but the sorta sideways thing that you lock thumbs and usually miss on the first attempt.

"Let's go to Tucson!" he announced.

Cliff had long straight blond hair and a thick beard. He was the epitome of a hippie. Wire rim glasses posed on his nose.

"Well, here we go. Back into the slush!" I thought aloud.

Cliff spoke in cliches. So, I'll always think of him as Cliche Cliff.

'Right Ons' and 'Far Outs' just poured out of the guy. And every other word was 'Like' or 'Man.'

Oh, Man.

"Hey, man, like I've got this killer weed. Wanna toke? It's far out, man."

"Man, like I know this chick, man. She's so far out, man."

It was like that all the way to Barstow.

It was far out.

It was late. Cliff said we'd stay at his friends' place.

There was a jeep parked outside. There was a building of sorts ... a mad collection of piled up rocks, bricks, aluminum siding, and cardboard. Two hippies exited the pad and hugged Cliff.

"These are my friends. Mars and Sunshine."

"Far out. I'm Mark. Pleased to meet you."

"Mars and Sunshine are getting back into nature. See their garden out there."

"Wow," I said seeing mostly weeds.

After introductions, we stepped inside of this crash site. It resembled a crashed airplane that you see in the papers. Candles and incense. No electricity. That's when I smelled the hint of heavy body odor exuding from our hosts.

"You guys have water out here?" I inquired.

"Yeah, man, like we have to carry it in pails. We got plenty."

Apparently, not enough for a bath.

But, their dope was first class. Nothing like getting useless for ten hours to propel the revolution. So we slipped into a haze. I fell asleep on some blankets. Cliff startled me awake in the morning.

"Hey, Mark. Get up, Man. Like, we gotta go."

"Far out."

I had sand in my clothes, in my ears, in my eyes, and in my shoes. Jesus, how can people live like this. No hope of a shower or any hot food. 'Living off the land.'

Well, that was interesting.

"Like, those people are people of the land, man. Dig? And they're gonna make it. Yeah, they're gonna make it!"

Cliff sounded so assured. I had my doubts.

Off to Tucson. At last. What pleasantries awaited there?

I was stiff and cold and my mouth felt like death. I stunk and I wanted coffee and a shower. Was that asking too much?

"Cliff, pull over here," I pointed to a convenience store. I marched in and purchased cigarettes, coffee, two doughnuts and a quart of chocolate milk.

"Far out man, all that shit's bad for you."

Yes it was. Fuck you, I thought to myself.

Phoenix and Tucson seem cradled in this vast desert scene. Flat mostly with some mountains or hills off yonder. Hotter than hell. Big city though. Freeways and traffic.

"Wow, man. I gotta drive now," exclaimed Cliff as he drew deeply on yet another joint. The guy had smoked more pot than I had in a year. And, he was driving. Where the fuck did Mark find this guy? The 'no dope' policy was out the window.

Oh well, beggars can't be choosers. Right!

We floated through Phoenix, a vast wasteland in the desert, and continued south into Tucson, a college town. Cliff drove to a poor section of town, mostly Mexican people.

"Here we are."

We entered a house. A mixture of pot and incense seared my nose. I sneezed a couple of times.

"Mark, this is Rocky, he's going to take you on to Texas."

"Pleased to meet you."

"Have you got the package? I have to drop that off right away and then we're getting on the road."

"Yeah, right. Here it is."

Another large manila envelope. Felt like mail.

"Come on with me," Rocky said.

"Thanks for the ride, Cliff. Good luck to you."

We hugged and Rocky and I climbed into his Chevy pickup.

No rest for the wicked but at least I wasn't driving.

Rocky dropped off the package at another house. He knocked on the door and handed it to a guy.

"There. That's that. That guy kept buggin' me for the package. I told him he'd get it when I got it. Probably full of money," he laughed.

Rocky was just the opposite of Cliff. Obviously more cautious and sober. Smoking pot and driving made me nervous. A cop could pull us over.

"How do you know Mark?" Rocky asked.

I had to be careful when talking about Mark.

"I met him through a good friend in San Francisco. I don't know him very well. He asked me if I could take these packages with me since I was on my way to Austin anyway. The trip here was on the way."

"Cliff made me nervous 'cause he was so stoned," I changed the subject.

"Yeah, I know. Don't worry about me. There are no drugs in this truck. We're drivin' through some pretty red neck states and the cops are assholes. You're not carrying, are you?"

"No way, man. No way."

We had a long drive to Austin. We drove all night through the Arizona desert. It was quite cold at night. The desert air chilled one to the bone. We made several stops along the way getting gas, the truck used a lot of gas, and buying coffee and smokes. All the usual pit stop items and body functions.

We reached the New Mexico border as the sun was rising in the east. Crisp distinct mountain tops silhouetted the horizon. It was very beautiful.

"Wow. That's quite a sight!"

"Sure is. I love this part of the world. My parents live in Tucson and teach at the University and I'm a student in Austin. I make this drive at least once a month and never tire of it."

"I can see why."

I made it a rule on these trips to not say very much about myself and to keep the topic as light as possible. I didn't want to get into any heavy political raps. I was just the messenger. It's not important what I think. Keep it low key.

I was beginning to put this puzzle together. Most of these drivers didn't know Mark at all. They had heard of him. Mark had somehow set up this network through trust. A friend of a friend. People entrusted to deliver messages, me, people who could drive people, Cliff and Rocky and the others, these people didn't know about each other. It wasn't like Mark had a yearly convention and all these folks would gather in the same place. No way. He had compartmentalized this network. How he did it and more over, what was in these packages, I had no idea and I didn't want to know.

We headed for Las Cruces and then south to El Paso. Every other vehicle seemed to be a pickup truck with a gun rack across the rear window. Rocky didn't have a gun rack. I felt like I was in a foreign land.

Texas was as huge as I imagined.

I had a funny thought: that original trip that Joe and I had embarked on where we would circle the outside states, well, now I had three more to that collection. I wondered how Joe was doing. The last I saw of him he was going to Winona State.

We were near the Mexican border. I grew up in the land of lakes and trees. This landscape, sans water and trees and mostly barren, was scary to me. I didn't care for it much.

Rocky was a most agreeable fellow. A good steady driver. I hadn't slept much in a couple of days and I must have just slipped off. I awoke somewhere near San Antonio.

"Good morning! You've been sleeping all day, man. You must have been tired. We'll be in Austin in an hour or so."

"Oh" ... I stretched as best I could in the truck ... "sorry man, I guess I was tired. I hadn't slept since Barstow."

"Quite all right."

I had to piss like a horse. I asked if we could pull over. I ran behind a bill board and relieved myself. Texas, I thought. Shit.

We pulled into Austin and it was like entering another universe. Hippies and people on bikes.

"Isn't this where that guy shot a bunch of people from a tower?"

"Yup, there's the tower right there."

"Wow."

"That was a weird day man, the whole town freaked out. The cops shot and killed the dude."

"I remember that."

"But, the place has calmed down since then. I think you'll like this town, Mark."

And I did from the first. We drove through the college campus. It was a huge school. We drove past the State Capital building and through the downtown area. How Austin was a part of Texas absolutely mystified me. From a land of red necks and cowboys to a liberal mecca on par with Berkeley and Madison. I love this country!

Rocky drove to a house in the student section near campus. It was like Mifflin Street in Madison. Rows of student housing. Rock music blaring from windows. The sweet scent of pot everywhere. Long hairs galore. Yes!

Rocky introduced me to everyone in the house.

"This is my old lady, Louise."

"Hi y'all. Make yourself at home. You can put your things in this room." Louise showed me a spare bedroom. It had a bed. A bed! Wow. A fucking bed!

First things first. I had a package to deliver. I mentioned it to Rocky. I showed him the address.

"No problem, amigo, he laughed, the dude lives across the street. Come on. Let's see if he's home."

He was home.

"Hey, Stan, this is Mark. He's got something for you."

"Oh, wow. Thanks man. I've been waiting for this."

He ripped the package open. It contained a stack of IDs and cash. I didn't want to see that but both Rocky and I did.

"Hey man," Stan said to me, "I'm still trying to get you a ride to Chicago. It might take a few days. Is that okay?"

I looked at Rocky and shrugged.

"Yeah, I guess so."

Rocky nodded.

I told Rocky that I needed food and a shower.

"Sure man. I know a great burger place around the corner."

I ate like a king. Texas size servings. The biggest burger I'd ever seen with a pile of fries and several beers. Rocky and I walked back to his place and I used the shower. It felt so good to wash the grime away. I laid down on the bed and slept for a few hours. When I awoke the house was quiet. It was dark. I found a book to read and went back to bed. I really needed some sound sleep.

I awoke the next morning. Feeling rested and human again. I needed to get back on my schedule again. Louise had made breakfast.

"Good morning, Mark," she drawled.

"Good morning."

"Sleep well?"

"Yes, I did. I feel human again."

"Mark, you can wash your clothes. We have a washer, no dryer, though 'cuz we don't need one," she laughed.

I took her up on that. I had a pair of gym shorts to wear and I put everything else in the washer. When unpacking my ruck sack I came across the little bag of whites. I'd forgotten about them. I took one. That and after several cups of coffee I was ready to go. I took the clothes out of the washer and hung them on a clothes line in the back yard. I really liked Austin. I felt at home.

Rocky was at school so I hung around the house. I helped Louise clean the kitchen and pick up. Louise was beautiful. Long blonde hair to her waist. Blue eyes. A dancer's body. Long and graceful. She was from Dallas. She was in graduate school working in social studies. She wanted to change the world and serve the poor and unfortunates.

We talked most of the afternoon.

"Come on, Mark. Let's go have a beer."

We walked to a really cool bar. I saw a stage set up.

"Do they have music here?"

"Oh yes. The Steve Miller Band used to play here. And The 13th Story Elevator and Doug Sahms and I can't remember who else. They all went to San Francisco. If you want, we could come down here later and see who's playin' tonight."

"That would be great!"

I told her about all the great bands I'd seen in San Francisco. Louise wished some of them would play down here.

"Probably afraid to come to Texas. I hear you get life in prison if you get caught with a joint," I noted.

"True."

"Really! That's fucked up."

"It is fucked up. This state is still fighting the Civil War. Very unfriendly to blacks and hippies and anything new or different. You gotta be careful down here."

Louise went on to caution me. Don't draw attention to yourself. Even though Austin was cool around the campus it was a different world as you distanced yourself from the sanctuary of the city center. Be cool around the Capital building and downtown. She likened the Texas Rangers to the Gestapo.

I understood.

Rocky was home when we returned. The other house mates were there also. We prepared a huge dinner. Burgers barbecued outside on a grill and potato salad.

My clothes were dry and I folded them and repacked my ruck sack. I was always ready to go in an instant.

Louise told Rocky about visiting the bar and wondered if we could all go out and listen to some music tonight.

"Hell, yes!"

We got to the bar at ten. The joint was jumpin'. A Texas swing band was in full swing. People were packed in like sardines, dancing and swilling 'long necks,' a Texas beer. I bought three beers after fighting my way to the bar. There was no place to sit. Didn't matter. You had to shout to be heard. No matter. I'd dropped two more whites for the occasion. Somewhere in here was a joint being passed around. If I closed my eyes I'd swear I was in San Francisco.

Rocky and Louise knew several people in here. I was introduced to several folks but couldn't hear their names. One girl, who I'd been introduced to, a striking woman. Long black hair tied back with a bandanna and wire rim glasses, grabbed me by the hand and led me out onto the dance floor.

Talking was out of the question. We danced among the hot and sweaty crowd. The music just made you dance. The band was great.

After several songs the band took a break. We found Rocky and Louise. They had found a table.

"What was your name?"

"Jacy, and you're Mark."

Jacy was a student at the University. She was from a little town in Texas. We hit it off. Rocky and Louise took off and left Jacy and I to our own devices. We guzzled several more beers and danced some more. She said she'd get me back to Rocky's house. She said she lived nearby so we ended up in her apartment. She had roommates and we found her bedroom. It wasn't long before we ended up in bed. I hadn't had sex in a long time and it felt wonderful. I was so drunk though that I soon fell asleep.

When I awoke the next morning there was a note by the pillow. It was from Jacy telling me to take a shower if I wanted and that she had class. She promised to see me soon. The apartment was empty. I took a quick shower and walked outside coffee-less. I wasn't sure where I was. I recognized the bar where we were last night and back tracked to Rocky's place. She was right. He only lived three blocks away. I must have some sense of direction.

As luck would have it, Rocky was home.

"Have a good night?"

"Yeah, I did. Jacy is a nice girl. I like her. What does she do? We didn't talk much last night. God, I was so drunk ... I'm still groggy."

"Jacy is a good friend of Louise and she's a student. We hang out with her a lot. I thought she had a boyfriend, but I guess not."

"Well, I hope I can see her again."

I was curious about how and when I would get a ride to Chicago. Rocky didn't know anything yet. I was getting anxious but decided to hold on for a couple more days before I called Mark. Patience is a virtue.

I needed coffee and helped myself to a cup. Rocky offered me some toast. I gobbled a couple of slices. That would hold me. I checked my gear and all was safe.

I was restless and decided to take a walk. I found a cafe and grabbed a window seat. I found a newspaper on the table and read the news. The war was raging and student protest seemed to be growing. Photos of Vietnam and cops with night sticks filled the front pages. This country was torn apart.

The scene here was vibrant to be sure but seemed to lack the revolutionary fervor offered in Berkeley or Madison. Football and school spirit seemed to rule even though a small hard core group did exist. The major pastime here seemed to be music. There was music everywhere. From Country Western to acid rock: Austin had it all. And that was a pleasant surprise.

I walked the campus and witnessed some anti-war activity. It was calm compared to other campuses. No wonder. Deep in the heart of Texas. I felt like any moment a herd of pickup drivin' maniacs would descend upon us and slaughter us. I didn't have a confidence or feeling of serenity that I had in other places. I really wanted to leave and get back to the Midwest. I couldn't wait to hear what had happened since I left.

Rocky and Louise were the perfect hosts. But, they seemed more interested in partying than anything else. Which was okay with me for a couple of days but I was getting itchy. No word from Jacy. A passing fancy, I suppose.

I did get a hold of Mark. He told me to sit tight. He would find another ride. It was too risky to hitch hike in Texas. It was against the law anyway.

I was feeling scared and abandoned. I had enough money to take a bus to St. Louis. I had some friends there. Maybe I should. At least I'd be out of Texas.

Finally after a week and a half Rocky informed me of a ride. I'd be leaving tomorrow morning.

I gave Rocky some money because I had eaten a lot of their food. I took him out for beers and saw Jacy. She was with another guy. She nodded to me and I nodded back as if to say 'that's all right.'

"That's the story of my love life, man. Hit and miss. Someday."

"I'm just really lucky, man. Louise and I are tight."

"You are lucky. I'm happy for you. I really am."

The beers rolled on. We smoked a joint outside in the Texas air.

I was up early and packed. I said my good byes to Rocky and Louise making impossible promises of sustaining a friendship.

My ride showed up.

A large Ford station wagon pulled up. Rocky introduced me to Tom and Mary. Both were med students at the University of Chicago. A very straight looking couple in appearances only, as I would soon find out.

"We're heading into Houston and then on to Baton Rouge, if that's okay with you Mark. We wanted to take the scenic route."

"Great. That's fine with me. The sooner we're out of Texas, the better," I chuckled.

Tom was at the wheel and I sat in back staring out of the window watching Texas pass by. I felt safe now and somewhat comforted by Tom and Mary.

"What brings you two to Texas?"

"My mom teaches at the University and we came down for a quick visit," Mary said.

"What does she teach?"

"She teaches biology."

"Oh yeah ... wow ... one of my favorite subjects. I attended St. Mary's in Minnesota and they are known for their biology department. Right on the Mississippi River, you know. Lots of subject matter to study there."

"And what brings you here?"

The kind of question I hated. I couldn't tell them the truth.

"Visiting a friend of mine who goes to school in Austin."

They seemed satisfied with my answer. It made me nervous that Rocky knew I was on my way to Chicago. I remembered what Mark had taught me about that. 'Never tell people from or to where you are going.'

It wasn't ten minutes later that Mary rolled a joint. I was surprised. Soon we mellowed into the vast Texas country side. I began enjoying the trip. In a few hours we passed through Houston. A huge sprawling stinky city. Oil refineries everywhere. The pollution was worse than LA. It was choking.

"It really stinks around here. How can anyone live here?"

"Well, people do. There's a lot of money here. The oil people. Millionaires galore," Tom stated.

It wasn't long before we reached the Louisiana border and everything changed.

"Good riddance," I pronounced as we left Texas.

"Amen to that."

We crossed a couple of rivers and the terrain seemed to hold more moisture. It was swampy in areas and the humidity was high. We were in the deep South. There didn't seem to be many towns just lots of shacks tucked off the main highway. I wondered how people supported themselves. It was like we had time-traveled back 20 years.

"We've always wanted to see this part of the country. We are going to be doctors and we want to work with the poor. God knows we see enough suffering in Chicago but this is like a third world country down here."

I briefly described my experiences travelling through some of the South registering black voters and how terrifying that had been.

"They murder civil rights workers down here, man. I feel like an uninvited guest," I said.

We needed to stop and gas up again. I told them I'd help with gas. People seemed friendly enough. I guess we didn't pose a threat. My hair was a little long but Tom and Mary were clean cut. Joe college types. We checked the oil and the tires looked fine. This was a sturdy car.

We bought some coffee and snacks and headed out. The place was lousy with mosquitoes. Smoking was the only way to keep them at bay.

Mary was driving now. We drove into Baton Rouge. A gorgeous city. Looked just like the magazine photos. I couldn't imagine living here but it was pretty. We were just a few miles out of New Orleans and then we headed due north for Mississippi.

"Look out for 'gators and red necks," Tom laughed.

In a few hours we were in Jackson, the state capital. I was amazed by the pure beauty of the place and the sudden squalor of shacks as we passed the black section. It was like two worlds. It was hard to understand how this inequality and contrast was allowed.

As we drove from Jackson I saw a sign for Winona. A Winona, Mississippi. I bet it's nothing like Winona, Minnesota. We whizzed by the town not stopping. It was getting dark and we were beyond tired. Mary suggested finding a motel for the night. It seemed like a good idea. I had money and a shower and a good night's sleep seemed in order. We found a little place and got separate rooms. Only cost $6 a night. We agreed to get some burgers and beer. We hung out after showering. After eating we were all tired. I retired to my room and slept like a rock.

This room had instant coffee. I ran the water as hot as I could and drank a cup as I showered. That's how you wake up. With a jolt of caffeine and hot water and whites. Tom and Mary were up also. We decided to grab a quick breakfast before hitting the road. They had omelets with grits and I had two eggs and toast. After a quick breakfast we gassed up the car and headed for Chicago. It was 7 a.m. Tom was driving. We might be in Chicago by late tonight.

"You can stay with us Mark until you find your friends."

"Thanks. It might take me a day to find them."

Neither Tom nor Mary quizzed me much on who I was and what I did. I told them I was a student at Stout State and that satisfied their curiosity.

It wasn't long before we drove through Memphis.

"Hey, doesn't Elvis live here?"

Tom decided the best route was to drive into St. Louis and then on to Chicago. We wouldn't be in Chicago until early the next morning. That was fine with me. Tom and Mary had a day before their classes started again. The weather and the roads were clear and we sailed through this hilly region. It was quite beautiful, hugging the Mississippi River most of the time. There is something comforting about water.

The communities along this river seemed so inviting. Ancient brick buildings rose from Main Streets populated with merchants and dime stores and cars parked at an angle and folks shopping. These river towns had been settled in the last century as the early country moved west and transported goods from the east. River boats and gamblers prevailed, as Twain wrote, marking this part of America unique. We passed dozens of barges filled with iron ore from Minnesota. I could have worked on one of these vessels if I'd stayed with the Merchant Marines.

Staring and dreaming out of the back seat window, I recall traveling up to Duluth to try and get on a ship. My dad had taken me up there a few weeks prior to get signed up in the Merchant Marines as a hedge to the draft. Once my ID and passport came in the mail I headed north. I waited in a dormitory of sorts for a couple of days waiting for a ship. I was terrified of some of these guys. It was like 'Terry and the Pirates.' Scary cretin looking guys from all over the world. Tattoos, gnarly beards ... a dangerous and tough looking bunch. Finally, a ship came in. A guy told me to grab my bags and get on board. They sent me to the kitchen. I was to be a cook's helper. I waited and waited. The same guy came and told me that I'd been bumped and to leave the ship. I went back to the dorm and waited another day before returning to Winona.

I heard later that the ship, filled with iron ore headed for England, had caught fire in Cleveland. So much for my Merchant Marine days.

Chapter 7

Chicago ... My Kinda Town

I'd dozed off. When I awoke we were well into Illinois having roared through St. Louis hours ago. Mary was at the wheel.

"Sorry I must have fallen asleep."

Tom looked at me and smiled.

"You haven't missed much."

It was dark. I had no idea what time it was or exactly where we were.

"I owe you guys some gas money," as I handed Tom a twenty dollar bill. He graciously accepted it.

"We'll be in Chicago in a couple of hours."

Mary masterfully drove to Evanston. It was very early in the morning and we had just missed the rush hour. Exhausted, we unloaded the car and carried everything into their apartment. We were not far from the Northwestern campus. I vaguely knew the neighborhood. Mary showed me to a small room where I could put my things. She fixed a modest breakfast and we all went to sleep.

I awoke first. It was mid-afternoon. I took a quick shower and looked through my phone book. I had to call a woman named Carol. Mark had arranged something with her. I knew not what.

Tom got up and looked the worse for wear. I wanted to grab a newspaper so I went out and found a *Chicago Tribune*. The entire front page was splattered with news of the Chicago Eight Trial, now the Chicago Seven, since Bobby Seale, a Black Panther, had arranged for a separate trial after being gagged and bound to a chair.

The trial was a fiasco. The eight had been accused of 'conspiracy to commit a riot.' I hadn't been following the trial that close but it had garnered national attention. I planned to go to the trial tomorrow. I had to see this.

When I returned to the apartment Mary was up. I showed them the newspaper and we discussed the trial at some length. In the middle of our discussion Tom blurted out. "Look, we know you're in some kind of trouble with the FEDS. It's none of our business. You're welcome to stay here until you find another place."

I was shocked and felt defensive. I swallowed my tongue and just nodded my head. I resisted the temptation to spill the beans. Rocky must have told them. I realized that this had to be a moment when I completely severed my ties. I wouldn't tell them where I was going next. I had to be discreet!

I found Carol's phone number and dialed. She picked up.

"I've been expecting you," she answered.

She gave me a time and an address to meet her tomorrow. I said I'd be there. I could check out the trial later.

I told Tom and Mary that I wanted to take them out for pizza and beer as a way of thanking them.

"Great! There's a great place around the corner. Can't be too late. We have class tomorrow."

We ordered two pizzas and a pitcher of beer.

"On me guys. Thank you for rescuing me from Texas!"

I told them how much I appreciated their kindness and for respecting my privacy. It meant a lot. They told me I could stay with them any time. Although, I doubted that would happen. I'd most likely never see them again.

We finished our pizzas and beer and returned to their apartment. I couldn't sleep so I read until I passed out.

Next morning everything seemed to go at a much faster pace. Both Tom and Mary looked frantic as they prepared for their day. I hugged each and said goodbye. I walked out into the humid Chicago morning to meet Carol.

She was waiting for me at a little cafe. She sat in a booth by herself. We had told each other what we looked like and what we'd be wearing. She wore glasses and had long brown hair. She looked to be my age. She was reading a book. She looked up and our eyes met. She took my breath away. I told myself that I had no time for romantic encounters. So, I dismissed my initial reaction as folly.

"Mark?"

"You must be Carol."

As we talked she revealed several pertinent facts as to how and why we were meeting. Her sister attended Cal Berkeley and was a good friend of Mark's. Carol had met him several times on visits. She was a student at Northwestern but planned to transfer to Madison in the fall. Her father was the Dean of Medicine there and she wanted to be near her parents.

"Mark thinks the world of you. He thinks you're the perfect message bearer because you're smart and honest and not a druggy. He likes that."

"Yeah, I'm the 'mailman' delivering parcels to people."

"That's what he said. You can be trusted."

Carol went on to describe that I'd be staying with her until more suitable arrangements could be made.

I mentioned that I needed to do laundry. She said there were washers and dryers in her apartment building. We walked a few blocks to her place.

"Oh shit, I almost forgot. Here's $200 for you from Mark."

Oh boy, did I need that. I'd spent a good amount on gas and motels and food and beer in the last few weeks. I was getting short.

Carol had a small room made up for me. She gave me a pair of shorts to wear as she ran off to do my laundry.

The clothes were washed in no time. I could just hang the other stuff up and let it air dry. It was very hot and muggy today. Her apartment was oppressively hot.

"Let's go to the trial. I have to check it out," I suggested.

I knew now that I had to gather information to pass onto Mark. He had told me 'everything and anything.' He would decide what was important. I had to take mental notes. I couldn't write anything down. It was bad enough that I had a phone book but I figured I could eat the pages if I had to.

Carol and I hopped a bus or two and we soon walked into the melee. Hundreds of National Guardsmen protected the steps to the courthouse as swarms of protestors chanted slogans and raised hell on the perimeter. Several held signs. One in particular held my interest. 'Bring the War Home!' I hadn't thought of that concept. I pointed that out to Carol. She nodded her approval. We moved mostly on the outskirts of the protestors. Chicago cops lined the streets. I noticed several undercover cops milling through the crowd. They were easy to spot. Older with short hair and raincoats. I wondered about the real undercover guys and gals. You couldn't trust anyone. I was assured I could trust Carol. But ...

The energy from the crowd was on the brink of exploding at any moment. Several small skirmishes broke out up front. We could here shouts and boos as arrests were made. I wanted no part of that. I was running a commentary in my head of this event. 'The whole world was watching.'

It was the cops on horses that scared me.

Carol and I walked out of there and returned to her apartment. She had a nice place which she shared with a roommate named Allison. Allison was a law student at the University of Chicago. Carol majored in economics, I found out later.

Allison and Carol prepared a huge meal of burgers and home made french fries and salad with plenty of wine. We stuffed our faces as we watched the evening news. The trial was big news. It was a farce. Bobby Seale had been bound and gagged to a chair because he wouldn't stop talking and Jerry Rubin and Abbie Hoffman, the court jesters, made a mockery of the court room with their antics. The other defendants were hardly mentioned. The judge, ironically, also named Hoffman, first name Julius, was this really old man. He looked totally out of place and couldn't handle these people at all. He looked like he should be holding traffic court instead. Still cameras weren't allowed inside so we had to rely on images made by a cartoonist.

Allison said that her entire law school was following this trial and that her classes were dominated by it. It was a far cry from the *Perry Mason* shows.

Our discussion focused on past events. The two women were up on everything. I'd been out of the loop for a few months and I had a lot of catching up to do. They talked about a conference that had been held in Boulder a few months ago by the SDS. They informed me that two factions had been created over a rift in the basic philosophy of the organization. One group had split from the main body and called themselves the 'Weathermen,' after a Bob Dylan lyric:

> *'You don't have to be a weatherman*
> *to know which way the wind blows.'*

The main group had remained steadfast in their non-violent resistance and protest but the Weathermen had wanted a violent revolution. Their tactics would include bombings and disruptive street fighting.

"Well, you could see that coming," I stated.

"After the black riots and assassinations and all the dead in Vietnam, it's no wonder," I added.

Both women fell on the side of peaceful change but I was torn. I wanted change now, not in a few years. I felt strongly that the working class of Chicago and the Midwest would be behind us if we overthrew the government. After all, I argued, they are the ones dying and paying for the war.

"Ever heard of Eugene Debs?" I asked.

Debs had been a labor movement leader and anti-war activist in the early 1900's. When he spoke against the draft before World War I, he was arrested for treason and sent to prison. It sent shivers through me. I faced a similar fate.

But, Carol and Allison knew nothing about that. In private later on, I asked Carol if Allison was cool.

"She can be trusted, believe me."

I did. I had to trust someone. Even Carol didn't know my real name or that I was wanted for draft resistance. Mark had told me that.

Staying with these two intelligent and mindful women demanded that I was on my best behavior. I was every bit the gentleman and volunteered to clean up and do the dishes.

I was restless. I filled the hours with reading and catching up on world events. I continued to struggle with the basic philosophies of the anti-war movement. To be violent or peaceful. It came down to that. I was willing to risk life and limb for the movement but what I was really searching for was a Zen moment or some kind of a revelation that would enable me to make up my mind. Most of Carol's friends were very political and I had a chance to mix with them and get info on what was happening in Chicago.

The prevalent mood seemed to favor a non-violent posture. Word spread through the grapevine that the SDS Weathermen were planning an action. Slogans like 'Bring the War Home' on posters were appearing on campuses. Another stated 'Days of Rage.' I passed this onto Mark. I hadn't heard from him in a while. We had an arrangement that he would get in touch with Carol. I didn't want to pester him unless I had to.

I had a pamphlet announcing the 'Days of Rage.' It stated where to meet, how to dress, the time, etc. What were these guys planning?

The day finally came. We had been told to wear a football helmet and bring a baseball bat! We arrived at Grant Park. The organizers had expected 50,000 people but I counted about 1,000. We marched downtown. Several speakers shouted through megaphones. Ranting and raving. Slogans sugared by flowing verbiage. Cops everywhere. Adrenaline rushing. Scared. Anxious.

Here we go!

I was swept up in the moment ... in the sea of shouting and thundering feet ... I was pushed into the middle of the street ... broken glass ... windows and cars smashed ... tear gas ... cops and protestors running amok ... chaos ... shoved along in the herd ... the melee ... I ran and ran ... fear ... eyes wide ... looking ... watching ... running ... cops hitting ... swinging batons ... people fighting back ... rolling and tumbling ... cops ahead and on the sides ... they were surrounding us ... I ran down a side street ... people trading punches with cops ... the shouts and the sound ... overwhelming ... escaping ... I ran and ran ... several others with us ... running ... someone shouted to 'get in the car' ... I dove into the back seat ... squealing tires ... two blocks away, three, four ... we're out of danger ... what about the others?

I didn't know anyone in this car. I asked them to drop me off. I was safe and out of danger.

I felt like a coward. I could have helped several people I passed who had been tackled by cops. I could have saved them as I ran by. I was scared. I was a coward. Guilt rushed through my veins. I hated myself. I should have helped those people. I should have.

That evening we watched our efforts on TV. The reporter said that only a couple of hundred rioters had shown up and that the organizers were very disappointed in the turn out. There was footage of us running down the streets and several episodes of people being arrested. I was very depressed.

Carol and Allison watched the news with me.

I didn't have much to add except there were more than a couple of hundred.

Click ... clack ... click ... clack ... peddling ... watching sidewalk cracks with little chamomile tufts ... like little trees ... blurred ... go faster ... ringing the bell on the handlebars ....click ... clack ... click ... clack ... bumping and making noise ... click ... clack ... click ... clack ... everything upside down ... tree tops down ... all is black ... big ones picking me up ... shards of pain in my head ... voices high-pitched and shrieking ... carried somewhere ... crying ... hear Grandma's voice ... then my mom's ... towel over my face ... in shock ... dazed crying, blood all over ... I'm scared and shivering ... pain ... oh, awful pain ... in a car ... holding me ... a hand ... comforting voice ... I'm screaming from somewhere down inside like it isn't even me ... someone else is crying ... I can see a small body covered in blood and towels ... kicking and screaming ... I'm floating ... picked up ... Mom is running ... put on a bed ... strange people looking at me ... can't see ... all goes black.

I awoke in a cold sweat from the nightmare. I wondered if I'd awakened the girls. Same old nightmares. Visions of today's riot danced in my head. I stared out of the window into the dark Chicago night. I was a coward.

I tried to go back to sleep.

The women were off to classes by the time I arose. There was supposed to be another march today. As an alternative, the Black Panthers and SDS had organized a peaceful demonstration. I elected to take part in that one too. Thousands marched in peace, chanting and carrying placards ... NO MORE WAR ... PEACE NOW ... OUT OF VIETNAM ... and the such. I saw no troubles at all. I walked with the people in solidarity and began to realize that maybe this was a more effective way to win over the American people.

The sentiment with most people I talked with seemed to think that the SDS had divided the movement. I didn't know yet. The faction that had broken off from the main movement didn't appeal to most people. Of that, I was certain.

What a contrast in the two demonstrations: one ugly and violent, the other peaceful and fun.

Many of Carol's friends had participated in the peaceful march. We had a lively discussion that night. Most were students and belonged to SDS. They were frustrated with the organization because it seemed elitist in that most students around the country weren't interested in joining. I agreed. We weren't reaching the average college student or high school student for that matter.

I made my report to Mark. He was all ears. I gave my impressions on the trial and on the so called 'Days of Rage.'

"Mark, I saw some cops running the other way. They were scared of us. We were mostly college men with helmets and baseball bats. Not docile passive weenies that, you know, they could just beat the shit out of ... no man .... yeah, man, they ran. But the main body of cops was ready for us. I saw several skirmishes with both cops and students fighting. It was a sight. It did bring the war home, I guess."

"I got out before getting tagged," I added.

"That was wise. You can't get arrested."

"Yeah, right, but I felt rather cowardly. You know. I should have helped some of those people."

"By doing what? Trying to wrest someone away from the cops? No. You did the right thing. I need you free, not in jail."

"Thanks, man."

"I want you to go to Madison. There's a guy there named Oliver. I want you to contact him. There are two brothers who are making waves and I need you to check them out. I think they're a risk but I want some more confirmation."

He gave me Oliver's phone number and I said I'd go over there in a couple of days.

Mark always gave me the confidence I needed to keep going on.

I told Carol I was going to Madison for a few days.

That night Allison invited some of her friends over and we had an intense discussion about the events of the last few days. But the conversation got interesting when one of her friends gave us a history lesson.

"It was just before World War I began. The Russian Revolution had ended and many Russians had exiled to America. Many of them wanted to incorporate the Communist model into American Politics. Among these new immigrants was Emma Goldman, a Russian citizen. She made several public and well publicized speeches. She was one of the founders of the American Communist Party. The Party advocated workers' rights and equality and human rights for all. They wanted to give women the right to vote etc. And there was Eugene Debs who spoke out against the draft and the impending war in Europe," she said.

"In the meantime, President Wilson, who was a weak president by the way, allowed some senators to form the first FBI. J. Edgar was a twenty year old up and comer but he wasn't the first head of the organization. These guys came up with the idea for what they called the 'Anarchist Exclusion Act' which allowed them, without any indictment or conviction, to exile any foreigners whom they deemed were advocating revolution. The rich manufacturers and the Carnegies and Roosevelts were really behind this. They didn't want to pay workers a fair wage. And the large banking institutions couldn't allow this."

"So, empowered by this Act, they exiled hundreds of foreigners including Emma Goldman. Some people spoke up saying this was against the Constitution and so forth. Their demands fell on deaf ears because the newspapers were all owned by the wealthy and they supported the Act."

"In the meantime," as I said, "the War was brewing and the draft was reenacted. Many thousands of anarchists were against the war and an anti-war movement was born. Probably the most known one was Eugene Debs. He openly spoke publicly against the war. Because of him, Congress passed the 'Espionage Law' which stated basically that anyone charged with 'anti-American rhetoric' (whatever that meant) could be jailed. Debs was a member of The American Socialist Party, along the lines with the Communists. Debs spent many years in prison. In fact, over 1,000 people were jailed under this law."

"So you see, this is nothing new in American politics. Same old shit ... the rich own everything and are running the Government."

This diatribe took the wind out of my sails. I'd never heard much about this in history class. What else hadn't they told us about. I felt comforted in knowing that I wasn't alone in my convictions.

I was left with the impression that the Government would stop at nothing to get it's way. It was obvious the Constitution meant very little to the people we had entrusted to uphold it.

Chapter 8

Madison

I spent several hours trying to find Terry, Curtis, and John. They had moved from their place on Mifflin street and the new people in the house didn't even know who they were.

I called Oliver's number but there was no answer.

So, I walked to the Student Union looking for them. I spotted John right away. He was seated in a corner booth sipping beer and talking with friends. He saw me too. I motioned for him to walk over and sit at my table.

After greetings and hugs I spoke.

"I'm glad I ran into you. Listen, A lot of shit has gone down and I need to talk to you in private. My name is no longer Mike, it's Mark. I've got a set of ID's with my new name on them. It's really important that you call me Mark."

"What happened?"

"I got drafted and resisted. I'm wanted by the FBI and I can't go home or to Winona. So, I'm hiding out here. Can you get a hold of Terry and Curtis. You're the only people in Madison that know my real name and you've got to promise me that you'll keep that to yourselves. I mean it, man. You can't tell anyone!"

"Cool man. You can trust us," John promised.

"I have to trust someone, you know."

"Just curious," I asked, "do you know a guy named Oliver?"

"Oliver? No, I don't think so. Actually, ... I'm not sure."

"I need a place to crash for a few nights. Can I crash with you."

"Oh yeah. No problem."

"Thanks."

Madison was much like Berkeley, very political and active. Students had been radicalized by the Vietnam war, of course, and by recruitment efforts by Dow Chemical, the manufacturer of napalm and by the ROTC and by the Army Research Lab on campus. Students demanded that they leave the campus. Over the years Madison had been the site of historic riots.

John walked me around the campus. He was a student and also worked at an underground newspaper. He showed me the office, if you could call it that, located above a pizza place on State Street. He showed me a copy. *Kaleidoscope*. He told me I could make ten cents for every copy I sold on the street. I read the paper and it rivaled the *Berkeley Barb* except for the sex ads. The paper had some excellent articles about recent demonstrations that had taken place in Madison. I was particularly moved by the photographs. I wanted to meet the photographers. I had some knowledge of photography and I had a brain storm. If I could get my hands on a Nikon with a telephoto lens I could photograph the cops and do surveillance on them. Mark had given me this idea of keeping tabs on the cops and FEDS. This way maybe we could spot infiltrators and print their photos to reveal who they were to warn people. I kept this to myself as John and I walked down State Street, the State Capital building visible at the end of the street. Hipsters and stoned people filled the street ... much like the Haight, I thought, but a bit less intense.

I would continue to attempt to contact Oliver and gave some thought about how I could get a camera.

I talked with Mark about my idea. He liked it. He suggested looking in second hand stores and pawnshops and camera stores for a used camera.

I talked with John about getting a camera. I would need a telephoto lens too.

I checked the pawnshops in Madison and I found an old Nikon F with a 50mm lens for $25. I bought it. They did have a 200mm lens too and I asked the guy if I could try it out and if it didn't work could I bring it back and he said no. "All purchases are final." So, I took a chance and bought the 200 for $35. The camera needed a battery and the meter didn't work so I bought a light meter and several rolls of Tri-X film at a camera shop for another $25.

My first camera! The people at the *Kaleidoscope* said they would process the film if I shot a riot. I was a photojournalist! I knew nothing about the craft. I had to practice. I took my new camera and used the light meter to get the correct settings. I quickly learned about depth of field and shutter speed. Now all I had to do was learn how to photograph. My first couple of rolls were interesting. I shot people and flowers on State Street. I learned from my mistakes. I went to the library and read a book on photography. It was one of those things that I understood.

The equipment worked!

After a week or so I was able to contact Oliver. An interesting guy. Long black hair parted on the side. Deep brown eyes behind thick black rimmed glasses. An intellectual sort. On the move. Restless. Talked a mile a minute. Lived with a bunch of people in a house off campus. He didn't walk ... he trotted. I found myself a stride behind him as we raced on. He didn't have time for small talk. He was a rebel.

When he finally slowed down I was able to discourse with him. He had heard that some guy was coming from Chicago (me) and that he was to educate that person about Madison.

"This town is full of wanna-be-revolutionaries and a few real ones. The Smith Brothers and the Armstrong Brothers are real. You'll maybe get to meet the Armstrongs but I doubt it. They don't trust anyone outside of their little group. They don't even trust me. I do know the Smiths. A couple of New York crazy rich guys. Their dad is some kind of Wall Street big shot lawyer or something. And, they are crazy. They really are. Their idea of a revolution is to fuck as many girls as they can and to get stoned every day and not get caught. I guess they figure that their daddy will get them out. But these two crazy motherfuckers want to blow up electrical plants and TV stations and all. The trouble with them is that they want to tell the whole world. They aren't cool. Besides, they deal drugs. Lots of pot and acid. So, they attract a lot of attention."

I was trying to absorb all of this. His rapid fire staccato diatribes were hard to follow, but, I got the gist of it. Oliver was a trip!

"Come on, Man, I want to show you something."

He raced home walked into his room and opened a box in his closet and he pulled out the biggest pistol I'd ever seen.

"This is a Colt .45."

I held it in my hands. It seemed to weigh a ton.

"I'm a sharp shooter. Won a bunch of awards for shooting. Someday I'll take you to the shooting range and I'll teach you how to shoot. My dad was into it and I learned from him. But, he died when I was 15."

With that expectation, I told Oliver that I wanted to return to Chicago in a few days. I realized I wanted nothing to do with guns. And, that was Oliver. Putting guns and his dead father in one thought.

Thanks Mark for introducing me to him. My first and lasting impression was that this guy was highly, highly intelligent and a maniac at the same time. My kinda people, I guess.

I shot a couple of rolls of the rear of the police station. I photographed cops coming and going. I don't think anyone noticed me. I saw several guys dressed in jeans and a couple of guys with long hair. I wondered if they were undercover. I dropped the film off and ordered contact sheets. This may come into play later. Oliver had told me of undercover cops who had infiltrated. Some of them had been seen behind police lines in demonstrations and then later on, marching with the students. They told me the film would be ready the next day.

I decided to pay John a visit at the paper. Terry and Curtis were there too. We ended up in the Student Union drinking beer and listening to Cat Stevens blasting over the speakers.

As we were talking we noticed some students rushing by the window. "What's that?"

"Let's check it out."

Students were gathered on State Street. Another demonstration was forming. I had my camera and asked Terry and Curtis if they could get me to the roof top above their paper. I had my camera with me and we ran around the block and entered the brick building from a rear entrance. It was an easy climb up the stairs to the roof top. I walked gingerly to the edge of the roof. I was directly above a police line on State Street. A mass of students facing them. There was a gulf of 100 feet between them. I noticed several long hairs standing with the cops. I focused and zoomed in on several of them. Terry and Curtis had split. I shot nearly a roll of film. I watched as a couple of the plainclothes men walked over to the student side. I got a clear shot of one of them nestled in with the students. Suddenly, he threw an object at the cops and it was on. The cops charged the students dressed in riot gear and began clubbing every one in sight. I could hear screams. Tear gas soon filled the air. I had to stand back because of the gas. I noticed several cops across the street. They had cameras too so I took a couple of shots of them. I had to get out of there. As luck would have it, I ran into John on the way down. "Here, take this to the paper." I handed him my camera and ran back into the alley. People were running everywhere. It was chaos.

I started to walk back to the Union when I was whacked in the side of the head. I saw stars. And heat. I couldn't breathe. I must have passed out. I sort of came to. A tear gas cannister was next to me and a big fat cop was telling me to get up. I couldn't. I saw his badge. #345. I felt my head and when I looked at my hand it was bloody.

Next thing I knew I was being tended to by a medic. She asked me where I was and I couldn't answer. Soon, a few more voices. They stitched up my head and applied an ointment to the side of my face. I was sitting up and began to focus. They asked me if I wanted to go to the hospital and I said no. I tried to stand up and made it on the second attempt. I felt my head and I had a bandage wrapped around my head. I was groggy but okay. I had a headache and my face burned like hell. I could hardly breathe. They put an oxygen mask over my face. That helped. I wasn't able to focus my eyes. They flushed my eyes with water. I was soaking wet. I slowly remembered being on the roof taking pictures and meeting John. After that things were a blur.

I finally managed to make it back to the Union. I got some weird stares. I walked into a bathroom and I realized why they were staring. My eyes were bloodshot. My head was wrapped in a huge bandage and one side of my head had singed hair. One side of my face was burned from the gas. Other than that ...

"What the fuck happened to you?"

"There I was, minding my own business ..." I tried to make a joke. I still couldn't focus my eyes. But, from the voice I knew it was John.

I told him the story. As best I could.

"I didn't even see the pig. But with my good eye I saw his badge number. #345. And I'm positive."

John said he had dropped the film off to be processed. He handed my camera back to me. I thought that if I hadn't run into him the cop would have taken my camera. Huh!

I told John that I had shots of 'hippie cops' mingling behind the police line and that I thought I got a shot of one of them instigating the riot.

"No shit! I'm going back to the paper right now and tell them that. Hold tight. I'll be back."

John came back in a few minutes. The riot had subsided.

"Come on. I'm taking you home."

John found Terry and Curtis and we went back to their place. I had a headache mostly. My sight was coming back and my lungs didn't burn as much. I didn't want any pot. I'd just cough. I drank some cough medicine and Terry gave me a pain pill and I drank some beer. I fell asleep medicated.

I must have slept all night. I woke up. The house was empty. I unwrapped the bloody bandage from my head. My head stung. There was another bandage over the stitches. They had shaved the top of my head. About 2 inches square. It would grow out. My face was still red but it looked okay. I took a shower without getting my head too wet.

John came home all excited. "Mark, you got some great shots yesterday. The paper is going to put your shots of the 'hippie cops' on the front cover and they printed posters of these guys to put on every telephone pole in Madison. It's so fucking far out, man."

"No shit."

"How are you feeling?"

"I'm okay. Take a day or two. But, yeah, I'm okay."

"You look better."

"Thanks. Still have a headache."

I recovered in a week. Terry took my stitches out one night. I had a bald spot but I felt no pain. My headaches were gone ... I was good to go.

I had told John and the boys about badge #345. That pig had blind sided me. It wasn't two weeks later and there was another riot. We had put the word out about #345. This night was pretty calm compared to most riots in Madison. I was with a bunch of guys who knew John and Terry. We had bandannas on and were ready for anything. We smelled tear gas and ran down a side street. Several cops were lining the street but let us pass by.

Then I saw him. It was badge #345. Standing by himself near an alley way.

"That's him. #345."

There were about six of us. One of the guys threw a stone at him and tore down the alley. #345 pursued. They ambushed him. Six on one. They tore his helmet off, took his gun and held him down. Three of the guys held him and made him sit on the side of the curb with his legs straight out. Another guy jumped on one of his legs. I could hear the 'snap' from ten feet away. #345 shouted out in pain and then they broke the other leg. It happened so fast. The cop was writhing in pain as several guys kicked the living shit out of him. The last I saw of #345, as I turned running down the alley, was a slumped figure silhouetted in a heap.

I later felt bad about that. I only wanted to ruffle his feathers. How did he happen to be standing there? Was it fate?

I hung out a few more days. Curiosity finally got to me. I wanted to know the reaction back in Winona and if the FBI had hassled my family. I told Oliver I was headed back to Chicago but instead hopped a bus to La Crosse.

Once in La Crosse I walked across the bridge to Minnesota and trekked off the road to the railroad tracks below. I walked along the tracks until a slow moving freight train approached and I hopped on. I was in Winona in twenty minutes. Emil was living on the farm by St. Mary's and it wasn't long that I appeared at his door. I knocked and I thought Emil was going to have a heart attack.

"Jesus Christ! You're okay. Thank God. Shit man, the FBI was asking everyone where you were. Nobody knew. Rumors were flying that you'd been arrested and stuff. Those FBI guys are complete pricks. They even took John and Mary out of school out in Pittsburgh and hassled them. Little kids. Fucking assholes, man. Shit. How are you?"

"Did they hassle you?" I asked.

"Oh yeah, and half the people in Winona."

"I guess I made a big splash ... huh?"

"They even put your picture in the paper."

"Really. I guess I better keep my head down. I just wanted to see what happened after I split. Don't tell anyone that I'm here. OK? I won't stay long. But, I'm okay and please tell Grandma and Grandpa and Mom and Dad that I'm okay. Your phone may be tapped so you should call from a pay phone. But, I suppose their phones are tapped too. I can't trust anyone. But, of course, I trust you."

"How's the band?" I asked to change the subject.

"Oh fine. Just playing all the time. We kicked Bob out of the band so it's just the four of us. We're thinking of changing the name of the band. We've been playing some Dead and jammin' more. Doing some Byrd's and Neil Young tunes too."

"I'd love to hear you."

"We're playing Uncle Charlie's in La Crosse tonight. Why don't you come along. Nobody knows you there. You could wear a big hat and sit in the back."

"Perfect."

As we drove to La Crosse I found out that several other guys had resisted the draft and now it was a daily event in Minnesota. This was comforting. He heard that a lot of guys were going to Canada.

Emil told me that two guys dressed in suits, short haired and very tense knocked on his door one day and really hassled him, asking him if he knew where I was and that they'd be watching his every move. I also found out that my mom had been bothered by the FBI. My family didn't know where I was anyway but it really pissed me off. They had nothing to do with this.

We pulled into the club and I helped them set up the equipment. The Marshall amps and speakers were really heavy. I borrowed a big floppy cowboy hat from Rick and hung out while they did their sound check. Emil had mentioned that they were considering changing their name to 'The North Country Band.' I liked it. Seemed way more hip than 'the Fabulous Ferrais.'

The club began to fill. I sat in the back by the sound board. I didn't recognize anyone so I felt safe. The band began their first set and I noticed a difference in their playing style. They had obviously listened to the San Francisco bands, especially the Dead. Longer extended songs with long solos played by Rick. Emil was the bass player and shared singing with Mudcat. Sam played drums. They were really good. It's too bad that they hadn't gone to San Francisco. They would have been famous.

People began to dance. Even dancing had changed. It was okay to stand by yourself, stand in front of the band and dance by yourself. Seemed more natural. I couldn't believe what I was seeing. The San Francisco scene, in all of it's accoutrements, long hair, beads, dope, had travelled to and embedded into the Midwest.

The band would play three sets. They were really great. The place was packed with hot sweaty fans. Pot filled the air. Beers spilled freely on the dance floor. It seemed we were stomping in puddles of beer as we urged the band on.

I told Emil that it was best I didn't return to Winona. He knew some people from La Crosse and I would stay with them tonight. I told them I'd would take the bus to Madison tomorrow morning.

I left with Emil's friends after the gig. Emil and I hugged. I never knew when I'd see him again.

Nice people. We stayed up for a while. I was tired and fell asleep on the floor.

I awoke the next morning. They were still asleep. I left a 'thank you' note and crept out of their apartment.

I found the bus station and bought a ticket to Chicago. I had told everyone that I was headed for Madison. I had to be sure no one really knew where I was going.

The trip was uneventful. I stayed on the bus when we arrived in Madison. Slim chance of being spotted but I took no chances.

It was great seeing Emil again. I'm sure he felt better knowing I was okay. I took a chance returning to Winona but it was better that I knew the score. The FEDS were after me!

I really had to be cautious. I trekked up to the North Side and waited by Carol's apartment. She was probably at class. I didn't know what my next step was.

Carol returned to her place after a couple of hours. She seemed pleased to see me. I couldn't tell her the specifics except to say that my little trip had been a success. She informed me that Allison was gone for the night and we would have the place to our own. We went out and bought some groceries. We made pasta with salad and lots of red wine. It was a most pleasant evening. We listened to her stereo. She produced a joint and we settled back. I'm not sure who made the first move but we made love on the sofa. I'd never felt anything so intense in my life. She was exciting to me.

I think we were both surprised. She told me that she loved me from the first moment she set eyes on me. Love at first sight. I was humbled. I hadn't given her much thought of that, at first, but I did like her. You meet hundreds of people in your life and most don't leave much of a mark but a few do. I had so much to think about and the stress of really not knowing what I was doing ... and now this! We made love all night long.

It's interesting how familiar people get with one another after making love to each other. Sometimes, of course, it's embarrassing but this time it was like I'd always known her. She was different from every other girl I'd been with. She was special and I knew that much immediately. I guess I figured that I never would have a chance with her so I didn't concern myself with that aspect.

I think she started it!

Well, this changed everything. I thought about telling her everything but thought, not yet. She knew me as Mark and such it would remain.

I told her what I could.

"Mark said I could trust you. My name isn't really Mark."

"Yeah, I figured. I won't ask you."

"Thanks. I'm kinda underground travelling around delivering messages and parcels and doing research, I guess you'd call it, for Mark. He gives me enough money to travel and feed myself. I don't know ... it's pretty weird. I met this guy a while back in California. He made an enormous impression on me and taught me a lot about the anti-war movement. He's older than I am and he's been around. He's like a walking encyclopedia on resistance and civil disobedience. So, I'm just his eyes and ears here in the Midwest. And you're part of it. We weren't supposed to fall in love but we are human."

I kissed her on the forehead.

Carol was cool. She didn't ask me any questions about who I was but she wanted to know what I was. In other words; what kind of a person I was. Hell, I didn't know myself. We had completely different childhoods. She was from a prosperous family and mine was middle class. Her parents sounded sane and sober. Mine were drunks. Smart, but drunks. Her parents were professionals. Mine were not. I felt like a low class stiff compared to her. She was a Princess and I was a Pauper.

What could she see in me?

Her life was a life I could only dream of. Summer vacations in France, hobnobbing with Senators and Governors, always having what she wanted and needed, and most of all, she had a loving family. What was that like, I wondered.

She took me downtown and we went shopping. She bought me new jeans and tee shirts and under wear and a couple of cool shirts.

"Carol, you don't have to do this," as I fake resisted her offer. It was fun and I wasn't used to someone caring for me like this. I was glowing.

"I want you to look good. We're going to a party tonight."

We arrived at the apartment downtown. It was a swank apartment building that had a doorman and a huge lobby. I had figured that we would sit in someone's living room on the floor smoking dope and listening to music. We entered the elevator. I was dressed in my new digs. She looked resplendent in jeans, a scarf, and a beret which couldn't contain her long thick hair. God, she was beautiful!

Getting off the elevator walking down a hallway with deep red carpet and mirrors and soft lighting, she knocked on the door. Another doorman answered and let us in. She knew him and introduced me. He was a butler!

Are you kidding me!

"Oh Carol, I don't know."

"Don't worry you'll be fine. Just follow me."

The butler took our coats and we entered the living room. I guess it was a living room. A huge space with dozens of people holding drinks and talking in small groups. The hostess ran over to us and hugged Carol.

"Oh my dear, I'm so glad you could make it. And who's this?" she added admiringly, regarding me.

"This is Mark from San Francisco."

"Mark, this is Gail."

"Very pleased to meet you. Thank you for inviting us."

"You're welcome. Now go mingle. I want you to meet some people here."

We walked into another room after passing through a small entrance way. You could smell the money. It was an older crowd. Strange bright paisley shirts and perfect fitting bell bottoms. The strong odor of pot and incense. A view of the lake. Priceless art hanging on the wall. Waiters with drinks on trays flashing by. A who's who of the rich North Side liberal society. A swirl of the red, white, and blue of the flag caught my attention. Standing in the corner surrounded by the enthralled stood Abbie Hoffman and sitting near him Jerry Rubin was rolling a joint. The deep resonant voice of attorney William Kunstler rapping off somewhere.

I was looking at two members of the Chicago Seven Trial plus their attorney!

I looked at Carol with my mouth agape.

"Jesus, you know these people."

"Yeah, my family is friends with Gail, and the hostess and her husband. I don't see them but we'll meet them later."

We grabbed our drinks and wandered to the food table. A vast spread of cheeses and meats and crackers and things I had no idea what they were.

"You've got to be kidding. People actually live like this?"

"You should see their place on the Wisconsin River. Next to Frank Lloyd Wright's Taliesin East."

"They know Frank Lloyd Wright?"

"Yep, they're neighbors. We'll go rafting with their kids this summer on the river."

I didn't know whether to be in awe or to just act nonchalant. Part of me wanted to flee and hide with my own people. Man oh man ... I was way in over my head. I hung to Carol's side like a scared little kid. She was in her world.

I was very nervous. Afraid I'd say something stupid or spill food on my new shirt and onto the million dollar carpet. I pretended to show interest in the art on the wall.

Carol saw some friends across the room and we hiked over there. The room was so huge that it was a hike. I was in a daze and wasn't listening. My eyes scanned the room. Who else was here. I wanted to hear what Hoffman was saying. He had a rapt audience. Rubin looked like he was drunk and stoned. He continued rolling joints. I grabbed one as it passed by. I noticed that it was really fat in the center and wasn't burning evenly. Jerry Rubin rolled a lousy joint. Carol poked me in the side and I came back to earth. The wine and pot calmed me down. I can't say I was enjoying myself. I felt like an alien from a different planet. The smiles seemed too big and eager. Insincerity ruled.

It dawned on me that these were the people who funded the anti-war movement. At least their hearts were in the right place. I held my criticism close and didn't share this with Carol. These were her friends and people. If I'd been raised like this they'd be my friends too. I had always resented people with money but I guess I was really just envious.

I spotted a few black guys wearing shades hanging out in a corner. Menacing. They seemed out of place also. I wondered if they were Black Panthers.

The real world seemed a million miles away. I walked to a large window and peered at the vastness of Lake Michigan. Imagine waking each morning and seeing this.

Was this what all the poor schmucks were dying for in Vietnam so some people could live like this?

I was out of place and really didn't want to stay long. Carol was in her element and easily moved among the other guests. She kept me in tow and sensed my unease. She said I was doing fine and that we'd only stay a little bit longer.

We did mosey near Abbie and Gail introduced us to him. He seemed like a nice enough fella. I sensed that the show he put on in front of the TV cameras was just that, a show. I suppose the left needed people like him. He grabbed a lot of attention and put several important issues out there in front of the American people. Just another crazy hippie to some, a crazy clown to many, the voice of the anti-war movement to most. They probably thought 'we' were all like that. He was clever. I have to give him that and he had balls. He and Rubin had made the trial into a farce. One day the two of them showed up at court wearing judicial robes. Judge Hoffman ordered them to remove them only to reveal Chicago police uniforms. Pretty funny, really.

But, on the whole there were some very serious issues. The war, poverty, the race riots, cops killing people on the streets; doing the bidding for the rich. And here I was atop the world in this high rent apartment surrounded by millionaires.

I couldn't help but feel envious of these people.

Carol and I left the party and took the elevator down to the lobby. I suspected we were being watched. I couldn't prove it and saw no evidence of it but I could feel eyes upon us. I pulled my collar up high to hide my face. Just to be on the safe side.

"Carol, I gotta ask. How in the world did we, or you, get invited to that party? My God, those are some heavy people."

"My parents know the Carlson's. It was their party. They have a place near my parent's cabin on the Wisconsin River ..."

"Yeah, yeah, you told me that. But Judas Priest ... Jerry Rubin and Abbie Hoffman and Bill Kunstler, I mean how ... I guess it just blows my mind, that's all. I hope I didn't embarrass you," I chuckled.

Carol just glanced at me and I was reassured that I didn't.

But, I had lots of questions I had to ask her. Like ... what was her connection with Mark and how did they know each other? Oh, yeah, her sister. Where did Mark get his money? Maybe I was better off not knowing.

It was chilly and too far to walk so we took a cab back to her place.

Carol told me that this party was really a fund raiser for the Defense Fund for the Chicago 7 defendants and their legal staff. Of course, it all made sense to me.

"Thanks for inviting me. That was amazing."

"Yeah it was. You know, all those people there and their money and clothes ... they are just people when it comes down to it. The people I knew tonight are actually really nice. You'll see some of them this summer on the river. You'll see."

We kissed in the back seat. Soon enough we were back at her apartment. Allison had some friends over. We joined them for yet another party. Why not!

Christmas and the semester break were in a couple of weeks. I asked Carol if I could stay here over the holidays while they went home for the Holidays. I didn't really have any other place to go. I promised I would clean the place and take care of the apartment. She ran this by Allison and she thought that was a good idea.

I planned to spend the next two weeks reading and writing and resting up. I read two Merton books. I didn't understand too much of what he said but was able to gather that passive resistance was a true path. The 'Days of Rage' had clarified things for me. It seemed that violence just begot more violence and created an endless spiral of harm and negativity. I vowed from now on to take and follow the roads of Ghandi and Martin Luther King.

I watched a lot of TV. One night I watched the program *The FBI* with Efrem Zimbalist Jr. I had heard that J. Edgar Hoover had approved of him in the lead role. The show was a white bread version of my impression of what the FBI really was; which was a reactionary organization bent on ruining the left and had categorized all pacifists as Communists and radicals. The show itself was about how great the FBI was in capturing a bank robber.

God, I hate being lied too. The FBI was just a bunch of bullies as far as I was concerned. Yet, another organization that let me down!

Mark had warned me again and again that the FBI was wire tapping and that no phone or room was safe from their prying eyes and ears.

I still had some speed left so I amped myself up and completely cleaned their kitchen and bathroom. I took the stove apart and scoured it sparkling clean and I did the same to the bathroom. I dusted and vacuumed the rest of the apartment. I cleaned all the windows. I couldn't get the outside of the windows. The place was immaculate. I spent ten days in aloneness bliss. Snow fell outside and it was pretty. One day I walked to the lake and took photographs. They weren't half bad. I needed to work on this craft. I bought a photo book at a bookstore and tried to get some tips. Couldn't find any books that covered 'How to Photograph FBI Undercover Infiltrator Pricks,' but I tried.

I thought about Carol constantly. I really was fond of her and for the life of me I don't know what she saw in me. I felt insecure in her presence. I wanted her to like me. Sometimes I wondered how I got into this mess. Where would I be today if I had gone into the Marine Corps? I was convinced I'd already be dead. When I was alone all of these bad thoughts came into my head.

I went for a walk and stopped into a bar. A basketball game was on as I drank beer.

I had that nightmare again. The one on the trike. I was being chased but couldn't pedal fast enough.

Carol returned home one afternoon. I was taking a nap. I felt a kiss in my ear. I opened my eyes.

"Oh, I missed you so much," she cooed.

We made love immediately. In a moment of passion she said she loved me. I completely opened up to her. I told her how I felt about her. How I was inferior intellectually and emotionally to her and that I wasn't who I said I was; but, she already knew that and how I couldn't tell her just yet who I really was not out of distrust for her or loyalty but that it was just best if she didn't know, then she didn't have to lie and she couldn't tell anyone anyway.

"You'd be better off with someone in your own caste. You know, someone from your society."

"Oh, fuck those twerps. Most of those guys are just spoiled brats and conceited anyway. No, Mark. I love you. You're honest and funny and believe it or not I know you are highly intelligent. You are well read and versed in what's going on. Mark saw something in you and so do I. My parents will really like you. They're down to earth and real."

I cried in her arms.

"Carol, I'm so scared half the time. I'm always looking over my shoulder. I'm just feeling sorry for myself. I want to be stronger for you."

"By the way," she said, "The apartment looks great!"

We had the place to our own for a couple of days. We exchanged Christmas gifts .She gave me a book of poems by Jack Keroauc, *Satori in Paris*. (I already had a copy but acted like I didn't.) And I gave her a 'Crosby, Stills, Nash, and Young' album. We played the album as we ate dinner.

I was on top of the world.

Chapter 9

1970

As the 60's ebbed into memory one couldn't help but feel a melancholy as this epic epoch of peace and love ended. So much had happened;

1960:
U2 plane shot down over USSR
Hitchcock's 'Psyco' released
First televised Presidential debates

1961:
Bay of pigs invasion
Berlin Wall built
President Kennedy's term begins
American troops arrive in Vietnam

1962:
Marilyn Monroe found dead
Cuban Missile crisis
John Glenn orbits the Earth
Port Huron Statement

1963:
Martin Luther King delivers 'I have a Dream' speech
Kennedy assassinated on November 22

1964:
Beatles and the British music invasion
Cassius Clay (later Muhammad Ali) becomes World Heavyweight
Boxing Champion
Civil Rights Act passes Congress

1965:
LA race riots in Watts ... 34 dead

1966:
Black Panther Party established
Mass Draft Protests

1967:
Che Guevara murdered
Thurgood Marshal becomes first black Justice on the Supreme
Court

1968:
Robert Kennedy assassinated
Tet Offensive
MLK assassinated ... April 4th

1969:
Woodstock Music Festival
July ... man walks on the moon
543,000 American troops in Vietnam

God only knew what was to come.

Carol and I spent a quiet New Year's Day watching football, eating, and making love. We couldn't keep our hands off each other. I felt grounded and confident. I was realizing the power of a woman. The power a woman can have over a man. A woman can make a man feel powerful or weak.

Carol made me feel strong and confident. I'd been raised feeling worthless and wrong and guilty. I didn't want to feel like that any longer.

It was time to contact Mark. It took two days before we eventually talked on the phone. He wanted me to go to Ann Arbor. He wanted to know about John Sinclair and the 'White Panthers.' Sinclair had been busted for pot and was in jail. It was causing quite a commotion.

I told Carol I'd be back in a few days. I caught a bus to Ann Arbor. The scene was reminiscent of Berkeley and Madison. Hippies and freaks dominated the campus. I was on my own here. Mark didn't know anyone so I had to wing it to find a place to crash. It was winter and I needed shelter. I found the Student Union and hung out. It wasn't too long before I engaged in a conversation with some people.

I had a ruck sack with me so it was obvious I was travelling. Some kind folks let me sleep on their floor for a couple of days.

John Sinclair had founded the 'White Panther Party.' I knew nothing about them but he had been busted some months prior for pot and had been in jail ever since. There was a benefit for his defense team featuring 'Iggy and the Stooges' and 'The MC5.' I witnessed two of the most raucous bands I'd ever heard. Iggy Pop was this little wriggling imp of a singer with a strong voice. The music was hard and raw. I couldn't hear anything but a white noise, brash and blasting. The MC5 were even louder. I checked out the scene and felt a profound difference here. These people were much harder and intense than the West Coast faction and just as political. Several speakers spoke about Sinclair in glowing terms asking for donations for his defense. It seemed that the FEDS were meaning to jail the entire anti-war movement one person at a time.

I left the benefit and my ears rang for two days. I would later tell Mark that the Ann Arbor scene was well and strong.

A few weeks later John Lennon showed up for another benefit. Sorry I missed that.

I had to get back to Chicago. I was freezing here. After a couple of days I hopped on a bus and split.

Alone, sitting and staring out of the bus window watching the frozen Michigan landscape pass by, wondering if I'd live to be 25. The violence around me would eventually claim me. I couldn't escape it. Black people who looked so angry glaring at 'the white boy,' older people despising the 'hippies,' some of the women in the 'Women's Movement' hating men, politicians lying to us about the war, the fucking war, everyday more and more GI's dying, the poverty of the inner cities, children disowned by parents in the big generation gap, our own government had turned against her own people, and even people in the movement bent on violence; no trust, no love, just hate and remorse.

When I returned to Carol's there was a message from Mark to go to Madison. She knew I'd been to Ann Arbor.

"How was Ann Arbor?"

"Interesting. To say the least. Ever hear of John Sinclair? They held a benefit for him and I saw a really cool band called 'The Stooges.' But the scene is just like Madison. Alive with revolt and dope. Ha."

"Meet any cute girls?"

"None as cute as you snookems."

Spent several days nesting before I embarked to Madison. Had no idea what Mark had in store for me.

I told Carol that I couldn't tell her where I was going and that I probably would not try to get in touch with her. I didn't know when I'd be back.

She understood. It must have been like this for so many other couples and families during war times. This was war!

It was 25 degrees below zero when I arrived in Madison. I had about ten blocks to walk to the Student Union and I thought I would just freeze to death. My feet were completely numb and felt like dead weights at the end of my legs. They stung as I warmed up inside. I looked for John or Terry but did see a guy who was a friend of theirs. He remembered me and he said we'd walk to their place as soon as I thawed out.

Mark wanted me to get in touch with a guy in town. I had an address and a name. Paul.

It was Paul from Chicago!

"Damn, what are you doing here?" I asked.

"Same thing you are, man. There's some heavy shit going down in this town. Mark seems to think that some of the 'Weathermen' are here and he believes that something really heavy could go down here. I suspect that there are many 'wanna be's' but you never know. Also, the FBI has infiltrated the movement. This is where you come in. You still have your camera?"

"Yeah."

"It may come into play later. It's so fucking cold that everything has calmed down. But, I got a feeling that everything is going to bust loose in the spring. So, Mark wants us to hang out and snoop around. You gotta be cool, man. You can't seem to eager. Just let it come to you. Some of these people get high and drunk and they like to brag at parties and shit. So, the two of us will be just hanging out for a while. Getting to know some people. You already know some freaks here, right?"

"Yeah. I know these three guys. But, they're mostly hippies. They go to the marches and stuff but I don't think they have any real links. I did meet this guy Oliver. He might be a source. We got along just fine. I'll run into him sometime. He has a gun, man. He kinda scares me but it's cool."

Each month more and more young men were evading the draft. Many were going to Canada. Canada accepted these men. Apparently many organizations had been created in Montreal and Quebec and Toronto to help these guys with housing and food and even securing jobs for them. There were rumors that some of these guys had even applied for Canadian citizenship! Paul and I discussed this phenomenon at length. I wanted to see how this worked and offered to go there myself. Paul said he heard that some guys from Minneapolis were taking guys up to the Canadian border in Minnesota and paddling canoes across the waters. There were miles of wilderness up there and I'm sure it was not patrolled. It was so cold that the lakes were probably frozen solid. You could walk to Canada!

I couldn't stay with Paul because he was crashing with people and there wasn't room. Besides, it was too risky to be seen together. I knew I could find Terry, John, and Curtis at the Student Union. And sure enough, I did. They were squatting in an abandoned building on Langdon Street near Frat Row. They said I could crash there but there was no heat and only one bathroom for about twenty people and oh yeah, there was no electricity. The temperature was hovering in the single digits. It was January in Madison. I met them that night in a room. They had candles and tons of blankets. It was freezing. I hadn't eaten and I was almost broke. There was a vending machine in the hallway. I jimmied the lock and got about ten dollars in change and ate some very stale Oreo cookies. I was starving and very cold. The guys were hanging out in the Student Union every day to keep warm. There were some other people upstairs. The bathroom down the hall worked, thank God, but there was no shower. John had a girl friend who worked at a restaurant and she was able to get scraps for us. She told me about a job cleaning out a doughnut factory. I talked to her boss, he owned it, and he said I could start right away. I reported to work at 5 a.m. The place was covered with a sticky sugary goo. I used a steam hose to clean the walls and the floor and the racks. It took three hours. He said I did a good job and could work 7 days a week. I really needed the money. He told me to take all the extra doughnuts home. I fed the boys with doughnuts. It got pretty sickening after a couple of weeks. I slept each night in the freezing room and walked to work at 5. I was able to clean myself in the bathroom at the doughnut factory. Then, I would walk to the Student Union and hang out all day. I kept an eye out for Oliver.

In a few weeks I had some money. But, not enough to go anywhere or eat everyday. I had to eat out and that was expensive. I always got my smokes at this little convenience store on State Street. I noticed that business was good all day but by nine p.m. it slowed down. There was only one clerk.

Motivated by hunger and desperation I made a plan to rob the store. The doughnut job kept me in cigarettes but there was little left over. I hadn't heard from Mark in a while. I needed something to eat. I found a ski mask and a large parka with a long hood. I 'borrowed' a bike. I was very nervous. I was living on 'whites' and Marlboros. I must have weighed 125 pounds, at most.

Fuck it, man. Let's do it!

Since it was winter, everybody was bundled up. You couldn't see anyone's face anyway.

I walked in. No one else here. "Give me the money." I demanded.

The clerk looked stunned. I poked my right hand with my index finger pointing in my parka. It looked like I had a gun.

"There isn't much in here. I just cleaned out the drawer."

He handed over a fist full of cash. I dashed out the door. The store was on a corner. I walked fast to the alley behind the store. I got on the bike and pedaled two blocks away. I threw the ski mask and the parka into a trash bin. I still had a stocking cap and a heavy coat underneath and of course, gloves. I looked behind. No one had noticed. I walked another several blocks. I could feel the money in my pocket. I'd count it later.

First things first. I walked into a restaurant and ordered a steak dinner with beer. I had a piece of apple pie for desert.

I counted $43. I felt really bad for scaring that kid and for taking the money but I thought I was going to starve.

Can't believe I did that.

(Six months later I dropped an envelope containing $50 through their mail slot with a note telling them I was sorry.)

I had enough money to get to the Twin Cities.

I didn't want to ever see that doughnut factory again.

I had to try to get a hold of Mark again.

I told John I was leaving again. I told him I was headed to Berkeley.

I arrived in Minneapolis and called Jeff. Thankfully, I had a warm place to stay. He put me up at a friend's apartment. I was able to reach Mark, finally. He said things were hectic and he would get some cash to me. He sounded really stressed on the phone.

Through Jeff I met a guy who was working with draft resisters who wanted to go to Canada. His name was Eric and he was an out-of-doors man. He had camping and fishing equipment and he had camped out on the Canadian boundary waters his whole life.

He was big and strong.

He and Jeff were good friends and he was a likeable guy. Eric told me he had explored Alaska and said he knew his way in the wilderness. We discussed the possibility of me bringing him candidates as well as travelling with him. He wasn't planning on any trips soon but he thought that this spring and summer would be busy. Eric said I could stay as long as I needed.

Mark was a saint. True to his word, he wired Jeff $200 and I was set for another few months. Jeff cashed it for me at his bank. I treated myself to a nice breakfast and a carton of cigs. I still had my camera with me.

It was the dead of winter and running around town was an effort. I saw Jeff a couple of times and planned to stay at Eric's for a couple of more nights. I missed Carol terribly. She said she understood but I was so tempted to call her but decided against it. My family and grandparents were in my heart and I missed them too. I sat down and wrote letters to everyone telling them I was okay. I figured I could mail them from here because I'd be long gone by the time the letters reached them. Mark taught me well. I had to assume that my mail was being opened.

Eric and I spent a quiet evening listening to music and having a couple of beers.

I slept comfortably in a sleeping bag on Eric's living room floor.

The phone was near my head and it rang. I picked it up on the third ring.

"Hello."

"The FBI were just here. They're looking for Tom and you. They are headed to Eric's place"

It was a voice I vaguely recognized but wasn't sure who it was.

"Eric. Get up. The FBI is on their way here."

"Fuck. What! Shit. Climb out the bathroom window."

I had my pants and a shirt on. No shoes or jacket. Eric helped me climb out of the small window. He threw my shoes, ruck sack and jacket out. His apartment was on the second floor and I was standing on a little ledge. It was 15 feet to the ground. The ground was still deep in snow and there was a slight hill in the back of the house. I threw my shoes and jacket on the ground and jumped. I landed on my feet and slid down the hill on my butt. I ran and hid behind the garage and put my shoes and jacket on. I was shivering. I ran down the alley and ran a few more blocks until I felt I was safe. Jeff's place was nearby and I took a chance. I was able to wake him up after getting the rest of the house up.

"Jeff. The FBI is looking for me and your friend Tom. I think they were headed to Eric's. I got out and ran over here."

"Fuck, man. You're half frozen."

He put some coffee on and I warmed up.

Jeff made a phone call.

"I found a ride for you. You must be the luckiest guy in the world. Carl is driving to San Francisco tonight and he said he'd take you along."

"I'm driving you to Carl's right now."

While waiting for Jeff to get ready the phone rang. It was Eric telling Jeff that the FBI had been there and they questioned him. He claimed he didn't know anyone by that name, Mike McAndrew, which was true. I was Mark. And that they left.

We drove to Carl's. I constantly looked out the rear window to see if we were being followed. It didn't appear that we were.

"Fuck. That was close. How did they know. Maybe just a lucky guess."

"Could be."

With relief we arrived at Carl's. He was a nice guy. He had no idea who I was or what had just happened.

"Carl, this is Mark."

"How do you do. Pleased to meet you."

Carl and I hit it off. I gave Jeff a hug as he departed. I never knew when I'd see him again.

"We'll leave in the morning. I want to stop and see some friends in Missoula and Seattle. I'm going to San Francisco. Pretty excited. I've never been there before."

"Oh, it's great, man."

Carl was busy packing his stuff. He had a 60's something Chevy. He said it was all tuned up. I just hoped the heater worked.

I'd left my sleeping bag at Eric's. Too bad. I'd have to get another one. The day was catching up with me. I came within minutes of getting caught. It was all I could do to keep from hyperventilating. I slept on Carl's floor. He had roommates but they weren't there. I didn't sleep real well.

Carl and I left early. The weather wasn't too bad. The sun was out but it was cold. His car ran great and the heater worked! Carl wasn't a great conversationalist but when he did converse it was important. He was one of those guys who didn't waste words with idle chat. He spoke in staccato phrases and was to the point. He wanted me as a copilot and a contributor for gas.

We saw a couple of hitch hikers on the way out of the Cities but Carl drove by them.

"Don't need any more people in this car. Besides, you never know who or what you're picking up. Can't be too careful. Ya' know?"

We drove all the way to Mitchell, South Dakota. Carl didn't want to spend the money on a motel so we drove up and down the main drag of Mitchell until he spotted some people with long hair.

"Hey man, know where we could crash tonight?"

"Sure. Follow us."

We followed their car out of town a couple of miles and drove to a farm house. There were several people inside. We introduced ourselves and said we were just passing through. Their hospitality was first class. They offered us food and beer and dope. We partied for a few hours. We both needed sleep. I curled up behind a couch in the living room. A woman loaned me a blanket and a pillow.

I was asleep and I felt someone crawl under the covers with me. It was the woman who loaned me the blanket. She didn't say a word. We kissed and the next thing I knew, we were screwing. Just like that. I didn't even know her name!

Carl and I arose early the next morning and thanked our gracious hosts.

"Those people were very nice, weren't they?"

"Yeah. There is something about Midwest people," I sighed.

Carl wanted to be in Missoula by tonight. He was hell bent and determined. I bought a tank of gas and we loaded up on snacks and coffee. It would be a long day.

Watching the scenery pass by. We entered the Badlands of South Dakota. It was one huge gravel pit. Flat and desolate it didn't appear that anything could grow here. Of course, this was an Indian Reservation. These people had been pushed into unlivable conditions by our government. This country was built on genocide and slavery.

"Hey Carl, I'd like to see Mt. Rushmore when we reach Rapid City. How 'bout it?"

"Yeah, okay, let's do that."

We eventually reached the western edge of The Badlands and on this straight road we could see a huge sign up ahead. It was too far to read it. As we neared the sign we could finally read it. It said in huge block letters, 'NO INJUNS.' It appeared to be a bar and music club of some sort.

Western South Dakota is beautiful. The grey flatness of The Badlands leads into mountainous pine tree country. The Black Hills. We found our way to Mt. Rushmore. We parked the car and joined other admirers. There they were. George Washington, Thomas Jefferson, Theodore Roosevelt and Abraham Lincoln. Two slave owners, a friend of the rich manufacturers and enemy of the poor and a false war hero along with Lincoln who probably was the only decent human being of the lot. It was an impressive piece of sculpture. The artist had defaced a once beautiful cliff of granite to make his masterpiece. This had once been sacred ground to Native Americans.

I watched other Americans gushing with patriotic fever posing for photographs that would end up in a family album.

Carl liked it and I kept my mouth shut. I'm too cynical sometimes.

I consulted the map and it looked like we had to drive northwest to get to Missoula. We could be there by late tonight.

I'd noticed a heavy New York accent in Carl.

"Are you from New York?"

"Yeah, I grew up in Brooklyn. A few years ago my friend, who'll you meet tonight, and I took a motorcycle trip. We were going to San Francisco. But, I had an accident and broke my leg. The bike was destroyed. I was laid up for several weeks. Jimmy, that's my friend, got as far as Missoula before his bike died. We'd always wanted to complete the trip but I met a girl and fell in love. I've been in Minneapolis ever since."

"Wow. So you two guys grew up together?"

"Yeah, he lived right across the street. We did everything together."

Carl went on to describe his new life in detail. It all came down to that he wanted to remain in Minnesota because the people were so nice. His family still lived in Brooklyn and he could always visit, he said.

Into Wyoming we zoomed.

It wasn't too long before we headed north into Montana, The Big Sky State. Indeed! The sky seemed to exist beyond the horizon.

"This your first time west, Carl."

"Yeah. It's fuckin' beautiful," he crunched his words in that delightful Brooklyn accent. The weather had cooperated. Crystal clear azure blue skies and moderate temperatures. We had lucked out so far. As we headed into the Rockies the temperature dropped but the roads were clear.

"How are you doing? Need a break? I could drive for a spell."

"No, no. I'm all right. But we need gas and coffee and I gotta piss!"

We stopped at the next truck stop. I could swear I'd been here before. We gassed up and stepped inside the restaurant to get some coffee. We ordered apple pie a la mode too.

"My dad always said to stop at the truck stops to eat because the food is the best," I exclaimed.

"This is fuckin' delicious!"

"Told ya!"

"You know, we've covered some miles today. We could find a motel and get some beers and rest up. One more day wouldn't matter, would it?"

Carl thought it through. The food and the stop and the day was catching up on us.

"Let's drive a little while. But, that's a good idea. We wouldn't get to Missoula until the middle of the night anyway. Yeah, that's a good idea."

We drove to Billings and found a cheap motel. It only cost us $10 for the night. We grabbed a couple of six packs of Coors beer and settled into the room. We ate at MacDonalds. Life was good!

We were in no hurry the next morning. We showered and cleaned up.

We only had a couple of hundred miles to reach Missoula. We drove into town mid-afternoon. Carl called his friend and Jimmy came and met us. We drove to his place. The town itself reminded me of Winona. A college town. This was some gorgeous country. Early spring was in full bloom and the temperatures were warm.

Jimmy, had a nice house that he rented. A few other people lived there too. Jimmy was a student at the University of Montana. He was so pleased to see Carl again. They both settled into their old routine, heavy Brooklyn accents and all. We ate like kings and swilled beer through old Brooklyn stories. It was a most entertaining night. I was pretty drunk by the time I crashed on the floor in the living room.

I wanted to sleep alone.

We stayed in Missoula for a couple of days. I had a chance to walk the campus and check out the scene. It was more sedate politically than Madison, of course, but people seemed hip and with it and there were plenty of anti-war signs. I thought this might be a good place to hide out. They'd never expect to find me here.

Jimmy took us to a hot springs in the middle of nowhere. We parked his car and we hiked a quarter mile or so into the woods. We could smell sulphur long before we got there. Jimmy had a flashlight and led the way along a path. We could hear other people there. We said hi and took our clothes off. The night had a chill. The water was hot and man, did it feel good! We soaked in the water for a while.

"Hey, I want to show you something."

Jimmy swam across the pool, maybe twenty feet.

"You have to dive under this ledge and swim fifteen feet underwater and then you come out in a cave. Trust me."

Jimmy dove under and Carl followed. Here goes. It was totally dark and much warmer. I opened my eyes and could see a flicker of light. I swam for the light. In ten seconds I came to the surface and sure enough, we were inside a cavern. The flashlight being the only light. It was scary as hell. Jimmy just laughed.

"Pretty cool, huh?"

We sat in there for a while. You could stand up and walk around. It was very warm and humid and the voices echoed some.

"Let's go back."

We returned to the open sky in the same order.

"You can see in the day time and it isn't so spooky."

"Thanks, man," I exclaimed, "that was really something."

"Yeah, these hot springs are all over the place."

We returned to Jimmy's feeling clean and weary. That hot water sapped all my energy.

I took a chance and wrote another letter to Carol. I'd mail it next time we stopped. I declared my undying love for her. I felt guilty about the other night but I didn't initiate it. I told Carol it was okay if she met someone else. It was nearly impossible to have a relationship like this. It was a rambling missive. I must have sounded half crazy.

In the meantime Jimmy and Carl continued to catch up on old times. We managed to stay pretty high the whole time. I did have a chance to check out the town and all though it was a college town and liberal, it didn't hold the fever that Berkeley and Madison had. Which was fine. It was a nice place. Like I said, it would be a good place to hang out in if I had to stay low.

"Nice bunch of people, Carl."

"Yeah maybe someday me and Jimmy can be close again. He was

pissed off when I had that accident. Not at me but at life, I guess. Oh well, life goes on. Let's go see Seattle!"

I thought twice of mailing that letter to Carol. I really didn't want her to see other people. I was a jealous guy. I couldn't help it. I knew I needed to reform and I didn't know how to do that.

"Carl, let me ask you something. If you found out that your girl friend was screwing another guy, what would you do?"

"I'd kill her!"

"No I wouldn't," after he thought for a second, "I'd kill him. No, I wouldn't do that either. I guess I'd really be hurt and pissed off at the same time. Why do you ask?"

"Cause I have a girl friend in Chicago and we are pretty serious. I've never had one this intense, and I worry about her finding another guy. I'm just jealous, I guess."

"Yeah, man. I can dig it!"

Miles and miles through the Rockies across the great state of Montana into a slice of Idaho. Another drop dead gorgeous spot.

Carl was digging the scenery too. A flow of constant 'wows' and 'check that out, man' rolled from his lips.

"I can just imagine the early settlers coming through here, like Lewis and Clark, you know. They must have been blown away."

We rolled into the flats of eastern Washington. Quite a contrast to the last several hundred miles.

We stopped and gassed up. My turn to pay. Bought cigs and filled the thermos with hot coffee.

In a few hours we came into the Cascade mountain range. Not as dramatic as the Rockies but none the less beautiful.

It was early evening. The sky was a twilight deep blue-green. The lights of Seattle loomed ahead.

Carl was a city guy and he wanted to spend a day and night here. I said sure. We drove into the city and his instincts took us to a district called Pioneer Square. Ancient-all-brick buildings of bars and restaurants and cafes and music. Sweet music. The smells of fish frying and pasta mixed with pot and the thumps of rock music.

He parked the car and found an old beat up hotel. We checked into a Victorian style room with high ceilings and creaky wooden floors. After a quick shower we both headed out the door for a night of carousing.

Immediately, one could judge that this was a very hip place. Hippies and blacks filled the streets. Carl was in his element. I tagged along as best I could and we settled into a bar that had a rock band playing. We paid the modest cover charge and sat in a booth. We ordered some beer.

This was a very old bar. Must have been 100 years old. The ceilings were twenty feet high. Smoke wafted over the patrons who were mostly young college students. We fit right in.

Carl wanted to dance and he asked a girl to dance and off they went. I was content to sip on my beer and people watch. It was a nice escape but my mind kept wandering to what would happen when I got to the Bay Area. I worried that I may not be able to find Brian. Mark knew I was coming so I didn't concern myself too much with him. The music blared and a sweaty Carl soon rolled into the booth with his new friend.

I needed something to eat so I told Carl I was going out to find something. I'd join up with him later. I walked the noisy streets and found a pizza place. I ordered two slices and a coke and sat in the window watching the passing scene.

Seattle was beautiful. An outline of mountains across the bay. Snow peaked. I walked and walked. Not wanting to get lost I wrote down the address of the hotel. I didn't wander far. I went back to the room and watched some TV. Carl came in soon there after. He looked stoned and drunk. He had a big smile on his face.

"Shoulda stayed. The band was pretty good and we danced a lot. She seemed pretty young though. I'm fucked up."

We drank the last two beers and fell asleep.

I was anxious now to get to the Bay Area. We still had at least a 24 hour drive. Carl wanted to see the coast line all the way down. This would take two days to get to San Francisco. It was all right with me.

We took a ferry across the sound and drove on Highway 101 through the Olympics and out onto the coast. Some of the most incredible scenery I've ever seen. High up in the mountains with mountain lakes and views to Canada and beyond. I wanted to stop the car and live here. I took some photographs out the window of the car. Won't be any good except for reference later.

The coast line was rugged and foreboding. Not a place to go wading. Rocky cliffs standing off shore with trees on top. Wow.

Carl was digging it too.

"Ain't nothing like this in Brooklyn. Can't hardly even find a fuckin' tree there."

We had stopped a couple of times to gas up and pee but we were making good time. We neared the Oregon border. Mysterious Oregon. The Dead played up here a lot in Eugene. Ken Kesey was from here and yet I found the state to be generally pretty conservative, especially the eastern side and the smaller towns. We did start to see VW vans parked along the beaches so we were again entering friendly territory.

Between 'wows' and 'far outs' I told Carl that he hasn't seen anything yet. The coast line was awesome all the way to San Francisco.

My mind wandered; I was so grateful to Carl for getting me out of Minneapolis, if only he knew and I kept thinking of Carol, I've got to write a letter to her. What lay ahead?

It was late April by now. Everything was green and alive. I remembered the last time I'd trekked these parts and it all seemed different. The scenery hadn't changed ... I had.

"Carl, what are you going to do once we reach San Francisco?"

"I've got some friends in San Jose. Figuring I'd drive down there and see what happens."

"How 'bout you?"

"I'm going to see about finishing up school and find a job and shit. I've got a place to stay in the meantime," I sorta lied. I wasn't going to school, I was trying to stay out of prison.

We drove all day and crossed into California.

"Hey, we could crash on the beach or find a cheap motel."

Carl opted for a motel.

"My idea of camping out is a Motel 6," he joked.

We drove another couple of hours. We stayed in Eureka.

I looked at the map.

"Lookit here. It would be faster to take 101 all the way down, but, the scenery is better on the coast."

"Let's decide in the morning."

We grabbed some beers and burgers and settled in for a couple of hours of TV before settling in. *The FBI* was on. What a joke!

Carl got up at 6 a.m. We hit the road by 7. We decided to drive down the coast line. We first had to drive to Leggett to catch Highway 1.

It was the right decision. We hugged the rugged coast line all the way.

"You were right, Mark. This is fucking amazing. When I was a little kid all we ever had was cement and sirens and buildings that blocked out the sun. I never thought I'd ever see anything like this. Wow! I love life!"

Told you so, I thought to myself. I never tired of the view either. The Pacific Ocean, a dark blue stretched to the horizon and beyond. It terrified me and excited me. Maybe there is a God!

I took out a pad and began writing to Carol. It was short.

> *Dear Carol,*
>> *I miss you and I love you.*
>> *I think about you all the time.*
>> *Please know that I will return to you as soon as I can.*
>> *Love, Mark*

I mailed the letter from Fort Bragg when we made a pit stop. All sorts of paranoid thoughts that she had found another guy, who could blame her, I'm so jealous, it was eating me up inside. Someday I vowed to tell her everything. I even thought of marrying her. Aaahh!

Carl was tiring. It was a hard drive. Because of the twists and turns he had to really concentrate on the road. I had vertigo most of the way. Sometimes we were just a few feet from the edge of the road with a 500 foot cliff looming. If I sat back in my seat all I could see was the ocean below, the edge of the car blocking my view of the road. But, Carl was a good driver and I felt safe.

We took a break in Bodega Bay before heading into Santa Rosa where the traffic promised to pick up.

We had an hour's drive into the City. At least we were travelling against the nightly commute.

Carl let out a 'wow' as we came upon the Golden Gate Bridge. There is no sight like it in the world.

As we headed on 19th Avenue through the Golden Gate Park I told Carl he could let me out anywhere.

"Are you sure, man."

"Yeah, I can make it from here."

Carl took a right turn at Geary Street. We parked on a side street. I got my ruck sack out.

"Thanks, man. I really appreciate the lift and it was fun travelling with you. Stay on this and it will take you to 280. At the airport, you'll see signs, take a left and you'll be back on 101. Shouldn't take more than 45 minutes and you'll be in San Jose. Thanks, again."

"You too, Mark. Take care."

Having made our farewells I walked down Geary until I entered the Mission District. I called Brian. He was home! I thought I might end up on the street somewhere. He was living in the same place. It wasn't long before I knocked on his door.

"Man, are you a sight for sore eyes," I exclaimed.

"Mark, you bastard, how are you, man? Come on in."

Brian, always the perfect host, had beer and pot in hand.

We talked it up. I told him of the close call in Minneapolis and how I narrowly escaped.

"All I can say is; 'With a Little Help From My Friends.'"

Brian laughed.

"Oh, it's good to be here, man. I have to call Mark, too."

"All shit has broken loose over in Berkeley. Nixon's been bombing Laos and Cambodia and there's been a riot every day for a week."

"Yeah I heard. Fucking bastard. I thought he wanted to end the war."

Brian showed me the latest papers. *The Chronicle* and the *Berkeley Barb* had lots of photographs of the carnage. Burned upside down cop cars. Every window was covered with plywood on Telegraph Avenue. It was a mess! The cops had made dozens of arrests. Also, the Draft Board in

Oakland had been the scene of several major protests and arrests. The cops were using helicopters spraying tear gas on the students. It only promised to get worse.

May Day was coming up!

Chapter 10

May 1970

I had to see Mark. It took me two days to reach him on a pay phone.

"Man, things are fucking heavy. Meet me at the cafe tomorrow at 1."

I was early. I sat at a table by myself. Things seemed somewhat calm today in Berkeley. The usual burn outs hung out on Telegraph. Mostly runaways looking lost. The 100 yard stare. Spare changers and druggies. Some of the windows remained covered. A tension hung in the air.

Mark slipped into a chair next to me. He was shaking his head with a smirk on his face. He held a newspaper to his face. He sipped on his coffee. He didn't look at me.

"I'm being watched. Don't look at me, just keep reading your paper."

"I want you to hang low for a couple of weeks. The riots are every day now and the FBI has infiltrated us. We caught one of them last week. We took a photo of him and posted it on every telephone pole in the area. Do you still have your camera?"

"Yeah."

"I want you to photograph a demonstration if you can. Here's my plan. We can put you on top of a building. I want you to take pictures of all the plainclothes men standing behind the barricades with the riot police. Some of these guys are easy to spot. They'll have long hair and jeans and shit. Keep an eye on them. We've seen some of these bastards cross the lines and stand with the students and they were the first to throw a rock and that's what started the riot. If you think you got something, take the film to this one hour photo place (he gave me an address of a lab in Berkeley) and make sure you give it to a guy named Steve and tell him it's for Mark. He'll know what to do with it from there. Got it?"

"Yeah."

This sounded familar, I thought. I had told him about photographing in Madison and the shots I'd taken of undercover FBI pricks.

"By the way, hi, how are you?" he asked.

"Oh, yeah ... um, I'm fine."

Mark slipped an envelope to me under the table. I coyly put it under my leg as I sat.

Mark got up and left. We never even looked at one another. I continued to read my paper. Someone else sat at the table. I got up to refill my coffee and as I did I slid the envelope into my back pocket. Spy shit, I thought.

I sat in the cafe for another hour reading the paper. I went into the bathroom and opened the envelope. It contained another $200 plus a two page letter. I read the letter and he wanted me to return to Chicago later this month but first he wanted me to cover the future riots. Most of the demonstrations amassed at Sproul Plaza and then went from there. Mark thought I could get in most of the buildings and reach the roofs by simply walking in and finding the roof.

May Day was in two days and a huge march was planned. I walked to the One Hour he told me about and bought five rolls of Tri-X. I looked behind me and was careful to spot anyone following me. I didn't see anyone. I took a bus back to the City.

I read Mark's note three times. It mentioned getting boys to Canada. He was in contact with people who had set up a network enabling draft resisters to find housing and employment and possibly citizenship. He wanted me to sniff that facet out. There were people in Minneapolis running guys up north. He also mentioned that I was doing a good job and that I should destroy this note.

I returned to Brian's and laid a few bucks on him. I asked him if there was any work for me from his landlord and he said that there probably was and that he'd check that out. I planned to spend a few months in the Bay Area, I might as well work and make some money. The exterior of the house looked beautiful but still had a lot of work to do inside. Most of the upstairs needed painting and the floors needed to be stripped and varnished, my specialty.

I tore the note up in little pieces and flushed it down the toilet.

"Hey, who's playing at the Fillmore tonight?"

Brian opened the *Chronicle* and found the listing.

"John Mayall and Miles Davis. Wanna go?"

"Yeah, sure. I love Miles Davis."

We stood in line and barely got in. Bill Graham himself was passing out apples to everyone. The Fillmore West was completely different than Fillmore East. For one thing you could sit on the floor and walk around. There were seats around and behind the floor and a side room with booths and a bar.

John Mayall and The Bluesbreakers opened with a set. Eric Clapton was long gone from the group but they played a wonderful set. It killed me that these white English dudes were playing American Black Blues. They put their own mark on the music and it was really good.

After a break Miles Davis took the stage. He had on a red leather jacket with matching red leather pants and large sun glasses with a huge hat. He played pieces from the *Bitches Brew* and *Jack Johnson* albums. It was a rock blues jazz thing obviously going after the young hip crowd. Brian met a buddy of his and this guy rolled a joint. I took a hit and went into a dream. What the fuck was in this. I felt sick. I told Brian I'd be in the bar. I needed air. I staggered into a booth and put my head down. After a few moments a woman tapped me on the shoulder and asked me if I was all right. I told her I took a toke off a joint and it made me sick. I was spinning. She brought me a glass of water from the bar. She told me that several other people were sick also. The joint was laced with heroin. A few minutes later Bill Graham came over to me with an apple and told me to take a bite. I did and it did help.

"Eat the whole thing, man."

I could finally put my head up and focus and I saw a dozen other people being tended to in same fashion. Bill Graham was a hero to me. He cared.

In the meantime Miles played on. He was a genius. It was beautiful!

I felt much better after an hour or so. I found Brian laying on the floor. Half conscious. I wanted to find 'his friend' and punch him out. I roused Brian and went and got some water and an apple for him. He felt better in a short time.

"Hey, man. Let's get out of here. Where's your fucking friend, man. I want to kill him. Fucking asshole. He put heroin in that joint. He made a bunch of people really sick. That's just not cool. Fucking asshole."

"I don't really know the guy. Don't even know his name. Just some guy I run into once in a while. Let's walk home man and forget about it. Sorry, man."

"Yeah, okay."

The fresh air helped and we walked twenty blocks back to his house. I love the Mission. It always aroused my senses to food aromas and music and the rumble of life. These people knew how to live life.

Tonight's episode was easily forgotten.

"Jesus, I've never been that high before," I groaned.

"Me too, man. The next time I see him I'm going to have words. I couldn't find him in there. He must have split. I dunno."

We stopped in a Mexican bar and had some cervezas and a couple of burritos. Almost felt normal again.

We both needed a good night's sleep.

I fell off with a sweet memory of Miles, back turned defiantly to the audience, trumpet raised in a revolutionary black salute.

When I finally awoke the next morning Brian was gone. There was a new flock of roommates. They seemed cool. I found a note from Brian saying he'd be back tonight. I cleaned up and decided to walk to North Beach.

I crossed Market Street. It was completely torn up by construction being done on a new subway system. The noise of jackhammers was incessant. I wondered how people who had to work down here could tolerate the din.

I walked all the way to Montgomery Street. The financial district. More huge buildings going up and up. God, it was noisy down here. The caverns between the buildings seemed to amplify and echo the sounds from riveters and cranes.

I edged through China Town. Again, food filled my nostrils as I got to Broadway. Carol Doda's tits flashed in a huge neon sign. Porn shops and cafes. I walked up Grant Street and suddenly was in Italy. Nothing but more cafes and bistros and Italian restaurants. I walked into a huge park with a majestic church on one side. I turned back to Columbus and crossed Broadway again and found City Lights Bookstore. This was a holy place. The Beats had hung out here. They had every Kerouac and Ginsberg book. I walked downstairs and more poetry books. I noticed a poster for a poetry reading in a couple of nights. I made a mental note of that. I wanted to be part of that scene. I walked back upstairs and bought Ginsberg's *Howl*, I'd never read it, and *Visions of Cody* by Kerouac.

I crossed the narrow alleyway and entered Vesuvio's. I sat at the bar and ordered a beer. I took my beer and sat in the window watching the cool hep cats walk by. Why can't life be like sitting in Vesuvio's watching hep cats?

I was born too late and in the wrong place. I was envious of people who had been here in the fifties. Must have been something.

I opened *Howl* and began to read it. I remembered being at St. Mary's and asking my professor if we could study the 'Beats' and he remarked that they weren't important to American Literature.

All I wanted out of art and literature was the fucking truth. Not the namby pamby bullshit of the English Romantics and most of the American 19th century writing. It was too safe. It didn't get inside enough. The Beats had the guts to tell the truth. The truth isn't always beautiful but it is beauty.

I read *Howl* twice. Only understanding parts of it. What I walked away with was Ginsberg's assessment of American culture. Drugged by TV and cars and possessions with no heed for spirituality and essence and meaning. We looked for meaning and direction from *Leave it to Beaver* and having the biggest car in the block without any thought that our government was killing people. Oh, is it just me? Why couldn't I just be some simple bastard who embraced the status quo?

Tomorrow was the first of May. I was going to Berkeley.

Got up at 7 and was in Berkeley by 9. I brought my camera. People were already gathering at Sproul Plaza. Police in riot gear gathered a block away. I meandered down the street and circled behind the police line. I focused on men who weren't wearing uniforms. I did spot one guy who had long hair and was talking to another guy. I shot a couple of frames with my 200 mm lens. I hoped I had a clear shot of his face. I soon lost him in the scurry of the cops. I didn't want to be spotted so I walked a couple of blocks away.

I looked for a building to enter but the cops were gathered mostly in a residential area.

May Day, of course, celebrated International Worker's Day and the rites of Spring. I presumed most people were here in solidarity with the workers of the world. Somehow, our movement hadn't attracted the working class of America. Most Communist countries observed May Day and that was another reason Americans didn't embrace this day.

It didn't take long before some speakers were reciting slogans and speeches about ending the war etc. Suddenly, some people began to march and the cops tried to stop them. I saw rocks flying through the air. The cops yelled through a bull horn to disperse because this was an illegal gathering or some bullshit. I couldn't see who was throwing rocks at the cops. A cloud of tear gas rose from the front and the stampede began.

From a peaceful demonstration to a riot in thirty seconds. I had no choice but to run with the crowd. It was loud as people yelled and the sheer din from this many people running. We saw cops ahead of us too. The crowd charged ahead. I had a bandanna across my face now. The hint of tear gas burned my eyes. Some people stopped and turned over a cop car and lit it on fire. I got a quick shot of that. Some of these people had balls, man. The Berkeley crowd was hard core. We ran and ran. It was a big game.

I didn't know where I was anymore. Just pure adrenaline flowing. Glass breaking. Helicopters overhead. We ran back onto the campus and I couldn't believe my eyes as I saw some students with books walking to class like there was nothing going on. The tear gas was getting thick and it made everybody change direction. I stopped to take a few photos and decided to find safety. I was a rookie compared to some of these guys. I saw guys run out and hurl tear gas canisters back at the cops. That took bravery. I ran inside a building. I found safety from the gas and cops. I looked outside to see cops chasing students with gas masks on and batons raised. They beat the living shit out of a guy and then dragged him away. I got shots of that. Jesus, I'd never witnessed anything like this. The 'Days of Rage' seemed calm compared to this. The Berkeley cops were better organized and prepared. I must have waited an hour before it looked safe to step outside. The damage had been done. I photographed a smoldering cop car and debris in the streets. Crews were already busy cleaning up the mess.

And just like that life returned to normal. Students crossing the quad with books under their arms. I guess people could get used to anything.

I dropped the film off at the lab as per Mark's instructions. I shot two rolls. I bought five more rolls of TRI-X as long as I was there. I left a message for Mark that there were two rolls at the lab.

The underground press continued to run articles about bombings in Laos and Cambodia. The *Berkeley Barb* quoted a source that we had been bombing them for years. I was always skeptical of the press, especially the underground press, because of an agenda wanting to promote the evils of our government. But, there was probably a speck of truth in there.

I returned to the relative safety of Brian's house. I was exhausted and one of the roommates noted the strong smell of tear gas on me. I took a shower and rinsed out my shirt and bandana. The stuff left an oily residue.

That evening I watched the local news and *KRON* had extensive coverage of today's events. I wanted to learn to be a better photographer and sensed that I needed to be closer to the action.

The tone of the report depicted the demonstrators as the 'bad guys' showing over and over students destroying property and in general running amok. I felt it was a biased report only showing half the story. It was obvious that the media was being controlled by the government. In order to change public opinion and eventually get most Americans to turn against the war, we needed the media on our side too. I had no idea how to achieve this.

I talked with Brian about this concept. He followed me absolutely.

"The media needs ads to pay for their programming or newsprint or whatever. And they don't want to offend their sponsors. Their sponsors need customers, the American people, to buy their shit. It's an endless cycle, man. You're right, Mark, changing public opinion is the only avenue. How we do that, I'm with you, I don't know."

"Maybe when people have had enough and they see their own sons and daughters being slaughtered this bullshit will end."

Things quieted down for a few days. Brian's landlord, Larry, came over and asked me if I wanted to help him on another project. I said sure. He had another property over on Hill Street, just a few blocks away. He said to come over at noon.

I arrived at the address on Hill Street. A serene little block crowded with Victorian's that had somehow survived the great earthquake and fire of '06.

I started upstairs on the floors. A crew was already busy painting the outside of the house. The floor had been stripped and I applied the first coat of varnish. The smell was over whelming and I wore a respirator over my face. This was a beautiful example of the 19th century architecture that dominated the early west coast days. He had about five days of work for me and that was perfect. I could use the cash.

I came back to Brian's everyday sticky and worn out by the work. I really liked doing this type of work because you saw the results of your labor. After a week Larry paid me another $200 in twenties. I was fat. I had $350 in my pocket.

It was May 4. Somebody called Brian and told him that some students had been killed in a demonstration on the campus of Kent State in Ohio! Brian and I immediately headed for Berkeley.

All hell had broken loose! The city was in a shut down. No buses and the streets were barricaded. Helicopters in the air. A million cops. Thousands of students running amok. I've never seen anything like this. Each new demonstration seemed to increase in intensity! Brian and I were in with a crowd. No one was in control. I snapped pictures. I must have looked like a press man because no one hassled me. Sirens blared everywhere. It was a state of siege!

I grabbed the latest *Berkeley Barb* and noticed one of my shots from the May Day riots. No photo credit, but that was cool. Mark came through again. I needed to contact him but there was no way. It was too dangerous to try to get anywhere in the melee. We saw smoke rising from a few blocks away.

"Fuck, man, they're going to burn the place down."

We made it to the western side of Telegraph and looked up the street in horror. Cops and students were holding a battle in the street. Tear gas was of course everywhere and something was burning. It was a cop car upside down in the middle of the street. Flames rose twenty feet. We walked up the street to a safe distance and I snapped some shots of the car. Shadowy figures could be seen scurrying hither and yon and tear gas canisters being tossed back and forth. A helicopter swooped low over the street and engulfed the rioters in tear gas. I heard what sounded like gun shots. Couldn't tell if they were or just explosions from the burning car. People were scattering. Many moved toward us. A swell of cops appeared behind us. We needed to get out of here.

"Come on, Brian, let's boogie."

Hundreds of us ran into side streets to escape the cops. They had the advantage of watching us from the air. I wanted to shoot those helicopters out of the sky. I was enraged. Rumors about Kent State filtered through the crowd. We heard all sorts of numbers. From 5 to 25 students shot dead. No one really seemed to know.

Somehow Brian and I had to get back to the City. We decided to hitch hike and found a ride immediately.

I looked out the back window of the car and saw smoke rising in several spots.

When Brian and I returned home we turned on the TV and *CBS* had a Special Report on the killings at Kent State. The details were sketchy, but, it appeared that four students had been shot and killed by Ohio National Guardsmen. Also, every major college campus in the country seemed to be in the midst of riots. The country was in chaos.

I had no way to drop the two rolls off at the lab. Brian and I felt lucky just to get out of there.

I decided not to venture to Berkeley for the time being. The film could wait. I worked a couple more days for Larry on Hill Street just cleaning up.

Brian and I kept a close eye on things. Campuses continued to riot. As much about the invasion of Cambodia as the killings at Kent State when we received news that two more students had been shot and killed at Jackson State in Mississippi during a protest gone bad. The police justified it by saying that black students had started fires and that they fired in self defense. Bullshit!

No arrests were ever made in each of these incidents.

It had been the bloodiest two weeks of the protest era. The Black Panthers were in a rage in Oakland and every day more and more GIs were dying and every day more and more young men were resisting the draft. The country was clearly split in half, polarized by the fucking war. I honestly thought we were about to see another Civil War.

I got a hold of Mark. We decided to meet in a couple of days. He said he had something for me.

I met Mark in the cafe. I gave him two rolls of film.

"Fuckin' week, huh," I shook my head.

"It's been intense," Mark concurred.

He showed me another package. "This has to be in Chicago as soon as possible. Give this to Paul. I checked the ride board on campus and found a guy who can drive you there. He's kinda crazy," he laughed, "but, he's cool."

"When can you leave?"

"Tomorrow okay?"

"How about tonight!"

"Yeah sure. I've got to return to the City and get my shit."

"Fine. He'll pick you up at Brian's at nine."

"Here's another $200 for gas. You'll pay for the gas. It was part of the bargain. This guy knows nothing about you. His name is Max."

"Should be plenty. Thanks, man. I'll call when I get there."

I got home and hastily informed Brian I was leaving tonight.

"Aw shit, man. We were just gettin' started," He chuckled.

"I know. But, I gotta go. Duty calls."

Max showed up on time. He was driving a brand new Dodge Charger with a 440 big block double-hemi fucking machine. It looked like a race car. It was loud and menacing.

"Hey man, get in. We're going to fucking Chicago. I'm in a fucking hurry."

I looked around and he had two cases of beer in the back seat and a pistol on the seat.

"Oh, excuse me. I'll move that. Here, put it in the glove compartment."

Oh shit, what was I in for.

"Relax, man. I only use that to relax," chuckled Max looking at the gun, "we ain't stoppin' 'cept for gas. Put this on," he continued.

It was a contraption that truckers used. You attached one end on your pecker and a tube ran down your leg to a jug. It was for peeing in. Max apparently hated pee stops, waste of time.

"Here, this is for you."

"What's that?"

"Pure meth crystal, man. Just lick on it. You can keep it, man. I got plenty."

It was a solid piece of crystal meth, speed, that was the size of a ping pong ball. I licked some and tasted the bitter sting on my tongue and was instantly more alert than I'd ever been.

"Thanks, man."

"You can call me Max. Some people call me 'Mad Max' 'cause I drive like a motherfucker. I like driving. Do you?"

"Yeah, sure."

And off we flew. And fly we did. We hit the Bay Bridge and ate it up. Soon we were headed east on 80. He drove in the fast lane all the way to Sacramento.

"Crack a beer, man. I'm thirsty."

I reached in the back and lifted two beers.

"There's a 'church key' in the glove compartment."

I gingerly moved the gun and found the 'church key' and popped two beers.

"Don't fuckin' matter if they're warm. Has the same affect."

He took a lick. I took a lick. The beer cut the taste.

Somewhere near Reno we stopped and gassed up. I emptied the pee bottle on the ground.

We crossed the Nevada State line.

"Now we can make good time. No speed limit." Although, he drove 85 all the way from Sacramento. He expertly worked the gears, down shifting to maneuver around trucks and slower traffic and then put it in fourth gear as we sped into the Nevada night. I took a peak at the speedometer. We were travelling at 100 mph. But, this car was made for it. And so was Max.

He was a tremendous driver.

"You should be a race car driver, man. You're really a good driver."

" S'pose."

He was too focused on the road to talk.

Lick lick, gulp gulp.

I was gaining confidence in Max's driving but I was terrified, curled up on the seat. We came upon a convoy of trucks. They seemed to be moving in slow motion. Max looked to pass having slowed down to 75. He moved into the other lane several times but there was traffic coming from the other direction.

"Fuck this."

The road was very wide with plenty of room on the shoulder, so Max pulled onto the shoulder and passed three trucks. He down shifted and floored it. The truckers were honking their horns at us. We passed the first truck and then the second and the third.

'Fuck me. I'm dead,' I thought.

"Aaaaaeeeeyyyyiiii!" he screamed.

Max just looked at me and grinned.

"Did I scare you?"

"Yeah, please don't do that again," I pleaded meekly.

"I won't. Guess that was a pretty dumb move."

The truck lights behind us soon disappeared. We were back to 100 mph.

The sun was coming up in the east. It was beautiful. The landscape was barren except for far off mountain ridges with vast desert like terrain in between. The road was straight and wide. We slowed down for the towns we drove through and it felt like crawling. Once on the outskirts, Max floored it again. Gas mileage was poor in this rocket so we stopped several times for gas. As fast as Max could refill the tank and a quick leg stretch we were off again. The trucker's helper was a great invention!

We likewise zoomed through Utah, only slowing down when we hit traffic in Salt Lake City.

"God, it stinks here. What's that smell?" he asked.

"It's the Great Salt Lake. It's a salt lake, see, and the only thing that lives in that water is brine. You know, like shrimp. That's what you smell. Dead brine."

I continued. "This is where the Mormons settled. I read about them. Wherever they lived the locals kicked them out so they settled here."

It was beautiful here except for the smell. The Wasatch Mountain Range loomed ahead of us. We were soon climbing into the elevations and we left the desert behind.

The radio didn't get very good reception. About all we could get were Christian stations and Country Western stations, 'cryin' music' as my dad used to say, so we listened to the wind through the open windows. The heat was repressive but the beer and speed tempered it.

"Those are the Rockies ahead. This car will chew them up and spit 'em out, man. You wait."

I was, by this time, grinding my teeth from all the speed. We both chained smoked and the ash tray was overflowing. Max showed me a paper bag in the back seat and I emptied it every three hours, making sure that the cigs were out so I didn't start a fire.

He didn't want to litter.

We were cruising about 80.

"Can't drive too fast out here. The cops will let you drive at 80 but no faster."

I never did see a speed limit sign.

By midday we were in eastern Utah and again began climbing. The western ridges of the Rockies were ahead. I didn't know if Max was political or not so I held my tongue on that but I kept thinking about Kent State and the families of those kids. I was full of hatred for our government and fucking Nixon. The bar had been raised. They were shooting at us. The war had come home. Everything had changed. There was a shift.

I was also anxious to see Carol. I wondered if she'd found someone else. I was so jealous. I had so much to do when arriving in Chicago. I had to see Paul first thing. Again, I wondered what was in the package.

I worry too much. Sometimes I was overcome with panic. Panic about everything. This ride. Max. Carol. Mark. The FBI, certainly. When is this going to end or will it ever?

The countryside blurred by. Max showed no signs of tiring. His eyes were bloodshot but he seemed alert. More speed. More beer. More!

I couldn't believe it when we entered Wyoming, seemed that we had just left San Francisco.

"I've made this run in 48 or 50 hours before."

This was when I suspected Max of running drugs. Why else would anyone drive like this between the Bay Area and Chicago? No way was I going to ask him.

"And we're makin' good time."

I inwardly laughed at the cosmic joke of this situation. What could I do but sit back and enjoy the ride.

"Do you know Mark very well?" I asked.

"Not really. I've done some favors for him in the past. Seems like a decent guy."

I'd been through the Rockies a few times and always marveled at the scenery. The road curved sharply in spots as it snaked through the peaks. We had to slow down because of traffic and because it was too dangerous to speed. Max could flat out drive and he punished that Charger, constantly shifting gears. He rarely used his brakes, the sign of a good driver. I was, by now, accustomed to his driving.

"Man, you can fuckin' drive, man. Where'd you learn to drive like this?"

"Just picked it up, I guess."

Max was very secretive and I respected that. Besides, I didn't want to push his buttons. My life was in his hands.

As we broke through the Rockies and neared Cheyenne we were able to pick up a decent Rock and Roll FM radio station. That helped pass the time. We stayed on 80 all the way. As the sun began to go down in the west, we entered the great plain state of Nebraska. Flat as a pancake.

"You can stand on your car and see all the way across the state," Max noted.

I laughed really hard at that one. It wasn't too much of an exaggeration. The speed signs all said 75 so Max drove 80.

The wide straight highway stretched ahead of us as far as you could see. Farmers raised great plumes of dust as they plowed the fields. The early settlers must have been awestruck by the pure vastness. It was like an ocean of solid land.

We drove into North Platte. It had taken us 19 hours. Max and I decided to pull into a truck stop to get a thermos of coffee and wash up in a rest room. We were both pretty grimy and stinky. Plus, we both needed to stretch and walk out the cramps. We gassed up and bought half gallon of coffee with two plastic cups. I didn't need any more beer. We still had a case left. I emptied the beers bottles in a trash can and cleaned up the car. I rinsed out the trucker's helper again.

It was early evening when we drove out.

"The hard part of the drive is comin' up. More traffic and we won't be able to drive as fast."

Which was fine with me. 70 MPH was fast enough for me.

"Yeah, Iowa's got all those hills, huh?"

"Yup."

That pit stop had rejuvenated us. A renewed energy. We both licked our meth crystal balls and sipped coffee. Chain smoking and rapping. Constantly rapping, Max was Superman behind the wheel. The Interstate wasn't completed in stretches requiring us to slow down and drive through the towns, which were numerous and frequent. Couldn't imagine living here at all. Nothing to do but grow wheat. But, these proud folks supplied the world with their crops. I would imagine that if this were your life it would be fulfilling. I don't know. Just day dreaming.

I consulted the map and figured we'd be in Omaha in a few hours. I remember being with my dad one hot August and watching a College World series game. That was really cool. And eating at Johnny's Steak House. The largest steak house in the world right in the stock yards. I had the biggest steak I'd ever eaten and it was good.

"You okay, man?" I asked.

"Never better."

"You're amazing. I've seen anyone drive like you, man."

"Aw shucks."

"No, I mean it, man."

We crossed the great Missouri River over an amazing bridge and entered Iowa. It was the middle of the night. Half a moon hung over the land making it possible to see the silhouettes of farm buildings. The road wound through early corn fields. In three months the corn would be 8 feet high and absolutely delicious, good enough to eat raw right on the husk.

I told Max a long rambling story about the time Dad took me on a road trip and we stopped in this little town in Iowa. It was a very small town. There were tractors parked in the street. We walked into a general store that had everything in the world in it including a bar and a restaurant of sorts.

We sat at a table and my dad said, "Look around this room. There is a man in here who owns over one million hogs and is probably the richest guy in Iowa."

I searched the room and even got up to look down the aisles. Everyone was in the bar. They were all farmers wearing bib overalls. Not one guy in here looked like he had two dimes to push together.

"Dad, are you pulling my leg?"

"No, look around. See the bartender?"

"Yeah." He looked like a hobo. Unshaven and red faced.

"He owns everything in sight including this place. I don't know what a hog is worth but that guy has millions. And look at him. He looks like the average farmer doesn't he? Just goes to show you."

"Wow. If I was rich I'd never show it either. Interesting story, Mark."

"Yeah and I'd never work again or live in Iowa. Nothing against Iowa but I'd rather live in San Francisco."

Once we crossed the Mississippi River we were in Illinois. Nothing of note in this part of the country, mostly farmland. It was late afternoon.

By early evening we drove into the outskirts of Chicago.

"I'm going downtown. Where can I drop you off?"

"Oh, anywhere is fine." I had to stick to my rules ... didn't want Max to know where I was really going.

Max pulled over.

"I don't know how to thank you for the ride. I'll never forget it! Oh, yeah, here's your meth."

"No man, you keep it. I've got plenty."

"You sure?"

"Yeah."

"See you, man. Thanks again."

And off he roared like a Zephyr, an unseen wind.

I was in Chicago in 48 hours. Unbelievable!

I called Paul.

"Are you here already? I wasn't expecting you until tomorrow!"

"I know. I'll tell you about it later."

Paul picked me up and took me to his place.

"You look like shit, man!"

"I need food and sleep. Here's the package."

"Take a shower and I'll fix you something to eat."

After cleaning up and eating a sandwich with a beer I was done. I fell asleep and slept for twelve hours.

I got up and for a few moments I didn't know where I was. Nothing looked familiar. It took several minutes and a quick peek out the window before I realized I was in Chicago. Paul was out. The place was empty. I made some coffee. Rinsed out my clothes in the bathtub, hand wrung them, and hung them up to dry. I found a pair of Paul's jeans. It was very warm and my clothes would dry in hours.

I felt human again. I walked down the street and found a pay phone. I called Carol. She wasn't home.

Paul would call Mark so I didn't call him.

I had no idea what or where I was going next. I needed a few days to recover from the drive.

I needed to find Carol so I walked over to the Loyola campus. I loved walking through this town. Once you left the city area the neighborhoods were lovely. Endless Maple lined streets.

I hung out in the Student Union for awhile but I didn't see her. She had mentioned once that she liked to study there. No luck. I walked across campus to a quad. Hundreds of students hanging out in small groups or some individuals leaning against trees lost in their books. I spotted the back of a woman talking with a group of friends. She turned around. It wasn't her. Then I thought that if I did find her she might think I was spying on her. Maybe I was. We hadn't seen each other in some time and I only wrote her one letter. Maybe she found another guy. Paranoia and jealousy ran through my veins.

I had given up looking for her when I spotted her. Walking alone towards me. She hadn't seen me yet. I leaned against a tree and waited. Her head was down. 100 feet away. She looked up and looked at me. Her eyes focused and she seemed to look again at me. She hesitated.

"Mark!"

She ran towards me.

"Mark, is that you?"

I just smiled.

"Yeah, it's me. Is that you?"

"Oh my God, I missed you. I didn't think you'd ever come back."

I'd never been kissed like this before. I actually thought I would fall down.

She said she had a test to take. I waited for her in the Student Union.

"Carol, I love you. I have to tell you something. Something very important. I've kept you in the dark ..."

"Are you married?"

"No, no, nothing like that. You have to promise me that you won't tell anyone, even Allison of what I'm about to tell you. I've gone over this 100 times in my head."

I swallowed hard and just spit it out.

"I'm a draft resister and am being hunted by the FBI and I work in the underground. That's all I can tell you right now. Don't tell your parents or your friends. Anyone. Understand. Because if you do I'll have to leave for good."

She stared at me in stunned silence. She took this as good news, I think because I wasn't married. And I wasn't a bank robber or anything like that.

"I love you too, Mark. I won't tell."

"I'm transferring to Madison next semester. I want you to come with me. Can you? Please say yes."

"Yes," I said without hesitation. I had work to do there as well, I thought to myself. I realized then that I really did trust her and moreover, I really loved her. Deeply.

I felt like the luckiest man in the world.

Carol had finals all next week and she had to cram but we found time for some serious lovemaking.

I showed her the crystal ball and she said it would help her study. She said lots of students were using that instead of No-Doz.

While Carol was in class I hung out with Paul. I told him about Carol and her plans to move to Madison. He thought that my relationship with Carol was a perfect front and I guess it was on one level but I truly did love her. He had to understand that. Paul said he was going to talk with Mark in a couple of days and that he would relay that information. In the meantime Paul told me to hang tight.

I could sense a major shift in this country because of Kent State. People who'd been on the fence with the war seemed to be favoring a withdrawal of troops and an end to the war. Maybe there was hope after all!

Chapter 11

Madison

Moving day came. Allison was moving with us having decided to transfer as well. Both women were originally from Madison and they were going home.

Carol rented a U-Haul truck and with the help of four other strong guys, we loaded the truck by 3 o'clock.

We were on the road by 5. Two cars and the truck. One of the guys drove the truck and Carol and I in one car and Allison in her car with one of the guys who was her boyfriend.

Carol's mom had found an apartment off Langdon Street in Madison. We all arrived by 9 something. We found parking and we began to unload everything. Beds and a couch and kitchen stuff and endless boxes of books and what have you. This apartment was half the size of the other one and I wondered if it would all fit. But it did. The place was a mess but we all worked through the night. We had the beds down.

The truck was empty and we all crashed. Exhausted.

We awoke late the same morning to chaos. We attacked the kitchen first, then the bathroom. Slowly, the place was coming together. We borrowed a neighbors phone and ordered pizza. Allison and her boyfriend, Roy, returned the U-Haul. I broke down boxes and kept clearing newspaper and such and made several trips to the garbage.

I hooked up the stereo and soon we had music. It was a cheerful scene.

There was a washer and dryer in the basement and we did several loads of wash.

By that night the place was looking pretty good. There were still odds and ends that needed to find a home, but on the whole, it looked like a home.

Carol and I couldn't keep our hands off each other. I'm sure Allison could hear us making love.

Carol had told me that her dad was the Dean of Medicine at the University. I knew her parents had a cabin on the Wisconsin River so they'd be around for the summer. I was afraid and at the same time looking forward to meeting them. After all, I loved their daughter!

When I got a chance to look the place over I realized we were not 100 feet from Lake Mendota. On North Henry Street. It was lovely. Carol knew Madison well and wanted to show me the campus. She gave me a thorough tour telling stories along the way when she was in high school about a variety of events that took place on these hallowed grounds.

We held hands.

I was thinking the whole time that I might run into John and Terry but I didn't see them. I knew Mark wanted me to find Oliver and see what he was up to.

In a couple of days Carol and Allison found waitressing jobs at the Holiday Inn. Carol had an early morning breakfast shift and Allison was taking a summer class as well, so I had the apartment to myself. I told the girls that I would do all the cleaning. The kitchen and bathroom needed the most attention. The living room was easy. Empty ash trays and clear empty beer bottles. The girls kidded me. I was 'the maid.'

I was getting pretty low on money and I hitched out to the cannery where I'd worked before and got a job on the spot. I even got my old position back in the warehouse. I found Terry and John working back in there as well.

"Mark!"

I heard my name. They were both driving forklifts. What luck. I could make some serious money in a few weeks. The Revolution had to wait.

I would be working from noon to about ten each night. Perfect. Terry had a car and he could pick me up each day. Carol was working anyway. We had our evenings together. I told them I could work six days a week but they said five days for now. The cannery didn't really get busy until August. It was only operating at half capacity. Most of the crew were students with a smattering of Mexican immigrant workers.

We spent a week cleaning out the warehouse updating the inventory. The books were a mess so I had John and Terry move out pallets of peas and corn so we could recount and also put the older stock in front so it would ship first. Last year's accident, (when a fork lift driver had bumped into a row of peas and like dominoes, leveled the entire warehouse) had jumbled everything up.

All the machines had to be repaired before the first harvest was ready. It was fairly relaxed and I enjoyed the work.

Carol and I still had our evenings together. We enjoyed walks on the lake and strolling across campus.

Things were quiet in Madison during the summer break. I knew things would get crazy again in the fall when 30,000 students returned to Madison.

One weekend Carol and I drove to her parents' cabin on the Wisconsin River. It was no 'cabin,' it was a small furnished home. I finally met her parents.

I was really nervous but they put me at ease. He was a doctor and taught medicine and Carol's mom was a political activist. I wasn't sure what that was except she had an office near the Capital building.

There was a lot of work to do at the cabin so of course I pitched in. We fixed a window that was cracked and did some painting and I cleaned out the swimming pool. Carol's mom had been out the week before and tried to clean the leaves out of the pool. Even though the pool was covered, the muck seeped in. She drained most of the brown water and then topped it with fresh heated water, but the drain was still plugged so I held my breath and dove down 10 feet picking leaves from the drain. I had a mask on, which helped. Carol's mom came out for a dip. It was sweltering hot. She was skinny dipping in the pool. I averted my eyes as much as I could. But, Jeez!

They were planning a big party for the next weekend so we worked hard. We had a big lunch and Carol said she wanted to show me something so we drove back to the main road and in five minutes we were looking at Frank Lloyd Wright's Taliesin East. Carol's family knew the caretakers and they gave us a tour of most of the house.

You see things in books and then you see it in person. Carol's friend took care of the house and grounds year round. He said there was endless work to be done. We walked into rooms that played with your perspective. Huge windows offering views of the river valley walking into spaces inside with gardens and rock paths and natural waterfalls. It was like being in nature yet protected from the elements. The structure seemed to grow out of the hillside.

He couldn't show us the entire house. I sensed that there was someone else in the house.

We toured the gardens outside. Cascading layers of native plants.

Carol said we had to be getting back. We thanked our host.

"Carol, that was amazing. I've seen photographs of it and the house in Arizona and they don't do it justice."

"I know. He never really completed it. He just kept adding on rooms. We didn't even see half of it!"

When we returned her dad asked me to rake the grounds. I started in the driveway and worked towards the small yard. It took me the rest of the day.

We had a huge dinner. Carol's mom had put out clean linen in each of the bedrooms. The house was pretty much put together. Her dad said we'd finish the pool and deck area tomorrow.

"Mark, we're having a party next weekend. Do you know how to tend bar?" her father inquired.

"No sir, I don't."

"Nothing to it, really. If someone asks for a drink just ask them what they want in it."

We all laughed.

I guess I'd be the bartender next weekend. I shrugged my shoulders and just laughed. They had a complete bar with liquors I'd never heard of. Hell, I just drank beer and there was plenty of that.

I had assumed I'd be sleeping on the deck or on a couch but Carol and I had our own bedroom. Boy, how times have changed.

After dinner we played scrabble. I held my own and didn't embarrass myself too much. They kicked my ass but we had a lot of laughs trying to make up strange words. I did impress them with 'ort.' A table scrap.

Carol and I went off to bed. I told her I just couldn't 'do it' with her parents in the next room.

"Prude!"

We all arose early. Carol's mom made breakfast and we made small talk.

After showering and cleaning up the kitchen we attacked the decks, scoured the pool, and washed all the windows. They were such a happy family doing all the tasks with glee. I remembered my dad when we had chores and how he made our lives miserable with his constant criticism. I was envious of Carol having been raised in a functional family. What was that like?

We stopped at noon and had lunch.

"We're almost done kids!" exclaimed the doctor.

We vacuumed and dusted and did a few loads of wash and by three we were all headed back to Madison. Carol told me on the way back that her parents really liked me. I liked them too.

Carol and I were pooped when we got home. We ordered a pizza and bought some beer home from the cabin. Watched some TV, made love and fell asleep early. We both had to be up early. Carol and I both had to work.

Terry and John picked me up and we drove to the cannery. I told my supervisor that I had to take Friday off and he said that was fine. The fields wouldn't be ready for the first harvest until next week and then all hell would break loose. The warehouse was almost ready for new production. I noticed that some of the Mexican workers were arriving, living in their horrible little shacks. I just shook my head.

It was pay day too. At lunch Terry, John and I cashed our checks at the bank. Had a couple more hundred bucks. Life was good! It was weird signing my fake name on a check. I always had to stop and focus when my name came up. My head still spun when I heard 'Mike' shouted out. I just had to be sharper and bury Mike McAndrew.

Carol and I spent Friday morning loading the car for the weekend. The party wasn't until tomorrow night but we had to get the cabin ready. Carol's mom called and said they were leaving and she wanted to make sure we were leaving too.

"Yes, Mom. We have it. Yes. Don't worry. Yep. Love you too!"

"My mom is a worrier. She always over plans. You know. But I love her. She's the only Mom I've got," she tittered.

I thought of my mom and almost started to cry. Her wasted life. Drugs and booze. She used to be smart and alert and ... I let it go without saying a word.

We arrived at the cabin. Carol's mom had taken charge. She wanted me to unload their station wagon. I opened the back of the car. It was full of food and booze. It looked like a liquor/grocery store on wheels. Most of the food went into the freezer and the fridge. Doctor was busy setting up the bar.

"Here's a booklet for you with the most common drinks."

"Thank you. I don't know anything about mixed drinks but I'll give it the college try."

"That's all you can do. Don't worry about it. These people are under-standing."

"You'll do fine," he added.

"Mark? Where are you? We need some help out here."

The pool drain was still plugged. The water looked clean and clear at least but it wasn't draining. I took my shoes and shirt off. I was wearing shorts and jumped in. The water was warm and felt great. They handed me a mask and I dove to the bottom. The drain was indeed plugged but I couldn't stay down for very long without having to come back up to the surface gasping for air. The doctor saw my problem and brought a garden hose.

"Here, breathe through this. Maybe it'll work."

It did. I held the hose to my mouth getting some air and with the help of a screwdriver managed to pry the drain cover off and I saw the problem. A mass of gunk had collected in there. I stirred it up and grabbed handfuls of the elusive stuff. But the drain was still plugged. I came to the surface and asked for some kind of a stick or prod to break through. The doctor ran into the house and came back with the poker from the fireplace, a nice heavy metal prod. I dove back down and within seconds the plugged drain was clear!

"It worked. My dad was a plumber."

Everyone laughed. Carol gave me a kiss.

"My hero!"

We barbecued burgers. The cabin was ready. The doctor showed me how to mix some drinks.

"It's pretty basic. Most of the men will want scotch or bourbon with a splash. A splash is a touch of water. Don't stir it. Put the ice in first, add the booze and finally water. The gals usually like wine or a soft drink. Don't worry about it. You'll do fine."

We hung out by the pool. The lights were on, lining the pool. It was a beautiful warm night and we had a nice evening assisted by several beers.

We all retired by midnight.

Carol and I were up early. The sun was up and it was going to be a warm day. Carol's mom made breakfast and after we cleaned the kitchen Carol and I jumped in the pool. That was our morning shower.

The first guests began arriving by 1 p.m. Within an hour the driveway was getting full. We had people park on the sides of the long narrow road.

I was introduced to several people but I immediately forgot their names. One man was a Federal Judge. Imagine, if he knew about me. I had to laugh at the irony. I was hiding out right in their midst.

Another couple were the two who hosted that party in Chicago.

I positioned myself at the bar. So far so good. Mostly gin tonics and beer. I was really busy. The doctor came in to help me out. Carol was busy busing for empty glasses and washing them out. Carol's mom put out platters of treats.

"I'd like a scotch and water."

"Comin' right up."

I looked up and it was Senator Proxmire!

"Thank you," he smiled.

By 3 o'clock the place was packed. The din of conversation and distant laughs and chuckles. The soon to be Governor, Patrick Lucey was talking to some people including Senator Nelson.

Wow!

I told the doctor I needed to pee and excused myself. The bar was packed and people were just having a good time. I peed outside in the bushes because the bathroom was busy. I ran downstairs and carried up two more cases of beer. It was still cool.

Steaks and burgers were frying on the barbecues. The pool was full of people. I grabbed a beer to sip on. I didn't have time to do much except serve the bar. Thankfully no one asked for any strange drinks. I was relieved.

We needed more ice so someone volunteered to drive out and buy it.

I didn't have a chance to really talk with anyone except one woman who was getting drunk on white wine.

"Honey, would you pour me another?"

"Sure."

I topped off her glass. She was an attractive older woman. She looked into my eyes and held her stare. I wasn't real comfortable with that.

"That's my asshole husband over there with the blue shirt on. He's a big shot judge. Whatdya think of that?" she slurred her S's.

The doctor had walked out to mingle with the crowd. Carol wasn't in sight.

"That's great!" I responded. I didn't know what else to say.

She was hunched over the end of the bar. She reached around with her hand and started to rub my leg. I had shorts on so there was no mistaking it. Her hand glided up to my crotch under the shorts. I froze for a second and then quickly moved away.

"Doris, stop bothering that young man."

One of her, also drunk, girlfriends rescued me.

"I can't help it. He's cute."

"Come on. Let's take a dip."

And with that I was saved. It always killed me when the older generation knocked us for our so-called life style of sex and drugs. Where do you think we learned it from!

Most people were by now out on the deck mingling or in the pool. People were lined up to eat so it was time for me to clean up the bar and to restock some of the booze. There were five empty scotch and gin bottles plus untold empty beer bottles. I ran the dishwasher again. We were low on glasses. We had plenty of ice. After an hour the bar was ready for round two. I noticed a large jar at the end of the bar. It was full of cash!

"That's for you Mark."

"Thank you, sir, but ... I don't think I deserve that. You paid for everything."

"No, no. That's yours," said the doctor.

I grabbed a handful and lined my pockets. I didn't count it. Mostly ones I noticed.

Carol's mom made an urn of coffee and put it out on the deck. It was late afternoon by now and several guests had departed. I didn't see the Senators so they must have left.

I took the glasses out of the dishwasher and put them away. I grabbed a beer and found Carol on the deck. She was talking with some people. She glanced my way and she motioned me over.

"Everybody, this is Mark."

"Hi. Pleased to meet you."

I didn't want to make small talk. I didn't know how to answer questions such as: "Mark, where are you going to school?" So I didn't say anything. I told Carol I had to clean up the upstairs so I excused myself. I felt inept and inferior in this crowd.

I tackled the stacks of dirty dishes and carried out numerous bags of garbage and bottles. I hid out in my work. Carol's mom looked exhausted.

"Why don't you go out and relax. I can get the rest of this."

"Thanks Mark, you're an angel."

There were only a few people left.

I counted almost $50 in tips.

It was getting dark and the pool lights were on. I was pooped. I sat with Carol by the pool and I nearly fell asleep. Carol nudged me.

"Come on Sir Galahad, you need some sleep."

"Good night, all."

Woke the next morning to a fairly clean cabin.

"Good morning. That was some party. I didn't realize you knew so many influential people!"

"Oh, they're just people. People who happen to be in the public eye."

"Well, I'll never forget it."

"Mark, you did a splendid job bartending. Everyone had a nice time." Carol's mom said.

"Oh, Thanks. And thank you for the tips. Whose idea was that?"

"Mine," Carol said. "We have a tip jar at the restaurant in the bar and I sorta put it out there as a joke but people put money in it."

We all laughed.

Here I was. I figured at least five federal warrants and maybe more, in the midst of the major politicians and judges in the State of Wisconsin. It was probably the safest place I could have been. The irony!

We loaded up both cars with garbage. We'd have to make a dump run.

It was Sunday and after a quick dip in the pool, we finished cleaning up and drove back to Madison.

What a party!

"Carol, you never told me your parents knew senators and judges. I figured it would just be a few close friends."

"I didn't want to tell you because we weren't sure if Proxmire and Nelson would even show up. Did that judge's wife make a pass at you?"

"Yeah, she freaked me out."

"She's done that before. She gets blasted drunk and flirts with guys. She's kinda crazy."

"I didn't like that, Now I know how women must feel when some jerk makes a pass. Hey, I've got $50 let's get some pizza!"

"We can't. We've got a car load of left overs," Carol said.

"Oh yeah, how about beer."

"We've got plenty of that too!"

"Well, all right!"

"I just want to watch some TV and go to bed early."

"Me too."

Monday morning and back to reality. We both went to work. Terry and John picked me up. We smoked a joint on the way. I decided not to talk about the party. It would sound like I was bragging.

The early peas were coming in. It took a couple of days to get production going. All the new people had to be trained and the machines ground to life after the winter's hibernation. I'd forgotten how much the peas stunk.

All we could do in the warehouse was wait for the first pallets to come through.

In the back of my mind, always there and not forgotten, were my duties to Mark in Berkeley. I told him I needed to work for a couple of months and save some money. I knew I had to find Oliver, somehow.

If I could last the summer season working here I could make a couple thousand dollars, maybe. I wanted to give Carol something for rent and food.

It was hotter than hell in the plant. The warehouse had to be kept cool to store the canned food. I was lucky. By late in the afternoon the first steady flow of pallets began rolling in. John and Terry were busy. The strong smell of propane exhaust filled the warehouse. My job was to log each pallet and number them and then enter that information into an inventory book. It was essential that the records be precise. The other two guys who did my job were equally adept at it too. At the end of my shift I showed the second shift guy where we were and he took over. John and Terry dropped me off.

"See you guys tomorrow."

And so it went for the rest of the summer. Carol and I were deeply in love. Allison stayed with her boyfriend most of the time so we had the place to ourselves. School was to begin in mid September. I planned to work until the end of August having saved a nice tidy sum. Students began filling the campus again. The protest movement had taken a summer break as well. The War was escalating however, as Nixon promised to end the war.

I hadn't heard from Mark in a couple of months. I assumed I'd have some more traveling to do.

It was the day before my real birthday August 24th, a Wednesday. It was very early. Carol and I were asleep as was most of Madison.

An explosion rocked our building. It woke everyone up.

"What was that?"

"Are you okay?"

"Yeah."

"That sounded like a bomb. What the hell ..."

People were scurrying in the hallways. Frightened faces. Panic. I ran into the street.

"What was that ..."

"It came from that way ..."

Nobody knew what was going on. I ran back inside and turned on the TV. The first reports were coming in. An excited local newscaster was saying that an unknown explosion had occurred on the campus. He advised people to stay in their homes. We could hear a myriad of sirens.

Carol tried to call her folks but all the phone lines were dead.

I decided to investigate. Carol wanted to stay home so I ventured out. Thousands of people were walking towards the campus. A huge plume of smoke rose over Lake Mendota. As I neared the site I could smell it. I thought it must be a fire because so many fire trucks passed by.

It was easy to find. Hundreds of police officers were ringing the area. It was one of the buildings on campus and it was gutted. The building was still standing but the insides were demolished.

News crews, cops, and thousands of bystanders ogled the building.

Was this an accident? I overheard somebody say that it was an Army Research building. Were they making bombs in there? There was so much uncertainty. I just hoped no one was hurt or killed.

I ran back home and told Carol what I'd seen.

"They said on TV that it was the Army Research building and they suspect someone bombed it!"

"Wow. No shit!"

The phones were still dead. I tried to call John. I didn't know if we'd work today or not.

John, Curtis, and Terry did show up. We drove to the plant chattering about the explosion. We worked that day as if nothing had happened. I'd given notice a week before and I was just going to finish off the week.

Rumors were flying around the plant. I couldn't wait to get home and watch the news.

Carol and I sat rapt as Walter Cronkite led the *CBS Evening News* with the story of the bombing. The FBI was looking for Dwight Armstrong and his brother Karl, and David Fine, and Leo Burt.

"Know any of those guys?" I asked.

"Nope. Sure don't."

As video of the building, identified as Sterling Hall, rolled by, Walter said that one man had been killed. Robert Fassnacht.

"Shit. This is serious."

The phones were finally working again. I had to reach Mark. I called him from a pay phone. I waited twenty minutes before he called me back.

"Mark, all shit has happened. You must have heard."

"Oh yeah. Listen up, here's Oliver's phone number. Call him right now. He's expecting your call. He's got a package for you. Get it to Minneapolis by this weekend. I can't tell you about it, but this is fucking heavy, man. You have money."

"Yeah. I've been working."

"Good boy."

"Call me when you get there. I've got something else for you."

I got back home.

"Happy Birthday to you ..."

The apartment was full of people. Carol had thrown a surprise Birthday party for me. Shit, I almost forgot. I was 22 years old.

Chapter 12

Oh! Canada

"Oliver, this is Mark. Can we meet somewhere?"

After telling Oliver what I'd be wearing and a general description, we met at the Student Union in the Rathskeller.

"Pleased to meet you Oliver. Oh, I remember you. Didn't we meet before?"

"Yes. It was a while back."

"Oh yeah, I remember now," I said.

"Mark speaks highly of you. Man, this town is swarming with FEDS. Mark said you could be trusted. I've got a package to bring to Minneapolis. Can you get it there?"

"Yeah, sure. Mark told me about you too. He mentioned the Smith Brothers again. And you know them? Right?"

"Yeah, couple of rich party guys that wanna be revolutionaries. Pretty nuts actually. I thought maybe those crazy fuckers were responsible for Sterling Hall but it was the Armstrongs. They're crazy too. Here's the deal. This package is for them."

"The Armstrongs?"

"Yep. Just some stuff from their mom, she lives in town. I think there's money in there too. When can you leave?"

"Give me a couple of days to get my shit together."

"Cool. Buy you a beer?"

"Why not. Are you being watched or followed?"

"I don't think so."

"Watch your back."

"Yeah."

Oliver and I hit it off. We laughed and had a couple of beers. I kept an eagle eye out for anyone watching us. I saw no one.

"I'll look you up when I return. Might be awhile."

"Right on," he said. "Oh, hey, can you come with me? I'm supposed to meet these guys. A few of us want to buy some pot from these guys. I'd like to have someone with me. We're just gonna talk for now. Won't take long. They're staying at the Holiday Inn down the street."

"Yeah, sure, ... I guess."

I stashed the package in my ruck sack and we walked a few blocks to the Hotel. Oliver knocked on their door.

"Who is it?"

"Oliver."

The door opened.

"Who's this?"

"My friend, Mark."

Three guys were sitting on a couch. The TV was on with no sound. They looked tough. Moderately long hair, jeans, ...

The one guy did all the talking. He said they had several kilos of hi-powered pot to sell.

"How much?"

"Depends on how much you buy."

As Oliver and this guy negotiated I checked out the other two guys. They glared at me. Not blinking.

"Got a sample?" Oliver asked.

Oliver took a joint from him and lit it. I took a hit too. It was very good. No doubt about that. The other three shook their heads when I offered to pass the joint.

I put in down in the ash tray.

I had a bad feeling. I wasn't even listening. Something wasn't right.

Oliver said that he'd get back to them.

We walked out.

"Oliver, those guys are cops! I can smell 'em. They were too clean. They didn't smoke the joint. They all were clean shaven. They're trying to set you up."

Oliver looked at me like I was from Mars.

"Tail 'em. I bet they leave here and go to the police station. I've got to get home."

I left Oliver in front of the Hotel.

When I saw Oliver next he said he waited outside for about fifteen minutes and a cop car picked them up. I was right!

The Bullshit Detector still worked.

I walked back to Carol's carefully checking my back to see if I was being followed. I wasn't or if I was I didn't see anyone. I couldn't be too careful.

"Hi, Honey, I'm home."

"I missed you. Where'd you go?"

"Had a beer with a friend of mine from work," I lied. I hated lying to her but I had to.

"Listen duty calls. I have to hit the road for a few days maybe longer."

"Oh. Where are you going?"

"East. I'm going east."

"Back to Chicago?"

"Maybe. It doesn't matter. But, I'll be back before you know it. Someday I'll tell you everything. I'm just trying to protect you. I hope you understand. There is no 'other woman' or any crazy shit like that. Please trust me. I really do love you."

"I trust you. I want to trust you."

We had a sad night together. I was fretting over what I had to do. I didn't know what would be waiting for me in Minneapolis.

As I sat on the bus I kept thinking about the bombing and how I wanted to distance myself from the violence. I simply abhorred violence. There was no way I could justify it and yet here I was possibly carrying letters and maybe money for the Armstrong Brothers. But, at the same time I couldn't say no to Mark. I'm sure I could have and maybe he would understand. It was that I was too weak to say 'no.'

Besides, I had to lie to Carol. I hated that!

I was so confused and really couldn't talk with anyone about this. Mark and I usually talked for thirty seconds on the phone. He didn't want to stay on the phone any longer than he had to. I couldn't blame him. Things were really heating up. I had to be cool in Minneapolis. People knew me there. My hair was really long and I was wearing sun glasses and a cowboy hat. Hopefully, this bad disguise would suit me.

I called Jeff. He was expecting me. Jeff picked me up.

"Hey man, how goes it?"

"Okay. Guess you heard about the bombing. Eight million cops, man. It's too hot there right now. The fucking FEDS have been really hassling people. I've heard of late night raids and shit. Dragging people out into the street in the middle of the night. Really fucked up, man. Other than that ..." I trailed off.

"You're supposed to meet this guy. I think his name is Gary. Anyway, I'm going to drop you off at his house. He lives in Edina."

"Cool."

Minneapolis, although not big in population is large in area. It took the better part of an hour to arrive at Gary's house. It was a nice middle class neighborhood. I'd been in this area before. I had cousins who lived in St. Louis Park which we drove through on the way.

Jeff and I made small talk on the way. He was finishing up in law school and was hoping to be a real lawyer in a year or two.

"That's great, Jeff. You can be my attorney when I finally get busted."

"Don't even say that. You won't get caught. You're too smart and careful."

"I hope you're right. I hope you're right."

"Well, here we are."

Jeff knocked on the door. The living room curtains moved. In a minute the door opened.

"Gary, this is Mark."

We exchanged pleasantries.

Jeff left. We said our good byes.

"See you soon, brother."

"Mark, want anything? I've got coffee, tea, soda ..."

"I'll have a coke."

"Got it."

Gary was intense.

"Nice place."

"It was my mom's. She left it to me when she died."

"Oh, I'm sorry."

"Yeah, it was tough. Fucking cancer. My dad got killed in Vietnam. He was a 'lifer.' So, I've got this great house."

It was sparsely furnished which made it seem even larger than it was.

"Listen," Gary said, "change of plans. Just say no if you don't want to do this. We're going on a camping trip. Fishing season ends in two weeks and we're driving up to Northern Minnesota near the Canadian border. Two other guys are coming with us. They are draft resisters and are going to Canada. We're going to go fishing and then take a canoe across the waters to Canada. Take the package with you. That's going to Toronto."

"Toronto?"

"Yup. Toronto. Still wanted to do this?"

"I wouldn't miss it for the world. When do we leave?"

"Right now. Don't worry, I've got all the camping gear packed up and ready to go. All you have to do is get in the camper."

Gary had a Winnebago camper with a canoe on top. Yeah, we were going camping. It was like a house on wheels. It had a kitchen and a living room and a bedroom and even a bathroom.

"Jeez, you could live in this thing."

"I do."

Jeff pulled out of the driveway.

"We ain't going to Toronto. Just said that in case the place is bugged. We're only going to cross the border and come right back. Take two or three days. I've done this a few times already. It's sweet, man. Got some people on the other side who'll pick these guys up and take 'em somewhere, don't know where and I don't wanna know. You'll give the package to one of the guys there. They know we're comin'."

Gary looked like Mr. Wilderness with his hunting hat on and a hunting jacket.

"War has killed my family. I was an only child. We moved all over the fucking place. Raised on Army bases. All I ever saw was death. It killed my mom for sure. All she ever wanted was a home. And my fucking dad was this gung-ho maniac. I loved them both but I never wanted any part of it. That's why I do this. To stop the madness."

"I can dig it!"

We crawled across Minneapolis and drove to a section of town off Lake Street. I remembered working with Native Americans in this part of town. It hadn't changed.

"Before we pick these guys up you have to know a couple of things. These guys have been vetted. You know what vetted is?"

And before I could answer.

"Vetted means that they were checked out. You know, to make sure they are who they say they are and shit. I ain't taken no fakers or murderers or FBI fucks over the border. They gotta be genuine. Certified! Ha, certified. I like that. I think I'll use that. Fucking certified, man. Fucking certified!"

"Well, let's pick up these fucking certified fucks and get 'em out of here," I laughed.

"Right on."

We were both laughing as we pulled up to an apartment building.

"Hey, Gary, before we pick these guys up I have some meth if you want. It's a chunk of pure crystal. All you have to do is lick it and it'll keep you going. Want some?"

"I knew you were good people."

"Oh, and another thing. Not a word about my package and the bombing stuff. Okay?"

"Oh yeah, mums the fucking word."

Since the day I had resisted, thousands more followed. I didn't know how many resisters there were. Many decided to go through the court system. They were routinely being sentenced to five years. Many of the Minnesota and Wisconsin guys were being sent to Joliet which was a hard core prison, full of murderers and rapists. Some guys were being sent to Stillwater, also a hard core federal pen. Unbelievable! The gentlest souls in the world sharing prison cells with psychopaths.

Gary and I picked up the two guys. They looked scared. I couldn't blame them. They were going into the unknown.

We introduced ourselves and Gary gave his little speech. No drugs and we didn't want to know much about them.

Michael and Joe took their seats in the back and Gary and I sat up front.

Gary headed for Highway 35 and we were on our way.

"There's pop and chips, help yourself."

Michael and Joe were pretty quiet for the first hour. I felt sorry for them. I found out that both guys were classified 1-A and assumed they would be drafted soon.

I assured them both that everything would be okay. It's scary the first time you leave home and even scarier when you don't know where you're headed. But, there's some kind of adventure lurking too and that can be exciting. It was exciting for me. Every institution from the church to my schooling to my family had been a complete disappointment to me. It was an easy decision to make.

Heading up Highway 35 into the early fall lush Minnesota country side. The leaves were just beginning to turn and there was a crispness to the air.

Michael and Joe seemed more relaxed now. They were talking to each other and enjoying cokes. I don't know if they knew each other before but I knew that this experience would bond them forever.

Trust was everything. Trust was an unknown. At this point in my life my very freedom hinged on it. As I looked back over the last couple of years I thought of the Acid Test and what it really meant. If you dropped acid with someone you bonded together. A trust was built. I just couldn't see an undercover FED or cop taking acid to gain our trust. But, realistically, you couldn't take acid every time you wanted to gain one's trust. So, I developed my own 'Bullshit Detector.' If something or someone didn't feel right then it probably wasn't. I felt 'right' with Gary and our two companions.

Gary needed to stop and gas up. Michael and Joe gave him some money. That surprised me a little.

We were about half way to Duluth. We still had a long drive ahead of us. Minnesota is a very long state. I figured we'd arrive to our destination very early tomorrow morning. I didn't really know what Gary had in mind. If we'd canoe in the daylight or what. I couldn't worry about that.

"You want a lick?" As I reached for my crystal. I kept it out of sight of the two boys in the back.

"Yeah. This shit helps. Keeps me alert. Could one of you guys pour me a cup of coffee?"

Michael reached for a thermos and poured Gary a cup. "Help yourselves." So we all had some coffee.

In a few hours we were just south of Duluth. We needed more gas and Gary needed to stretch. We all peed and refilled the thermos with coffee. We drove through Duluth and reconnected with Highway 61. I thought of the Dylan tune; "Where do ya want this killin' done ... out on Highway 61." This is the great Iron Range of Minnesota. Train loads of iron ore are trained to St. Paul where it is loaded onto barges which float down the Mississippi River. Billions of tons of the stuff in an endless supply of energy. Superior, Wisconsin is next door. We hugged Lake Superior for a few hours. It was magnificent. I'd never been up this far north before. It was like an ocean. Couldn't see the other shoreline.

"We still have a good drive. We're only half way there," Gary stated.

By now, the boys were laying down and resting.

"It'll be their last night in the US. Let 'em sleep."

We drove to Grand Marais and turned off on Highway 12.

"I wouldn't want to be up here in the winter. I bet this road is closed a lot."

"It can be after a big snow fall. But, these guys know how to clear roads. I've been up here at the cabin when it's -30 below. Fucking cold, man."

"No thanks."

"A few more hours and we'll be there. We can rest up during the day. It's supposed to be clear tonight with a full moon. You won't believe how serene it is up here. Total silence except for rustling leaves and critters."

"Bears and wolves?"

"I've seen a few. My dad bought this place years ago. Mom didn't like it that much. She could only stand a couple of days so Dad and I used to come up here all the time. We'd ice fish in the winter and fish all summer. We didn't hunt though. Dad hated guns."

"But he was in the Army."

"Exactly."

Some 12 hours after we left the Cities, we arrived at the cabin. The last miles being on a dirt road that was very bumpy. It woke our passengers up. I couldn't tell you where we were. Hadn't seen another human in an hour.

"Gary, this is great!.

The cabin was on the lake with a dock.

Gary unlocked the door and we packed our things in. The boys were quiet.

We had plenty of groceries with us.

"You guys hungry?"

Gary fired up a Coleman stove and made some burgers and hot dogs. Tasted great after the long drive. He went out to a shed and started a generator. We had lights.

"We'll have hot water in a few hours."

"We don't want to attract any attention so you two stay inside. It ain't like there's anybody around, but just to be on the safe side. Mark, you and I should probably try to get some sleep. But, first help me carry the canoe down to the dock. It isn't really that heavy."

The two of us easily managed to carry the canoe down.

"You see that clump of trees over there?"

"Yeah."

"That's where we're going. Make sure to bring your package."

"Right."

"They'll be waiting for us."

"You've done this before?"

"Yep. This is my third trip. So far, so good."

"Now, get some sleep."

Michael and Joe slept in the camper and Gary slept in the bedroom. I curled up in a sleeping bag and finally dozed off. I thought maybe I should go to Canada too. Here was my big chance. I tallied up the pluses: I'd be free, I could use my real name again, I wouldn't be living in constant fear of being caught and going to prison ... and the minuses: I was helping other people, I'd be 'chickening out,' ... and Carol.

After what seemed like several hours, I heard Gary in the kitchen. He was making coffee.

"It'll be dark around 7. We're supposed to meet them between 8 and 9. The moon will be up by then too."

I got up and woke the boys up. We drank coffee and were further perked up with speed. It was time to go.

"Okay. Here's the deal. Two guys row on each side and we row together. That way the canoe travels in a straight line. It takes about fifteen minutes to reach the other side."

Gary blinked his flashlight and two blinks returned.

"They're ready for us. Got your package, Mark?"

"Yup. Right here."

"Let's go!"

Gary got in first and sat in the back. The two boys in the middle and I was in front. We rocked a bit at first and after a few unsteady rows we found our cadence and moved away from the dock. The moon was bright, the air still and the water calm. We moved with surprising speed across the lake. Gary was right. It wouldn't take very long especially with four guys rowing.

I noticed that bugs weren't bad. Must be the fall weather.

Gary had told us not to talk because sound traveled so well. We whispered to each other counting out our cadence. "Row" ... "row" ... "row." I wanted to break into 'Row your boat' but thought better of it. This was fun.

Gary knew where he was going. He blinked his flashlight again and we could see that we had to veer to the right so Gary quietly told the other two guys to pull their oars and Gary expertly put us on course.

We glided onto the shoreline. We were in Canada! One of the Canadians pulled the canoe up onto the shoreline and we all managed to get out of the canoe.

"Hey boys. How's it going?" Gary said.

There were four guys. All had long hair. Gary didn't bother introducing everyone.

"Hey Thomas, Mark here has the package for you."

I really couldn't see that well. Thomas' face partially hidden by a large hat.

"Thanks, man," he said in a deep voice as I handed over the package.

I was free of that obligation. Aiding and abetting. That's me!

I was caught up in the moment. As we hugged our two comrades good by and good luck I knew I'd make the return trip. The two hapless boys, Michael and Joe thanked us over and over. That made me feel so good and reinforced my decision to return. I wanted to do this again!

The return trip took a little longer because there only two of us rowing. But it was relaxing out here. It was so beautiful.

We docked the canoe and went inside.

"Come on in Mark. Let's finally relax."

Gary promptly produced two beers and fired up a joint. He even had some music playing on a small stereo system.

"You know. We could stay up here for another day or two. If you want to, that is. I would like to fish some and enjoy this place. I may not be up here until next spring."

"Yeah. Okay," I said.

We listened to the Beatles and got pleasantly stoned. The night was perfect and we sat out on the deck and watched the moon silently crossing the sky.

"Hope those guys will be all right."

"They'll be in Montreal or Toronto in a couple of days. I've been there and their hosts will take good care of them. They'll find permanent housing and jobs for them. They can still see their families. Canadians are cool!"

"Man, that's a load off. I didn't have a good vibe with this package. I just wanted to hand it off and get rid of it."

"I know what you mean. I feel better getting those guys safely over. I don't really know if it's against the law to help these guys if they haven't been indicted yet. But, I suppose some prosecutor somewhere would make a case out of it."

"Yeah, no shit."

"Hey, let me ask you something," I inquired. "Are you going to be doing this again? You know, getting guys over the border. Because if you are I know some people who work with draft cases and would like to know you. If not just say so. I won't tell anyone. Until I write my great novel about these times, that is," we both laughed.

"Well, let me think about it. The more people who know about this, the more nervous I get. But, yeah, anything to help. If a guy came from you personally ... definitely!"

We settled back as the moon lit the lake. A bright reflection dancing on the waves.

"Goodnight, Gary. I gotta crash. See you in the morning."

It was so nice out that I slept on the deck and dreamed.

I heard foot steps on the deck. I could barely open my eyes. The sun was just coming up. Gary walked down to the dock and I heard the gentle clicking of a fishing rod casting.

I finally roused. Gary had made coffee. Had a cup.

I heard a yelp and watched Gary reel in a fish. Ten minutes later he had another one.

"Hungry? Got two lake trout. Can't believe it. It's usually hard to catch 'em. Breakfast will be in half an hour."

Gary cleaned the fish and fried them in butter and his 'magic batter.'

"Oh my God, this is the best fish I've had in years. My great grandpa used to fish and he was a fly fisherman. Trout is the best."

We dined on the fish as well as some fried potatoes with gravy. We sipped our coffee. I cleaned up the kitchen.

"Wow, Gary. That was really good."

"Thanks, man. This is why I love this place. No one around. You see a boat once in a while or a plane. You can live off the land up here but it can get lonely after a time."

"My dad could fuckin' fish, man. He'd reel in a Great Northern or a Muskie once in a while. Terrible tasting though so he'd throw 'em back. Just loved to fish. I miss him sometimes."

"So Gary, can I get personal? Like, what do you do and stuff."

"I broke my back in a car accident when I was 18 and was fucked up for a long time. It was the other guys fault and I got a settlement. So, that keeps me out of the draft."

"I did notice a limp."

"Yeah. Anyway, then both of my parents died, as I told you before, and they left me everything. I'm pretty blessed I guess. Just need to find the right gal to make me whole. How 'bout you, Mark?"

"Well, yeah, I came from a pretty fucked up family and was raised a Catholic. Fucked my head up bad. But, that's another story. Seems religion has killed more people than any other institution! Can't stand the thought of killing another human being or even an animal for that matter. Oh, it's okay that you fished because we ate them. You know, we go to the store and buy hamburger and shit, you know. That's different. I mean, killing out of hatred or just for the hell of it or 'cause your government tells you too. That's fucked, man! So, I guess I'm just trying to stop the war and all the killing and the racism against blacks and all the rest. My dad was in Iwo Jima and that totally fucked him up. He wakes up in the middle of the night screaming. He drinks all the time. I think just to quiet the noise in his head. And, I don't want to be like that. Oh, yeah, I've got a girl. A woman, I should say. She's smart. Smarter than me, that's for sure. And I love her. She could be the one. We always hear that. You know, 'the one.' Maybe she is. I'm lucky, man. Really lucky. And she doesn't know what I do. I feel like I'm lying to her ... I can't tell you all the shit I've done just 'cause. You know? I just can't tell her," I teared up.

"Oh cool, man. I don't want to know either."

"But I've never hurt anyone and never will," I added.

"Fuck it, man. Let's have a beer and some dope."

"Good idea, Ollie!"

We spent the rest of the day sitting on the dock and watching the day pass into night.

Gary said we'd leave in the morning instead of staying on any longer. That was fine by me.

Gary and I got up at sunrise. We packed up the camper. He turned everything off and double checked, just to make sure. We moved the canoe inside the cabin. "No room for it in Edina."

We headed out.

"We lucked out with the weather. It can get nasty up here. I don't think I'll be back until spring. The roads are so fucked up, especially this one." We bounced along the dirt road and eventually found a paved road.

"I'd get lost up here," I laughed.

"Believe it or not, during the summer this place is full of people. Campers and fishermen flock to this area. It's generally called the 'Boundary Waters.' I've seen planes land out there and we do have neighbors. Not many but some. A few cabins here and there. Maybe next spring we can get some more guys over. The lake usually freezes over in the winter. Shit, you can walk to Canada!"

Same long drive back.

"Those guys looked scared. Huh?"

"Yeah. They'll be fine. I was thinking that maybe next time we could go all the way to Montreal or Toronto. That way you could see for yourself how this is set up. I don't want to get into bringing real criminals up here though. Just draft resisters."

"Got it."

As we neared the Twin Cities I mentioned I wanted to catch the evening bus to Chicago. Gary dropped me off on Hennepin.

"Til next time brother. You'll be hearing from me."

We hugged each other and I walked to the station. Wow!

I walked to the ticket counter and bought a one way ticket to Madison. I called Carol and told her I'd be home in a few hours.

"Mark, I missed you. Are you okay?"

"I'm fine! I missed you too. I should be there by midnight. I love you."

"I love you, too."

I didn't mention I was in the Cities. She didn't ask, she knew better.

The bus was over half full. I found a seat in the back and tried to sleep. We drove through the center of Wisconsin on 94. We stopped in Eau Claire. Fond memories of my great grandparents. And Tomah and a few other small towns before mercifully arriving in Madison. I walked to Carol's apartment. I didn't know whether to knock or not. I knocked and opened the door. Carol and Allison were watching TV.

"Mark!"

Carol kissed me passionately and I returned the favor. God, I love this woman.

I was starving. Carol heated up some hot dish and we talked in the kitchen.

"Someday this will all be over and I can tell you about it. I hate being mysterious but I can't tell you stuff ..." I trailed off.

"I understand," Carol soothed me.

It was around midnight and Carol and Allison had classes tomorrow.

We went to bed and felt her body wrapped in my arms. I slept contented.

Carol and Allison ran off to classes. I didn't know what to do with myself. I was worn out by the trip but I needed something to do so after I cleaned up I went out for a walk. Winter was in the air. The campus was calm. I walked out to a point on Lake Mendota and day dreamed. A crisp wind made white caps on the water. I was discontent. I couldn't put my finger on it.

I walked back to the Student Union and didn't see anyone I knew. I had a beer. Cat Stevens (still) on their stereo. This semester was winding down.

I had to call Mark. I found a pay phone. I left my usual vague message with the phone number. 15 minutes later he called.

"Good job, Mark. Sorry about all the last minute changes but we had to be really careful with that package. Stay tight for the time being. I'll have something in a few weeks. Call me just before Christmas."

"Okay," and hung up.

I shuffled along State Street. Walked into a bookstore and read some Kerouac. Even that didn't cheer me up. Found a record shop and bought *Anthem of the Sun* by the Dead. I walked back home and put it on. I was dancing in five minutes. That's what I needed!

Allison came home so I turned down the volume. She went into her room and said she had to study. So I turned the stereo off.

Carol came home soon after.

"Mark, we need to talk."

Oh, oh!

"I couldn't tell you last night because you looked so wiped out. I'm going to Europe!"

"Huh?"

"I'm going to Europe next semester. I'm going to Lucerne in Switzerland to study for a semester and then I'm transferring to Bryn Mawr in Philly."

"When did this ... I mean ... what!" I was shocked and thrown off balance. "I thought you were going to say you met another guy."

"No, no. Nothing like that. My dad knows all these people and he wants me to study over there and my mom graduated from Bryn Mawr so she wants me to finish school there. I know this comes as a shock to you and it's really unfair to you but, I'm going to do this and if our love is strong enough we will survive this."

"I had this bad feeling all day. I just knew something was wrong."

I had been so happy the last few months with Carol. I knew it was too good to be true.

I had to find a place to stay. Rent was paid up until December 31. I found Oliver at the Student Union.

"How'd it go."

"Oh, just fine," I didn't tell him I had been in Canada.

"Everybody has been hassled by the FBI. We shouldn't even be seen together."

"Yeah, you're right. I'm going to go someplace until things cool down. By the way, Carol is going to Europe for the winter. She's going to school in Lucerne."

"Really, you must be bummed out. Sorry, man."

"Yeah. Listen, I'm going to split in a few days. I'll be back. Can I look you up again? Might be a while."

"Oh yeah, just let things cool down first."

I walked back to Carol's. We spent a few days packing her stuff and cleaning out the apartment. Allison needed to find another roommate.

"Oh Mark. Are you going to be okay?"

"Yeah. I love you so much. I'll see you next summer. I'm just feeling sorry for myself."

"I love you, too. I need to do this. And, except for you I'm really excited about this opportunity."

The semester was over. Carol and I said our good byes. Her parents picked her up. They were very kind to me. They got in the car and drove off. She was flying out of O'Hare.

Allison and I walked back into the apartment. She said I could stay until she found a roommate. But, I had other plans.

I called Mark from a pay phone. I told him I was coming out. I also called Brian in San Francisco.

I hopped a bus to Chicago. Too fucking cold to hitch.

It took me most of the day to get to O'Hare. Wouldn't it be weird to run into Carol. But, she was long gone.

I purchased a student stand by ticket to San Francisco. I waited all day and that night. The first flight left early tomorrow. I had missed today's flight. The airport was old and funky but safe. I bought a sandwich and curled up on the floor by the gate. I was actually able to sleep. Nobody bothered me. I only heard a few voices in the night.

I awoke abruptly to the sound of passengers going to their destinations. I had to pee and I splashed my face with cold water. I brushed my teeth. I almost felt human again. I walked to the gate and waited. I crossed my fingers that I'd get on. I did.

I'm outta here!

Chapter 13

1971

Brian and I celebrated New Year's Eve in style. Saw the Dead at Winterland. Bill Graham was dressed as 'Old Man Time' as he rode high above the crowd on a tight rope cable at midnight. The Dead always cheered me up. The show lasted half the night. We were righteously high when we finally stumbled out onto Post Street. We walked to the Mission to Brian's place. By the time we got home we were straight again.

"Man, that was great!" I exclaimed.

"It was, want a beer?"

We sat up the rest of the night talking in the kitchen. It was 6 a.m. when I finally went to bed. I had my own room. One of his roommates had gone home for the holidays.

I had the best sleep in a long time. My thoughts were of Carol and I felt a tinge of pain in my heart. She's probably in Switzerland by now. Fuck it! Got to move on.

Got up.

Brian was still asleep so I took a quick shower. Made some coffee. Smoked a few cigs. Didn't know what I'd do today. I was waiting for Mark to contact me. I loved being back in San Francisco. It was chilly but not like Wisconsin. I didn't think I could survive another winter there.

Oh, yeah. It was 1971! I almost forgot. It was New Years Day. Just kick back and watch football. It probably wasn't cool but I loved watching sports. Brian woke up and found me in front of the TV. It was early afternoon and a game was on.

"Morning."

Brian looked like he was in pain. He was hung over from last night. After a few cups of coffee and a couple of smokes he was able to talk.

"Whew. That was some night. Fun though. I love the Dead, man."

"Me too."

I went out and bought some beer and a few slices of pizza. When I returned Brian was his old self.

"Oh thanks man. Do I need this. A little hair of the dog," as he poured a beer down.

Watched Notre Dame beat Texas in the Sugar Bowl. That was great. Told Brian about my dad's years at Notre Dame. The other games were a blur. We drank and smoked dope and then walked out into the Mission. We found a neat old bar and drank more beer. Life was good. My troubles and broken heart numbed. I needed this.

"So, my friend, what's next for you? How long can you keep running?"

"As long as I have to I guess. They almost got me once. I was lucky. And the other thing is that I can't be in a relationship right now. I don't know what I expected. Shit, I couldn't tell her anything, man. She'll just find another guy anyway. It's tough, man. It's tough."

"You'll be okay. We've all gone through this shit. Somehow we get on. So will you. Time heals, as they say. Another beer."

"Definitely."

I just hung out for a few days. Brian and I had the flat to ourselves for another week. It was nice. I even went out and took pictures of the City. I loved taking street shots. People lost in their own little time and space racing through the day in a daze. The energy was powerful. What were they thinking at the moment I snapped the shutter? Were they happy or sad? Had they lost someone recently? It was my therapy.

Mark called. We'd meet tomorrow.

I watched the news every night. One could feel the country tiring of the war. Large anti-war protests were an everyday thing. This pleased me greatly. There was a shift.

I saw Mark the next day. He looked tired and worn out.

"Happy New Year," he said.

"I hope it will be."

"Sorry to hear about your girl friend. I guess we have to have a life, too. Things are dicey right now. I'm being followed and watched. I can't trust anyone anymore. Except you and a couple of other people. You did a great job going to Canada. I'm sure you'll be up there again. We have to get these guys out of the country. Everyday there are more and more of 'em. The Government and Nixon are losing. Fucking Melvin Laird is a psychopath and the rest of 'em are just plain liars. The American people are starting to see this and more and more people are speaking out. I'm encouraged. But, we have to fight on, man. I've got a big trip planned for you if you want it."

"Always."

"Good. That's what I thought you'd say. I haven't worked out all the logistics yet but basically you're going back to Tucson and Austin and maybe to Boston and New York. I'm getting some drivers together as well as some stuff to deliver ... you never look inside do you?"

"No, I've wanted to but just knew better."

"That's why I trust you, Mark. Anyway, as I was saying ... I'll have some money for you. How are you holding out?"

"I made some money last summer but I am getting low again. I have a couple hundred and I need to give Brian some. He's been great by the way. He always takes me in and I'm able to have some fun and relax. I trust him."

"Oh, I meant to ask. How was your trip with Max? He's a trip huh? But good as the day is long."

"Shit, man. He scared the shit out of me for the first 100 miles and then after that I got used to moving at 100 mph. We left the City and I was dropped off at the Loop in 48 fucking hours! Do you believe that! That fucker can out right drive."

Mark laughed.

"You said you were being followed. Are they watching us now?"

"Nope. I slipped out of the house clean."

"How'd you do that?"

"State secret. No, I wore a wig and a fake beard and then I darted into a bookstore and walked out the back. I'll retrace my steps on the way back. If they were watching me they will think I'm still in there."

"Have you ever been followed?" he asked.

"Not that I know of," I hoped.

"Well, listen my friend. Good to see you again. I'll be in touch."

"When will I leave?"

"Soon. In a week. No more."

"Peace."

I hung out and finished my coffee. So much to think about. Telegraph Avenue was a zoo. So many street people; runaways druggies, musicians, panhandlers every two feet, crazies. No wonder hippies had such a bad reputation. Some people called this place Berserkley. For good reason I thought.

Returned to Brian's.

"Mark's got another assignment for me. I'll be leaving in a few days, I guess."

"Bummer, man."

"If I stay in one place too long I get moldy," I joked.

His roommates returned so it was a good time to leave anyway. I asked Brian if he could keep all my processed film here. It was beginning to accumulate. I couldn't carry everything anymore. My ruck sack was brimming. I managed to clean all my clothes again. I still had the crystal in my pocket. I was using it more and more. It made me feel good.

A few days passed. Didn't do much. Just hung out and read. I was reading all the Beats. Catching up. They wouldn't let us study them at St. Mary's so I did it on my own. Besides the obvious authors like Kerouac and Ginsberg, I also found Corso to be enlightening.

Mark called. I was to be in Berkeley tomorrow morning. I'd meet him at the same cafe at 10.

I didn't sleep very well. I was emotionally spent. I was heartbroken over Carol. Every woman reminded me of her. It was better to be busy.

Mark was on time, as usual. He introduced me to Bill.
"Mark, meet Bill. He'll be driving you to Tucson and onto Austin."

"Pleased to meet you," I said extending my hand. We did the hippie handshake. He seemed like a nice person. Rather large with shaggy blond hair.

Mark passed me another package in a large manila envelope.

"This is for you," he handed me another $200 for gas.

Bill was driving a brand new Cadillac.

"Wow, nice car!"

"It isn't mine. It's a drive-away car."

"What's that?"

"There's an agency in Oakland. You can go there to drive someone's car for them. Let's say you're an old couple and you move to Texas but, you don't want to drive. This agency will find someone to drive their car for them. That's me. We only have to pay for gas and oil. We have to follow a certain route but they said I could go through Tucson and then onto Austin. No sweat, man. This car is awesome. It has air conditioning that actually works!"

"All right! Let's move," I said.

The car still smelled new. It was immense. We could easily sleep in here and stretch out.

We were going to Arizona and Texas. I put my crystal ball carefully wrapped in plastic and I dropped it into my Afta after shave container.

I just had a feeling.

I gave Bill my 'no drugs in the car' speech. He agreed. Two hippies in a new Cadillac and all. I heard tales of the cops in Arizona and especially Texas. A life sentence for having one joint for Christ' sake. Wasn't worth it.

Bill wanted to take Interstate 5 so we drove to Sacramento first and then headed south. Even though it was late January, we had the air conditioner on.

"This thing doesn't get great gas mileage but at least we're comfortable."

"Did they have any other cars?"

"None going our way. That's the trick. You gotta find one going where you're going at the same time."

"Yeah, I got it. Tricky."

We laughed.

Found a decent radio station. 5 was a major aorta connecting Central California to Southern California. The traffic consisted of mostly trucks. Bill was an experienced driver as well. I don't know where Mark found these people but he was always spot on. Getting together people.

"We're going to pick up two people in Tucson and take them to Austin. No worries, though, I know 'em. A young couple on their way back to school. You'll like 'em."

"We don't have to return the car for five days, so we can spent a night and a day in Tucson. Ever been there?"

"No. Oh yeah, passed through once. I've been so many places. I can't even remember," I joked.

We pulled into a huge truck stop in Bakersfield. This town scared me. All I saw were pickup trucks with gun racks. It was like the deep south. Nothing but red necks. After filling up and peeing we walked inside to have a snack. We had coffee and apple pie. No one really paid any attention to us except for a couple of dirty looks. I was used to that by now. Bill was kind of a large burly guy so no one hassled us.

"Oh man. That was good!" exclaimed Bill.

We checked the map and decided it best just to bite the bullet and drive through LA and down to San Diego before heading east to Tucson. It was getting late so we figured if we hit LA at ten p.m. the traffic wouldn't be too bad. We drove over the mountain on the insane stretch called the 'Grapevine.' The Caddy just ate it up like nothing. Bill weaving around a continuous string of semis. Going up the mountain, some of the trucks were only going 10 mph. There were six lanes so he was able to traverse in between and around the mammoths.

"Jesus, what a horrible road."

"I'm okay," said Bill, white knuckled.

Coming down the other side was hair raising as well. We hit speeds of eighty and so did the trucks.

"Fucking A, man."

And just like that the terrain flattened out somewhat and we hit the freeways of LA. At least it was moving. Six solid lanes of tail lights. Unbelievable! What are all these people doing out here driving at the same time.

"We missed the rush hour. At least we're moving. I'm going 70 and so is everyone else."

I consulted the map and told Bill which lane to stay in so we wouldn't get on the wrong freeway. But, I think Bill knew the way. How can people live like this?

"I hate this place. I really do. Too many people," I complained.

"Oh, I don't mind too much. LA is great as long as you stay off the freeways. The neighborhoods are great. I grew up in Pasadena and my parents still live there. I love it actually."

"Sorry, man. I didn't mean to insult you or anything. I just get too uptight sometimes."

"Oh, no sweat, man. You're cool. I know how you feel. It takes getting used to. I know what you're saying. It's cool. You know, if you don't know LA like I do I can see what you're saying."

"Pasadena ... isn't that where the Rose Bowl Parade is?"

"Sure is. I've been to a million of them."

"Wow, that's cool, man. When I was a little kid I watched it on TV. I grew up in Wisconsin and it was 20 below outside. Fuckin' sucked. As I watched the parade I vowed that I would live here someday. Where it's warm and you can wear a tee shirt in the winter."

"And so did 7 million other people."

"Ha. Good one."

Cars and lights all the way to San Diego. Too many people. We reached the outskirts of the city. We passed by the Marine base Camp Pendleton. This is where my dad was nearly 30 years ago before he was taken to fight the Japanese. And here I was, in defiance of everything he stood for and believed. I felt like an asshole. Like a coward. Like a traitor. And in some sense I was but to my core, I couldn't fight in a war. I just couldn't do it. What was wrong with me? I had doubts. To be sure. Who wouldn't when just about everyone you knew didn't agree with you. It's too late now. No turning back. I'd crossed that bridge.

I didn't care if I was right or wrong. Who could really decide that? I had to be true to myself. I was a selfish bastard. Narcissistic. Self centered and vain. Maybe I should of just gone off and gotten myself killed. Maybe I was better off dead anyway. Who would even notice.

Hidden thoughts deep inside.

"Now we head east, young man."

I came out of my coma and consulted the map once again.

"We gotta find 8. Takes us all the way to Tucson."

We'd be in Tucson by midday.

The stretch between San Diego and Tucson was a long lonely desert. Mexico was right there. I pondered that I'd been in Canada a few short weeks ago and there was Mexico. Travelling man!

We needed gas, again, and we coffeed up and used the rest rooms.

"We've got another ten hours or so. I reached in my ruck sack and pulled out my after shaving lotion bottle.

"Bill, I've got some speed if you want some. It'll help you stay awake."

"You do! Yeah sure, I could use some. The fuckin' road is straight and it hypnotizes you."

"Yeah it does. I keep it wrapped inside here," I pointed to the bottle.

"Clever," he said.

"We're coming into Yuma pretty soon. The fucking cops down here are assholes. I'll drive the speed limit."

It was totally black except for a few lights off in the distance. We watched the endless highway movie and listened to cowboy songs on the radio.

'Welcome to Arizona ... the Grand Canyon State.'

Yuma was on the California border. It was good to see lights and life again. We cruised through. Traffic seemed to pick up, mostly semis.

We drove through the night. The speed helped. Long drive.

The first rays of sunlight gradually broke the darkness. The desert was beautiful. The colors softened and yet saturated in gentle Earth tones. I snapped a couple of pics with my Nikon. Black and white. No matter. I would remember this moment. The air outside warmed. I could wear a tee shirt in January!

"Tucson comin' up."

It was midday. The sun was high. We had the air conditioning on. Tucson was larger than I expected. A University town. Very spread out and vast.

Bill drove to the college district and pulled into a neighborhood of one storied shacks and adobe houses and an odd assortment of other buildings.

"They live down this street. Funky huh?"

"Yeah. I like it, though."

I met Jerry and Mary. A young couple. After introductions and hugs between Bill and our hosts we settled into the living room. It was an adobe house. Built to remain cool during, I'm sure, the unbearably hot summers.

"You guys must be hungry. Or do you want to clean up first?" said Mary.

Bill was hungry and I asked if I could take a shower. The smell of coffee and cigarettes and sweat was overwhelming. Boy, did that feel good. I lathered up and stood under the shower for a few minutes and actually felt human.

I dried off, dressed, and walked into their kitchen. Mary had made some burritos and they were chowing down on them. I soon caught up while Bill took a shower.

"Where are you from, Mark?"

"Wisconsin. Where it's 20 below zero right now. This is awesome. What is it? 70 ... 75?"

"This is the best time of the year. It really gets hot in the summer. Over 100 degrees for two straight months. Mary and I rented this place because it stays cool," Jerry added.

"Jerry and I graduated this semester and we are going to Austin to get our Master's."

Wow. That's great," I had a tinge of jealousy.

"What's your study," I asked.

"We're both going to be teachers. Jerry wants to be a history professor and I'm an English major. We decided to take this semester off and move to Austin and then start classes in the fall. We needed a break."

"We're going to Austin to find an apartment and then we'll come back and move our stuff."

They were an awfully nice couple. Bill soon rejoined us. We were both exhausted. Mary showed us to a spare bedroom and they also had a study. I took the study and unfurled my sleeping bag and fell asleep.

"I'll wake you guys up in a few hours. We should go out tonight."

Bill and I slept fast. It was more like a nap. We were both groggy when Mary woke us up. Bill looked pretty rough and I felt as bad as he looked. But, after a cup of coffee and a lick on the crystal ball all was well again.

"There's this great bar and restaurant downtown and they have a Mariachi Band that plays Mexican torch songs. It's on us."

An offer that we couldn't refuse. Bill looked at me with raised eye brows as if to say. "Yeah, why not!"

Jerry's car was a piece of shit VW bug that had seen it's better days so we piled into the Caddy.

"Wow, man this is great!" Mary and Jerry sat in the back.

Jerry told Bill where the place was. We could hear the music blaring from inside. A waitress seated us outside on a deck. The place was over half-full. Mostly students from the University of Arizona.

We ordered margaritas and chips with hot sauce, not too hot, I begged. Trumpets and guitar players strolled through the restaurant. A man with a huge sombrero on and an even larger bass guitar with a singer belting out sorrowful love songs in Spanish. I had to take a second look at the singer.

"Is that a man dressed like a woman?"

"Yep. He's great though. Huh!"

"Yeah, he is," I chuckled. You don't see that every day.

The food came and another round of drinks. We all ordered different dishes and we shared each others food. It was a feast!

Without noticing, the place filled up.

"This is our favorite place. Jerry proposed to me here."

"Are you guys married?" I asked.

"Going on two years, now."

"Must of been the margaritas," chided Bill.

"It was," Mary giggled.

We all laughed.

"On the serious side. When we hit the road don't take any drugs with you. It's one of my rules. Okay?" I asked.

"Yeah, we won't."

"Promise?"

"Promise."

We clicked our glasses together and managed to get properly slushed. It was a great night.

We were all hung over the next morning. Mary had coffee and eggs and toast made when I got up.

"Feel like a train wreck," Bill moaned.

"This'll fix you up," as Mary handed him a mug of coffee.

"What's the matter, Bill. Goin' soft?" Jerry didn't look much better.

But, we were all in a good mood.

After eating and washing up Bill told us we should leave late in the afternoon.

"That way we'll be in Austin tomorrow afternoon."

We all agreed that sounded like a good plan. Too much in pain to argue.

Jerry and Mary started packing and Bill and I lay down and tried to sleep. I just closed my eyes. Didn't really sleep.

Bill came in and said we should start packing the car. We put everything except my ruck sack, in the trunk. Mary made sandwiches and brought several bottles of water. Good thinking, I thought.

We headed out. It was warm so Bill turned on the air conditioner.

"God, this is great," cried Jerry from the back seat, "travelling in comfort for a change."

I reminded them of the 'no drugs rule.' "No problem."

We had a long drive ahead of us. About 1,000 miles.

Bill gassed up before leaving town Jerry threw $50 unto the front seat. "That's for gas."

"Looks like we stay on 10 all the way to San Antonio and then head North," I said.

We drove through some beautiful country. All desert.

"I wanted to drive in the afternoon so the sun wouldn't be in my eyes," Bill said.

"Don't blame you."

In a couple of hours we were in New Mexico. Long endless vastness. It was hard to believe that anyone lived out here. But, people did and had for thousands of years. Looking out the window seeing a mirage. My first. It looked like there was a lake out there. I'd seen so many western movies where the guy thought he saw water. It was beautiful, especially when the sun was setting behind us and the mesas did look painted in bright reds and orange.

Wouldn't want to run out of gas out here.

"Shouldn't be long and we'll hit Las Cruces. Isn't that where they had the Manhattan Project? You know, where they developed the Atomic Bomb?" I stated.

"No, that was Los Alamos. Different part of the state," Jerry corrected.

"Oh, anyway, once we get to Las Cruces we head south along the Rio Grande River into El Paso, Texas," I said to Bill.

"Yeah, we'll stop and gas up there."

We rode into El Paso. A God forsaken place. Dusty and old. Drove through a junky neighborhood.

"There's a station ahead. We'll gas up."

We stopped. I opened the door and the heat hit me like a truck. I looked for a rest room. Had to walk through the garage. A guy pointed to it. I was met with hostile stares from a few guys hanging out in the back of the garage.

"Hey, hippie boy, give me a kiss."

I pretended not to hear him. The bathroom was filthy. There was a condom vending machine and a toilet that had been neglected and never cleaned. Don't touch anything I thought to myself. I pissed and flushed the toilet with my foot. Didn't bother washing my hands. I walked out and Bill was standing there awaiting his turn. Jerry was behind him.

"Next!"

I walked back through the gauntlet of red necks.

"Fuckin' hippie queers."

I laughed.

"What's so funny?" one of them asked.

"Nothin."

I walked back to the car. The attendant was just finishing up. He filled the tank and checked the oil. The tires looked okay.

"Don't pay no attention to those assholes. They don't mean no harm. That'll be $5.60."

I handed him a five and a one.

I glared back into the garage. I could have taken them. Little greasy fuckers. But, four on one was a different matter. Bill and Jerry ran the gauntlet as well. Luckily, Mary's rest room was inside by the cash register.

"Jesus H. Christ! Is this Texas? Fuckin' cowboys, man oh man. Wish I had a couple of my old football friends with us. We'd a kicked their asses," I rambled.

"Settle down, Mark. Peace, brother," Bill chided.

"Peace my ass ..."

"Let's get out of here."

It wasn't fifteen minutes later when a police car, sirens and lights, pulled us over.

"Everybody keep cool," Bill said.

It was a Texas Ranger. Sunglasses.

"Whose car is this, boy," his Texas drawl menacing.

"This is a 'Drive Away,' we're taking this car to Austin for some people."

"What people?"

"The people who needed their car but, didn't want to drive all the way."

"Yaw'l got papers to prove that?"

"Mark, get that packet out of the glove box, would ya'?"

I handed the packet to Bill. He handed it to the Ranger.

In the meantime two more cop cars showed up. They surrounded the car and were peering in the windows. Cowboy hats and sunglasses. Big guns on their hips. We were fucked!

"Everybody out of the car. Now!" he shouted.

Without protest we got out. They made us put our hands on the top of the Caddy. The roof was hot. They frisked us and told us not to move. Then, they put us in the back of the two cop cars. Bill and I in one car, Jerry and Mary in the other. They drove us to a police station. Is this how it all ends, I thought. In a fucking dust bowl shit town in Texas.

"Are we under arrest?"

"Not yet."

They put the four of us in a room.

"What's going on? What did we do?"

They let us smoke and go to the bathroom. We sat in a windowless room. We asked one of the cops what was going on.

"They're looking for illegal drugs. Sit tight."

I had my ruck sack in the car. Fuck. I was worried about the speed inside my after shave bottle and the manila envelope. Would they find them?

"Nobody's carrying, are you."

'No's' went around the room. Maybe they think the car is stolen. After all, four hippies driving in a brand new Caddy.

"Where are we anyway?" Mary asked.

"I think we're in Clint, Texas," I responded.

"They must be checking out the car. I wasn't speeding," Bill pleaded.

We sweated it out. Hour after hour passed. I thought of my rights. Ha. That's a joke. We asked for some coffee. They obliged. I was pacing. They had checked our ID's. Hope they didn't look too deep. Mark Heddington had been dead for twenty years. I had a 2-S student deferment Draft Card. Hope the others were solid as well. Fuck, how long is this going to take? I thought of making a run for it but knew that was hopeless. Two more hours. We'd been holed up for over three hours.

Bill opened the door and asked one of the cops if we could go now. Nice try.

Finally, after five hours, a cop came in. He was actually nice.

"We thought you folks we're in a stolen car. But the car checks out. You're free to go as soon as the car is returned to the station."

Sighs of relief.

"Thank you, sir," Mary said, meaning it.

They directed us to a bench outside. It was very late. The air had cooled and the evening air felt good.

We waited another hour before the car showed up.

"Jesus! Welcome to Texas!"

"What was that all about?"

We were all talking at once as we got into the car.

"This car has been vacuum cleaned!" declared Mary, "Look, you can see the rows the vacuum made on the carpet."

"Yeah, you're right."

"They were looking for pot. They were looking for pot seeds, man," laughed Jerry.

I checked my ruck sack. Everything was there. They hadn't found the stash or rifled through the envelope.

"I need a drink!"

"I'll second that!"

And yes, we were in Clint, Texas. We headed out of that hell hole. Fifteen minutes later. More red lights and sirens. More Texas Rangers.

The cop asked Bill for his license and the paper work. Again. Two more cop cars pulled up. They menacingly peered in the windows at us. Nobody spoke.

We waited there by the side of the road for another 30 minutes. Finally the cop approached the car.

"Y'all can go. Drive safely."

Bill rolled up the window. He handed me the papers.

"Fuck man. Are we going to get pulled over in every bum fuck town in Texas?"

We were more pissed off than scared. Bill slowly crawled back into the traffic. He was driving below the speed limit. Afraid to even pass anyone. There wasn't much traffic.

We drove to Van Horn and gassed up. We stopped in a huge truck stop and nobody even noticed us. It was the middle of the night and only the weird were out anyway. And we made it to Ft. Stockton without getting pulled over again.

"You know. I think it was one of those assholes at that garage that called the cops. Probably told the cops that we were hippies and had drugs driving in a stolen car," I said.

Everyone pretty much agreed on that.

"Ah fuck it, man. We're okay," Jerry said, "Just to change the subject, he continued, "Did you ever know how many great musicians have come out of Austin?"

"No, I didn't, but, tell me."

"Well, let's see, it's a long list; The Steve Miller Band, Janis Joplin played here a lot, The Sir Douglas Quintet, Willie Nelson and Roy Orbison, The 13th Floor Elevators, ever hear of them?"

"Yeah," I said. "They played in San Francisco. The first Psychedelic Rock band, right?" I asked.

"Yeah, Mark. You pass the test. The band was led by a guy named Roky Ericson. He was busted for having one joint on him. They gave him the choice of life in prison or to be sent to a Psych Ward. He chose the latter and we heard they gave him electric shock treatments and totally fucked him up."

I thought of my mom at the Mayo Clinic.

"He was the first to use feedback from his amp. Everybody copied him. The Dead, Jimi Hendrix. All of 'em. Anyway, there's a long list of musicians who have played in Austin. There's a hundred bars with music every night. It's great. Oh yeah, plus a whole slew of blues guitarists. It's the best scene, I think, in the country. Everybody says San Francisco is but I say Austin, Texas."

"I didn't see the Elevators. I guess I got to San Francisco too late, but I remember a friend of mine telling me about them. He had an album of theirs. Sorry I missed 'em. Too bad about Roky. Life in prison for one joint. Are you kidding me? That's ridiculous!" I cried.

"They wanted to make an example out of him."

Jerry and Mary were really into the music scene. They couldn't wait to move to Austin. I had to say I wasn't very impressed with Texas. The cops, the people I'd met so far were hostile. The landscape boring and hot. I just wanted to leave. This was 'America, Love it or Leave it' country. Gun racks and angry stares all the way to San Antonio.

Then we headed north to Austin. It was early in the morning at first light. My first impressions of Austin were mixed. But, this was my second visit and I was glad to be here.

We drove by the campus. I saw that tower where some years ago a maniac had opened fire on people below. And then I noticed tons of long hairs. In the middle of Texas. Imagine that! This place would be all right after all.

We could stay at Jerry and Mary's friends' house. We also had to return the car but that was Bill's job. I had a phone call to make. Their friends house was dark when we pulled up. We were supposed to have been in this afternoon but we had been delayed by Texas' Finest. So, Jerry suggested that we head out and get a bite to eat. We had to wash the car anyway. It was early morning.

We found a funky little place nearby. We needed food. We loaded up on omelettes and biscuits with gravy and bacon and hash browns juice and coffee all the way around. We could relax now. We were safe. This was a University town with young people on bikes and flowers in their hair. I was munching away when I noticed a naked woman pedal by. "Oh, yeah, she rides around like that all day. If you're here long enough you won't even notice her."

Jerry and Mary went on to tell us that they had spent several summers here taking classes. They knew the scene.

Bill needed to return the car. He called the car agency and they wanted the car cleaned. We drove to the outskirts of Austin and found a car wash. We vacuumed the car and made sure that we had all of our stuff out of it. The four of us made quick work of it. We drove the car through the car wash, sitting inside and enjoying the process. The car agency was just a couple of blocks away and Bill took the keys and the paper work inside. Shortly afterwards a man came out and checked the car out. He said everything looked okay. He gave us a curious look before going back inside with Bill. Ten minutes later he came out with the deposit on the car.

"I called a cab so we can get back into town," Bill said.

The cab came and we rode to Jerry and Mary's friend's house. They were awake by now. We carried all of our stuff into the house. I was introduced to Fred and Louise. It was their house. They were very nice and older. I found out later they were both professors at the University. After introductions and several minutes of chaos I asked Fred if I could use his phone. I called the number Mark had given me to drop off the package. There was no answer. I'd call later.

Meanwhile, everyone was hanging out in the living room. Jerry, Mary, and Bill and I could stay for a few days but I needed to get going and find my own place to stay.

An hour later I called again and got someone. I asked for Larry. "Just a moment, who's calling?"

"Mark."

"Mark?"

"Yeah, I've got something for you."

"I was expecting you. Where are you, I'll pick you up."

I gave Larry the address and ten minutes later he picked me up.

I thanked Bill and said good bye to Jerry and Mary and wished them luck. Bill said he was going to hang out in Austin for the summer.

"Here you go," I said first thing as I got into Larry's car.

"Thanks," he said as I handed him the envelope, "need a place to crash?"

"Yeah."

"Stay with me and my old lady."

Larry was a very serious dude. Short cropped hair, a white tee shirt and jeans. He looked like an anarchist cowboy.

"So, you some kinda mailman or what."

"I guess so. I'm the Mailman."

"You're a fuckin' legend, man."

"A legend?"

"Yeah man, in the Underground you're a fuckin' legend. I've been hearing about you for a couple of years now. My old lady can't wait to meet you."

Every alarm and 'red flag' went off in my mind. Notoriety wasn't part of my resume.

"Don't worry, Mark. You're secret is safe with me."

"Hope so, man."

Larry lived in the student section of Austin. It reminded me of Mifflin Street in Madison. Tightly rowed houses full of hippies and rock and roll and weed.

"Come on in."

"Honey, this is Mark from San Francisco."

"Hi."

Her name really was Honey. She was absolutely stunning. Long blond hair to her waist and an open beautiful face. She radiated.

"Hi, Mark. I'm so pleased to meet you. We've heard an awful lot about you."

"Pleased to meet you too and thank you for letting me stay with you."

"You can stay as long as you want. And don't worry, we know how to keep our mouths shut. You're our friend from San Francisco and that's all people need to know," she drawled in the most pleasant Texan accent.

Feeling reassured, they showed me to a room in the back of the house with a bed and dresser. I looked in the mirror and I didn't even recognize myself. My eyes were sunk into my head with dark rings around them. My face looked like death. I was very slim anyway but I looked like someone from a concentration camp from WWII. I was decaying.

"You look famished!" Honey stated.

She made me a tuna sandwich which I devoured in seconds. That hit the spot.

I needed a shower and some clean clothes. Honey showed me the bathroom as I showered and she washed all my clothes.

"Here, put these on," she handed me a pair of jeans and a tee shirt and underwear and socks, "They belong to Larry but keep 'em. He's got plenty of clothes."

I went back into my room and saw my reflection again in the mirror. I was just a clean version of death. I brushed out my hair and pulled it back into a ponytail. I had a month old beard and I looked old so I went back into the bathroom and shaved it off except the mustache. I kept that. I wanted to look like George Harrison.

The jeans fit perfectly. The tee shirt was baggy but it looked good.

I walked back out into the living room. *Crosby, Stills, Nash, and Young* were on the stereo. "4 dead in Ohio ..." That's more like it. Larry offered me a toke and I took it and went into a dream.

Larry told me all about his relationship with Mark from Berkeley. They had known each other for years and they were best friends. They met at school in Berkeley several years ago and they both became heavily involved with the Free Speech Movement with Mario Savio. They became radicalized together over a period of time. They protested together and marched together. They were more than just roommates, they were brothers. Both had dedicated themselves to the peace movement.

"Me and Mark went through a lot of shit together. When he told me about you and all the good work you've done. I couldn't wait to meet you. He said you're the most reliable person he ever met. That's high praise from him, man. High praise."

"I just hope I can live up to that."

"You already have. Ever wonder what's in the packages?"

"Yeah, I do, but I've never peeked."

"Letters, man. Mostly. Sometimes cash. Correspondence from families to their kids who are hiding out from the pigs or letters from the kids. Money to see them through. The pigs are trying to lock up an entire generation, man. And it's because of cats like you that we can resist them. Resistance is the name of the game. We can't send these letters through the regular mail because the pigs will intercept them so we use the Underground. You're a fuckin' hero man. I can see that it's taken a toll on you."

"Yeah, I used to play football and weighed 170 pounds," I joked.

"We're gonna out last 'em, Mark. You wait."

"I know you're right, Larry."

"So, my friend. You are safe here and mum is the word. In a month or so I'm traveling to New Orleans and then onto Atlanta, Athens actually. I'd be honored if you'd stay with us until then and I could get you to Athens."

"I'd have to talk with Mark."

"Already have, man. It's all set."

"Well, yeah. Okay then. I need a rest anyway."

"Mi casa su casa."

I eventually spent a couple of months in Austin. Got a taste of the great music scene. I saw the naked lady pedal by often. Jerry was right, I hardly noticed her anymore. I wrote dozens of letters to Grandma, my family and friends and to Carol. I didn't mail them right away because I feared they might be intercepted and traced back to Austin. I missed everyone so much it hurt but I wanted to reassure everyone that I was okay. This was a special place right in the heart of Texas.

Larry and Honey took good care of me. I put some weight back on and was feeling much better although I continued to use speed. I just couldn't stop. If I waited to use it I felt like hell and trembled. I knew I was addicted to it by now.

Mark sent some more money to me and I was set. I had almost $500 and it kept me in cigs and food. There were protests on campus but nothing like Berkeley or Madison. But, it was reassuring to know that the anti-war movement even touched here. I didn't follow the news too much. It was so depressing and besides it just made me angry. But, I did come across an article about the rising numbers of draft resisters. Yeah, 'What if they had a War, and nobody came?'

There were early rumblings about the Presidential campaigns for 1972. God, they started already. After the 1968 election year this should be interesting. Names like McGovern and McCarthy and Muskie and Humphrey for the Dems and of course 'Tricky Dick' Nixon for the Reps. Somebody had to beat Nixon. I liked McCarthy from the start because he was from Minnesota and because he was against the war and said so over and over again. But, like I said, it was early. I wanted to be in Madison next summer and fall for the Primaries.

Larry, Honey, and myself spent many evenings talking about things. Not always political. They were a wonderful loving couple. I wanted to have someone like Honey. She always seemed upbeat. She was one of those people who had a permanent smile on her face. She was even happy on cloudy days. I told them as much as I could about my upbringing and I spoke of Carol. Honey said that, "If it was meant to be then it will be," referring to Carol. I knew she was right but I was doubtful it would work out with her. "She's probably already met someone new," I despaired, "and if she has" ... "you'll meet someone someday," Honey retorted.

On that note ... there was no use in speculating.

I was treading water. I felt useless and I needed to get back into the action again. One day Larry announced we were leaving the next morning for New Orleans and then onto Athens. Mark had informed me that there was another package to pick up in Athens and take to Boston!

Larry, Honey, and myself decided to go out and paint the town red ... and green ... and blue. We started at a great Tex-Mex restaurant and finished up at a couple of bars and danced to music. We got fairly plastered and had too much fun. I think I had a crush on Honey. Had to get that out of my mind. She was the prettiest and smartest woman. We got home at 2 a.m. and had a nightcap. Now, I hated to leave but knew I must. I found out that Larry wanted to go to New Orleans to see his brother and then onto Athens because he and Honey were thinking of moving there and Larry wanted to see about getting work at the University there. Honey worked at the medical center on campus and couldn't get any time off.

Tried to sleep but the room was spinning. I must have fallen asleep because I awoke in a start. I was having a nightmare. I was being chased on my trike and the faster I pedaled the slower I went. It was the same bad dream I've always had. The bad guys were just about to nab me when I woke up. I got up and went to the bathroom. I was drenched in sweat. I splashed my face with cold water and drank a glass. I felt better. I took two aspirin and went back to bed. I was lonely and scared.

I wanted this saga to end. I wanted to be me again and be able to walk down the street without always looking behind me.

"Up and at 'em."
"Oh, my head. What time is it?" I asked.
"Time to go my friend."
"I need a quick shower. Five minutes at the most. Okay?"

I hung my aching body under a spray of cold water. Brushed my teeth. Brushed my hair. Got dressed. Packed in ten minutes. Honey had coffee and toast ready.

"Honey, thank you so much for everything. I'm going to miss you."

She put her arms around me and we hugged for a good minute. Then she kissed me on both cheeks. My knees were weak and I had to hold on to something.

"Now, you boys behave. I packed a basket for you with lots of goodies. Water, cookies, sandwiches. And Mark, Larry and I love you and this is for you."

She handed me a card. I read the front. It was a handmade card. It said; "From the bottom of our hearts, all the best to you in your travels. May you find peace." Love Always. Larry and Honey. I almost started to cry. And then Larry gave me $100.

"What's this for?"

"It's from Honey and me and that's for you, my friend. It ain't much.

Just a token of our appreciation."

"I can't ..."

"Shut the fuck up!"

We then got in a group hug.

"If there were more people like you in the world ..."

"I know."

Larry and I got in his car. Actually, it was Honey's car. A newish Ford Fairlane. And off we went.

"Jeez, that was some night. I feel like I'm too sick to die."

"Me too," I moaned.

"I don't usually do this but would you like some speed? It'll make you feel almost human again," I offered.

"Yeah, under the circumstances ... yeah."

I dug into my ruck sack and found the crystal.

"Here, man. Lick it ... like this," I demonstrated.

"Oh, okay."

After a couple of minutes Larry said, "That's got a kick to it."

"Sure does. I need something for those long hauls. Besides, it keeps my mind limber."

Larry looked at the crystal ball.

"Where'd you get that."

"From a guy I rode from San Francisco to Chicago with. We only stopped to get gas. He was a trip, man. Think his name was Max. He was mad."

"Mad Max! What a name!" Larry chortled.

I stashed the speed. We cut right through the middle of Texas. Larry didn't need a map. He'd driven this before to see his brother. Larry said we wouldn't stay long because his brother was a little crazy. He just wanted to see him.

We made good time passing through these little Texas towns. So remote. Made me melancholy. A sad feeling came over me. To think people lived here. I wanted to know what their lives were like. I suppose, as in most small towns, they distrusted outsiders and the city slickers and especially Yankees. I was anxious to see New Orleans and some of the Southern States. It looked like I was completing that trip that Joe and I had begun some years ago. It seemed like an eternity ago, now. This is one big country, man.

"We should be in Houston soon. Let's pull over and gas up and piss."

We were ten miles or so out of Houston. We stopped at a service station and filled the tank and drained our bladders. We pulled to the side and found a shady spot to park.

"Let's see what Honey packed."

Larry and I found a cornucopia of goodies. Soda pop and tuna sandwiches and chips and candy bars. We feasted. There was plenty left.

"Honey's a good woman. Met her in Berkeley. Won her over with my charm!" he laughed.

"You're a lucky man, Charlie Brown."

"Yes, I am," he said seriously as we climbed back into the car.

I lit two cigarettes and we sat back and watched the horror of Houston. Spread out like LA with endless miles of oil refineries. Smoke belched from huge towers and large flames emitted everywhere burning off the gas. Reminded me of Gary, Indiana. Another hell hole.

"It fuckin' stinks here."

"Tell me about it. It's pure money for the millionaire oil men. Pure gold."

"How can anybody live here?" I wondered.

"Jobs."

"You're in for a treat. Louisiana is a jewel. It's another country. From now on all the way to Athens we're going to see such abject poverty you won't believe it. People wearing rags and barefoot, man. No teeth. Old cars and dogs crossing streets. You see their ribs. Most of these rural folks have never been out of their county, much less seen the world. It's another world."

He was right. We entered Louisiana just as darkness came. It was like someone had hit a switch and everything changed. Texas was fucked but it was affluent. This was where all the poor people lived. Shacks that looked like they'd just fall over if you leaned on them. Junked cars in yards. Garbage piled everywhere. People hang dogged, heads drooped, shoulders slunk. A pallor fell over these small towns.

It was depressing.

"Like this all the way to Athens. Might as well get used to it."

I realized now that Joe and I would have hated this part of the trip. People didn't seem very nice. But, when you're travelling like this you aren't apt to meet the gentry.

"My brother lives in a Mental Hospital just outside of New Orleans, so we'll stay in a motel for a night or two."

"Okay."

Larry went on to tell me that, George, his older brother had been diagnosed with Paranoid Schizophrenia. He had troubles as a child and the family finally had him committed when he was a teenager. "He couldn't go to school or be around people. He would seem fine around the family but if someone came over he'd run and hide claiming they were trying to kill him and stuff. I was 8 years younger than him and didn't know what was going on. I love my brother. The poor guy has been locked up for years. We were living in the Bay Area then and George has been in several hospitals. My dad and mom finally found this place a couple of years ago and he's doing pretty good. Mom and Dad moved to New Orleans to be near him, so you'll meet my folks too."

"Just you two kids?"

"Yeah. My poor parents. They just couldn't take care of him anymore. They had him in the Mayo Clinic and they gave him electric shock treatments which totally fucked him up."

"Hey, man, same thing with my mom. She was in the Mayo too. They gave her shock treatments and she's never been the same."

"Really?"

"Yup."

"Sorry man."

"Aren't we going to stay with your parents?"

"They are old and frail. Dad was 42 when I was born. Don't worry, man, I got us covered."

"Thanks. I was just wondering."

Many of the towns had French names. It was curious. The French had once occupied this territory and left their mark. I was excited to see New Orleans. So much great music had come out of that town. This wonderful country never ceased to amaze me. It's diversity. We were all Americans.

"We'll be in Baton Rouge in a couple of hours. How's that speed holding out?"

"Need another lick?"

"Yeah, I'm tired. Let's pull over and get some gas and coffee."

"Good idea."

Larry pulled over into a service station with a diner next door. We filled the gas tank first and then ambled into the diner.

"Well, look at that. Two girls." One of the patrons cried.

"Let's get out of here," I said.

"Yeah."

We hopped back into the car and flew out of there.

"Jeez, scary," I said.

"Yeah, the coffee can wait. Like Easy Rider."

"Hey, do me a favor. I want to mail these letters. Next chance we get."

"No sweat."

There was a mailbox just ahead and I dumped the bunch into the mail box. I had put 'Mars' as a return address on each letter. The FBI would see Grosse Tete on the Post Office stamp. Big Head, Louisiana. Ha. Yeah, man, this is where I am.

"I was thinking. Let's stay in Baton Rouge tonight. I'm wiped out. We'll get some beers and finish off the food in the basket, watch some TV. We can easily drive to George's place tomorrow. I'll call my folks and we'll all meet there tomorrow."

"Okay."

After driving all day in the heat and humidity, it felt good to take a shower and relax in an air-conditioned room.

Larry called George and then his parents. They set up a time. We would meet at George's.

"If you want me to get lost for a few hours so you can be with your family ..."

"No, no. That's cool. You'll like my folks and George too. In fact, it's better if there is someone else around. Keeps things light."

Larry was wiped out so we called it an early night.

We hit the road early and were at George's hospital by 11 a.m. We sat and waited on the lawn for someone to bring George. He and Larry hugged. Soon after, their parents walked up. Larry looked just like his dad. After some chit chat a doctor joined us and talked of George's progress. I felt like I shouldn't be there but no one else seemed to matter. Then, the doctor and the parents walked off in one direction and the three of us in another. Other patients dotted the campus. Some people looked in pretty bad shape. I just prayed I wouldn't end up like this.

Larry and George walked ahead along a path and I followed behind. It was obvious that Larry loved George.

We soon were rejoined by the parents. They invited us to lunch but Larry declined. He said we had a long drive ahead of us and needed to hit the road.

"Hope that was okay with you Mark. I love 'em all but I can only take them in short spurts."

"Yeah. I understand. Hope you didn't leave early on my account."

"Oh no. It's all on me. Let's boogie."

We were just north of New Orleans. We drove into the city at one point hugging the Mississippi River and then crossed the longest bridge I'd ever seen and eventually drove into the State of Mississippi.

"I have an idea. I don't know about you but I'm pretty tired of looking at all the poverty in the South, so how about we take the scenic drive. We drive all the way to the Atlantic seaboard, you know, through Florida and then head up into Georgia."

"Sounds like a plan," I said.

I was excited by the prospect of being on the coast line as long as possible. It was out of our way. But, hell, Larry's driving.

Larry went on a diatribe about his family. How he loved them but couldn't be around them for very long. His mom ran the show and was very 'bossy.' "She just can't let anything be, man. It's suffocating. And my dad just sits there and lets her do everything. Then, my mom complains because nobody helps her. Hell, she won't let anyone help her!"

"Anyway, fuck it, I've done my duty for the next six months."

I fumbled with the maps and drew a course. Larry wanted to hug the coastline as much as possible. We drove through a series of beach towns along the Gulf of Mexico. The sea breeze was welcomed. The air smelled fresh and it wasn't stifling hot like Texas. We stopped and gassed up. The people actually seemed nice. "How y'all are?" Asked one gas station attendant as we filled the tank. "Thank you, ... you boys drive careful like, ya' hear?" Spoken in the most extreme Southern accent I'd ever heard.

"Did you hear that? 'How y'all are?' Are you kidding me. I love it. The guy looked like one of the characters from the *Andy Griffin Show*. You know, what's his name?"

"Gomer?"

"Yeah, Gomer."

The people on the coast seemed much friendlier. It was probably because these were tourist towns and they were exposed to a diversity of people. Fishing seemed to be the big business down here. I saw a sign that said 'Live Bait' and I laughed. "Can you imagine being Live Bait!?"

"Yeah, bummer man."

We drove into Biloxi.

"Lots of great blues men from this area," Larry remarked.

We drove in silence through long neighborhoods of abject poverty. The black sections. Racism ruled the roost.

"You know what I think? I think the real problem in this country is poverty."

"And racism." I added.

"They go hand in hand, man. When people are repressed they revolt. Happens every time. Look at South America. Look at the race riots here. It's poverty man. We shouldn't be fighting poor people in Vietnam we should have a war against poverty."

"The Middle Class is scared shitless by the lower classes so they just sit on the fence while the rich just laugh at us and rule everything. It's like my mom, she runs everything and ends up driving people away, except the poor people have no place to run to."

"All these poor black guys can't go to college so they get drafted and get their asses blown off and if they come back it's the same old shit. What is it? Something like 20% of the population is black and 40% of the troops in Vietnam are black. That's fucked up, man."

"You and I are two well-off white guys who are privileged, compared to them. It isn't just. It isn't fair. We Americans always pride ourselves on fairness ... give me a fuckin' break!"

"Then, you've got these fuckin' idiots in Washington putting lies and fear and hate into everyone's mind. Parents sending their own sons off to get killed so they can retain the 'status quo.' This country has gone insane!"

Larry reminded me of Mark. He made sense to me. Finding the words to express my personal angst.

And it was like this all the way to Florida.

The little tip of Alabama was a blur. Mobile was interesting but behind us.

"Now, Florida is a trip. It's still 1945 in most of these towns. Nothing has changed in all those years. We'll drive to Jacksonville and stay the night. You'll like it there. It's a college town. In fact, it was one of the places Honey and I considered before deciding on Athens. Nobody will give us any shit there."

We drove through miles of fruit orchards and farms. It was hot as blazes and the sun beat down. The Ford didn't have air-conditioning so we had the windows down to get air. The radio was blaring Top 40 hits.

After several hours and a couple of pit stops, we entered the outskirts of Jacksonville.

"This place is huge."

"That's why Honey and I didn't want to live here. Too many people. We like the smaller towns."

Larry drove over to the University district and found a cheap motel. We both needed a shower and some cool air.

After cleaning up Larry wanted to show me the water front. There was a huge Marina on the bay that lead to the Atlantic Ocean. Yachts and sailboats lined the docks. It was a sight.

"Let's eat, man. You like fish?"

"I do sometimes."

He was right. College towns were cool. No one even noticed us as we walked in a restaurant. After we were seated a waitress approached.

"You boys ready?"

Larry spoke, "We will both have the shark and a couple of beers."

"Shark?" I protested.

"Trust me, man. You'll love it."

And I did. Flaky and tasty. It was delicious.

"This is great!"

"Told you."

After dinner we walked along the Marina and looked at the boats. It was a wonder. I thought of living on one and going out to sea. They'd never find me.

We grabbed a six pack and headed back to the room. We were bushed.

We arose the next morning. Packed the car. Bought some coffee and headed out. It was a gorgeous August morning. The blazing sun lifting over the Atlantic. I wanted to sail across it someday.

"We can be in Athens tonight. So, let's drive up the coast line to Savannah, then we'll head northwest into Athens. We don't have to drive through

Atlanta."

"Want some crystal?" I asked.

"Sure. Can't hurt."

We each took generous licks. I could feel the blood rushing through me.

We followed 90 North keeping the ocean in view most of the way but sadly losing sight of it from time to time.

Savannah was an old city. Lots of Civil War history here. What had that been like? Americans fighting against each other. In some cases brother against brother. Just awful. Could happen again.

Georgia was a pretty place. We saw huge mansions tucked in groves of trees. White picket fences. Soft rolling hills. Farms. Plantations. The first white people who settled here must have thought this was Heaven.

I didn't know what I was going to do in Athens. Frankly, I wasn't very excited about being here. Larry said that Mark had something for me in Athens. It was another package, I assumed. Where was I going next? Boston?

I had no idea.

We drove through a semi-mountainous area. Rolling hills with valleys and meadows.

At last, we drove into Athens. An absolutely gorgeous town. For the first time since we'd left Austin I saw hippies again. We drove into the downtown area.

"I can see why you wanted to live here. This is really neat!"

"Honey and I fell in love with this town at first sight."

Larry drove to a large Victorian house.

"This is where we'll stay. These are my friends Phil and Marcy. You'll like them. They both teach at the University."

It was hot and muggy. I got out of the car and stretched. Larry knocked at the door. A man answered.

"You made it! Come on in."

"Mark, this is my good friend Phil. Where's Marcy?"

"She'll be back in an hour. She had a class. Come on in you guys. How was the drive? Hot I bet. Mark, Larry has told me about you. Don't worry, you're safe here. Grab your stuff and bring it in. I'll get you guys settled. Want a beer?"

Phil was talking a mile a minute. My mind couldn't keep up with his chatter.

"Oh Mark, Mark from Berkeley called. He wants you to call him ASAP. You can use the phone in the kitchen."

Wow. What had I walked into? The guy was a machine gun rapper. I walked into the kitchen. What a great house. Found the phone and dialed

Mark's number, which I had memorized.

"I'll call you right back."

I waited ten minutes before the phone rang again. Phil picked it up.

"It's for you."

"Hey, what's up?"

"Things are so heavy here. I'll wire you some money and an airplane ticket to Boston. Hang out in Athens for a few weeks and I'll get back in touch with you."

"I'm going to Boston?"

"Please!"

"Oh yeah, I'll go to Boston. I was just asking. Are you all right?"

"Yeah. Yeah. I'm fine. The pigs are getting close. The Panthers are going nuts. They're out there posing with their stares and shotguns and the pigs are fuckin' freaking out. I've been trying to work with them but they're tough to talk too. Anyway, that's not your problem. I'm going to have another package for you soon and we need the people in Boston to get this. So, I'll be in touch."

"Okay Mark. I'll do my best."

"I know you will. I know. Stay cool my friend."

"I will. Talk to you soon."

"Everything okay?" Larry asked as I joined the others.

"Yeah."

Soon, Marcy walked in. Larry and Marcy hugged each other.

"Oh, you must be Mark. Pleased to meet you."

"Glad to meet you too. You have a lovely house."

"One of the perks of teaching at the University. Make yourselves at home."

We drank some beers as Larry and Phil and Marcy caught up with the news. They were going to help Larry find a house for he and Honey. I was envious. I wished my life was so. I felt sad and left out. But, I put up a brave front. How did my life get so fucked up? I knew I shouldn't feel like this but I did. I was so lonely and I missed Carol. Oh Carol.

Marcy showed me a bedroom I could use. Larry and I both needed a shower. Marcy and Phil made a big spaghetti feast with numerous bottles of wine. I was ready to pass out and sleep. It must have showed because Marcy mentioned I could go to sleep if I wanted to. I did. I apologized and excused myself. I climbed into the bed and fell instantly asleep.

I dreamed I was asleep. It woke me up. I didn't know where I was. Then I remembered. I had to pee. Where was I? I thought I was at Brian's in San Francisco. I walked down the dark hall way and found the bathroom. Oh yeah, I was in Athens. I'm losing it.

I crawled back into bed. I couldn't sleep. I found a light and read Thomas Merton poems until I slept. I woke in the morning with the light on and the book on my chest.

I woke before the others so I sat in the room and waited for them to rise. I heard someone in the hallway and the bathroom door close. It was Marcy. I heard her walk downstairs and I waited a few minutes and followed her.

"Good morning Mark! How did you sleep?"

"Morning Marcy. Just fine, Thanks."

"I'm making coffee. Help yourself. There's cream and sugar if you want."

I lit a cig and poured two cups of coffee. Soon Phil joined us. He just nodded when he walked in the kitchen. Marcy gave me a knowing look that said Phil was moody in the morning. It was already warm so I walked out onto the back porch. A dog was barking off in the distance. Soon, the cobwebs cleared and I was beginning to wake up.

I heard Larry's booming voice from the kitchen and some laughter. The house had only one shower so we took turns. Phil had to go to school so he went first. Marcy second and then Larry. I soaked my aching head and body under cold water. The water heater had run out of hot water. It was okay. I just wanted to be clean.

Larry was excited to start house hunting and he wanted to show me the town. We drove downtown and Larry bought a newspaper and scanned the want ads. We stopped in a cafe and had breakfast. We were both feeling better. This seemed to be a neat little town. The town was wrapped around the University. I saw lots of long hairs and felt comfortable. Austin and now Athens. Surprising. I was anxious to hear from Mark and whatever he had for me. I asked Larry how long he was going to stay in Athens and he thought maybe a week. I didn't know what I'd do after that.

"Here's a place. I'm going to call them."

I waited in the booth. Larry came back in a few minutes. He was excited.

"They said to come by and look at it."

We finished breakfast and drove to the house. It was near downtown and close to campus. The house was an old Victorian. It was in pretty good shape. It had a picket fence around the front yard and a huge porch in front.

"Should I stay here?" I asked.

"No, no. Come with me. I want your take."

The landlord met us at the front gate. It was being rented until the end of August. I realized that my real birthday was in two weeks. The current tenants were home. They were an older couple who seemed unfazed by two hippies invading their domain. The landlord was a kindly gentleman and seemed interested when Larry mentioned that both he and his wife would be working at the University. The house itself had two floors and two bedrooms and two bathrooms plus a large kitchen and dining area. The living room was spacious as well.

We walked through the house and then to the back porch which led to the Garden of Eden. A sidewalk split the yard and led to an alley and on both sides were roses and several fruit trees, a little grotto sitting area. That's what sold Larry on the house.

"When can we move in?" joked Larry.

"Three weeks!"

The landlord and Larry sat down in the grotto and pounded out the details. I walked around the side of the house and waited by the car.

Larry was animated when he sprinted around the corner of the house and ran to the car.

"Gotta call Honey and give her the good news. Wow. How lucky can I get! Do you believe it?"

"That was quick," I said.

"I've got a great idea. Would you like to help us move? We have two cars so I'd leave one here. We could fly back to Austin and then drive my car out here. The University will move us so all we have to do is go back and start packing. Think about it, in the meantime I have to go meet with a guy in the Administration Building and arrange all the details for the move. I'll call Mark and tell him about it. I'm sure it will work out. I can pay you too!"

"Well ... yeah ... I guess," this happened so fast my mind couldn't process.

Larry was happy. We returned to Phil and Marcy's house.

"Hey, guess what. I got the house. It's over on Hall Street. We can move in at the end of the month. I'm going to call Honey and then I have to meet this guy at school. Oh boy!"

"Oh, that's wonderful," exclaimed Marcy.

Larry went off to the school and I went for a walk. Lovely tree lined peaceful streets. I found a cafe and huddled around a long cup of coffee. I watched the hustle and bustle of students clamor by. This was a rather peaceful campus or at least I hadn't heard about any riots here. Well, I guess I'm going back to Austin. I had to talk with Mark first. Larry said he'd call Mark so I'd wait for that. I remembered in *On the Road* about how Dean wanted to just live in the moment. I guess I'd achieved that.

Larry was waiting for me when I returned.

"It's all set. I talked to Mark and he thought this was a great plan. The college has reimbursed me for the trip here plus ... they will pay for two airline tickets to Austin plus ... paying for Mayflower to move us plus ... the drive back plus ... $500 for expenses plus ..."

He collapsed on the couch laughing.

"Let's celebrate!"

The five of us invaded a bar/restaurant and ate like Henry VIII and drank like Dylan Thomas. What a night!

I awoke and heard Marcy stirring in the kitchen.

"Are you hungry Mark? I made some eggs and toast."

"Good morning. No thank you. I can't eat yet. I need coffee."

"Suit yourself," she said.

I felt pretty good considering how much I'd eaten and drank last night. It was fun. Larry paid for everything. It was nice to be with people talking about happy stuff instead of the horrors of war and resistance.

Larry came into the kitchen. Just a ball of fire. We were leaving tomorrow afternoon flying from Atlanta to Dallas and then onto San Antonio. Honey would pick us up at the airport and we would drive to Austin. Sounded like fun and I was anxious to see Honey again. I would keep my attraction to her to myself.

Marcy offered to drive us to the Atlanta airport tomorrow. Phil had to work.

After cleaning up I just wanted to spend a quiet day reading Merton. His poetry calmed me and I was learning to accept and to forgive and to love. Later, I fell asleep on the couch, reading.

Early evening. Marcy made a chicken and potato delight. We sipped wine by candle light. I made a toast thanking Phil and Marcy for their kindness and to the future of Larry and Honey. I helped with the dishes and we slept early. We had a big day tomorrow.

We left early. It was a couple of hours drive to the airport. I sat in the back of the car and watched the Georgia countryside pass by. It was hot as blazes so we had the windows down. I couldn't hear the conversation from the front seat. We had two hours until our flight left. Larry picked up the tickets at the front desk and we proceeded to the gate. Finally our flight was called and we boarded the plane.

The jet gently lifted into the air. The non-smoking light went off and we all lit up. They served lunch and we each had a beer. It was a short flight. Couple hours. We landed in Dallas. A huge airport. We walked to another gate and caught a puddle jumper to San Antonio. Honey was at the gate!

"My boys are home," she declared as she hugged and kissed us both. I wanted to tell her that I missed her but I played the role of a mere friend. Just being happy to see her and being safe on the ground again.

"Mayflower dropped off a ton of boxes ... clothes boxes ... boxes for books, and we have a million books, boxes for clothes ... you should see the house ... it's a fucking mess. Dishes ... oh my God ... do we have dishes ...

Mark, you're going to be busy," she giggled.

Back in Austin. The house was a mess. Like she said, boxes everywhere.

We ordered pizza. We had a week to pack. It was a daunting task. I took charge. I began packing boxes of books. I wrote on the outside of each box a list of what it contained. For example ... Adams to Bennett etc. That way when we unpacked we could put everything back into some sort of order. I moved each box into the garage. I called it 'the staging area.' Larry and Honey were intellectuals and not adapt at organizing stuff. They could conceptualize vast ideas into an order but ask them to put the kitchen together and they looked back at you with a vacant stare. It was beyond them.

"Mark, you're amazing. We couldn't do this without you!."

"My pleasure, Honey. It's the least I could do. Let's start on the kitchen."

We carefully wrapped glasses and plates in newspaper and packed them. Honey decided to give a lot of this stuff away. She sorted through everything and put some of it aside in a separate box. We would take the unwanted items to St. Vincent DePaul.

After a few hours we had made a dent in it. We were going to have to make several dump runs. There was a growing pile of trash in the driveway. Larry had a buddy with a truck and they made two trips. Honey and I continued to add to it.

And books. Oh my. They had a small library of books. Hundreds of them and they wanted to keep them all. I counted ten boxes already with many more to come.

The garage was filling up. We stacked everything in the middle so we could get to all the stuff in the garage. Larry had a complete set of tools, garden equipment, a lawn mower, rakes, shovels, yard chemicals, paints, ladders, etc.

"Mark, can you help me with these clothes?"

Honey had a pile of their clothes to take to St. Vincent DePaul's. We loaded Larry's VW and drove to the store. They knew we were coming. We unloaded everything. The woman seemed grateful. Most were women's clothes. Somebody could use them.

"We'll be back," promised Honey.

"Oh, Mark, I couldn't do this without you're help."

"You're welcome," I tried not to look at her with affection. I hope it didn't show.

Back to the house. What a mess! Honey started packing knick knacks and I stayed on the books. I had most of them packed. The thing about packing books, of course, is that you can't put that many in a box because it's too heavy, hence, the boxes were small, holding twenty hard bound books per box. The paperbacks held more. Being sure to label each box.

"We're going to need more boxes, Honey."

"I know, I'll call Mayflower."

Larry and his buddy returned from the dump and they loaded up the truck again.

By 5 p.m. we were pretty worn out and Honey ordered some pizzas. We took a long break and ate. As we ate all of us surveyed the progress we had made. We still had a long way to go but it was beginning to clear out. By this time tomorrow we could maybe start to clean the rooms. We were supposed to completely clean the place before we left which meant we may have to stay another day just to clean once the movers had filled the moving van.

"I have an idea ... let's clean as we go, in other words, once we empty a cabinet or a room we clean it out. I think it'll go faster that way," I said.

"Good idea," they both agreed.

I was a good cleaner. My dad had taught me well. After we ate we weren't too energetic. We drank some beers and listened to the stereo for the last time.

We crashed very early. My body ached.

Day two. Coffee, cigs and speed. Honey and I worked in the kitchen most of the morning. I volunteered to clean the oven and defrost the fridge. I unplugged the fridge and opened the doors. There wasn't any food left. Honey had given it to the neighbors. I used Easy-Off to clean the oven and the stove. The stuff really worked and eventually it was clean. Now the fridge. The freezer still had two inches of ice in it so I put a pot of boiling water in there. I saw my mom do that so I guessed it would work. It did. Took some time but I was able to chip the ice away. Honey was busy wiping down the cup boards and she put fresh lining in them. We did the floor last. It was sparkling when we finished. We also needed to wash all the windows in the house. I did the kitchen first using Windex and newspaper. They gleamed!

"This kitchen wasn't this clean when we moved in. You're a good house cleaner, Mark."

I blushed.

Larry was out in the garage packing his tools.

The Mayflower guy came and gave us more boxes. We had used most of them. I still had two bookshelves of books to pack.

We broke for lunch. Larry drove to some place and came back with burgers and fries and a case of beer.

After lunch, I needed a nap.

"Hey, I need to take a nap if that's okay."

"We all do."

I went back to my little room and crawled under the covers and slept for an hour. Woke up refreshed. Washed my face. Ready to hit it. I didn't hear anything stirring in the house so I quietly grabbed the Windex and washed the windows in my room and the back hallway. Soon enough the two woke up.

Coffee, cigs, and speed. We tore it up for another four hours. The kitchen was done. The bathroom was clean. All the books were packed. About all we could do was wait for the movers. They were supposed to be here the day after tomorrow.

We swept up and had another load for the dump ready to go. I washed every window. We moved furniture and vacuumed. We dusted. The land-lord came over and seemed pleased with our progress. He said he wanted to paint the place before new tenants moved in. I thought of volunteering for that but decided not to. How would I get back to Athens?

Larry and I moved several pieces of furniture into the driveway so we could clean the rooms. It wasn't going to rain and no one would take any of this stuff.

Larry had a car rack for the VW so we attached that to his car. It would hold our suitcases and such.

We three were so wired from the work and the speed that we were just walking in circles looking for something to do. It was funny.

We went to a burger spot. We had to eat.

"Just a few more loose ends. We can basically hang out tomorrow. This went faster than I thought it would. Thanks for your help, Mark. Can you help us on the other end?" Larry said.

"Oh yeah. I'd love to."

As I chomped on a cheeseburger I saw the naked biker ride by. Fitting, I thought.

The next day Larry's friend with the pickup came by and we made one more dump run. That was that!

Honey and Larry invited some of their friends over for a 'going away party.' People brought food and beer. We hung out in the back yard because the house was stuffed. Some of the neighbors even came by to wish them good luck. Mayflower was supposed to be here tomorrow at 7 a.m. so we didn't get too stoned.

I slept on the floor in my sleeping bag. Last night in Austin.

We got up early. About 5 I think. We took our showers and Honey made a last pot of coffee. I wiped the bathroom down.

Sure enough a huge truck showed up. Three burly guys came in and started moving everything onto the lawn. Two more guys showed up and they methodically loaded the truck. As each room cleared, Honey and I did the final clean. It wasn't but a few hours and the house was empty. It was clean.

Larry was busy loading the car rack. It was stuffed. We still had some room in the car and in the front trunk.

By noon the movers had most of the stuff loaded. There wasn't anything else for us to do so we hopped in the VW and headed to Athens.

"Everybody in?" Larry said, "let's boogie."

"Did you see that one guy? He picked up the TV like it was a loaf of bread."

"I know. They were very careful though. Hope everything makes it okay," Honey said with slight concern.

I sat in back. I was crunched but comfortable. Larry had serviced the car recently and it just purred as we headed to Athens. Larry decided to take a more direct route than our previous trip. Less scenic but quicker. We headed towards Houston but skirted just north of there and drove into Beaumont. It was unbearably hot. Honey had a jug of water which we drank volumes from.

We found a cheap motel somewhere out of Baton Rouge. It was late and we were exhausted. Larry and Honey in one room and I had a room to myself. I took a long shower and turned the air conditioner on all the way. We hadn't eaten since this morning so Larry drove and came back with some burgers and beer. We sat in their room and ate. We were so tired that we hardly spoke.

"See you in the morning," I said as I walked next door and crashed.

I fell asleep realizing that it was my birthday. I was 23. I think.

We packed up. Coffee, cigs, and speed.

Honey wanted to drive for awhile. We felt that we could make Montgomery, Alabama by night fall. It was so hot we just couldn't push the car that hard. We stopped several times to gas up and cool off. Larry made sure to check the oil each time.

We drove through some pretty desolate areas. Miles and miles of cotton fields. People picking cotton out there in this heat. Shacks that black people lived in. Alabama was a very poor state. There was little evidence of vitality. It seemed that most of the rural people were black. What was it like to grow up like this? I was so fortunate.

I sat in back the whole way. The windows were all down in an attempt to stay cool. It was a losing battle. We were drenched in sweat and felt grimy. It was hot and dusty and everything stuck to us.

We drove through one little town and a sign on a bank said it was 95 degrees.

At last we entered Montgomery. A large city. We must have looked like hell. Larry found a motel and we again had separate rooms. First thing was a long cold shower. Felt great. Larry, again, went out and bought burgers and fries and beer. We ate and watched some TV in their room. When I left their room I opened the door and it felt like a blast furnace outside. My room was nice and cool and I had no trouble falling asleep.

Coffee, cigs, and speed. Day three and the final leg into Athens. It was really hot again, even at 7 a.m. We gassed up and got some more water. I figured we could be in Athens by this afternoon. We had about 300 miles or so to go. We drove all the way with only one stop.

"Home sweet home," Larry cried.

We drove to Phil and Marcy's house. Marcy was home and expecting us. Big hugs all around. Larry and I drove to the new house. The movers weren't there yet so he called the landlord and picked up the keys. The movers were supposed to call Marcy's house when they got in town so all we could do was wait for them. They were also expected today.

"I bet those guys didn't leave until the next morning. They only work 8 hours a day, right?" I conjectured.

"I'm not sure. Tomorrow would be okay too. I'm bushed," said Larry.

"Should we stay here or at Marcy's?"

"Good question. Let's see what Honey thinks."

So we drove back to Marcy's. Phil was home by now and it was really nice to be with these people again. I felt totally safe and wanted.

"Honey told me you worked your ass off, Mark."

"Oh ... yeah ... I guess. It was fun really. Just glad I could help out," I responded. I felt shy. I never could accept praise. Just my nature I guess.

"Should we stay in the new house and wait for the movers?" Larry asked Honey.

"Did you check the electricity? Is it on?"

"Yeah, I got the keys from the landlord and he said the place was ours. The lights worked and there was hot water. What do you think?"

"I think we should stay there. We can borrow sleeping bags and some pillows for the night. It'll be fun."

Marcy packed up the sleeping bags and some pillows and let us borrow a coffee maker and some coffee and cups for the morning.

"Life isn't worth living without coffee," she joked.

We drove to the house and the movers were there! They said that they had just shown up and were going to call. Wow! Here we go again.

It was the same three guys from Austin plus they hired two guys from Athens to help. They opened the back door of the moving van and I couldn't believe it. It was stuffed. There wasn't a spare inch of room. They really knew how to pack.

They began to put boxes on the front lawn. When they came to a piece of furniture Honey told them where she wanted it. Honey hadn't seen the house yet and in ten minutes she had a plan for everything. I helped where

I could but I'd have to wait until more things were unpacked. I couldn't touch the books yet because they hadn't found the bookcases. The living room was taking shape. They had both couches moved in. It was a nice house with hard wood floors so it was easy to move things. They put the kitchen dishes in the kitchen so I helped Honey with that. We just unwrapped and put things away. No need to clean them because they were already clean. A neighbor lady stopped by and welcomed us to the neighborhood. She brought some cookies. She was nice.

Larry was in the garage putting his tools away. It seemed to go fast. Unloading was faster than loading. It was hot as hell and I was dripping with sweat. It felt great. I could feel my muscles coming back to life. I was dying for a beer. But it was best to hold off.

Phil and Marcy came by and they helped too. The guys had emptied the truck by now. All the furniture was in. The beds weren't made yet but they were in. Larry and Phil put the master bed room together. I could hear them laughing as they did.

Larry thanked the movers as they drove off. Man that was fast. Marcy and Honey put as much of the kitchen stuff away as they could. There were boxes everywhere. I broke several dozen boxes down and put them in the backyard. Out of the way.

Phil and Larry took off and came back with pizzas and beer and Honey's car. At long last. We could stop for a moment. We sat on the back porch. It was cooler back here.

"We can stop for the night. That's enough for one day."

Music to my ears.

I slept on the back porch. It was screened so the bugs weren't too bad.

I slowly awoke the next morning. Everything ached. I took a lick first thing. Honey was already up and had coffee made.

"Ugh! I fell like shit. Any chance of getting a shower?"

"Go ahead. Larry and I took one last night."

While I was showering Larry came in to pee.

"It's just me. I won't flush."

I didn't even towel off. It was already hot and my skin enjoyed the coolness of the shower.

Drank two cups of coffee and took another lick. I was ready.

"Where do you want me to start?"

"Anywhere!"

The phone man was supposed to come by today and hook up the phone. Larry had some business at the school. Honey wanted to finish the kitchen. She wanted to reline the cup boards.

"We left the other house cleaner than this. Let's do one cup board at a time." I had to reach in front of her to grab some plates and I accidentally brushed her breast. She touched my cheek and gave me a kiss on the lips. We were both stunned, I think. Frozen in time. I looked at her and cleared my throat and looked down.

We both said simultaneously, "I'm sorry."

A million thoughts raced through my mind and I'm sure hers as well.

'No. Stop right there.' The little voice in my brain shouted.

We were both embarrassed. But, giggled and continued working as though nothing had happened. Nothing did happen and yet everything happened!

"The landlord said we could paint the inside of the house and he would buy the paints. I want earth tones. What do you think?" she had completely changed the subject. It was a relief!

"Oh, yeah. Earth tones. Greens and browns. I guess."

The awkward moment had passed. But, deep down inside I wanted to throw Honey on the floor and fuck her!

"Honey, we should do it now while we can still move things around. Er ... paint that is."

Honey laughed at the double entendre.

"Let's go to the paint store!"

I told her of my experience in San Francisco of restoring old Victorians and how the soft mauve colors looked the best. She asked the neighbor lady where a good hardware store was and off we went. The guy was very helpful and after selecting the right colors and getting the paint mixed and brushes and paint thinner and rollers etc. We were off.

We started in the living room. I carefully taped off the edges for the trim and put the drop cloth over the furniture. I started on the ceiling. It would take two coats. Honey worked on the walls. The rollers made fast work and the trim was easy because it was taped off.

"Boy, will Larry be surprised when he gets home!"

"I'll say."

The first coat would be dry by tomorrow. Honey chose an off-white. The room was already brighter.

Larry returned and seemed overjoyed! "I got reimbursed for the move and I cashed the check! Wow! You guys are painting! Looks great! Hey, Mark, here's $300 for you."

Larry handed me a wad of twenties. "Oh my God! What's this for?"

"For all the work you've done, stupid."

"Thank you," it was already in my front pocket.

"Mark and I decided to paint the house. The landlord will pay for the paint. It really needs a fresh paint job," Honey said.

Just then there was a knock at the door. It was the phone man. He connected two phone lines in the house. I remembered I needed to talk with Mark.

I wanted to start in the kitchen and bathroom. Honey had chosen a very faint yellow for both. The paints were a heavy enamel and I told Honey that it was best to paint in this hot weather. The kitchen would be difficult. I taped off all the windows and emptied half the cabinets. I wouldn't get the entire kitchen done for a couple of days because there was so much stuff to move so I'd do it in shifts. The bathroom was hard also but I managed to get a coat on the walls. I'd do the trim last.

I had paint in my hair and all over my hands and arms and my jeans were heavily speckled also. I liked my jeans. They looked artistic.

I cleaned up. Carefully cleaning the brushes and rollers in turpentine.

The kitchen was a mess so we called for pizza. Larry had plugged his stereo in. We gratefully listened to tunes. It was a happy time. I managed to get a call in to Mark. He'd call me back. In the meantime Honey and I planned our assault on the house. Room by room.

The next morning I finished the living room as Honey worked in the kitchen. I moved to the bathroom. Managed to get the second coat on as well. I started on the long hallway which ran the length of the house. Honey chose a tan color. Subdued. She wanted to buy a long carpet for the hallway. I managed to get the first coat on. By nightfall we were halfway done with the house. Only a couple of rooms remained downstairs.

Honey still had a few days before she had to go back to work and we desperately wanted to finish this huge task before then. I told her I would stay until we finished.

Finally, that evening, Mark called and told me I had to go to Boston and there would be another package to take to Portland, Maine.

"This is a 'biggy.' "

He gave me the phone number of a guy named Bruce in Boston. I was to contact him and then travel to Portland. There was an urgency in his voice. An airline ticket was in Atlanta.

I worked until midnight. I don't know why. I just had to finish this. Mark wanted me in Boston next week. I had enjoyed this brief break from the 'Revolution.' Painting was a metaphor for my life. I wanted to cover all the bad with good.

Carefully and methodically I applied paint to the trim in the hallway. Honey was already hanging pictures on the wall. It looked so nice! Larry will be pleased.

I went to my room that night and started to cry. It came from no where. Tears streamed. The emotion from somewhere deep inside. I was blindsided. Why. Why was I sobbing? I justified this outburst, I was weak, not strong enough, pull yourself up, man. Get a grip. Men don't cry. I was trembling. Afraid the others would hear me, I crushed my face into the pillow. I wanted to die. I wasn't a man. This charade! The fear! Oh God, the Fear. Where could I go? I was lost. Alone. Who was I to question The

Man? I was a piece of shit! Not worthy. I felt so stupid in the midst of the smart people. I had flunked out of college. I didn't merit. I was ugly. I had pimples. I'd let everybody down who I'd ever loved! I was a leech living off the goodness of others. I was a 'taker' not a 'giver.'

I fell asleep.

Woke early to the strong scent of coffee. Honey and Larry were already up and eating breakfast.

"We let you sleep in, Mark. You've been a trooper."

"I really like doing this. No sweat. You guys have been so nice to me ... it's the least I could do. I'm leaving next week. Can't tell you where I'm going but could you give me a lift to the bus station? I have to catch a flight out of Atlanta."

"Shit man, I'll drive you there. You don't have to take the bus."

"Really? Oh, that would be wonderful."

"We can finish the downstairs today ... I think," said Honey.

"The place is shaping up. You two have worked hard. Keep it up. I'm off to work," and Larry got in his car and drove off.

"Well, what's next Mark?"

"Let's finish the kitchen and the office and bedroom then do the stairway."

The stairway was difficult. I had to use a different ladder and when I turned it sideways I put some books on the lower stair. I hoped it would hold. I remember that night my dad fell painting the stairway in Ohio. I didn't want to do that. It was perilous but I managed. I got the first coat down. One to go.

The downstairs was done! Honey was putting the finishing touches on the living room. Pictures hung. Drapes back up.

"Jeez, it looks great, Honey!"

"Come on with me. Take a break. I want to see if I can find a long rug for the hall way."

We measured the dimensions. Honey found a carpet store across town. It was a huge store. They had carpets and rugs galore. A salesperson showed us a bunch of different throw rugs. Honey told him what she wanted. We looked through several piles until she found it. It was an Oriental rug about 20 feet long and four feet wide. It was perfect. The guy gave her a good price on it because it was used, although it looked new. It had been cleaned too.

She was thrilled. We got back and we unfurled the rug.

"C'est fini!"

"Wow. That's perfect, Honey!"

She gave me a big hug. "Let's have a beer!"

We sat on the back porch and sipped a beer. It was hot as hell. I didn't want this day to end.

Larry got home.

"The house looks great, you guys! I love the hallway. Where'd you get that rug? It's gorgeous. Hope it didn't cost much!"

"We lucked out. It was used," I remarked.

"Careful of the staircase. I had to leave the ladder there."

The next day we moved the show upstairs. Two bedrooms, an office, a bathroom and the hallway. We finished in three days. Luckily, the paint dried quickly because of the heat.

Honey started work on Monday, tomorrow. I was leaving on Tuesday. The landlord came over and praised our work.

"This house has been in our family for several generations. I just knew you were the 'right' people for it. I'm going to give you a month's free rent because you did such a nice job. I couldn't be more pleased!"

Larry and Honey and myself were so happy. It's nice to be appreciated.

"Mark, just for that here's another $100. You earned it my friend. Honey and I both love you and will worry about you. Try to stay in touch with us. It goes without saying that if you ever need a place to stay ... you stay with us!"

My eyes welled up and I was speechless. Group hug.

Monday came and I carefully packed. I had three pairs of shorts and socks and shirts, two pairs of jeans, a camera, some film, two lenses, speed and cigs, plus a shaver and soap and deodorant. That's all I had in the world plus about $700 in my pocket. What else does a guy need.

I hadn't forgotten Carol. On the contrary. She might be at Bryn Mawr by now. What should I do?

All I knew was that I had to get a package from some guy named Bruce, and deliver it to Portland, Maine. Mark had seemed on edge. It must be an important one.

Larry and I left early the next morning having said goodbye to Honey in a tearful exit. We drove to Atlanta and found the airport.

"Just drop me off, man. I'll be okay. You don't have to see me off."

We hugged in his VW and I grabbed my ruck sack and entered the terminal. He had no idea where I was headed.

I walked to the United Airlines ticket desk and waited for an hour in line. I told the woman I had a ticket here for Mark Heddington. After several minutes and a phone call she produced the ticket. A one-way flight to Logan in Boston.

I received my seat assignment and we filled the plane. There wasn't an empty seat. We took off. Good bye sweet friends!

Chapter 14

Boston, New York, Maine, Nova Scotia ?

I arrived. There was no one to pick me up. As arranged, I took a cab to the address Mark had given me. It was in a really seedy part of downtown. An old warehouse district. I paid the cabbie and knocked on the door. A woman answered.

"Who are you?"

"I'm looking for Bruce."

"Come on in."

The apartment was on the 4th floor. No elevator. It was dark and dingy. Bruce was a big guy with long hair and a black beard. He looked menacing.

"You Mark?"

"Yeah."

"I've been expecting you. This is for you," as he handed me a large envelope.

"I don't know what's in it and I don't give a fuck. Wanna a beer?"

The woman disappeared momentarily and returned with three beers.

The apartment was barren except for two chairs and a mattress in the corner. I didn't see any other rooms except a kitchen and I assumed a bathroom. There was no light.

I was fearful. I drank my beer and said I had to go.

They were not very friendly. I walked back to the street. I was lost. It was getting dark. I walk passed groups of scary black guys, but none hassled me. Soon I found what seemed to be the center of downtown Boston. I had to find the bus station. I asked several people, most seemed alarmed when I asked them where the bus station was, a cop, of all people, Irish I could tell, kindly directed me. I was only three blocks away. A bus for Portland left in five hours. Midnight. What luck. I would wait it out here.

I put the package away. I found my note. I was to meet a guy named Allen. I had his phone number. I decided to call him.

"Hello."

"Allen?"

"Yeah, who's this."

"Mark. I'm in Boston. Can you meet me tomorrow at the bus station in Portland at 10?"

"Oh, yeah. Mark. Yeah, man. No problem."

"I'll be wearing a jean jacket and work boots."

"Um ... I'll wear a Red Sox hat. See you then."

I hoped that was cool. I took a chance calling ahead. Mark had told me this was important. I couldn't fuck up.

It was late September and fall was in the air. The coolness felt good for a change. That had been one of the hottest summers ever for me. The bus came by. I got on.

I fell asleep in the back of the bus. It was only half-full. We pulled into Portland by 7. I would wait for Allen. I walked around a bit. Nice town. Completely different than Austin or Athens. Hugged the Atlantic. First light. Sun rising over the water. A pretty sight.

Walked back to the bus station. No one was following me or even noticed. My hair was pulled back. Wearing glasses. I grabbed some coffee and seated myself so I could see the front door.

Right on time. A guy with a Red Sox hat walked in obviously looking for some one. I stood and approached him.

"Allen?"

"Oh yeah. You must be Mark. Pleased to meet you. Come on."

We drove out of town and into the country side. It was gorgeous! Some trees were just beginning to turn to their fall colors.

"Wow. This is some beautiful country, Allen."

He was a very kindly hippie boy with long hair. He drove his VW van with care.

"Sure is. Born and raised. Wouldn't think of living anywhere else. Do you have the package?"

"Sure do."

"Great. 'Cause we're going to drop it off right now," we drove down a lonely dirt road to a farmhouse.

"Wait here."

Allen walked to the house and the door opened before he even knocked. They must have heard us. Not one minute later Allen exited.

"Glad that's over. And you don't want to know."

"No, I don't," I agreed.

"Okay. Now we can relax. Those are some heavy people. Bad vibes, man."

I was blissfully lost in this wilderness. The trees touched the sky. We drove back into Portland.

"Mark wants us to call him as soon as it's delivered."

We found a pay phone and Allen made a quick call. How did Mark know all these people? It just amazed me. His Underground Network. I should write a book about this someday, I mused.

"I just left a message. 'Job done'. He'll probably call me in an hour or so. So, we should get to my place. It ain't much but it's warm."

We drove into a driveway. The nearest neighbor was a few acres away. It was an old or should I say ancient farm house. When we entered I was surprised to see indoor plumbing. Allen told me all about the property. It had been in his family for several generations and it was his now since his grandma passed away. He'd been coming here all his life. He lived alone.

"Do you smoke? Pot, that is."

"Yeah, sure," I said.

He rolled a perfect joint. And we got stoned.

"I grow this out in the green house. Come on, I'll show you around."

It had once been a real farm with cattle and chickens. Allen wasn't into that. But, the barn still stood. Albeit, slightly leaning and in need of repair. The green house was newer. He had built it a few years ago. Several big pot plants were growing in here. It was hot and humid.

"Almost harvest time," he declared.

We continued walking and we walked down a long well-worn path. We came upon a small lake.

"It's well stocked with trout. I don't fish though. They keep the lake alive!"

"Does it freeze in the winter?"

"Solid."

"In about a month this place turns colors you won't believe! I hope you can see the trees then, Mark. I don't know if you believe in God but it's God's hand, man."

"Sometimes."

"Sometimes?"

"Yeah, sometimes I do believe in God."

We both laughed and walked back to his house. I noticed a slight chill in the air and it was refreshing.

Allen shared a devotion to the Grateful Dead and he had everything! We played *Anthem of the Sun* several times on his super fine stereo system. Allen must have known too because he had a case of beer.

Called it an early night.

Eventually, I slipped into my sleeping bag. Fell asleep. Had the trike nightmare again. I was being chased and I couldn't pedal fast enough. They were closing in. I awoke in a sweat. Where the fuck am I?

"Morning, Mark. Made some coffee."

"Oooh," I was still asleep, "what time is it?"

"Six."

"Mark never called. Did he?"

"Nope. He will."

I lit a cig and found the bathroom. Pissed like a horse. Grabbed a cup.

"Thank you. I need this," as I poured a cup.

"Sorry to wake you so early but I drive a school bus and I have to get going. Gotta get the kiddies to school. So just hang out and answer the phone if it rings. It'll probably be Mark. I'll be back in an hour or so."

He didn't mention that he drove a bus. Oh well. It was Monday morning. Allen didn't have a TV so I turned on a radio station and listened to Top 40. Elvis! Elvis? Are you kidding me? Elvis. I turned it off. I yearned to know what was going on in the outside world. Honey and Larry didn't have their TV hooked up when I was there so it had been a few weeks since I had watched the news. Maybe I was better off.

I showered and picked up the house. I noticed Allen had a washer and dryer. I should wait to ask him if it would be all right to wash my clothes.

Allen returned.

"Oh, thanks for cleaning up. I have to go back out at 2:30 on the bus again. Did Mark call?"

"Not yet. Should I call him?"

"Maybe, if he hasn't called by this afternoon."

"Allen, can I wash some clothes?"

"Be my guest. I've got some too."

I didn't want to leave the house until Mark called. Allen had a vast library. I noted several books I had read and many I wanted to read. He also was a fan of Kerouac. Allen had some chores to do out in the barn so I curled up with Merton.

The phone rang. I answered by the second ring.

"Mark?" a voice said.

"Yeah. Hey, Mark. What's up?"

"Oh ... you know ... the usual. Hey, listen, I need you to return to Boston and get in touch with Bruce again."

"Okay. He was kind of a jerk."

"Yeah, that's just his personality. Once he gets to know you ... he's solid, Mark. He's got another package for you and it needs to get to New York. He's got the contact information for you. I'll talk to him. Then, I want you to get back to Boston and sit tight. Can you do it?"

"Anything for you, man."

"Honestly, I don't know what I'd do without you. You're the only person I know that can move around like you do. Most people I don't trust and secondly they just don't have the balls! It takes balls to go from place to place and keep their heads right."

Mark was giving me one of his 'pep' talks. That was okay. My ego could use a boost once in awhile.

"Thanks. Should I call you?"

"Yeah. Give me a jingle when you get to New York."

"Will do."

"Is Allen there?"

"Yeah."

"Let me talk with him."

"Hold on. He's out in his barn."

He and Allen talked for about ten minutes in hushed tones. I didn't listen in.

"I'm driving you to Boston tonight!"

Allen made his afternoon run. I packed my ruck sack. Clean clothes.

We drove to Boston. The same seedy apartment building. I told Allen that I'd see him again. I didn't really know if I would. Thanked him. Rang the buzzer. The door opened. Walked up the long flight of stairs. Winded, I knocked on the door. Bruce answered. It was obvious from the start that he had a different attitude. He was nice.

"Mark! Come on in. Sorry I was such a 'dick' before. I just don't trust anybody until I know 'em."

"No problem. You've got something for me?"

"Yeah. Here it is," he showed me the package and the address and name.

"Hey, maybe you can help me. New York is a big place and I'm afraid of getting lost. Can you give me directions?"

"Oh yeah."

He wrote out an intricate map showing me which train to catch. The address was on the Lower East Side.

"After I drop this off I'm supposed to call Mark. I may be coming back here. I don't know. Is that cool?"

"Oh yeah."

The next morning I took a commuter train into Grand Central Station. I was scared. This town is too big! I followed Bruce's map and caught a subway train and got off in the Lower East Side of Manhattan. God hadn't been kind. It was a slum. It was grimy and dirty. The buildings were made of iron and brick. Winos littered the sidewalks. I found the address and rang the buzzer.

"Who is it?"

"Mark."

The buzzer released the lock and I entered the building. I looked for an elevator but found none. I walked up six flights of stairs. 606. I rang the bell. I heard a series of locks being opened.

A black haired bearded guy opened the door.

"John?"

"Yeah. You'se got somthin' for me?"

"Yeah. Here it is."

"Want some coffee?"

"Please."

The place was just a room. A kitchen, a very small table in the corner. Junk everywhere. Windows closed and shaded. A menacing space.

"Ain't got no sugar or milk."

I thanked him and sipped on it. At least it was hot.

"You'se can't stay here. Mark told me to put you up in the Village. You'se know where that is?"

"Nope."

"Ain't far from here."

He told me how to get there. I could walk. I got the unquestionable feeling John wanted me out of here. I finished half my coffee and excused myself. I walked down the dark stair case and thought that if there was such a thing as a Mafia Hippie ... I had just met one.

I followed John's directions and found East 9th Street. It was about six blocks away. I got a glimpse of the Empire State Building. God, that was high. A marvel.

Here it is. An old Brownstone with a flight of stairs to a landing. I rang the buzzer. A woman's voice answered. "Who is it?"

"Mark."

"Oh great ..."

The buzzer unlocked the front door. #110. Must be on the first floor. A woman was waiting in the hall way. "Mark?"

"That's me."

"Welcome."

"My name is Anne."

"I just came from John's place."

"He's a brute but a sweetheart once you get to know him. You can stay here for a few days. This is your room. The bathroom is down the hall to your left. Put your things down and join me."

We adjourned to a small living room. She served coffee. She was, I'd guess about 30. Long brown hair, passed her shoulders. Blue jeans and a white blouse.

"It is a pleasure to meet you in person, Mark. Your reputation precedes you."

"Really. I'd rather be anonymous."

"I see your point. I've just heard about you through the 'Grapevine' as it were. You're called 'The Mailman.' "

"I'm sure you've only heard an embellishment. I'm just a guy who hates the war. Kinda fell into this."

"You're way too modest. Is this your first visit to our City?"

"No. I was here several years ago with my dad. It's a big place."

"Yes. It can seem that way. However, we 'Village People' find it quaint."

"Quaint. Now that's a word I would never expect to hear when de-scribing New York!" I laughed.

"Have you lived in New York long?"

"My whole life. Mother and Father were both professors at NYU and

Columbia respectively, I grew up in this neighborhood."

"Did you see any of the Beats?"

"I did. I was younger then, of course, I recall seeing Ginsberg and Kerouac several times."

"Wow."

"However, I was more involved with the student takeover of Columbia. My Father taught Mark Rudd in one of his classes. I was on campus for most of the takeover and got to know some of the people quite well."

"You knew Mark Rudd?"

"We spoke a few times. Yes."

"Wow, again."

"What do you do now, Anne?"

"I'm still going to school getting another Master's degree and I waitress at a restaurant a few blocks from here."

"And it's okay if I stay here?"

"Of course. Be my guest. Stay as long as you need to. Anything for the Revolution," she giggled and raised a clenched fist.

"Come on. I want to show you the Village."

Anne rapped non-stop showing me historic coffee shops and bistros where the Beats made their name. Several cafes where Dylan played and the folk scene was born and finally, the house that 3 SDS members had blown themselves up last year. They called themselves 'Weathermen' after the Dylan song.

"That's where I draw the line, Anne. I'm against violence."

"I think most people would agree with you."

"Let's go in here and have a slice of pizza. Best in the City."

We each bought a slice. It was out of this world. I've never tasted anything like it.

"My God this is good!" I cried.

We sat outside on a bench in a park. I could hear the hum of this great City but it seemed peaceful. Fall was in the air. It was chilly.

It was getting dark and we walked back to Anne's.

"Anne, if you don't mind. I'd like to crash. I'm tired."

"Of course. If you need anything ..."

I walked to the back room and actually slept in a bed. I don't remember falling asleep.

I awoke the next morning looking at a tree outside the window. The leaves were turning. Early light saturated and embellished the reds and yellows. It was the most beautiful sight ever. I wanted to stay in this lasting moment, but nature called.

I found the bathroom. The door was open. I relieved myself and trod to the kitchen. Coffee, cigs, and speed. That was all I needed.

Anne sat at the kitchen table.

"Oh, you poor dear. I'll get you some coffee. Did you sleep okay? Are you hungry?"

"Just coffee. Good morning. I wanted to thank you for showing me the Village last night. That was neat!"

"You're welcome. I have to work today. Here's an extra key if you want to go out. Be sure to lock the door if you do."

"Thanks. I think I'll just stay in and catch up on my reading. I'm kinda worn out."

"Suit yourself. I have to run."

She gave me a peck on the cheek and scurried out the door. I was left to my own devices.

I took a long hot shower and drank volumes of coffee. I snuggled up with my Merton and eventually fell asleep again.

Anne returned smelling like a restaurant. She hopped into the shower. Her head wrapped in a towel. Dressed only in a bathrobe smelling like a flower I was attracted to her but, she was above my station. For sure. Get over it. I told myself. Get over it. I did.

"I thought you might want to hear some music tonight."

"Hey, that's an idea."

We hopped on the subway and went somewhere and she took me to a bar in Mid-Town and we listened to and danced to some rock band. After several drinks and hours of sweaty dancing we headed back to her place. It was late and we were both pretty stoned. We slept together. It was the first sex I'd had since ...

When I awoke the next morning I realized I'd told Anne things I shouldn't have. Like ... I was a draft resister and that I delivered packages etc. What was I thinking. "You're secret is safe with me," she had said.

Dumb ass!

"Anne, all those things I told you last night ..."

"I know. Don't worry. I won't tell anyone."

"You can't. You just can't," I pleaded.

She went off to work. She kissed me as she left. It was a passionate kiss and it lingered. But, I had fucked up!

I fretted all day. Would she tell anyone? Of course she would! People like to make themselves big by bragging about the people they knew. The things they'd done. I paced. Then I thought she wouldn't. No, she's cool. Nuts! It's my own fault. I thought of writing a note saying that I had to go but I poo-pooed that idea. Christ! I wanted to go out for a walk but was afraid I'd get lost and I couldn't navigate the lock system anyway. I licked more speed. I was restless. Tried calling Mark. Left a message. Tried taking a nap ... couldn't sleep. Laid on the bed watching the leaves rustle and turn in the wind.

Anne worked a short shift and returned. She smelled like grease. She took a shower. When she finished I heard her on the phone talking to someone. She had a boisterous voice and it carried.

"Yeah, no shit, he's a draft resister ..."

I heard it.

When she finished I asked her who she was talking to.

"Oh, just my mom."

"I overheard you tell her I was a draft resister ..."

"Oh, she's cool. I tell her everything."

"I thought you told me my secret was safe with you?"

"It is!"

"No it isn't ... you just told your mom for fuck's sake."

I was pissed.

Anne was apologizing, she admitted to telling her friend at work too!

"Anne, look at me, I'm not angry with you ... but, I need to go. I can't stay here any longer. I don't want you to feel bad but, I know you will. Next time though ... it was all my fault, I should never had told you. I was drunk, but that's no excuse! It's all my fault ..." I trailed off.

I had my bags packed anyway and headed out the door.

"Thanks for showing me the Village."

The last I saw of her she was crying holding onto the door.

I'm an asshole. A selfish arrogant stupid asshole!

Argh!

I walked up 9th. I didn't know where I was going. In a City of 7 million people I knew only one person. How could that be. What are the odds. Fuck it. I found the Subway and guessed where I was going. I had to get to Grand Central, I guess. Where would I go? Boston, I guess. Yes, back to Bean Town. At least I knew someone there!

I asked one of the passengers which stop was Grand Central and he didn't even acknowledge me. New Yorkers! I looked at the map above our heads and sort of figured it out. Eventually, I got off the train and walked up the stairs. I was in Times Square. I knew I was close. I saw a cop standing there and I asked him. He was kind and helpful. Shortly, I was in the huge terminal. I looked around. A million people. Running for their lives. No eye contact what so ever. Finally I found a ticket window and bought a ticket to Boston. It left in thirty minutes. I waited.

I was running. Poor Anne. But I wasn't going to hang around to see what happened. I wondered if Mark ever called back. I had to call Bruce when I got to Boston. What a joy he is. Well, better than prison, I thought. There was a chill in the air. It was nearly October. World Series time. Thinking of the World Series calmed me. It looked like the Orioles and

Pirates. Wow! A Series without the Yanks!

The train came by. I got on. Packed is not the word. Commuters. Suits. Perverts. The working class!

I stood for an hour before I finally found a seat. What's next? I don't know. I just don't know. I'm living in a scary movie, a bad novel. Is this real? I wanted more speed so I walked to the bathroom and licked up. My veins stood up. I was on high alert! I noticed that I still had a ton of that shit left. Nice!

Thank God, Bruce was home.

"Sorry man for the short notice. This is Mark. Can I crash with you?"

"Oh yeah, grab a cab. Come on by, man."

This time, Bruce was as gracious as the Royal Family. I guess Mark had set him straight.

"What happened?"

"The chick told her mom and a friend I was staying with her. I panicked. I probably over reacted but I split, man. I can't trust anyone, you know."

"Easy man. Smoke this. Wanna beer?"

"Yeah. Thanks."

"Thanks, Bruce. I hate to crash on you, man ... but ..."

"Hey, man. It's cool. Mark told me about you. You're a fuckin' king in my pad, man. It's a fuckin' honor, dude."

"I've got some bread for food and shit."

"Cool."

We spent the evening listening to his record collection. He had everything. I always enjoyed someone sharing their music. I could learn a lot about a person that way.

His flat had no heat or hot water. The electricity consisted of an extension cord from somewhere. He had a hot plate and hot coffee. That was it. The temperature had sunk and it was cold in here. I would need the sleeping bag tonight. Bruce didn't mind. He was as tough as nails. I started to really like him. Around the tough edge and hard mannerisms lived a soulful brother. Salt of the Earth kinda guy. No bullshit! I liked that.

I fell asleep in the corner on the floor. A long cry from the warm sheets of Anne.

Woke up in a shiver. Had steam on my breath. Bruce just shrugged it off, No big deal. It's 25 degrees in here and he acts like it's fucking Miami. I had to chuckle. If the FEDS broke in here right now they'd freeze before they could make an arrest. Too cold. It was cold!

"Here, have some coffee. That'll warm you up."

"Fuck, man I'm freezin'."

"It's all in the mind."

Bruce turned the hot plate on and put a clay pot for plants over it.

"Place will warm up. Just wait."

It did warm up. All the way to 45 degrees. It acted like a small radiator. Inventive!

I called Mark. Left a message.

I had to wait here in this ice box for him to call back. At least the beer was cool.

Finally, I had to eat. Bruce usually ate at a shitty diner down the street. All I can say about this place was that the cock roaches seemed well mannered. They waited until I finished eating before they invaded. But, it did warm me up a bit. I could feel my feet again. We walked back up to Bruce's place and hung out. Bruce was a strange sort. He didn't say much. Consumed by a book he was reading.

Mark didn't call that night.

"Bruce, are you okay in here? I mean, it's cold, man."

"Yeah. No problem. Wait until February. Then it gets cold!"

I couldn't imagine.

"How do you bathe?"

"I heat some water and take a sponge bath. I call it a 'whore's bath' or I go to the YMCA."

We didn't venture too far from the hot plate. I had a blanket over my shoulders. I was getting used to it.

Woke the next morning. It was much colder. This is how poor people live. I thought. No heat, no hot water, no fridge or oven, no privacy, no rights, no fair! This is America? I found out last night that Bruce had been to Vietnam. He saw a lot of action. It had fucked him up. He was against the war and when he returned was treated like shit from people. His family wanted nothing to do with him. He didn't seem to have any friends except that woman I met the first night. I didn't want to pry. He needed help but where was he going to get that? He was a 'Baby Killer.'

My heart opened to him. Another casualty of the war. No, he wasn't dead or maimed, physically. Emotionally. I hadn't thought about that aspect. The emotional side. But, I could remember my dad on several occasions screaming out in the middle of the night. He was a war casualty too. And all those GIs from WWII coming home with grave emotional issues and raising their kids. No wonder! No wonder!

World War Two GIs came home as heroes. They were given the GI Bill and were basically given free homes. They wanted everything plain and simple and ordered. Then their kids grew up and rebelled. Of course we did. I know why. So did they, but couldn't admit that their value system of Maytags and Doris Day wasn't what we wanted. We wanted truth and justice. The status quo of racism and bigotry and injustice wouldn't suffice. The very idea that America was the 'Police' of the world was ludicrous to us. This country was being ruled by an elite super white super rich minority. For the most part, their son's didn't serve in the military. We just thought it would be nice if everyone had the same rights as them. I saw poor blacks, no teeth, shoddy clothes, hungry ... I saw women being raped and the courts blamed them ... I saw gentle people beaten by police ... I saw people not given a chance because their skin was dark ... I saw babies living in squalor ... I saw hate and I saw love.

And the propaganda machine was in full force preaching their lies that it was 'Un-American' to protest against the government ... to be against the war. I wondered what Thomas Paine and some of our Founding Father's would have thought of that line of logic.

Rambling thoughts as I watched Bruce read.

The phone rang. It startled both of us. Bruce picked up.

"Doin' okay. How about you?"

There was a moment when Bruce was listening.

"Yeah, he's right here."

He handed me the phone. It was Mark.

"Hey man. How are you."

"Cold, but holding up."

I looked at Bruce with an apologetic look.

"Sorry to hear that. I gotta cut this short. Listen. Stay put for a few days. I've got a big one working. Can you do that?"

"Of course. I'll just wait for you to call ... right?"

"Yeah. Hey, Mark. Thanks," he said.

And he hung up.

"Everything okay?"

"Yeah. He wants me to hang out here for a few days if that's all right with you?"

"Yeah. Fine. It might be cold but it's safe. Let's go to the Y. We can clean up there. I go once a week for a shower."

We walked several blocks to the YMCA. Bruce was a member. He flashed his card. I was his guest.

The shower felt great. My clothes were dirty but didn't smell too bad. At least I was warm again. My hair was still wet from the shower as we walked out. I borrowed a stocking cap from Bruce and we headed to a bar. We watched the Celtics and ate a burger and drank beer. The Celtics lead by John Havlicek and Dave Cowens were playing the Knicks. Everybody was screaming at the TV. Great fun.

We walked back to Bruce's flat. We were both quite warm by now. The flat was warmer than outside. He turned on the hot plate and within a few minutes it did seem to warm up ... some.

The temperature had dropped to the teens. Cold for this time of year. I grew up in Wisconsin, this is nothing, I thought to myself.

Bruce and I got into a routine. We didn't stay in the flat much. I found a cafe/bookstore to while away the hours and stay warm. Bruce went off somewhere. He was a man of few words and at first I felt ill at ease around him but I adjusted. He was a troubled guy though. I figured if he wanted to talk he would.

A week went by.

Mark called.

"Here's the deal. I need you to go back to Portland and meet Allen. This is heavy. He'll take you to where you're going. God's speed, Mark."

There was a tinge of panic in his voice. I sensed that this was an important delivery. But, they all were. This is just another one.

Bruce told me to wait here. He returned in two hours with another package.

"This is for you," he handed it to me. Neatly wrapped and heavily taped, I put it in my ruck sack.

I told Bruce I was leaving in the morning. He didn't respond in a normal way. He just shrugged his shoulders and continued reading.

The next morning I awoke shivering as usual. Bruce made some coffee.

"Hey, thanks, man for letting me stay here. I appreciate it."

"No big deal."

I just walked out of the room. No big goodbye or anything. I could have been insulted but I felt sorry for him. He couldn't help it. I thought of him often in the years to come living in that God awful place. No heat.

Caught the train to Portland and was there in a few hours. Allen even met me at the station. Nice!

"Great to see you, man," big hugs were exchanged.

"We got us a big trip. We're leaving tomorrow for Nova Scotia!"

"You're kidding!"

"Nope. And it's no problem getting across the border, if that's what you're thinking."

I was.

"Just show 'em your student ID with the student deferment on it. Piece of cake. I do it all the time."

"You're sure?"

"Positive, man."

It was snowing when we got up. Not too hard. It was melting as soon as it hit the ground.

Allen had a newer Ford truck that he kept out in the barn.

"We should take the truck. It's great in snow!"

We headed out. I was just amazed by the trees. We drove for an hour or so and drove into Brunswick. It continued to snow. And it was sticking.

"I can't believe this, man." Allen sighed.

We had the radio on and the weather reports were not encouraging. They expected blizzard like conditions later in the afternoon.

Allen decided to take the scenic route on Highway 1 against the rugged coast. He figured it would be snowing less than inland. It was getting difficult to see. There was almost no traffic. It was late November, a few days before Thanksgiving. I guess you had to expect this. I watched the ocean. It looked menacing. Huge white caps. Strong waves. Fall in Maine. The trees were psychedelic adding to the adventure.

"Allen, I think this is one of the most beautiful drives I've ever been on."

"It is pretty up here. Especially this time of year. Fuck, man, it's really coming down. But the roads are clear so let's keep going!"

We had a long drive ahead of us. We didn't expect to reach our destination, Saint John, New Brunswick, before tomorrow anyway. We weren't really going to Nova Scotia after all. The people were going to meet us there instead. Change of plans.

As we were driving I got to thinking about the package and who it might be for. I was guessing the Armstrong Brothers (again) but couldn't be certain. Maybe it contained letters and money from their mom. I'd seen their pictures in Post Offices on the FBI's Ten Most Wanted list. I was small potatoes compared to those guys. But, then again. Stop thinking about it. Forget about it!

"Jeez, Mark. I don't know. The road is starting to ice over. Maybe we should pull over in the next town and find a motel. What do you think?"

"I think that would be a good idea. We were going to stay overnight anyway. Better to be safe than sorry."

We crept along the highway for another ten miles and came to Belfast. We found a motel and checked in. The town looked deserted so we had no trouble getting a room.

"I'd better call those guys."

Allen called them and explained what was happening. Apparently it was snowing up there also. All the roads were closed and they expected a couple of feet of snow.

"This calls for pizza and beer, my friend."

There happened to be a pizza place in town that delivered and they had beer too! Perfect.

We enjoyed the rest of the evening eating and drinking and watching TV. There was at least two feet of snow on the ground and you couldn't see across the street.

Allen fired up a joint just to put the finishing touch on the night.

A Winter Wonderland!

Everything was white.

Obviously, we weren't going anywhere. The news had said that the entire East Coast was blanketed in snow.

But, it had stopped snowing.

The proprietor of the motel was trying to shovel the walks. The poor bastard was overwhelmed. The parking lot ... forget about it!

We stayed another night.

Allen's friend was still in Nova Scotia. I didn't know where. Didn't want to know.

We were going to be here for a few days.

Big change of plans, again. Allen's friends would drive down here to meet us. I got to thinking. That was better. Didn't want to risk crossing the border.

Allen and I spent Thanksgiving with the motel manager and his wife and a few other guests in the motel. It was pleasant enough. They were very nice people and we had a feast. Ended up watching football back in the room. At least we were well fed and warm.

By the next day it looked like they were getting some of the roads cleared. Allen talked to his friends again and they were going to leave tomorrow. We would wait.

The weather finally cleared by the next morning. The roads were dry and clear again. Allen's friend called and they were on their way.

The managers of the motel were really nice folks. They offered us breakfast. We accepted. Allen and I decided to drive around the town just to check it out. It was beautiful. The neighborhoods neat and tidy and of course the trees which I couldn't get enough of. I only had Tri-X with me, black and white film, so I didn't attempt to photograph.

We found downtown. Allen wanted a beer. We walked into a bar and ordered a couple of beers. Several locals were present but they didn't seem to mind us. We munched on peanuts. This place reminded me so much of Northern Wisconsin. Lots of water and the same kind of trees. I was homesick!

"They should be pulling in some time tomorrow afternoon. It was nice of them to meet us here. Saves the driving."

We spotted a couple other 'long hairs' in the bar. They paid us no mind. I was relaxed.

"Two more, gentlemen?"

"Why not!"

After several rounds Allen and I headed back to the motel. The sun made a peek at one point. We drove down to a boat harbor.

"Allen, I love this place. You know, sometimes things are just meant to be. There's a reason we got stuck here in Belfast. It must be Fate, you know."

"Sounds like the truth to me," he giggled.

"Or, maybe not. What the fuck do I know."

We happily returned to the motel. We ordered a pizza and more beer.

"What's on?"

We found a Celtics game and enjoyed the rest of the evening yelling at the TV set.

Allen's friend called. It was around noon. He wanted to meet Allen at a service station on the outskirts of Belfast.

"They must have driven all night. They want to meet me. Alone. Stay here, man. Give me the package. I'll be back."

"Okay."

I gave Allen the package. I would have given my eye teeth to know the contents. Off he went. I waited for an hour. He returned.

"That's that. Let's check out and go home."

We paid our bill and thanked the manager. We were gone.

"How'd it go?" I asked.

"Fine. I guess. He grabbed the package and we talked for a while. He wouldn't tell me who it was for so I sensed it was somebody heavy, man. Somebody heavy. I've known this guy a long time and he was scared, I think. I don't know. It was like he was afraid he'd fuck up or something and the blizzard set him off. The delay, you know. He likes things to go mellow like. He'll be home by tomorrow. It's better if we just forget about it!"

I sat looking at him in the front seat. I just had to let it go. I could tell he was tense. He was tense because his friend was tense. I just knew that this had been the most important delivery yet. I just knew it!

I had to let that go. Forget about it! I'd done all I could.

This time, I witnessed the last of the beautiful autumn. Shimmering trees showing off like proud colorful children in a dance of yellow and red hues.

"Allen, this is something! Is it like this every year?"

"No. Some years it's even better," he laughed.

The roads were clear and dry. We made it back to Allen's in due time. We were bushed but it was nice to be back. We unpacked.

Allen said his friend would call when he made it back.

Allen fixed up a huge pasta dish and we fed our faces with a great meal.

I called Mark and left a message to call back.

Allen's friend called the next morning and said everything went okay. What a relief!

I wondered what Mark had in mind for me? I really wanted to return to San Francisco. I didn't want to deal with the winter.

Mark did call. "Good job, Mark. Have any difficulties?" he laughed because he knew about the snow storm.

"We got it done, man. What's next?"

"Nothing right now."

"I'd like to return to the City. I don't have the right clothes for winter."

"Yeah. Good idea. See you soon."

I told Allen I had to leave in a couple of days. Christmas was coming up and if I flew out now I could catch a flight before the holiday melee. I didn't tell him where I was headed. He looked a little crest fallen. We had had a good time. But, I had to go.

"Maybe I could stay a few more days and help out around here to get ready for winter."

"You can stay as long as you like."

"Thanks, man but like the song says 'I'm goin' where the weather suits my clothes.' I'll probably end up in Texas. (I lied). Mark's got some stuff for me there," (I lied again).

"Yeah. Well, if you meant what you said you can help me put bales of hay around the house. This place is like a wind tunnel in the winter and you can help me get the fireplace going again and carry some wood. Yeah, I could use the help!"

"Thanks, man," I said.

I liked to work. Made me feel useful.

Allen gave me a pair of work gloves and we loaded up a wagon in the barn with bales of hay. God, these were heavy. I remembered years ago with my cousins in New Richmond trying to lift bales of hay. It took two of us then. Now, I was able to lift and swing the bale. Allen hooked up a tractor and we motored up to the house and stacked the bales three high around the house. We put storm windows up too. Two stories.

Allen had a huge wood pile out back. We toted a load of wood and stacked it by the back porch. All in a day's work.

"Would have taken me two days to do this. We did it in one."

"What else?" I asked eager to help Allen.

"Nothing else today. I'm bushed."

I knew I would ache tomorrow. Hadn't worked that hard since the monastery.

"Got a real treat ... if you're up to it..."

"Yeah, what's that?"

"I've been sitting on two hits of blotter acid."

"Fuck yeah!"

"First, let's go out and get some beer. I've got pot here, too."

We ran into town and Allen bought a case of beer and some chips.

"To peace ... down the hatch."

We let the acid melt in our mouths. It had a bitter taste which was soon erased with a gulp of beer.

Allen lit a fire in the fireplace and we waited for the acid to come on. And come on it did. At first I felt a faintly sickly feeling in my stomach soon followed by a shakiness in my limbs. And it came on and on. More intense by the minute. My senses were stirred. Just kind of laid there watching the flames. Every time I moved it seemed more intense. Allen and I didn't talk. Once in a while one of us would mutter ... "shit" ... like a groan. I couldn't even move. Powerful surges through my body. Wasn't hallucinating yet. Just a full on body rush that would have brought Superman to his knees.

"Where'd you get this from, man?" I slurred.

"A friend in California brought it."

"Figures ..." I giggled.

Allen somehow managed to put on *Crosby, Stills, Nash, and Young*. Very nice. The rush was fucking intense. I felt like I was trembling inside my body. Things started to look weird. I knew we were in for a night!

Allen was perfect to trip with. He didn't freak out and get crazy, he just went along with the ride. We decided to go outside and walk around. The night was still. It was cold but not bitter cold. There were a few clouds. We saw clear stars in between the breaks. We walked out to the barn. It seemed so different in here. The cold air helped. Things were moving and dancing out of the side of my vision. Allen brought his guitar and started to strum some chords in the barn. It was magical!

"I'm too fucked up to play."

He handed me the guitar. I started to play. I only knew a couple of songs. I played *Cold Rain and Snow* by the Dead for like an hour.

"Keep playin', man."

"I can't feel my fingers," I laughed.

We walked back to the house. It was very warm inside and immediately felt the rush of the acid return.

We were tripping at a thousand miles an hour. Everything was funny.

"Wanna beer?"

We drank our beers with gusto. Then another. And another. Almost felt human again. We smoked a joint and it began again. Not as intense. It was mellow and perfect. We both kind of slumped on pillows on the floor and listened to the stereo.

After several hours and beers I was more drunk than anything. I fell asleep on the floor. Allen must have put a blanket over me.

"Morning, Mark."

"Ooooh ... ," I moaned ... in confusion and pain.

Allen handed me a cup of coffee.

"Damn, that was fun. Good acid, huh?"

"I'll say."

I had to pee. I still had all my clothes on, I noticed. I stood up and was dizzy. I sat down in a chair and waited for it to pass. Soon, I was able to make it to the bathroom.

"All right?"

"Yeah," I laughed.

"That shit kicked my ass."

I sipped coffee and took a lick. In an hour I felt like a human being again. Took a shower and ate some breakfast.

"Whew. Man, can't do that too often."

Allen was in great spirits.

"Acid cleans out the pipes, man. I feel re-born," he laughed at his own joke.

I said, "Let's finish up our chores. What else is there to do?"

"Not much. We just need to haul some more wood."

Allen had a rather large stack of seasoned wood neatly stacked out back. The tractor would do most of the work.

After a few minutes we had taken our coats off. I was plenty warm, sweating heavily. The acid-beer-speed hangover vanished quickly from the hard work.

"I'm all set for the winter. Believe it or not, I'll burn all that wood up."

We drove into town and bought another case of beer. We had somehow polished the other one off. Allen and I went into a grocery store and he bought a shopping cart full of food. Enough for an army. He insisted on paying.

"No man, you're my guest. Besides, you'll need it for the road."

I couldn't argue with that. But, I felt guilty none the less. Guilt was my constant companion.

We drank and ate that night. In the back of my brain ... conflict. I wasn't sure what to do next. Or where to go. I thought of Carol. She never left my thoughts. I alternated between believing we were still together to sudden thoughts of anguish that she had found someone new. She would be back from Europe by now. I think. I could call Bryn Mawr and see if she was there. I don't know. That was a stupid risk. I just couldn't get her off my mind.

In the haze of dope and beer I decided to risk it and go see Carol. I couldn't rest until I knew!

Chapter 15

Carol and San Francisco

I awoke early the next morning, the birds having their morning conversations.

Allen, of course was already up and had coffee for me.

"Allen, I'm going to split. I've got stuff to do for Mark and ..."

"Stay one more day ... can you?" he interrupted.

After a moment I considered it ... what's one more day. "Yeah, sure."

"Oh good. I've enjoyed your company so much. It gets lonely out here."

Actually, I wanted to stay and never leave.

"That's really cool, man. You understand though. I have to get back to New York."

"Yeah, yeah, yeah ... I know. We can just kick back tonight and listen to music and rap."

"Sounds good."

Allen fixed dinner. Had a few beers. Had a few tokes and listened to some old Beatles stuff and reminisced about the 'old days.' I told Allen about the day after the Beatles had been on *Ed Sullivan* and how the school Principal had told us students that no 'Beatle boots or Beatle haircuts' would be allowed.

"Now look ... half the people under 25 have 'Beatle' haircuts. It's a fucking joke, man, telling us how we are supposed to look, act, and most importantly think. Fuck 'em," I added.

"Yeah, fuck 'em."

"This fucking war has split this country in two. With the fucking politicians in the middle telling us that we are traitors and cowards while telling their side that God is on their side and that they are patriots and heros. Fuck them, man."

"Remember that whole thing about 'Question Authority'?" ... I continued, "you can't trust 'em, man. You just can't trust the motherfuckers."

I was getting agitated now. I took a deep breath and another toke. Relax, I told myself. Relax. It's your last night here. Just relax, man.

"Fuck it ... got any Stones?" I asked.

The next morning Allen gave me a ride into town and dropped me off at the train station. I told him I was going to New York.

"Thank you for everything Allen. You're a true friend. Thank you."

"Anything for the 'Revolution' man. I enjoyed you're company and thanks for the help around the farm. Anytime you need a place to stay ..."

We hugged and gave each other the 'thumbs up' hand shake.
I waited for the train.

I did end up going into New York. I found a phone booth and dialed information. I got the number for Bryn Mawr and I dialed that number. A woman answered and I asked her to ring Carol's room. I wasn't even sure she was there. I heard a dial tone and Carol picked up.

"Carol?"

"Who's this?"

"It's Mark!"

"Mark. I've been worried sick about you. Where are you?"

"Grand Central Station."

"I'll come get you!"

"But ..."

"It's only two hours away. Wait there. Can you, darling."

"Yes. Of course. I'll meet you at the gate where you're train arrives."

"Okay. I love you."

"I love you, too."

We hung up. Wow!

My mind was racing. I had two hours to kill. I watched a million people parade by. Their lives, I wondered. What were their lives like. How different each of us is yet, we all want the same things: love, food, air, ... we are born innocent and dependent.

I enjoyed the methadrine crazy rush of people. Eyes blazed and focused on getting somewhere fast. Coming or going, who knew. It occurred to me that this would not be a good place to trip.

I looked at the big board. I found the gate that Carol's train would arrive. I found a seat and continued to wait and enjoy the show.

Eventually, her train pulled in. A thousand people scurrying. Hard to find anyone in this mass. I spotted her before she saw me. I focused my eyes on her. I didn't want to lose her. She looked ahead and she seemed to be looking right at me but I didn't see that look of recognition in her eyes until she suddenly jolted and shoved her way to me.

She leaped into my arms. It was like a movie kiss ... complete with violins and flashing lights. I almost lost my balance.

"I missed you so much ... I thought of you every day," I stammered. I just couldn't believe my eyes.

"I missed you, too."

"How was Europe?" I asked.

"Spent most of the time in school but it was wonderful. The Swiss are just like us so most of the time it felt like the States. But, enough of that. We can catch up later. First things first. We're going to check into a hotel and go sightseeing tomorrow. We'll have all the time to catch up."

"Okay."

I felt helpless around her. I truly loved this woman.

We swan upstream through the throng and finally went outside. It was a brisk late fall afternoon. We walked across the street to a huge hotel. Carol was used to such settings. Unbeknownst to me, she had booked a room for the night.

"Don't worry, it's on me," Carol said.

I only had my ruck sack and Carol had a small suit case. We walked into the room. We were on the 16th floor.

I opened the drapes.

"Look at this view!" I exclaimed.

"Look at this view," she cooed.

I turned around and Carol was naked.

There was no comparison!

A couple of hours later, we woke up. We showered together. We couldn't keep our hands off each other. I had never felt so uninhibited with any other woman.

It was dark by now and chilly. The excitement of Manhattan was exhilarating. We were hungry. We found a burger place. Sitting in a booth across from each other. A noisy busy place. I didn't notice anything else except her.

"Who is she?"

"Who ... what?"

"Who's your new girlfriend?"

"I don't have one. It's only you."

"Well, I have a boyfriend back at Bryn Mawr. Nothing serious. He's rich," she laughed.

I sat in silence. I wasn't surprised. I guess I just didn't know what to say.

"Are you jealous?" she inquired.

"Yeah ... I screwed somebody one night. All I did was think of you."

She seemed unruffled.

I guess I wanted her to get pissed and upset. She just kept sipping her milk shake.

"What about us?" I asked.

"You look like a puppy dog. I don't know. I love you and all that but I'm too young for anything serious. I just want to have fun."

There was a long pause.

"Yeah, and I have all this shit hanging over my head. Besides, we're from different sides of the track. I'm just a jealous guy ..."

"It's okay, Mark. I like you just the way you are. Let's just have a good time tonight and tomorrow. You can come to Bryn Mawr with me if you want."

"Really?" I said hopefully.

"Sure, you can stay in my room. The college is very liberal. Katherine Hepburn graduated from there."

"Really?"

"Yup."

"Well, yeah, okay."

We walked back to the hotel and fucked ourselves to sleep.

Morning came. We showered and packed our things. Carol checked out. We needed caffeine. Found a cafe down the street full of pissed off New Yorker's all trying to get their coffee at once. It was a noisy rude place. People pushing and shoving, yelling, swearing ... I liked it. As my dad used to say, "He's not an asshole, he's from New York."

Just getting a cup of coffee was an event. We had several trains we could have taken. They ran all day long to Philly. Carol opted to spend the day in Manhattan. We started to walk towards Central Park. It was a marvel. I was used to small town parks that one could easily walk in ten minutes. Not this! It was endless! Carol and I carried our things and still managed to hold hands. We came upon a horse drawn carriage.

"Oh, let's!" Carol exclaimed.

We rode in the carriage across the Park. The driver was a friendly Irishman with a heavy Brogue accent who told us silly little jokes as he pointed out various historic spots in the Park. It was wonderful.

Time came to catch a train. We bought our tickets and waited for the train. It was packed to the gills. Carol and I stood for most of the ride. I wouldn't want to live like this. When we got to Philly we had to transfer to another train. It was called the 'Main Line.' First, I thought of shooting smack and secondly, of that great Hepburn-Grant movie ... *The Philadelphia Story*. The Main Line.

Luckily, this train was empty except for a few people. Carol and I sat together. The landscape had changed dramatically. I saw affluence and estates. Large homes hidden behind iron and brick. It was a different world.

The college was just a couple of blocks from the train station so we walked. It was a cold brisk afternoon. Getting dark. I was at an Ivy League school. I saw ivy everywhere.

Carol led me into a dorm and we walked up the stairs. It was all women. Wow! She knew everyone and I was introduced to so many girls I couldn't keep up. They seemed very curious and interested in me like some rare specimen that had been discovered.

We got to her room. She lived alone! It was small and spacious at the same time. There was no kitchen or bathroom ... those were down the hall. They, of course, only had a woman's bathroom so the first thing she did was to instruct me on the proper use of it.

"Mark, first you knock ... real loud ... say 'man coming in' ... wait a moment ... and then enter. Here, I'll show you."

Each toilet had a private stall. There were sinks. And showers. A few girls were already in there and they didn't even react when I walked in.

"It's okay. They're used to men coming in. Especially on week ends."

This would take some getting used to.

We walked back to Carol's room. A few girls were hanging out in her room.

"So, this is him!"

"Hi. My name is Grace."

"Hi."

After several other introductions like this I was surrounded by beautiful smart women.

"Keep your hands off, girls ... he's mine!" Carol joked.

I sat in a window seat and looked out into a quad. This place was gorgeous! Sidewalks crisscrossing. Trees. And ivy draped from ancient brick buildings. This was Bryn Mawr.

Carol showed me around campus. Wow! I was impressed. It was very old but I could feel the prestige and importance of this campus. Indeed, this was a 'rich girl's' school. I had to pinch myself and remember from Merton that I was only a humble servant and all that shit. Yeah, right.

That night Carol and I ate at the cafeteria and hung out in her room. She had finals next week and needed to study. I fell asleep in her bed as she studied.

The next morning I had to pee something awful. Carol was still asleep. I dressed and walked to the bathroom. I could hear them inside. I knocked and cracked the door and said very loud ..."Man coming in" ... I heard giggles and laughter and then a voice saying ... "come in" ... I entered tentatively.

Every sink was occupied with a half dressed woman, applying make up or brushing their teeth, some had only a towel draped around their waist, tits exposed, showers running, toilets being flushed, several "Hey, Mark's" ... they all knew my name ... I shyly found an empty stall and peed. Now, I had to walk back through the gauntlet. My eyes focused on the floor, trying not to ogle the seven or eight half-naked ladies.

I ran for my life back to Carol's.

Carol was awake when I returned. She also had to pay a visit to the ladies room. Less dramatic than my visit, I'm sure. When she returned she told me that all the women were talking about me and how cute I was and how shy I seemed. She got the biggest laugh.

"I'm not going to drink or eat anything while I'm here just so I don't have to do that again," I joked.

"You're precious."

We crawled back under the sheets and began the new day just right.

"Let's go take a shower!" she proclaimed.

"Okay. Just so I'm with you."

"Man coming in, ladies" ... we found a shower and bathed each other. The hot water and smooth slippery soaped skin just turned me on again. What better place.

We dried each other off and scampered to her room. We entered the busy cafeteria and grabbed our trays and helped ourselves to eggs and bacon and toast, juice and coffee. The black woman serving the food giving me a knowing smirk. I just shrugged my shoulders as if to say 'when you got it ... you got it.'

"Darling, I have to go to class. Do what you want. You can hang out in my room ... or whatever you want to do. Just be here when I return."

God, I love this person.

I went back to Carol's room. Took a lick and climbed into Merton. Carol had a coffee machine in her room. Thank God for the little things. I brewed a pot and kept myself busy and alert until Carol returned.

Carol was tired when she returned from class and wanted to lay down for a nap. I told her I'd take a walk and return in an hour. I walked around the campus by myself. I had this overwhelming feeling that I shouldn't be here. These people came from different stock. They were the chosen ones.

Later that night several other students gathered down the hall in another girl's dorm room. There were a few guys as well. One of them was the guy that Carol had slept with. I forgot his name. His eyes pierced into mine and as soon as he began to speak in his high Manhattan ... 'Fuck you, I'm rich, accent' ... I knew my time was up. I tried to swallow my pride but I knew I didn't have a chance with this guy. You know the saying, 'Money talks and bullshit walks' ... well, that was me. I knew as soon as I left that they would get it on. I wasn't mad at Carol. I wasn't even angry with smarty pants. I was angry about the situation; the fact that I couldn't stand and fight for her, I couldn't provide for her, I wasn't worthy of her. I was merely an adornment on her resume. Nothing more than that.

The conversation in the room turned to the topic of where everyone was going for Christmas vacation after finals. One girl mentioned she was going to Paris 'to see Daddy.' Daddy was the Admiral of the Mediterranean Fleet for Christ's sake. One other girl was also going to France to ski. Carol was going back to Madison. I was going to hell.

Carol and I retreated back to her room. We had a long talk. I told her that I loved her, of course, but that I needed to get going again. I told her I couldn't tell her much but that I had important business to do for the 'cause.' I almost told her my real name. The girl doesn't even know my real name for fuck's sake! She was really busy with school anyway and she had a couple of papers to write and cram for finals and all that. But that was just an excuse. I was jealous as hell and my heart hurt.

I left first thing the next morning with a vague promise of keeping in touch. I never saw her again.

I walked in the cold rain to the train station and retraced my steps back to Grand Central Station. I took an airporter to Kennedy Airport.

It was a long lonely trip. The excitement of moving again and trying to figure out which airline I needed to get to distracted my broken heart.

I figured that TWA was a good bet to catch a flight to San Francisco. I was in luck. They had a flight in fours hours. A non-stop. I flashed my fake student ID's and bought a student stand by ticket. It was still only $48 one way. I waited by the gate. Not knowing if I'd get on or not. Made my adrenaline flow. I read Merton to pass the time and kill the pain.

I watched the masses of people coming and going and I realized that each of us has a story and that nobody cared about mine. Somehow, that was reassuring.

They called the passengers for the flight. I lucked out again and got a seat. It was in the non-smoking section but I didn't care. I just wanted to get out of here.

They served dinner and a snack. I bought a beer and sat back and tried to close my eyes. I luckily had the window seat. The guy next to me was a businessman. Nice enough fellow. He grilled me about hippies. He wanted to know everything; especially the drugs and sex part. I was amazed how the media had portrayed 'us.' As a bunch of hedonistic air heads high on pot and acid all the time and fucking like monkeys. Wasn't quite like that I told him. He seemed disappointed.

About half way there, somewhere over Kansas, I needed a smoke so I squeezed myself through the seats and went into the rest room. I did have to piss and as I peed we hit an air pocket and I lost my balance and spun around and managed to pee all over the rest room. I had a cigarette dangling from my lips but managed to keep that in place never loosing a puff. I tried my best to wipe up the mess.

I returned to my seat after finishing the cig. Feeling refreshed, I climbed back into Merton for the rest of the flight.

We landed and I grabbed my ruck sack from above my seat. I got outside in the warm California air and took a deep breath. Yes! I took the airporter to the City and walked to Brian's.

"My man!"

"Oh it's good to see you. Can I stay a few days?"

"Of course. Hungry? Thirsty? Horny (can't help you there). What do you need."

"A foot high beer and a joint."

"Comin' right up."

"I didn't call, I know. You're the only person who would understand that. The East Coast ain't for me, man. Too uptight. I did meet a couple of cool cats, but for the most part ... oh, this hits the spot," as I gulped on a beer.

"Here, have a toke. You're home, man."

"What's new around here?"

"Lots. You remember San Francisco State? Well, that's calmed down but the crazies in Berkeley are just tearing the place up. I talked to Mark a couple of days ago. He's paranoid as hell. He says he's being followed all the time. Can't even wash his fuckin' clothes without a tail. I don't think you should meet up with him anymore."

"Really!?"

"Yeah, no shit. He was worried about you back east. He said the package got through okay. Great job, by the way! Oh fuck, I almost forgot. This is for you."

Brian handed me an envelope.

"What's this?"

"Dunno."

I opened it. It was another $200 from Mark with a note that said; 'Great job. I need you in Madison by the spring. Keep an eye on the Smith Brothers. They're up to something. Stay safe. Mark.'

"Let's go out."

"Yeah," I said, "I could use a burrito or three."

"I'm actually glad you're here. I'm going home for Christmas and so are the other roomies. It would be perfect if you could stay and watch the place for a week."

"Oh sure. No problem. Yeah, that is perfect. I need some space right now anyway. I think my girl and I are broken up. And other things have been kinda tense, you know. Yeah, man. I'll watch the place. Thanks."

Brian and I were the perfect friends. We fit each other just right. But, most importantly I trusted him. Someday, I reckoned I would figure out Mark's network. I now knew several people in several cities, but I was certain I didn't know the half of it.

It was cold and raining tonight in San Francisco. We caught a bus to North Beach to look for fun and music. The strip houses on Broadway with barkers encouraging lonely guys to see the delights within. Brian and I weren't interested. We walked into Tosca's and had a couple of 'Irish Coffees.' Mario, the bartender, knew Brian and he introduced me to him. He made his 'Irish Coffees' using an old steamer from Italy, I was told.

"Now watch this, he doesn't use gloves to heat up the glasses. Everyone else has too. His hands are so used to the heat, I guess," Brian pointed out.

Mario made drink after drink and they disappeared as a waitress would fill her tray and then return empty to fill it again.

"This is a famous place. If you sit here long enough you'll see the VIPs, man."

I didn't doubt it for a moment.

Caruso was playing on the jukebox. Caruso!

We jay-walked across the street and scanned books at City Light's Book Store. I found a couple of obscure Beat books and bought them. I found another copy of *Naked Lunch* by William Burroughs. I'd lost the other one. Then we crossed an alley and spent the rest of the night drinking beer at Vesuvio's.

I love this town.

We took a cab back to Brian's. Smoked a bowl and listened to music until we both passed out.

Brian was leaving tomorrow and he thought it would be a good idea to introduce me to the neighbors. On the left lived a Mexican family. The kids spoke English and Brian said I would be staying there for the week. On the right lived a bunch of hippies who probably wouldn't notice anyway.

I left a message for Mark.

Brian had gone home. Just to keep busy I cleaned their kitchen. The fridge was the worst. Things with green tops and black meat. The freezer was an ice berg. I found frozen things back in there too. It took two days to defrost. I threw away lots of things. The oven and stove were pretty bad too. Nothing a pick axe couldn't fix. I scrubbed the floor at least four times until the water wasn't brown anymore. I bought some floor polish. I cleaned out the cup boards and wiped everything down. I didn't go into the bedrooms. I figured that was a private sanctuary. I did do a deep clean of the living room and hallways. After three days the place looked good.

Merry Christmas! A day spent alone and buried in my new book *Journey to the End of the Night* by Celine. It was wonderful! It blew my mind. I immediately saw a correlation with Kerouac. The 'stream of consciousness' style. The free flowing thoughts and words.

Brian had some William Blake around too!

For my Christmas present to myself I walked all the way to City Lights and found some more Merton and another book of poems by Corso and I bought a copy of the *Berkeley Barb* and a copy of *Ramparts*.

It was New Year's Eve and the revelers were already out. I walked into Vesuvio's with my bag of books and had a couple of beers.

I returned to Brian's well before midnight and watched the ball drop in Times Square.

It was 1972!

Chapter 16

Hiding Out in Amerika

Mark had called and he wanted me back in Madison. It was the first time I had told him no. It was too cold back there right now. I told him I would go back in March. He actually seemed okay with that. He laid some more money on me. (I always wondered where he got it from.) So I bided my time.

As I spent these first days alone in the house I thought of all the events leading up to this day. I thought of JFK and his brother Bobby, I thought of Fred Hampton and Kent State and Jackson State, the horrible race riots and fires and killings in Watts, Newark, and Detroit, of the dead student in Berkeley shot on a roof top, of the days in Golden Gate Park with Joe, about all the draft resisters now numbering over 100,000 and climbing, of this country torn in half by this fucking endless war, and of Carol, the one that got away, of my family and parents who I hadn't seen in I don't know how long, of my early hopes of playing second base for the Yankees, of all my friends, some lost but not forgotten, of the returning vets from Nam who were being called 'baby killers' and how I was torn about how I felt about them, most of them being draftees, how Reagan was Governor of California and had responded to the protestors of Berkeley by saying, 'If they want a bloodbath, then let's give 'em one,' how the Black Pan-ther's had been totally misrepresented by the media, that Nixon was still President and had 'a secret plan for peace,' how each night I agonized with the 'trike dream' of being chased, this Watergate business, whatever that was about, the Dems running who? Against Nixon, where would all this bullshit end?

How one night I'd gone to Stanford to hear Stokely Carmichael speak at this conservative University and how he worked the crowd into a frenzy getting us all to chant, 'we ain't goin', referring to Vietnam and the high-light being ... 'Fuck Mickey Mouse' ... referring to Governor Reagan.

Oh, there was so much ... the Pentagon Papers and some guy named Daniel Ellsberg alleging that the Gulf of Tonkin never happened and the ensuing cover-up and lies, the Berrigan brothers, Draft Board burnings, I recalled the day on the steps at St. Mary's, it seemed like a life time ago, when I held up my sign and a guy spit in my face. And when they installed the new Draft Lottery system and my number had been 286, no doubt safe from the draft, but it was too late. If I would have just stayed in school. I thought of the loss of my religion, the loss of my family, the loss of myself. And then there was Carol again in my mind. Always in my mind.

Chapter 17

1972

And suddenly it was 1972. New Years Day. Several football games were on, the best being the Rose Bowl. Stanford beat Michigan 13-12 in a thriller. But I wasn't really interested in games. It just passed the time.

The house was looking spiffy when Brian returned.

"Wow! The place looks great. You'd make a great wife, Mark!" he joked.

The two other roomies wouldn't return for another week.

"How was your Christmas?" I asked.

"Same old family shit. It was okay, I guess. My mom and dad both think I should cut my hair and meet a nice girl etc. They don't understand me at all but I love 'em. They're the only parents I have."

I felt a pang in my heart about my own family. They were the only family I had too.

I was getting low on my speed. I asked Brian if he knew anyone who had some whites.

"Yeah, sure do. How many do you want?"

"I don't know ... what does $20 get you now days?"

He made a call. He left and came back within an hour with a baggy full of them. They were cheap.

"I think there's a hundred in there. My buddy owed me so he gave me a deal."

"Thanks. I need 'em."

I took one and offered one to Brian. We sat in the kitchen and talked over coffee. It was a cold and wet day. San Francisco could be inhospitable sometimes.

"Mark wanted me to go to Madison but I told him I didn't want to spend the winter there. I think he understood. I'm not sure what I'll do."

"You can stay here. We have room. You remember my landlord. He's cool. He's painting the inside of another Victorian over on Hill St. Not far from here. I'll give him a call if you want some work."

"Oh yeah. That'd be great!"

"Oh, I meant to ask. How were the neighbors?"

"Never saw 'em."

Brian went in the other room and called his landlord.

He returned in a few minutes.

"Hey, good news. His partner is working on a house on Hill Street like I said. Walk over there tomorrow morning and he'll give you some work.

His name is Duke. He's cool."

"Oh, Thanks man."

Brian wanted to go out tonight.

"Where to?"

"Let's go to North Beach," I said.

"Done."

We took a bus across town. I loved the bus system. Assorted freaks and a mish-mash of people rode the bus. We skirted the Tenderloin District and there was a fire. The bus stopped in traffic so we got out. There was a hotel fire. Lots of fire trucks, cops, onlookers, and ... men dressed like women ... whaaa ...

"Transvestites," Brian said.

Apparently their hotel had a fire and they all had to exit the building. Only in San Francisco, I thought.

"Come on, Mark. We'll walk the rest of the way."

We started the trek up Jones Street zig-zagging until we reached China Town. What an amazing city! I told Brian that when all this bullshit was over that I wanted to live here.

I wasn't long before we strode into Speck's Alley. A little hole in the wall beer joint. I'd been here before. Brian knew about the secret passage-way in the men's room for the strippers upstairs in the 'Nudie Bar.' We ordered beers and sat at the bar. It was cold and rainy and the place was packed. Seemed everyone else had the same idea as us.

After our beer we walked across Broadway and walked up Grant Avenue and heard some blues. We walked into the 'Saloon' and paid a 75 cent cover and listened to a blues band. After an hour or so we walked back to Vesuvio's for a night cap. I didn't want to get to crazy because I had to work tomorrow. We were home by midnight. I fell soundly asleep.

Got up early, Thanks to Brian's alarm clock, and walked the few blocks to Hill Street. I found the house and walked in and asked for Duke.

"I'm Duke. You Mark?"

"Heard you could paint. We've got lots of work. I'll show you around."

Duke took me to the second floor. The house was being remodeled for apartments. It had originally been a house for a family, so they were in the process of dividing up the house into four apartments.

"This street is where the fire from the earthquake stopped. There were pastures between here and the fire. So it burned out. These homes need to be upgraded. All the electrical and plumbing needs to be done. Our group is buying a couple more of these homes plus a few in Noe Valley and the Castro District."

I knew this from before but I let him talk.

"Mark, I want you start in this room."

The task was daunting. There was a ladder and rollers and cans of paint and a huge drop cloth. The floors were hard wood. It seemed to be a bedroom. The windows must have been eight feet high with window seats. It was beautiful.

"I'll get started Duke."

I climbed the ladder and prepared to apply the first coat to the ceiling. The ceiling was 12 feet high or so. Duke had supplied me with a painter's hat and he gave me a pair of coveralls to wear. The room was good sized; 25x25 feet or so. One edge was cornered off at an angle because of the fireplace. I taped off the molding as I moved the ladder. I would do that last in an enamel. It took me a couple of hours to do the ceiling. And that was just the first coat. I started on the walls which were a tone darker that the ceiling. I was a neat painter. I prided myself in not spilling or dripping. Duke's rollers were first class professional and worked very well.

After a while Duke came up to see how I was doing.

"You've done that much! Wow. Good job!. Listen we usually break for lunch about now. Did you bring anything to eat."

"No."

"You sure? I'm buying."

We walked to 28th Street to a Mexican restaurant and I had a coke and two burritos. Duke had a beer but I thought that might be pushing it.

He said I was doing a good job and if I wanted I could work for several months. I took him up on that.

I worked at least five days a week for the next two months having saved up about $700. I was able to pay Brian rent and buy food and beer and dope. The weather was horrible so it didn't matter. I was waiting for spring anyway.

We had finished one house on Hill Street and had begun another in the Castro. It was a wonder that so many of these gems had survived. But, man, did they need work. I not only painted but assisted with finishing the hardwood floors and even doing some plumbing. I wouldn't touch electrical, though.

I felt strong and almost whole after these months. Coming home to Brian's to join in the family on Capp Street. I was walking a lot and felt strong again. I was using a lot of speed but not as much as before. I was becoming dependent on that shit. If I didn't drop a couple of whites I felt irritable. I made several attempts to stop but I did manage to cut down. By half.

I had my own closet that I set up as my room. It was off the hallway and was very large for a closet. I had a mattress on the floor and ran a light in there so I could read. I liked it and felt safe.

I even had time and money to do some photography. I wasn't very good but I enjoyed it. I walked to Adolph Gasser's Camera Store one day and bought a Nikon 24mm wide angle lens. It was 'used' but in good condition. I shot a couple of rolls of TRI-X and had the film developed and proofed. Not bad. Just some street shots of people in the city. I found that if I pre-focused say at ten feet at F11 almost all of the images were sharp. I could use this technique in riots shooting the cops. I could hold my camera at chest level never bringing it to my eyes, that way they wouldn't even know I was taking their picture. With some street noise to silence the shutter.

I practiced my new method until I had it down. I could be the next Walker Evans!

The weather was beginning to warm. I had talked with Mark a few times just to stay in touch.

He wanted me in Madison for the Democratic Primaries and to keep an eye on the Smith Brothers.

It was late March. Usually still pretty cold in Wisconsin. I called Mark for a meet.

We met a few days later in the same cafe. Mark looked haggard. It was good to see him. He had grown a beard and his hair was long. Dark hollow eyes.

"Mark, are you feeling okay?" I inquired.

"Yeah. Just haven't been sleeping. Never mind that. Listen. I need you to get back to Madison and Minneapolis and Ann Arbor. My people tell me that some shit is going down. They have plans to hit a couple of Draft Boards and to break some guys out of prison. Fuckin' heavy shit. I want you to tail the Smith Brothers in Madison. They are a couple of crazy mothers. They could really fuck up some people. Also, and this is vital, I need you to get to Canada again and check out how some of these guys are being treated. I've heard that some of the boys have been having a hard time because of some bullshit about them being bribed or some shit by the Mafia. Seems that some of the guys ran into the wrong people and they want money from them to remain safe from the FBI. The mob guys would kidnap them and deposit them in the US. I think, myself, that there is some crazy connection between the FBI and the mob. I can't be more specific right now. I think, and this is all conjecture, that the mob wants to tell the FBI about our underground so they can continue their bullshit. You know, drugs and shit. I don't know. Just see if you can find anything on this."

"The war seems to be winding down and fucking Nixon is in trouble with the Watergate business, you've undoubtedly heard about that, but the shit endures, man. The Panther's are in jail. That Chicago trial thing is a fucking joke. It makes us look like a bunch of clowns. Fucking Abbie and Jerry are a disgrace. The Weathermen have done more harm than good for the cause. The media has got it so wrong but that's what most Americans believe. I don't know man, I'm tired. There is no truth anymore. None at all. It's all bullshit!"

"Anyway, how are you Mark! It's good to see you my brother," he added after a pause.

"I'm doing well. I have some money and I'm feeling strong. I've been working painting houses in the City. Yeah, I'm okay. I'll leave for Madison in a couple of weeks, if that's all right with you."

"Yup. Here's some more money for travel. Can you fly back?"

"Yeah."

Mark laid $200 on me. Fuck. I was fat. I had about a grand on me. I could have run right there, but I didn't. Mark was paranoid and scared. He wasn't the same guy I knew. Something had happened to him. I left the cafe and said farewell to my mentor. As it turned out, I would never see him again.

I got back to Brian's in the City. I really didn't want to leave. I had a job, a place to live and now I was going back into the fray.

I talked to Brian about leaving. He also noticed that Mark had changed his demeanor somewhat. Brian just shrugged it off to stress.

And before I left, Mark had measured my finger. He said he was making rings and would make one for me. I didn't think too much of it at the time.

That next Monday I informed Duke that I was leaving in two weeks. He seemed disappointed but added he'd hire me back in a second. I finished working for him on the second house on Hill Street. I found out that there were about 25 investors who were buying up old Victorians, fixing them up and then selling them at a profit. Clever.

I had almost $1,100 after paying Brian.

I flew to Chicago in the second week of April. I took a bus to Madison and arrived late at night. Since I had some dough I stayed in a motel near downtown. There were still a few un-melted snow banks here and there but for the most part, spring was in the air. I needed a day's rest before I went out looking for Oliver and John and Terry and Curtis. If they were still here at all. I hadn't watched much TV in the last few months. It was nice to relax and watch an old movie.

I checked out the next morning. I walked to the campus to the Student Union. On the way over everything reminded me of Carol. I walked into the building looking for a familiar face. None to be seen. Walked into the Rathskeller, thought I saw John but it wasn't him. I decided to find a seat in the back of the room so I could view the entire room and read a book and wait. Occasionally, I looked up. No one. I got up and walked around. I left the Union and walked over to Mifflin Street. I saw some familiar faces of people that I didn't know. I stopped one woman who I had seen before and asked if she knew John and Terry and Curtis. She did! She told me that they were still in town but that they had moved. She didn't know where to though. It was a start. I walked back to the Union.

I saw Terry from across the room!

"Hey, man, remember me!"

"Mark. Where have you been?"

"Here and there. What's up, man?"

"Ever since the bombing the place has been crawling with heat. But, it's mellowed out some. Mifflin Street got too hot so John and Curtis and myself found a house on the other side of the lake. Hey, you need a place to crash? You can crash with us. No sweat. The other guys will be glad to see you. But, no shit, man, where did you go? I mean you just disappeared."

"Terry, I went back to San Francisco after Carol went to Switzerland. I was bummed and everything reminded me of her. Dig?"

"Yeah. I can dig that."

"Hey, I was wondering ... have you seen Oliver around?"

"Yeah, I see him once in a while."

"Do you know where he lives?"

"I do."

Terry gave me his new address and told me to come over there tonight and he told me where Oliver lived.

I told him I'd catch up with him later and walked to Oliver's. A big green house on Jefferson Street. He didn't know the exact address but I found a big green house. I looked at the mailboxes in the lobby and took a chance. I walked to the apartment and knocked.

"Who is it?" a male voice answered.

"Mark."

I heard several locks being unlocked.

The door opened.

"Mark, you fucker!"

It was Oliver all right.

"Come in."

"Am I glad to see you!" I exclaimed.

"This is my lady, Emily."

"Pleased to meet you."

Emily seemed to be rather shy and she excused herself to the kitchen asking me if I wanted some coffee.

"Yes please, just black."

Oliver rolled a fat joint and got me caught up on the happenings in Madison. Seemed the FBI had scoured the place looking for information on the bombing. Several people had been harassed, hassled, harangued, searched, questioned in some half-baked attempt to find the Armstrongs. Nobody knew shit. They operated on their own. But the damage had been done. Paranoia hung over this city like a plague. In the meantime, the Democrats were sending in their candidates on a daily basis each begging for votes as the primaries had begun. A strange vague process that challenged explanation. McGovern seemed to hold an advantage in Wisconsin. No surprise there. He was from the nearby State of South Dakota. Humphrey was old news. George Wallace was nuts and Eugene McCarthy had worn out his welcome with his elite intellectualism, no one could understand what he was talking about. Oliver was very involved with McGovern's campaign. He'd even met him on his last visit to Madison. Oliver soon got me up to speed on the candidates. The primaries had already begun in New Hampshire.

The primary vote was in two days. Muskie was to hold a press conference tomorrow afternoon in a last ditch attempt to save his candidacy after the so-called 'Canuck Letter' and some rumors that his wife drank paint thinner. Oliver asked me to come. He wanted to heckle Muskie.

I stayed at John and Curtis and Terry's place that night but made plans to meet Oliver the next morning. By this time these guys were professional students. They could pass their classes with a minimum of work and study. Terry had a paper to write so he stayed in his room typing while John and I and Curtis drank beer and listened to music. They had rented a house in a nice neighborhood surrounded by normal people, away from the bedlam of Mifflin Street.

I was pretty worn out from my travels so I crashed early on the back porch.

I got up stiffly the next morning. I hadn't slept very well. A barking dog had kept me half-awake the whole night.

John had a class so I walked with him to the campus. I walked over to Oliver's place. He was up. We drank a cup of coffee.

"Two of my buddies are coming with us. One of them will drive the get-away car."

"What?"

"You'll see."

We drove to a hotel downtown. A throng of people were gathering outside. We walked into a huge ballroom and Oliver and I found seats directly in front of the podium. One of his buddies stood in the back of the room while the driver waited outside in the car. I didn't know what to expect from Oliver. He was a totally funny, irreverent, daring, smart guy.

We waited and waited. Finally some guy came out and addressed the crowd. The room was mostly full. I noticed TV cameras and several photographers standing in the wings. The guy droned on and on about a new America and bringing the war to an end etc.

At last, he introduced the candidate. People rose to their feet and applauded and whooped it up. Senator Muskie took the podium and began to speak. God, he was boring. He looked old and tattered. I thought to myself why would anyone want to be President?

I didn't even hear what he was saying. Just a monotone voice reciting the same old bullshit.

Suddenly Oliver stood up. We were right in front of Muskie. Had to look up to see him. Oliver lit a joint and offered it to Muskie. Muskie stopped speaking, he was frozen, glaring at Oliver in a shocked look. Oliver offered the joint to Muskie. Camera shutters clicking. I sat next to Oliver looking at this surreal moment. I grabbed Oliver by the arm and we ran out of there. I looked back at the disarray. People were scrambling. Didn't see any cops. Muskie just stood there looking shocked and stupid.

We three ran to the car and were gone in ten seconds.

"Fucking A, man."

"Did you see the look on his face?"

"Everybody was so stunned ... the room got real quiet for a minute and by the time they realized what had happened we were gone."

"Oliver, I gotta hand it to you. You're fuckin' nuts, man."

"Thanks, Mark."

No one was following us.

"Let me out here," Oliver demanded.

Oliver and I got out of the car three blocks away. We walked down the street like nothing had happened except that we were both laughing like hyenas.

We walked across town back to Oliver's apartment.

"Christ, I didn't know you were going to do that. I just thought you were going to heckle him. I hope you don't get busted for that."

"Me too."

Oliver and I spent a couple of hours catching up on stuff. He gave me the low down on what had gone down since the bombing. Everyone was laying low. Friends of his had been taken off the street and interrogated, ripped out their beds at night, etc. Oliver knew Mrs. Armstrong. Their families were friends. It was a nightmare for her. Her phones were tapped and she was tailed everywhere she went. To church, to the supermarket. Everywhere. Oliver said he had known the brothers, of course, and never expected this from them. They were pretty quiet guys apparently who had few friends but made no waves in the Madison scene. Guess you just never know. Oliver knew that I had possibly carried some letters from their mom to them and vice versa. I didn't really know that for sure but I had a feeling. I let it go. It was pure speculation and I didn't pursue it.

I told Oliver that I had to go and find John and Terry and Curtis. The truth was I was just a little paranoid that the cops might be looking for him. I didn't want to hang around.

I met up with John at the Union and told him what Oliver had done. He was amazed and started to laugh. It was getting on in the afternoon so we walked out to their house. It was a walk. A few miles. But it was a pleasant afternoon, rather warm and muggy, but pleasant.

"We should watch the news to see if Oliver is on it."

"Good idea."

We turned on the TV. The *CBS News* was first with Walter followed by the local news.

The lead story on *CBS* was more misery from Vietnam. The country was now anesthetized by the daily killing and death. A commercial for Ford Trucks. Walter spoke about the Democrats and their puzzling primary and then there was a piece from Madison showing Oliver offering a joint to the dumbfounded Muskie. You could see the side of me for an instant. My three seconds of fame. The piece focused on the problems Muskie had had on the campaign trail blah blah blah.

"Holy shit!"

Next, we watched the local news and they showed the same clip. It wasn't a good shot of me because the cameraman focused on Oliver.

"Well, there should be something in the paper tomorrow too," I said. Again, a bit paranoid that the shot might show me.

"Shit, everybody knows Oliver, I wonder if he'll be arrested," John asked.

"It happened so fast and we split in seconds. I think it's too late. Oliver could always say it was tobacco. But it was weed, man. We finished the joint in the car," I laughed.

"Speaking of which ..."

Terry rolled a big one. Their other roommate, Curtis came home. We sat around the stereo and listened to tunes the rest of the night. I felt safer not being around Oliver right now.

The next day I walked to the campus. Oliver and Muskie were on the front page of the Madison paper as well as the *New York Times*. It was a tight shot. I wasn't in the shot. I was relieved.

Oliver was all the talk. He was laying low. But, he was not arrested or even hassled by the cops. Wow!

I hung around for a week or so. Frankly, I was bored. Couldn't get close to Oliver until this thing blew over. And wouldn't you know it. Just when I thought things would cool off both *Newsweek* and *Time* magazines ran the photos in their issues.

I decided to get a hold of Mark. I wasn't doing any good here.

When we did talk I told him about Oliver and how I was right next to him. He knew about it and chuckled. I told him I wanted to go to the Twin Cities again. He said that was fine.

I didn't want to risk hitching so I took a bus. I took a bus to La Crosse. I wanted to see Emil, my brother.

I walked across town and easily caught a ride to Winona. It was late afternoon. The ride dropped me off on Highway 61 and I walked through the East End to downtown. I was sure no one saw me or would even recognize me anyway. My hair was down to my waist. I wore a base ball cap and sun glasses. I figured that if Emil had a gig tonight he wouldn't be found but if he had a night off he'd be in Charlie's Bar. Bingo! I saw him sitting at the bar. I walked behind him and tapped him on the shoulder. He slowly turned and it took a second before he recognized me.

"Brother!" He shouted.

"Emil."

We hugged and he grabbed me by the shoulders and just stared into my eyes.

"You fucker! The FBI has been here a hundred times looking for you. They said you were making bombs and shit. That true?"

"What? Those fuck heads ..."

Several other familiar faces gathered round to see the 'Big Radical Weatherman' ... whatever.

"No man, I ain't done shit."

We all laughed. I don't think they believed me. They wanted to believe that I was a dangerous man on the run. I think.

Emil threw his remaining beer down and we walked to his pad. He now lived above a dime store on Third Street. He had several crazy roommates. I knew them all. The place was just a nudge above squalor. Five male hippies usually doesn't make for a comfy home. There were porn mags in the kitchen. Dishes piled two feet high. Crusty food remnants stuck to everything. Would need chisels to clean them. Beyond hope. Mattresses strewn in the living room. And no hope for the bathroom. Bacteria laden towels hanging here and there. You'd be dirtier after taking a shower. The toilet was covered in feces and other unknown matter. I was afraid to open the fridge.

Home sweet home!

Emil had his own room. If you could call it that. Everything was on the floor. I assume there was a floor underneath all the junk. He had guitars and papers and clothes strewn in a confused mess. His mattress was on the floor. Dirty sheets. Stained, no doubt, from excessive love making to his adoring female fans.

This apartment had managed to break every hygiene law known to man.

"Fuck, it's great to see you," Emil chimed as he rolled a joint and took a swig out of last nights beer. I think there may have been a cigarette butt in there.

"I just had to see you. Just to let you know I'm okay and to see if you are too. How's the family?"

"Well, Dad's the same, you know, pissed at the world. Mom's kinda wacky but I love her. The kids are all right. They told me the FBI had been to their school and pulled them out of class to ask about you. Psssst. Here, this is some great shit. I don't know. I guess they're okay. I was back home for Christmas. Wasn't the same without you."

"Yeah. Tell them that I'm okay. Will ya?"

"Yeah. You look awfully skinny though. Jesus."

"Yeah. Whatever. Know anybody can get me to the Cities tonight or tomorrow?"

"Yeah. I think so. Let's get some beer."

"Might as well."

As far as I knew, Emil was still underage but that posed no problem. He was an old soul and walked in a liquor store to 'Hey, Emils' and bought two cases of beer and a fifth of whiskey. "Adds a little punch."

"Put it on my tab."

"Will do. Thanks Emil. Good to see you again."

He was a marvel of modern something or other.

Back to his place.

The apartment was filling with his cult. I've never met a funnier or more humanistic person than my brother, Emil. He was something. I felt remorseful having missed the last couple of years of not being around him. My little brother, my best friend. So said about 1,000 people. My best friend. I was always 'Emil's brother' never Mike. I was Emil's brother and that was fine with me!

The party began. The beers disappeared. The joints floated. I floated. You floated. We floated.

The word got out. There was Snipe. There was Twig. There was Mud-cat. There was Linda looking swell with a new beau.

I found a ride. Carl could take me tomorrow morning. I told him I had money for gas. All he said was, "Fuck you and your money, brother. It's on me. It's an honor, fuck head!"

I'm a 'fuck head.' I could cry. I love these sweet souls.

I must have passed out at some point. I woke up in my clothes on the floor. Some party.

Emil was asleep. A second bump under his covers. Didn't want to bother him but I did.

"Emil, wake up. I gotta go."

Two half opened slant eyes. He jumped up. Naked. Hard on.

"Love you, Mike. Take care and be safe. Fuck the FBI!"

With that I departed and waited for reliable Carl. He picked me up and we were off to Minneapolis.

Up Highway 61. My favorite stretch of road. The Highway passes

right through several small towns, Wabasha, Red Wing hugging the Mississippi River most of the way. Barges and locks and dams. Bridges spanning
the great river. Bluffs on the west side the river to the right. The Wisconsin
drive is great too but I prefer the Minnesota side.

Carl and I chatted most of the way up. He got me caught up on all the
news-gossip of Winona. Who was doing who and so forth.

"Carl, can you drop me off in Dinky Town? It was great to see you
guys again. I'm sure you'll be visited by the FBI again. Word'll get out."

"Fuck 'em." Was Carl's reply.

Carl dropped me off on University Avenue SE. He wouldn't know
where I was going. I had to find Jeff. He had moved. Maybe he was a real
lawyer by now. I walked to his apartment and saw his name on the mail
box. I buzzed his apartment. In a few seconds a voice ... "Who is it?"

"McAndrew."

The buzzer let me in. I walked up to his apartment and knocked.

"Holy shit! What the fuck are you doing here?"

"Came to see you."

"Come in."

"Mike, how are you, man? You are hotter than hell. The FEDS are
telling people that you are running guns and drugs and making bombs and
shit. True? As your attorney you can tell me."

"No, none of that. It just isn't true. I'm 'The Mailman.' I deliver packages to people. That's all. Honest. I wouldn't hurt a fly. I'm non-violent.
Remember?"

"But, call me Mark. Okay?" I added.

"Oh yeah, right. I forgot. Mark. Right. I didn't think so. I know you
better than that. Have you seen Gary? Remember him? The guy who takes
guys to Canada? He'd like to see you, I know."

"Oh, yeah. I remember him quite well. Good man."

"How's school coming?"

"Almost there. One more semester. I got through torts okay. That was
the toughest. I'm going to be doing Criminal Law. You'll be one my first
clients."

"Can't wait. Are you living alone?"

"Yeah. Why?"

"Can I stay here?"

"No. It isn't safe. But I know a place that is."

"Sorry to just drop in like this. But, you know how it is."

"Absolutely no problem, man. No sweat. I'm going to summer school
right now and it's pretty mellow. I don't have any classes today anyway.
Let's hang out 'til dark and then we'll move."

"Hungry?"

"Always."

Jeff fixed a couple of burgers washed down with a beer. We caught up on stuff. Minneapolis was a fairly quiet place. A few demonstrations on campus but nothing like Berkeley or Madison. It was a blistering hot day and Jeff's apartment luckily faced north with a commanding view of the river and the other side of the campus. We sat out on his deck ten stories high taking it all in.

"Seems that Gary and his friends are planning to raid a Draft Board. Don't know where or when. There are some serious people up here and they put me in the loop to advise them on the legal shit. They don't plan on getting caught. Like, they're not going to call the police and the papers and wait to get arrested."

"Good. Never liked that plan. If they get away they can do it again."

"Right."

"I just bet Gary would love to have you in on this."

"That's all I need," I laughed.

"Are you serious?" I asked.

"Yeah. I'm serious and so are these guys."

"Even though there's a lottery?"

"Even though."

"Can I meet them?"

"Sure."

Jeff brushed back his thick black hair, adjusted his wire rims and looked me right in the eye. "We could use you on this caper. These guys don't know what they're doing."

"What the hell makes you think I do? Well, okay, I'll meet with them but I can't promise anything. I'm in enough shit as it is."

"What's one more count?" Jeff mused.

"I s'pose." I conceded.

Jeff made a phone call. In ten minutes he walked back onto the deck.

"It's all set. We'll meet tonight."

"Where."

"Here."

A knock on the door. Six guys walked in among them my old friend Gary.

"Hey Man, it's good to see you. How have you been."

"Great," I said.

Gary introduced me to everyone. I didn't want to know their names. Beers were cracked open and we sat around Jeff's living room.

After some small talk the meeting began. This other guy seemed to be the leader. His name was Greg.

"Here's the plan. We want to hit the Draft Board in Wabasha."

I almost fell out of my seat.

He rambled on for a few minutes. Finally I spoke.

"Have you cased the place? Do you know where the 1-A records are? Can you get into the building and into the office? Do the cops patrol the neighborhood? You'll need gloves ... no prints. What do you plan to do with the records once you have them? How are you going to get away? Who else knows about this? Ask yourselves ... who else knows?"

Greg spoke. "We have cased the place. We know where the records are kept. They're in a file cabinet. It's locked but we can break the lock. Steve here knows how to open locked doors and stuff. We'll bring some card board boxes with us and put all the files into them. It'll be easier to carry."

"The cops?"

"Don't know about them. It's a little town. They probably only have one cop patrolling."

"Check that out."

"We have to get some gloves."

"Get surgical gloves from a drug store," I advised.

"Right."

"The get away?" I asked.

"Well, we haven't gotten that far yet ..."

"Listen," I interrupted, " You guys need to have a 'dress rehearsal.' You can't leave anything to chance. I would also recommend that you think hard about getting away. Like, you could have two cars waiting for you on the Wisconsin side. You could dump the records off the bridge. That way you'll be split up in three cars with no evidence on you. Toss the gloves too. Just an idea."

They showed me a crude drawing of the draft office. There was a main room with a secretary and a larger room behind a locked door with another desk and a table and several file cabinets.

"How do you know about the back room?" I asked one of them.

"I was in there when I had to register. Each cabinet is labeled."

"When was this?"

"About a year ago."

"What's your lottery number?"

"36," he answered.

"Bummer."

I continued. "You should go back to them. Make up some bullshit about applying for a CO or something. See if you can get back in there. They could have moved shit around. And don't touch anything. No prints."

"What else?" I added.

"I don't know. It's just these two old ladies. They wouldn't suspect anything."

"They close at 5 p.m., I assume."

"Yeah, I guess."

"I think the best time to do this would be on a Friday night. Not too late. When the bars are still open. Is there an alley in the back of the building that you could carry everything out?" I asked.

I had to say it. "I don't think you guys are ready yet. You need a plan. Get back to me when you think you're ready. Practice doing this. Run it out. Those records are heavy. You can only make one trip. Time it."

They looked at me and nodded their heads. They would have been busted in ten minutes. And they knew it.

After some small talk the guys left. I looked at Jeff and just shrugged my shoulders. He nodded. We both knew this was a disaster waiting to happen.

"Are those guys for real?"

"Yeah, I think so."

"I don't know. I got a weird vibe. I don't trust them," I said.

"What do you mean?"

"I don't know. Do those guys check out. I mean is one of them a FED or a cop? I just get a strange feeling. Maybe I'm just paranoid. I think I should split."

"No, Mark. Don't do that. It's okay."

"I gotta go. Better safe than sorry."

"No wait. Mark, let me make a call.'

I sat on the deck. It was late. I was tired. I was scared. It just came over me. The Fear. This underlying constant Fear. It never went completely away. Sometimes it was intense. It was intense right now.

"I found a place for you. It's in the building. He's my buddy at law school. You can trust him. He doesn't know anything and won't ask any questions. Don't worry. He's coming up right now."

"Thanks. I'll calm down in a couple of days. I shouldn't have come to Minneapolis but I'm running out of places."

I met the gentleman from downstairs. He had long hair and was a good friend of Jeff's. His name was Peter. Peter said I could stay with him for a few days.

We took the elevator down to the 7th floor. His place was exactly like Jeff's except he had different stuff.

"Come in, Mark. Wanna beer?"

"Thanks. I could use one."

"I'm one of Jeff's good friends. We've known each other a long time. Don't worry, you're safe here. I'm a draft counselor and I volunteer my time with NAACP, ACLU and with Native Americans. Don't worry, I'm on your side."

"Jeff's told me about you, Mark. You're a real patriot as far as I'm concerned. And a Pacifist. I like that. I've studied Ghandi and his methods. And Martin Luther King. I believe peaceful passive resistance is the only way."

"Me too," I concurred.

Peter grabbed two more beers. I was calming down.

My mind was racing. I could just see Gary telling those guys, "You know who that was back there? That was Mike McAndrew. He's wanted by the FBI for blowing up buildings and running guns and bombs. Yeah man. He's the one."

Fuck!

"Peter, could you get Jeff to come down. I need to talk to him."

Jeff appeared in a few minutes.

"Can you guys get me out of town. I shouldn't be here."

Jeff and Peter looked at each other. It took a moment.

Jeff spoke. "It's late but they'll be up. Let me make a call."

He was back in ten minutes.

"I called my buddy in Wisconsin. He's totally cool. He lives on a farm outside of Ladysmith. I'll drive you there tomorrow."

"What did you tell him? Does he live alone?"

"That I have a favor to ask. I told him I have a friend who needs to hide out for awhile. No questions. Don't tell anyone etc. He knows the drill. He's also brought several guys to Canada. He knows Gary. But, he'll keep his mouth shut. I think it's just him and his old lady."

"We'll leave in the morning like I said. Stay here with Peter tonight. You'll be okay."

"All right. Thank you. Good night."

Pedaling as fast as I can ... they're gaining ... the cracks in the side walk a blur ... faster ... faster ... upside down ... spinning ...

I awoke in a sweat. I must have shouted because Peter was there asking me if I was okay.

Just a nightmare. I was drenched in sweat. I had to get up. Peter looked concerned.

"I'm okay," I tried to assure him, "I'm okay. Sorry I woke you up, man."

Peter wished me a good night again. He walked to his bedroom and I stared at the ceiling in the dim Minneapolis night. I couldn't sleep at all. Strange new night noises in a strange building. I got up and found a beer. Took a lick and stared out the window. This was a nightmare too.

The sun blinked it's first light from the east. I'd been up since 3 a.m. It was about 6. Peter got up.

"Sleep okay?" He asked.

"No, I never went back to sleep."

"Bummer."

Peter made a fresh pot of strong coffee. It smelled great and tasted even better. I drank two cups to his one.

"Sorry about last night, man. I'm just really uptight right now."

"Don't worry about it."

I was embarrassed. I was losing it. I took some more speed. I had a long day ahead. Jeff showed up. I thanked Peter and we were off.

"I woke up Peter last night. I had a nightmare and was screaming, I guess. I feel bad. Man, I'm slipping!" I was feeling sorry for myself. Again. Get it together, man. Get it together.

Jeff and I pulled out of the Cities and I felt better. We had a two or three hour drive. We drove through my country. I grew up here. Across the St. Croix River into St. Croix Falls and the beautiful bridge spanning Minnesota and Wisconsin. From here it was a straight shot through green rolling hills of Northern Wisconsin. Farmland. Dairy farms. Huge black and white cows by the thousands. Immense cumulous clouds shaped like faces and dinosaurs. Azure blue skies peeking through. Barron. A few miles from my birth place. The town of Ladysmith. Old fond memories of swimming and summer camping trips with Dad.

We drove a few miles north out of town.

"This is it."

A lonely old farm house upon a hill. A barn. Fences and a long gravel road lead to the house.

A barking dog greeted us. A tall lanky long haired man waved.

"Jim, this is Mark."

Jeff introduced us after several lusty hugs and greetings.

"Welcome. Pleased to meet you."

We shook hands in the hippie thumbs up style.

"Mary's in the barn."

Jeff and Jim had grown up together in Edina. Gone to high school together. Dated some of the same girls.

I felt safe again.

Chapter 18

Ladysmith

Mary was a healthy looking big boned blonde gal. She was milking one of their two cows when we walked into the barn.

"Oh, hey. Howdy. Mark is it? Welcome."

She was milking the cow by hand.

"I thought you had to milk cows early in the morning and then later towards evening," I asked. It was mid-afternoon.

"Yeah. Usually. Except this one has been sick with an infection and we've had to milk her a few times a day. She can't get it all out. The milk is no good. She's old. We may have to slaughter her if she doesn't improve."

Jim walked us around the spread. They had 40 acres and grew some corn and wheat besides having the two cows and a Collie. They had some chickens running around. The place was neat and tidy.

"Even have a swimming hole over there."

He pointed but I didn't see any water. Jim explained to us that he bought the farm after both his parents were killed by a drunk driver. He bought the farm with the settlement. He was also injured in the crash but survived. He was an only child. They had put in plumbing and electricity and had refurbished the house and painted it. They were still working on the place.

"Jim, I like to work. I spent time as a kid on a farm."

He cut me off. "No bother Dude."

I still had some money left and I offered to help with expenses.

"Your money is no good," was his reply.

But, I would work and help out as much as I could. I promised myself. Jeff had to get back to the Cities.

"Thanks. Sorry I kinda freaked out."

"I understand. Stay in touch."

Jim took me into the house. The place reminded me of my Aunt Bid's place. All wood. Old wallpaper. Small rooms downstairs. We walked up a creaky stairway. He showed me the room I'd be sleeping in. The ceiling slanted down towards the window. A single bed and dresser with a night stand and a lamp, a small closet. I dropped my gear down and we walked downstairs.

"We don't have a TV but we have a radio in the stereo. No washer or dryer. We do the clothes by hand. I put the bathroom in last year. It's about the only modern room in the house. It used to be a pantry. I want to fix up the kitchen this summer. Replace all the cabinets and counters. Can you do carpentry?"

"Some."

"Great. It would be cool if you could help me with that."

"I'd love to."

"The fridge and oven are new but Mary wanted to keep the wood stove."

"Is that how you heat the place in the winter?"

"You got it. Someday we'll put some heating in here but this thing keeps the house warm. Can you paint?"

"Yeah. I'm really good at that."

"We need to paint the outside of the house."

"When do we start?"

Mary came in from the barn. She started to make dinner. She was making a huge salad from fresh vegetables picked from their garden. Jim uncorked three bottles of homemade beer. Jim and I sat at the kitchen table while Mary fixed dinner.

"Jeff told me a little about you. Don't worry, Mark, I'm not going to ask a lot of questions except one. Have you ever hurt anyone?"

"Only in football."

Jim and Mary laughed out loud. Jim had a mouthful of beer and nearly spit it out.

"No, seriously. I'm a pacifist. Non-violence is my creed."

Mary turned round from her duties and smiled.

"Us too."

"Jeez, this beer is strong," I commented.

"It'll kick your butt. We make our own beer and wine. Ever had dandelion wine? We got gallons of it. Here I'll show you."

We walked to a side room off of the porch. It was surprisingly cool in here. Jim showed me bottle after bottle of wine. Some had balloons on top. They looked ready to burst.

"When the balloons pop the wine is ready. So if you hear what sounds like a gunshot, it's just the wine."

"Cool."

Jim grabbed a bottle for dinner.

We had steak and corn on the cob and the best salad I'd ever had with wine. The wine was sweet but once you got used to it ...

After dinner Jim rolled a joint and we passed it around. This would be my home until the fall.

I fell asleep in my new room. No dreams.

The sun woke me up. I heard noises from downstairs and smelled the coffee and bacon. Mary and Jim sat at the kitchen table.

"We thought we'd let the 'City Boy' sleep in."

It was 7 a.m.

"That's the best night's sleep I've had in a long time. Wow," as I yawned and stretched.

"Hungry?"

"Oh yeah."

I helped myself to eggs toast and bacon and a volume of coffee.

I offered to clean the dishes. Mary let me. She had to tend to the sick cow. She had already milked the healthy one.

I finished the dishes. It was going to be a warm day. Into the 90's. A good day for painting. Jim set up a couple of wooden telescoping ladders. We had to scrap the old paint off first. After years of neglect the house was a bleached white. I hated this part. It was hard work. But eventually we finished one side of the house by noon. We broke for lunch. Mary fixed a couple of sandwiches. We drank homemade cider.

"We'll work in the shade this afternoon. Too hot in the sun."

We continued scraping the old paint until I couldn't hardly move my arms. Man, this was work. Luckily, Jim had an old floppy hat and a pair of bib overalls for me to wear. We were both covered in paint chips which stuck to us because of the humidity and our own sweat. By six we had finished the long sides of the house. We'd do the narrow sides tomorrow.

"You're a good worker, Mark. Sure do appreciate it."

"Man, it's the least I can do. I'm staying in your house eating your food. Fuck, man, I like it. I really do. Keeps me busy. Makes me feel like I'm accomplishing something. I should thank you and I do."

"That's a different take. I like it. You're all right. Let's eat and get stoned."

"Good idea, Ollie."

There is something about farm life. You work your ass off all day and then eat a delicious meal. No nonsense. You're usually so tired that there isn't time for much 'malarkey.' Just work, eat, and sleep.

Mary and Jim discussed the doings of the farm. The barn needed fixing. The one cow was so sick. The Vet had been out twice giving the cow some shots. That cost plenty. Jim had purchased the paint for the house. More money. Jim had the trust fund but he couldn't get at it. The monthly allotment was just enough. Jim popped a beer and rolled an excellent joint. He just laughed and said everything would be fine. Their personalities were forming in my mind. Mary was a worrier and Jim was a dreamer. Mary being the pragmatic one in this formula. Perfect balance, I thought.

"We wanted to paint the house last summer but we didn't have time. Too many other things to fix first. You're a Godsend Mark."

"That makes me feel good. I don't know what Jeff told you about me but I don't want you guys telling anyone. Not your families or friends. Please, just let it abide and stay here. It's enough to say that I'm in deep shit."

The pot and beer were taking affect.

"We understand. Mary's brother is AWOL from the Army. So we know."

Feeling reassured. Again.

"Man, I don't know about you but I need a shower," I said.

"It's all yours."

The shower felt so good. Paint chips washing down the drain. I didn't take long. Save the water. They had a well and there was only so much water. I got out and toweled off. Changed into some clean clothes. Didn't take but ten minutes.

Jim was next. I had a chance to chat with Mary. A strong committed woman. I really liked her and felt comfortable around her. She had a degree in economics from the University of Wisconsin and used her skills on the farm. She and Jim had big plans for the farm. They had both decided to hold off on having children until the farm was stable. Like I said, she was pragmatic.

"You guys don't have a TV. How do you get your news?"

"We don't."

"Maybe next time one of you go to town you could pick up a Tribune for me. I'm addicted to news," I laughed.

"Yeah, sure. I'm going to the market tomorrow. I'll pick a few news-papers up for you," Mary said.

I handed her some money. She just shook her head. She rolled a ciga-rette and handed it to me. Jim came out and we finished the evening with another round. I passed out fully tired and content.

Today was just like yesterday except we scraped the narrow sides of the house.

If nothing else I was getting a nice tan on the backside of my body. I could feel the strength returning to my body.

We finished scraping by late afternoon. Both of us were bone weary.

"Hey, Mark, follow me."

Jim led the way across a pasture where it was obvious the cows grazed. We climbed through a barbed wire fence and followed a small pathway covered by huge Elm and Maple trees. We soon came to an opening and lo and behold. A pond. A swimming hole. Wow!

Jim and I didn't hesitate. We stripped off our clothes and jumped into the cool water. Man, did that get the blood flowing.

"This is great!"

"This was one of the reasons we bought the place. We couldn't use it for the first couple of years because the previous owner let his cattle down here and it was so full of cow shit that it took that long before it was safe again. Sometimes Mary and I come down here and listen to the frogs at night," He winked.

"Bet it freezes in the winter."

"It does. Not big enough to skate on though."

We splashed around for awhile and were soon joined by Mary who was soon equally naked. We soon churned the murky bottom up so that the water was brown. The bottom was full of old decaying tree branches which made moving around a slow task. No matter. It worked. The days labor in the past. Clean enough and certainly cooled down. We just put our clothes back on, wet as we were. Walking back to the house we worked up a sweat.

As we neared the house and it came into view Jim and I admired our work.

"There's some patch work to do but we can start the primer tomorrow. Isn't supposed to rain for at least a week."

"And then two more coats ... right?" I asked.

"Uh huh."

Mary still had to milk the cows. I asked how the sick one was and she said 'not good.' That night at supper Jim and Mary discussed putting the cow down and selling her for the meat. That was sad.

I cleared the table and did the dishes. Mary appreciated that.

Jim grabbed some beers and rolled one. We sat outside trying to catch a breeze. The mosquitos were plentiful but they didn't like tobacco smoke. That was the only way to keep them away. Jim and I walked around the house. He pointed out several areas that needed patching. He wanted to take the eaves down and clean them out and paint them. We still had a ways to go.

It was so hot in the house, especially upstairs, that I slept outside under the stars. The bugs settled down after awhile. I slept soundly.

I awoke with the sunrise. Birds clattering to each other. I was covered with morning dew. My sleeping bag was wet.

I walked into the house.

"How'd you sleep?" Mary greeted me.

"Great. Just great."

Coffee, eggs, toast, bacon, coffee. Did I say coffee?

Jim came down.

"Are you ready, Freddie?"

"Yeah, let's get an early start before it gets too hot."

The sun was still in the tree tops when we began. Jim wanted me up on the ladder with the primer. But first, we had to remove the eaves and that was a bitch. When we finished that I began painting while Jim patched up some sore spots. The paint spread easily as the morning warmed. I had a ten inch brush and a paint bucket hooked to the ladder. It went surprisingly fast. We finished the broad side of the house by noon. We broke for lunch. It was so hot that all I wanted was a beer. The sun was high up with almost no shade and little breeze. The paint dried in an hour. Amazing. I told Jim I wanted to really push and get the house half-done.

We moved the ladders and paint around to the other side. Jim had finished all of the patch work and had removed the eaves so he could help paint too.

By 8 p.m. we had put the primer on the entire house. It looked great. Kinda of a flat white.

"Hell, we can start the first coat tomorrow."

"I think so."

"Last one in is a rotten egg!"

Mary came dashing out of the house and we three raced to the swimming hole. I was laughing so hard I couldn't run. I was a rotten egg!

God that feels good. All the heat and sweat washed away in an instant. Nobody cared about the muddy water.

"Hey, I didn't ask. What color are we painting the house in?" as I splashed in the pond.

"Mellow Yellow."

"You're kidding. Is there a color called 'Mellow Yellow'?"

"Yeah. Just like the Donovan song."

"Too much!"

After dinner I slept outside again.

Another dreamless night.

Jim gave me a full bucket of paint. It was a pretty color. Mellow indeed. Another scorcher. The paint flowed easily. Mary made her rounds and ran into town. She promised to buy a newspaper or two for me. I was in such a different world far from my worries. I welcomed it. I embraced the work with a joyful vengeance. I thought of Carol but without the pain in my heart. I saw the revolution from a different perspective. I was able to see for the first time in a long time. I wondered how the Dems were doing, who they would select. It had to be McGovern and the Republicans of course, would run Tricky Dick Nixon again. Jeez, I disliked that man. I wished I could vote but that was out of the question. My mind drifted and I was day dreaming as I worked. I looked over at Jim and we were about to meet in the middle.

This paint had a shine to it. A gloss. It didn't dry as fast as the primer but it would be dry by tomorrow.

"Hell, man, we can get the first coat today, easy."

"I think so."

I took a break and walked back across the lawn. Rolled a cig and looked for missed spots and noticed how nice it looked.

"Hey, Jim. Check this out," I called to him.

We took a moment to admire our work. It would take two coats. The trim was to be a hi-gloss white to really set it off. We had all the storm windows to do and of course, the eaves. But all in all, we were flying and the weather was cooperating.

Mary came back with loads of groceries. Jim helped her unpack the car. I continued painting. I could see it now. My son asks what I did during the Vietnam Era. 'I painted.'

"Mark, I got your papers."

We broke for lunch. Again, I wasn't really hungry. It was just too hot. I saw the papers, the *Minneapolis Tribune*, the *St. Paul Pioneer Press*, and a local paper. I scanned the headlines. McGovern had chosen Senator Eagleton to be his running mate at their convention. Another article about the Watergate. I put the paper down as I finished lunch.

I'd read them later.

"Jim, I think we'll finish the first coat by 4."

"Think so. It'll have to dry before we can put the second coat on. Hopefully, it'll be dry by tomorrow because we've got some weather coming."

"When?"

"Next week. You know August around here. Stormy weather."

We did finish. I checked the other side of the house. The paint was still tacky.

I grabbed a beer and sat under a tree and ended up taking a nap. Just plain worn out. An occasional car would pass and I noticed they would slow down and stare at the house. Huh!

I asked Mary about that and she said that people were gawking at the hippies.

"We're a roadside attraction. Last summer we had a whole bunch of friends up here for a week or so. One Sunday afternoon we were having a good time and cars were driving by. I'd never seen that much traffic here. Hell, if we get a car an hour that's traffic. Anyway, some cars stopped. Car loads of people. One of Jim's crazy friends decides to really give them a show. He's like 6'3 and has hair to his waist. He played football for the Badgers. Anyway, he's athletic, right, so he takes all of his clothes off and starts doing cartwheels across the front yard. It was a fucking hoot. Mom's were covering the eyes of their children and they couldn't get out of here fast enough. Fucking hilarious. About an hour later the Sheriff showed up and gave us some shit but he couldn't do anything about it."

"So, yeah, we still get an occasional gawker. I just wave at them now. Like we're good neighbors."

I walked back to the pond by myself and soaked with the frogs.

A nice breeze greeted me on the walk back. The grasses swaying. I figured the light wind would help dry the paint. The house just gleamed.

"We're having corn on the cob and chicken tonight. I made an apple pie too," Mary exclaimed.

I was hungry. We ate and chatted through supper. The breeze had cooled things down.

"You're right, Jim. I can feel the weather changing. Hope we can finish this thing on time. You know we can always do the storm windows and eaves in the barn."

"Yeah. Good idea. Pass the butter, would ya'."

We had a very pleasant evening listening to music and drinking beer and smoking joints. I wanted to read the papers. I read all the articles on the front page. Wondering about this Watergate thing. Was Nixon involved?

He had to be. Maybe this would derail his candidacy. Wishful thinking. I read the sports pages. Then I read section two of the Tribune. My heart jumped right out of my chest. A headline read, 'Draft Board Raided.' The article detailed how the Wabasha Draft Board had been broken into and all the records had been found later floating down the Mississippi River. The FBI was handling the break in and they had several suspects in custody. My name jumped off the page! One of the suspects was a 'Michael McAndrew, a known member of the SDS Weathermen.' What? I wasn't even there. I wasn't a Weatherman. How did they get my name. The article mentioned that they had matched a footprint of mine to the crime scene. What? I always wear shoes. I'm never barefoot. The article mentioned that they had arrested three members of the break in. How the fuck did they get my name? I just felt something was not right with those guys. I had met with them and offered suggestions. That's all. One of those fuck heads was a FBI plant. Had to be. He must have recognized me.

I read the *Pioneer Press*. Same article basically. Except they posted pictures of the suspects. Mine included. It was a high school graduation shot. Thankfully, it didn't remotely resemble me. Fuck!

I tried not to show my chagrin.

"Enjoying your papers, Mark?"

"Yeah. I am. The Oakland A's are rocking. Nixon's the One."

They both laughed.

I had to think. Gary was cool. Jeff was cool. Only Jeff knew I was here and Jim and Mary didn't know who I was. I really wanted to call Jeff but I couldn't risk the phone call.

I thought maybe I could call Mark tomorrow in town from a pay phone and call Jeff too. I'd always heard that it took several minutes to trace a call. I hope I was right. But, I didn't want to put a call in from here. Maybe I could get Jim to call Jeff.

I had to think. I pretended like everything was okay. I went for a walk. I congratulated myself in following my instincts. But that was besides the point. I walked down the path to the pond and sat. I watched huge clouds gathering. I remembered as a boy in Wisconsin laying on my back watching these same clouds. If only I could retrace my steps and do a couple of things differently.

I figured I had to trust Mary and Jim. I walked back to the house with my mind made up.

"Hey Mark, did you see this?"

Jim showed me the article about the break in.

"Yeah, I saw it. Cool huh?" I responded.

"Is this you?"

He showed me my photo in the paper. I couldn't lie.

"Yeah."

"You're Michael?"

"Just call me Mark."

"You're my hero, man. I can't believe it. A celebrated revolutionary man in our house!"

"No, I'm not. The article is a fucking lie. I was never there. I know nothing of this break in. The entire article is untrue. Honest!" I cried.

"Dude, you can hide out here as long as you want. We haven't told a soul about you. Ask Mary. No one even knows you are here."

"Except Jeff."

"Yeah, well, he's cool."

"I saw the article earlier. I've got to think. I did meet with those guys at Jeff's and I told Jeff that I had a bad feeling. Like, one of them was an FBI agent or something. I was right. This is what I want you to do. I want you to call Jeff and say that your 'friend', that's me, needs to see him. I need to see Jeff face to face. I can't trust the phone. See if he can come over for a visit. The last thing I want to do is endanger you guys. Besides, I want to finish painting the house."

"Secondly," I continued, "Mary, can you give me a lift into town to-morrow. I need to use a pay phone."

"Sure thing."

Jim picked up the phone.

"Sound casual."

And dialed Jeff's number.

"Hey man, how's it going ... our friend wants to see you. Read the papers lately ..."

Jeff was all over it. He knew the shit was hitting the fan. He told Jim he was coming over now. Which meant he'd be here in two hours or so.

"Might as well eat while we wait," Mary said.

"By the way, how did you recognize me from that old photo?" I asked.

"Looks just like you, except now you have long hair. And I noticed the shock on your face after you read the article. As soon as you left for your walk I picked the paper up. It was Mary who suggested that perhaps that was you."

"Good eyes, Mary," I said.

"And I ain't no Weatherman either. I'm a fucking pacifist! Pass the spuds," I laughed.

In a couple of hours we saw headlights in the driveway.

"Must be Jeff."

"What's new!" I exclaimed.

"Oh, nothing," Jeff mused.

I showed him the papers. Of course, he'd seen them too.

"You were right. Something did stink. I think I know which guy it was. It must have been the guy with the blonde hair and glasses. He was just too perfect."

"My guess too."

"Were you followed?"

"No."

"Do you think anyone knows I'm here?"

"Besides us, no."

"I smell paint."

"Yeah, we've been painting."

"Jeff, I wasn't even there. I was here. Painting."

"I know."

Mary and Jim listened to us speak and moved their heads back and forth like at a tennis match.

"What about the three in custody?" I asked.

"They probably talked."

"Fucking great!"

"And what's with the foot print?"

"That's just bullshit. Propaganda," Jeff observed.

"My fucking grandma reads the *Tribune*. She'll see that article. What about the TV stations? Did *WCCO* air it too?"

"Yeah. It was the lead story. Never mind that. One thing is for sure. They play dirty. Now listen, Mark. I'm positive no one knows you are here. Stay put. Jim, Mary, keep him here until I say let's move. As you're attorney I strongly advise you to stay put. Got it! Mark, You've told me of Mark in Berkeley, do you want me to contact him for you?"

"Yeah. Just tell him the basics. He's hot too. So don't stay on the phone long."

"Fuck!" I sighed.

Jeff wanted to get back to the Cities. I thanked and hugged him. He was a good man. Jim and Mary did the same. After he left I looked at my two hosts and shook my head.

"Wanna beer?" asked Jim knowing the answer.

"Don't worry, if they come I'll swear that I answered an ad in the paper and am just a hired hand."

"You're not a hired hand, Mark, you're family," assured Mary.

With that we all hugged and proceeded to get stoned.

The pot put a nice haze over everything. It put me at a distance from things. God, I hate bullies. People in power just stomping the less fortunate. The rules were stacked in their favor. They had all the marbles in their bag. And this was like some big game of 'hide and seek.' But, it wasn't a kids game anymore.

"Mark, what do you want to hear?"

"Huh," I said rising out of my coma.

"Oh, yeah. *Anthem of the Sun* by the Dead. And play it loud."

Jim put the vinyl on the stereo and boosted the volume. The first notes put me in the right state of mind. I needed this. Mary passed me a joint and I was in the dream.

I finally passed out. I slept outside again. Felt safer and it wasn't so hot. Didn't mind the mosquitos at all.

Woke the next morning. Had a couple cups. Wasn't hungry. I almost forgot about the painting but I soon remembered. Thank God for that. It got my mind off.

Jim and I walked outside to check the paint. There was still a morning dew so we had to start on the east side of the house where the sun had dried it. The paint from yesterday was dried. With any luck we could start on the trim tomorrow. If I wasn't in jail, that is. The thought of jail sent shivers up my spine.

Every car that passed scared me. I had a plan that if needed I would run to the woods.

Man, the second coat really got it! No more streaks, just an even tone. It just shined. Jim and I would easily finish by this afternoon.

Lunch came. I still wasn't hungry.

"Mark, you have to eat something," Mary said.

I halfheartedly munched on an egg sandwich. Swallowed a beer.

For the first time I thought of those poor guys in jail. The article had said three of them. I couldn't remember their names but I felt for them. Attorneys and cops. What a drag that must be. In a holding cell with 50 other degenerates. No smokes. That would suck.

Jim and I did finish the second coat. The only heat being from the sun. We started on the storm windows next. They needed to be scraped of old paint and primed. That took up the rest of the day.

We stood back and stared at the house. She shined, man, she shined. It was a thing of beauty.

"That's enough for today, Mark."

We got back inside. Mary had two glasses of iced tea for us. It hit the spot.

The phone rang. Mary picked it up.

She handed the phone to Jim. "It's for you."

All I heard were a bunch of 'uh huh's and ok's' and after a couple of minutes he hung up.

"Good news. That was Jeff. He said that they aren't really looking for you that hard. He's got some lawyer friends, I guess, who told him that the FBI figured that they got their men. They arrested the other three guys today. Apparently they said you weren't there. Maybe you're off the hook."

"Then why did they put my name out?"

"Good question."

"I still think that one of those guys was a plant. I'd like to get my hands on him."

"And what would you do if you could."

I hesitated. "Nothing." Actually, I don't know what I'd do. Never thought of that.

"Did he mention talking to Mark?"

"No."

Finally, I was hungry. Maybe the heat was off for now.

We raced to the pond. This time Mary was the 'rotten egg.'

As we soaked in the pond Jim spoke. "We still have a few more days of good weather. Let's finish up the house and then take a few days off. Mary and I have invited some friends of ours up from Madison. They'll be here in about ten days. You'll like 'em."

In all the commotion; Mary had sold the sick cow to a farmer down the road. He was going to use the meat to feed his hogs. They had a couple of acres of corn that needed to be harvested and a few acres of wheat to cut and bale. There was lots to do around here. They had to get ready for the winter. The winters were long and hard. I'd be long gone by then.

It was a pleasant evening. I was dead tired. Just needed sleep. I slept in the house tonight.

It wasn't as hot when we woke up. The heat spell was breaking. In fact, it was overcast and very humid. Jim and I made fast work of the trim but we'd have to wait a day to apply a second coat. We had moved the eaves and storm windows into the barn so we began working on them.

It looked like rain and smelled like rain but the front blew over. By late afternoon it was sunny and clear. All we needed was one more day.

Mary had run into town for more supplies. She had a couple of news-papers with her. After dinner I scanned them but found no mention of the break in. That was good. But one article did alarm me, apparently there were reports that McGovern's running mate, Eagleton, had been in a men-tal institution and had received electric shock treatments. I didn't think too much of it except maybe this was another 'Dirty Trick' by Tricky Dick. And another article about this Watergate business. Nothing like an election year to throw shit at the fan.

I felt better not seeing any more articles about the break in.

Mary also bought tons of beer and some wine.

As we ate dinner we talked about their lives and how they met and their future plans. Mary had a teaching degree and wanted to teach at the local high school and Jim had studied engineering but still had a couple of years to get a degree. They had enough money for several years from the settlement but they both wanted to continue to work.

"Jim maybe you could work for the City or for the State. You know, on planning commissions and the sort."

"I'd like too, actually. I'd have to go back to school for that. Not many colleges out here. I might just be a farmer."

"We just really need to get this place fixed up first before we think about jobs," he added.

"Besides, we might have kids."

"Don't start with that!" Mary laughed.

"What about you, Mark? Gotta a girl?"

"Had one, but she got away."

"I don't want to talk about that right now. It's kind of a bummer for me. I mean, I'm all right and stuff but if things had been different ..."

"You mean because of your situation?"

"Yeah, for sure, I should have fought for her and I wussied out. She was pretty high class. Her parents being very influential and wellheeled. I felt low class around them. They liked me and all but I could just tell that they didn't want me for a son-in-law. I don't know. A relationship is about the last thing on my plate right now. Speaking of which, pass the peas."

Another splendid meal. I was getting healthy again. Good food and hard work will do that for you.

We lucked out with the weather. We were able to finish the second coat on the trim. Jim and I stood back and admired.

"Look's nice, man. Real nice."

"Thanks to you. You're fucking awesome!" Jim said.

"Am too," as we laughed like two school kids at our private joke.

Storm clouds were gathering to the north. They would probably miss us though.

Jim needed to get that wheat cut before it rained again or he would have to wait until it dried. That was enough hay for the lone cow. And most of the corn he sold to his neighbor with the hogs. His neighbor would harvest that himself. It would only take a couple of hours, Jim said.

Jim called Mary out to admire our work. She hugged us both.

"Good work you two. You should see it from the road. It shines!"

So, I did that. I walked down the road a bit. Down a hill and back up a hill. I was two miles away. It was beautiful. I walked back along the road and I felt like a little boy again. Kicking stones and just lollygagging along. Not a worry in the world.

I don't know why but at that moment I was overcome with a feeling of joy.

Huge storm clouds, all ugly and mean, rolling purple and green and yellow, to the north of us.

I got back to the house and told them about the storm clouds. We were expecting some rain and hail, maybe, from that front. Jim and I went down into the storm cellar. We brought water and an extra flashlight and some blankets just in case. I saw a portable radio sitting on a table.

The skies above us were still clear but one never knew in this part of the world. The wind could shift in a minute.

"Just want to make sure we can survive the night in case that storm comes over us," Jim looked at the sky and noted, "it's beautiful though, isn't it?"

"God, I'm glad we finished the house when we did."

"Me too," Jim added.

This was tornado country. Not as well-known as Oklahoma but they got their share up here. Mostly though, these storms turned into raging thunderstorms and hail storms.

We turned the radio on and there were tornado warnings to the north in Sawyer County. We were just to the southern edge. The air felt quiet and still. Mary fixed dinner and we had a nice chat.

There was a nervousness in the air.

As it got dark we could see lightning strikes to the north but not a drop here.

"Well, we'll keep an eye on it but I think we're okay. We need to get the house ready for our guests."

"How many people?" I asked.

"I don't know ... four or five."

"Any kids?"

"No. At least, I don't think so."

"Hell, they could sleep out in the barn if the weather's okay," I suggested.

"Ha, I can just see Susan sleeping in a barn!" Mary jabbed.

"We'll figure it out. It'll be fun," she added.

"You guys, you can't tell them anything about me. Just say I'm a friend of a friend and I am helping you guys out or say that you hired me or something."

"Don't worry. We promise."

"But, that's a long way off. They aren't coming until next week."

The radio station alerted citizens of the weather. Again saying that the storm was headed east and was centered 50 miles from here.

We were expecting rain tomorrow.

The humidity seemed to be 100%. It was unbearable. Nothing a few cold beers couldn't tame down.

The storm had passed us by. Seemed like a lucky omen in that most storms seemed to miss me.

Jim and I spent the next few days finishing painting the storm windows and with much ado managed to reattach the eaves. The house was finished.

Jim and Mary's friends pulled in. Two couples and a lone woman. Amongst hugs and introductions the beers flowed and joints were passed.

We all sat in the living room as everyone spoke at once catching up. Jim and Mary were so proud of their house. They gave everyone an impromptu tour. They seemed impressed.

I felt left out, which was fine with me. I had forgotten all their names so I asked them again. There was Mary Jo and Tom, Linda and Jerry, and Susan. They were a group of highly energized and intelligent people. I was introduced by Mary as a friend of Jim and Jeff's. Good enough. They were all students and grad students in Madison. All I knew is that there would be plenty of food and beer and dope.

It was hot and muggy so everyone headed to the pond. Within minutes we were all naked sitting in the muddy water. I tried not to stare at the women. Boy, were my eyes full. Susan, who seemed moody, had a beautiful body. Long straight blonde hair. Tall and graceful. I was afraid of getting a hard on so I stayed in the water a long time.

I felt rather awkward because Susan and I were the only two people that were unattached and the dynamic of the arrangement unintentionally pushed us together. Susan and I talked on the way back to the house. She asked me several questions about myself that I brushed off like a politician would. I asked her about herself turning the conversation around. She was a grad student in social work. She wanted to help people, she said. It's kinda weird talking with a complete stranger about stuff when you've seen them naked.

The women went into the kitchen and started making a feast. We guys sat on the front porch drinking beer. It's interesting how men and women gravitate to their roles. No matter how liberal or conservative, enlightened or not, men and women seem to fall into their roles. It must be some evolution development. It's got to be genetic or something. What if we guys prepared the food. It just wouldn't seem proper.

We discussed the news. McGovern's campaign was in the toilet. The Eagleton affair had made him look incompetent. Fucking Nixon was going to win again. I asked about the Watergate break in. No one knew too much about it but we all wondered what it meant. The Republican Party had hired these guys to break into the Democratic Headquarters. Was Nixon behind this? And what about Daniel Ellsberg and the Pentagon Papers. Round and round we went. The cigarettes piled with empty beers. It was time to eat.

It was a feast. It was like Thanksgiving in August. We sat outside to eat. It was too warm in the house. Jim praised me for the work I'd done. I'm sure I blushed. That was nice of him. The house looked brand new. Could still smell the paint in fact.

The conversation turned onto school things, which was perfect. Talking about classes and certain professors and future job prospects. Their futures looked bright. I asked Susan if she wanted to teach and she said she wanted to go to work at a social agency of some sort. She was thinking of working in Chicago with inner city kids. I looked at this tall blonde athletic blue-eyed woman and somehow didn't see her fitting into the inner city projects of Chicago.

It seemed that the other folks all wanted to teach. I was envious. I would have made a helluva great American Lit teacher.

The weather was oppressive. Jim and the other guys hauled a horse tank to the front of the porch and Jim put a hose in it and started to fill it with water. If you sat on the edge of the tank you could dangle your feet in the water. It kept you cool.

Later on a small cool breeze whipped up. It helped. Wish I was in San Francisco right now. I'd be wearing a sweater.

Jim and Tom ran into town to buy some more beer and ice. We'd keep the beer cool in the horse tank.

I started to clean up the dishes. Mary and Susan helped put the food away. The fridge was stuffed. There were so many dishes that I had to change the dish water and I needed help drying the dishes. Susan helped. I could feel a spark between Susan and I. I didn't know if she felt one too. Women were very hard for me to read. Proust was easier.

Jim and Tom came back with two cases of beer and several bags of ice which were all promptly dumped into the horse tank. Jim was nice enough to bring me a paper. Same old news. Again, nothing on the break in.

McGovern wanted to appoint a commission on the Watergate Break In and it looked like he was going to dump Eagleton. What a mess. Nixon and his 'Meanies' were gathering in Miami for their convention. What I wouldn't give to be there. There was a new movement of returning vets from Vietnam who were opposed to the war. The winds were changing. When is this fucking thing going to end?

Even Muhammad Ali had resisted the draft. The 'Greatest' had said, "no Vietcong ever called me nigger." I didn't know the exact numbers but there were now about 200,000 draft resisters. 30,000 of whom had migrated to Canada. The new Draft Lottery would begin in 1973. So, Conscription as we knew it would end. I didn't know what to think of that. The right wingers were praising it saying that 'only those who wanted to serve' blah, blah, blah. But, it seemed to me that mainly the poor would serve because it was the only way to get a job and an education. But, there was still the lottery. The unlucky bastards with the wrong birthday would still get drafted.

I even read the Sport's page. Old habit. Look at those White Sox and the Reds. I really missed baseball the most. My dreams of playing second base for the Yankees. But, they already had a second baseman. Bobby Richardson. He was pretty good. Oh well. Nice to dream.

I joined the others on the porch.

"What's new in the world?"

"Looks like McGovern has screwed himself into the ground. This Eagleton thing. Nixon has taken that to the bank. I keep wondering about this Watergate thing though. I guess time will tell."

No one seemed interested in the outside world right now. Just watching the clouds pass by.

I went upstairs to my room to sleep. Our five guests did opt to sleep out in the barn.

I fell asleep reading Merton. I love his imagery. Made me feel good inside. Don't know why. His spirituality touched me. I thought of my family, all of them, and how they must worry about me. I missed them so much. I said a prayer for each of them. And one for myself.

And, I thought of Mark. Poor Mark. I had to talk to him soon. I caught myself weeping as I feel asleep. A flood of emotion welled up in me. I was so alone and so scared. Every time I thought of the future I got sick to my stomach. Merton taught me to see the moment. I had to constantly remember that. It just went against my grain, I guess.

"Good morning."

The smell of coffee and bacon and eggs and toast. My, oh my.

It was hot and sunny. The farmer from next door was already up and cutting the wheat. I wanted to help but the cut would have to dry out before baling. I asked Jim about the corn. There really wasn't that much of that but it would be done with a machine as well. I wanted something to do. I was restless. For no reason at all I started to jog down the road. I had a pair of cut-offs on, no shirt and a pair of work boots. Pony tail bobbing. I must have run half way to Ladysmith. Several cars passed and gave me unsure stares. I just waved and let the sweat run.

I got back to the house and the others were staring as well at this curiosity.

"Just needed to run off some steam."

That seemed to satisfy them. I walked back to the pond to rinse off. I felt great!

By now everyone had settled in. The rush of a new arrival having worn off. I looked over at the fresh cut field. God, that smelled good. Jim was right, it had to dry out first. How long, I wasn't sure. The farmer had also shucked the corn and was in the process of cutting that down. His hogs would be happy. Mary grabbed a few dozen ears to eat later.

"How many bales of hay will that make?" I asked the farmer.

"Hundred, maybe more."

Jim and Mary's cow would be fed for the Winter.

I rolled a cigarette and grabbed a beer and sat on the davenport on the porch. The clouds were mighty today. Lots of dragons and dinosaurs. I feel asleep.

I awoke to voices in the kitchen. I must have slept an hour or so. The skies were overcast, the air still.

"Feels like rain," I said.

It was the middle of the afternoon and it was as dark as night. They had the radio on and the forecast called for thunder storms and possibly hail. But, this time the storm was headed directly at us. Mary and Jim had a stash of candles and flash lights, just in case. The electricity was still working.

A few drops of rain began to fall, and then a few more. It hadn't rained here in a few weeks so I'm sure the farmers were pleased. The rain gradually increased. A crack of thunder could be heard in the distance. Soon it was flat out pouring. The sound of the rain drops deafening. Another crack of lightening. The lights dimmed and then went out. By this time we were all gathered in the kitchen. Mary lit some candles. The house shook from another bolt. The storm was right over us. I walked into the living room and sat in a big chair by the window. Another crack, this one sounded like it hit the house. My hair was standing out from the static electricity. The air smelled like ozone. I heard a loud thump from outside. It was dark but it looked like a tree limb laying on the ground, smouldering. Holy shit. The lightening was constantly lighting up everything. It was scary. And it was pouring in torrents.

I wanted to be in it so I ran out the door to the barn. I grabbed a flashlight so I could see. I climbed the ladder to the hay loft and walked toward the open door.

"Hey."

A voice startled me.

"Who's that?"

"Susan, ... Mark?"

"Yeah, jeez you scared me. What are doing out here?" I asked.

"Same thing you are. Digging the storm."

"It's a doozy."

"Sure is."

She was laying in the open window on a mattress of hay.

"Mind if I join you?"

"Not at all."

I laid next to her and that's when I noticed that she was topless. I noticed because another bolt of lightening lit everything up. She looked so beautiful. We watched in silence as the storm marched across the Wisconsin fields.

"Did you see that!"

"Yes, I did."

"That was a funnel cloud. Let's keep an eye on it."

Another strike and the cloud was moving away from us.

"Should we tell the others?" I asked.

"Not yet. Let's just see where it's headed."

"Okay."

We waited several more minutes. Another strike. It was gone. Large balls of hail began to fall. Big ones. The size of ping pong balls. The noise was deafening. Susan put her arm around me and hugged me close. More out of fear than eros.

The hail storm only lasted a couple of minutes. The dark green and angry purple skies were gradually giving way.

I kissed her. She kissed me back. We tore at each other's bodies with a hunger.

The skies cleared. The birds returned. The rain subsided.

We joined the others inside.

"Where were you two?" Mary asked in an accusative voice. Giggling.

"Out in the barn watching the storm. We saw a tornado!"

"I'm sure you did," she answered sarcastically.

It's like they all knew.

"Hey, Susan, you're tee shirt is inside out," someone pointed out.

I knew my face was red even though no one could tell in the candle light.

We walked outside. The horse tank was full of hail.

"They don't believe us about the tornado," Susan gasped.

"Why should they," I laughed, "just look at us, soaking wet with our clothes on backwards. Would you believe us?"

"Guess not," she conceded, giggling.

"I'd say it's time for beer and dope, everybody," Tom exclaimed.

Just then the lights came back on.

The voice on the radio said that a tornado had been sighted near Ladysmith but hadn't touched down.

"See, we told you we saw a tornado!" Susan said.

"Holy shit."

That got a good laugh from everyone.

Tomorrow was Sunday. Our five guests were leaving. I didn't think Susan and I would get together. I think we were both slightly embarrassed by our encounter. It just happened.

We had another huge feast. We made a bonfire that night. Since everything was so wet Jim thought it would be safe. Watching the embers float into the night sky. Sitting next to Susan. Half of me wanted to return to Madison with her but I knew better. It just wasn't the right time.

Susan went off to the barn to sleep. Alone. We thought it best.

It was sad seeing everyone leave. It was the best of times.

"Are you going to see Susan again?" Asked Mary.

She couldn't wait to ask me.

My expression answered her question.

I went for a long walk.

When I returned Jim informed me that Jeff had called and was driving over.

"Did he say why?"

"Nope."

The Fear!

Why was he coming here? What was going on?

Jeff showed up in a couple of hours.

"Hey, man. What's up?"

"The pigs are asking questions about you. All those guys got arrested. They were real amateurs. Fuck, they bragged to their friends that they were going to do the break-in. Half the fucking state knew about it. And the cops are claiming that you were the ring leader. You gotta get out of here. It's only a matter of time before they figure out that you're a friend of mine," looking at Jim, "and they could show up here."

Jim, Mary, and myself sat stunned.

"Excuse us a second."

Jeff led me outside. "I talked to Mark. Here's some money for you. I'm going to take you out of here right now. Mark is freaked. Where do you want to go?"

"Can you get me to Milwaukee? We'll tell Jim and Mary that we're going to Minneapolis. Got it!"

"Okay. I can do that. I got you into this mess anyway."

"Aw, it wasn't your fault, man."

"I'm so pissed at those assholes. I trusted Gary, he's cool, but those other guys ... jeez."

"Anyway, all right, let's go back inside and tell Jim and Mary."

Jeff spoke. "Listen, I'm taking Mark out of here right now. We're going to Minneapolis. If the pigs show up just tell them the truth. That your friend Jeff brought this guy over who was having a hard time, whatever, and you put him to work on the house etc. I don't care what you say because you don't know anyway. Blame it on me, I don't care. I can take care of that shit."

I packed my meager possessions. We gathered in the kitchen.

"I can't thank you guys enough. Thanks for everything. The house sure looks good."

We embraced. Mary was crying.

"I love you guys," I said. I meant that. I did love them. A complete unknown coming into their lives. They shared. They gave. They were what Merton always talks about. They were the real deal.

"Mike McAndrew, you are a pain in the ass."

"Yes, I am. I take that as a compliment."

"Yes, it is. You are a pain in the ass," he repeated.

Onto Milwaukee.

Chapter 19

Madison Redux

Off into the darkness we drove.

"Gary was cool but he didn't choose his posse carefully. I'm so fucking sorry, man. It's really on me. You know. I should never have included you in that shit. Fuck. I'm just angry with myself," Jeff said.

"You know what they used to say in WWII ... 'Loose lips sink ships' ... It's true, man. You gotta learn the shit, man. Like, when we just left Jim and Mary's ... we said we we're going to the Cities ... see what I mean. Mark taught me that. It's the little details, man. You gotta think and you gotta think ahead. It's spy shit for sure but it makes sense. Now, if the pigs show up in ten minutes they're going to look for us traveling to Minneapolis and I'll tell you right now I ain't gonna be in Milwaukee long. Get my drift," I was rambling.

"As my attorney, or future attorney, they called my name out of order and they never gave me a CO hearing. Just remember that. Fuck. I liked those people, please tell them that. Promise?"

"Who ... Jim and Mary?" Jeff asked.

"Yeah."

"Those fuckers are never going to catch me. I'm going to be the biggest thorn in J. Edgar's ass of all time. That's my goal."

I was ranting. I knew that. Jeff just let me riff.

"Aw shit. I didn't want to leave there, man. Anyway, I'm calming down now. Have you talked to Mark? Oh, yeah you said you had. What did he say?"

"Just to get you out of there and to give you some money. Oh, there was one thing. I didn't know what it meant. He said he wanted you to see the Smith Brothers."

That meant Madison. And Oliver. I was considering heading back west or even east but not Madison. I would have Jeff drop me off in Milwaukee by Marquette and then catch a bus to Madison. Too risky to hitch. The bus would be okay.

As long as I had a plan my mind settled down.

Maybe I'd run into Susan. Wouldn't that be the cat's meow.

Across the Wisconsin night. Little towns with their little stories. People sleeping this night away.

"Hey, man, Thanks for getting me out though. You're a good friend!"

"T'was nothing."

"So, what's going to happen to those guys, especially Gary?"

"Not sure at this point. Most probably they will get 7 to 10 years, with suspended sentences. Probably end up with five years."

"Fuck. That's a long time."

"Sure is. The worst part is that they will most likely do their time at Stillwater."

Stillwater was where the murderers and psychopaths went.

"Cripes, that's awful. For destroying pieces of paper."

"Yup," Jeff agreed.

"And in Texas you get life for one joint."

"Justice my ass."

We were an hour out of Milwaukee. Jeff pulled into a service station to fill up. We both needed to pee. I bought some coffee and a couple packs of smokes. I paid for the gas too. Least I could do.

"No, man, I got it. I'm fat. And here's another twenty for the drive back."

"You sure?"

"Yeah, yeah, yeah. Shut the fuck up and drive," I laughed.

I liked Milwaukee. A bar on every corner. Beer came out of the faucets in your house. I had considered going to Marquette and was accepted way back when but it just didn't work out. My cousin Rob was here as well as two other guys from my high school. No chance of running into them.

Jeff dropped me off on campus. It was early morning. Not much activity. I remembered where I was and would walk the distance down town to the bus terminal.

Jeff and I embraced. Don't know when I'll see him again.

I was in luck. A bus left for Madison in two hours. I grabbed a newspaper and read it. Did the crossword puzzle and got on the bus. It was nearly full but I found a seat on the last seat by the bathroom. My favorite.
Got in a conversation with a student from Madison. Made up some bullshit story about working for my uncle for the summer and getting back to school at Stout State. Wanted to see some pals in Madison first. All bullshit.

It isn't a long ride to Madison from Milwaukee. Arrived mid-day. Figured I'd walk to the Student Union. Might find John and those guys. If they were still in town. They may be working at the Cannery.

No luck. I walked to a pay phone and called Oliver's number. He actually answered the phone.

"Oliver? It's Mark. Remember me?"

After a pause, "Yeah, hey, man. Haven't seen you since I smoked a joint with Muskie."

"That's right."

"Where are you?" he asked.
"At the Rathskeller."
"I'll be right there."
"Man, you are one crazy fucker. I saw your photo in *Time* and *Newsweek* and shit. That was incredible. You got balls, man. I'll say that for you."
"My mom almost died. All of her friends, you know. But that's been forgotten. It looks like fucking Nixon is going to win. McGovern picked the wrong guy and now he wants Sargent Shriver to run as VP. It's a real mess. But, hey, where are you staying?"
"Just blew in."
"Stay with me and Emily. No sweat."
He continued. "A bunch of us were going to go down to Miami for the Republican Convention but it fell through. No money."
As we walked Oliver became more and more agitated by the current state of events.
"That fucking Nixon is going to win in a landslide. Mark my words. Have you seen this Watergate business? There's something to it. I tell you. That fucking prick and his 'dirty tricks.' Did you hear that the so- called shit about Muskie and his wife was bullshit. Yeah. I'm telling you Nixon has to be stopped but outside of shooting the fucker there's no way to stop him. And I ain't goin' there, man."
The election was just two months away.
"Mark!"
"Hi, Emily. Great to see you again."
"Are you hungry?"
"No, I'm fine. Thanks though. You look good. This guy been treating you okay?"
"Oh yeah. You look good too."
"Oh Thanks. I worked on a farm all summer. Painting mostly but hard work."
It was getting to the point that it was becoming impractical not to tell some people some things. We walked into the living room and Oliver fired up a bowl. I told them about the fiasco in Wabasha. They had heard about it, of course, but didn't know the gory details until I told them.
And I told them more about Mark from Berkeley.
"So, you see," I said when I had finished, "I'm hot right now and can't be seen much. But, here's the rub, Mark wants me to check out the Smith Brothers. Don't know why. You guys have to swear to secrecy. You can't tell another living soul. I felt that I could trust you and also felt compelled to tell you and honestly, I need your help."
"How can we help."
"Glad you asked," I smiled, "first thing is to keep quiet about what

I just told you and secondly, help me with a safe place to hide out for awhile."

"Well, you can stay here for as long as you want ..."

"Thank you. That means a lot to me. I do have money so I wouldn't be a burden in that way and I can always disappear when you guys need privacy."

"Yeah, I was thinking ... we know lots of people who we trust ... maybe we could find other places too. You know, just in case," Oliver added.

"Hey, I was just curious. Did you ever get hassled by the cops for that Muskie thing?"

"No, can you believe it. I think they thought it was funny too. You know, this town has changed. We have a new mayor and City Council and they passed an ordinance that the city cops have to live inside the city limits and they can't recruit southern hillbillies anymore. The cops have seemed nicer."

"Wow, really. You know Berkeley did that too!"

"Who's the new mayor by the way?" I inquired.

"Paul Soglin. Remember him? He was very active in student's rights."

"Yes, I do. You're in good hands."

"Man, what a little organization can do, huh? I've always felt that the real power starts at the local level," I added.

They were both attending classes. Emily had a part time job in a restaurant as a cook and Oliver helped his mom out with the family business. His dad had passed away and left the flower shop to her. Oliver helped with deliveries and making flower arrangements. That explained the numerous bouquets around the apartment.

"Mark, I have just the job for you. You can be our butler. We'll call you James if you prefer. But, seriously, we could use some help around here just cleaning up and stuff. You don't have to ... but ..."

"Hey, great idea. Thanks Emily. Yeah, sure, I'll do that. You can call me James. I don't care."

We all laughed. Oliver refilled the bowl.

The apartment was small by most standards but there was a large walk in-closet off the living room. That would be my room.

I slept in there and moved some stuff around. I slept on the floor for now. It was fine with me.

I woke the next morning. Oliver was already gone and Emily about to leave. I smoked a cig and drank a cup, took a shower and had a lick from the shrinking crystal. I still had several whites left.

I started in the kitchen I washed every dish and dried them and put them away. I scoured the sink and cleaned out the oven. I used my own judgment when I cleaned the fridge. Anything suspicious I threw away. I mopped the floor three times before the water was clear. I scrubbed the walls and ceilings. I had told Emily before she left that I was going to 'clean the kitchen.' I don't think she had any idea how extensively of a job I would do.

Next the bathroom. This would be a challenge as well. The shower stall had never been cleaned. Rust spots and mold everywhere. Luckily, they had plenty of comet and SOS pads. I scrubbed and scrubbed until eventually the stains surrendered. I also cleaned the walls and floor. Again, the floor took three changes of soapy water before it was clean.

Oliver came home.

"Jesus H. looks great! Thanks. Emily is going to love this."

"I had to throw away some of the food in the fridge because it was old and green shit was growing on it."

"No problem. More room for beer."

"How was work?"

"Busy. I have to make a delivery to the hospital every day and that takes time. And the store is always busy. It's good, though. We're making a living."

"Hey, listen," he went on, "I'm doing some volunteer work for the McGovern Campaign. I was wondering if you wanted to come along?"

"You know, I think not. I should just hang low for a bit."

"Yeah, maybe that's best. I won't be long anyway. They're so disorganized that half the time nobody knows what to do. The people are pretty discouraged with the whole thing anyway. Most people have quit. Aw, you know what. I'm not going either. It's just a bummer, anyway. Tell you what, I'll go out and grab some beers and we'll just stay home tonight, how's that sound?"

"Fine with me."

Oliver left the room and walked into the bathroom.

"Holy shit!" I heard him shout as he discovered the clean bathroom too.

"You must have worked all day."

"I did."

Emily came home. She was bushed. She had a bag full of left over food from the restaurant. She carried the food into the kitchen. I looked at Oliver and winked. It only took a few seconds.

"Oh my God! Look at this kitchen!"

I heard her open the fridge and another joyous outburst.

"Wait 'til she sees the oven," I chortled.

Emily returned from the kitchen. Very excited and gave me a big hug.

"Thank you so much, Mark. You must have worked all day."

"I did."

Then she kissed Oliver. They were a loving couple and he worshipped the ground she walked on. It was a very comfortable relationship. This is how 'normal people' live. I thought. I wanted to be a 'normal person' too.

They had a small black and white TV and we watched the *CBS News*. The country seemed to be for ending the war now. Nixon was projecting himself like a 'peace candidate.' This guy has no scruples. The Watergate thing was gaining momentum. McGovern spoke on TV about forming a commission again. But it was too late. With the election just weeks away Oliver and I both thought that Nixon would win and win big. McGovern just wasn't 'Presidential.'

Over the next several weeks I managed to clean the rest of the apartment as well as maintaining it. I only went out at night and then only to walk around the block but I did manage to finally meet the notorious Smith Brothers, again, and made a visit to their ramshackle house. Oliver took me over there a couple of times. It was a party house. A complete disaster. Garbage and broken furniture. Dozens of people hanging out smoking dope and drinking. They described themselves as 'Zippies.' A take off from Hippies and Yippies, I guess. They said they were into guerrilla theater staging weird events and acting out funny and embarrassing actions mocking the establishment. Oliver's stunt was an example of that. They liked to get their group and dress up as mimes and prance around in front of the National Guard. Oliver showed me the basement. It smelled like gasoline. I saw dozens of empty wine bottles. Were those Molotov cocktails? And Oliver showed me a stash of guns and ammo and a work table with boxes and wires. Were those bombs?

These guys, the Smiths, struck me as two guys who were out to screw as many women as they could by impressing them how 'radical' they were. They disgusted me. They had a big poster of Che in the living room as if that proved their point.

And besides their lack of sincerity and all that. The whole fucking world knew they had this shit!

And their dad was some high powered Wall Street attorney who was bankrolling these two idiots while innocents died in Vietnam.

These guys were just two spoiled rich kids who thought that the revolution was a fucking fashion show!

I advised Oliver to keep his distance.

I had to tell Mark. For fuck's sake, even Mark knew about these two, 2,000 miles away!

Oliver and I left the house in a pot daze. We could hear the music blaring a block away.

"Oliver, stay away from those two. They're trouble. They might as well put a sign up in front saying 'Come arrest us!' "

"I know. But I like 'em. You met Dana right."

"Yeah."

"Well, he's pretty heavy. He's the guy who wants to create a new Party called the 'Zippies.' "

"Oh, that's the guy. You know, this is weird, but he picked me up hitch hiking last time I was in town. And I remembered him asking me what I thought of the term 'Yippie.' And I thought that was nice. Then he asked me about the term 'Zippies' and I asked him if he was running out of letters. I don't think he remembered me though. Seriously, man, are they planning to blow something up? Fucks sake. The whole town knows about it!"

Oliver just shrugged his shoulders and we walked back to his place.

I planned to call Mark ASAP.

The next day was like the last day was like this day. I was bored hanging around the apartment. It was cold out. I wore a stocking hat and I borrowed a muffler which partially covered my face. I was being paranoid, I knew, but it made me feel safer. Besides, it was cold. In the twenties. Another Wisconsin winter.

I walked to the Union and called Mark. Left the call back number and waited. Just hoped no one would use the pay phone so I sat there with my finger on the switch and the phone to my ear, like I was talking to someone. Eventually Mark called. I told everything about the Smiths. "They're fucking crazy, man. Drugs everywhere and gasoline in the basement. I'm not getting near them."

I told Mark that I wanted to either come back out there or head east. I didn't want to shiver for the next 4 months. He told me to hang tight. To call him in two weeks. He was working on something.

I got back home and Oliver wanted to fire his gun. He said he was out of practice. We drove out to his firing range. By now the sun had come out and it had warmed some. He set up some bottles and cans. He didn't miss one. I tried and if I aimed very carefully and let my breath out and squeezed the trigger ... I still missed. He had a new gun. A .25mm pistol. It was smaller. We fired that for the first time. The recoil wasn't too bad. I tried and had better luck. Oliver probably fired 50 rounds or so. He should be in the Olympics I told him.

"Yeah. It's the only thing I do well."

The Elections were tomorrow and we planned to spend the night in front of the TV. I was excited. We both felt Nixon was the one, though. I figured the country got what it deserved!

Oliver and Emily went out to a movie. I wanted some privacy. I fell asleep reading.

Woke the next morning to an empty apartment. I hadn't heard them come in I was so tired. I cleaned the place up and took a nice shower. It was clear and chilly outside. I took a long walk around Madison remembering my times with Carol. I didn't want to run into John and those guys. I wanted my presence here kept to a minimum. I chanced a walk down State Street passing the store I held up. I can't believe I did that! I ducked into a bookstore and got lost in the store. I wanted to buy about twenty books but alas alack. Going back outside walking with the herding crowd of students. Maybe when this bullshit was over I could go back to school. I just wanted to fit in instead of always feeling like an outsider.

Luckily, I didn't see anyone I recognized. It was mid-afternoon. I took a nap.

I awoke when I heard Oliver come home. He had a case of beer under his arm. I helped him with several bags of groceries. Emily soon followed. We ate some burgers.

Oliver turned on the TV. The *CBS Election Coverage* was just beginning. Walter sat in a white shirt with a big board of numbers behind him. The voting booths back east were just closing so they had very few numbers. We three sat there watching hoping against hope. Oliver rolled a joint.

Within an hour the slaughter had begun. State by state went to Nixon. It looked like D.C. might go for McGovern, but that was it. Apparently, Americans didn't want to change leaders in the middle of a war. It was horrible to watch.

By 8 o'clock *CBS* called it. The voting booths were still open in the west. Why bother even voting.

There was nothing else on TV. All the networks were covering the debacle. We turned the volume off and listened to music.

Oliver said he wanted to go over to the Smiths. He asked me if I wanted to come along.

"No way," I said. It was a fateful decision.

Emily and I sat there for awhile staring at the screen. It wasn't going to get any better.

"I wish he wouldn't hang out with those two. Of all of Oliver's friends those are the two I don't like. They're creepy, you know," she said.

"I don't like them either. I'm going to crash early. Good night Emily."

I crawled into my closet and kept the door ajar for some heat, turned on a light and read. I sighed as I realized four more years of that prick.

I heard Emily in the kitchen the next morning. She was really upset.

She had been on the phone and she was crying. Through her sobs I managed to get her story out. Oliver hadn't returned last night. He was in jail. He had shot three policemen! The Smith Brothers had tried to fire bomb an insurance company building. It made no sense to me at all. I had to think fast. I couldn't stay here. I was amazed the cops hadn't been here already. I grabbed my shit, gave Emily a hug and ran out the door.

What the fuck was going on? The paper didn't come out until late in the afternoon. I decided to walk to the Union. Maybe somebody over there would know. Wish I had a radio.

Rumors were flying around that there had been a shoot out with the cops. Was Oliver okay? What did the Smith Brothers have to do with this? All I could do was wait. I had all my gear in my ruck sack. Now, I was looking for John or Terry or Curtis. I knew I couldn't return to the apartment, the cops would be all over that place. Fuck!

I just blended in with the student body. But, I figured they wouldn't be looking for me, I just needed a place to crash.

I sat way in the corner of the room so I could see the comings and goings. There was a TV near me mounted on the wall. There was a news flash update on the Madison station. The reporter laid out what they think happened. The cops had followed the Smith Brothers to an insurance company building and had witnessed them setting up what looked like explosive devises outside the building and then had hurled Molotov cocktails through some windows setting fires. The cops arrested them immediately and the fire department put out the fires. Three plainclothes officers raided the Smith Brother's house and they were fired upon and shot. Their injuries were unknown at this time. More cops showed up and a suspect surrendered. That was Oliver. They showed the suspects mug shots on TV. There was a third suspect, a woman, who was with the Smiths. Oliver's face was swollen and he had a black eye. He wasn't wearing his glasses. He looked terrible. The other three had grins on their faces. It was surreal. The Union got very quiet during the short news flash.

My prints were all over that gun!

I had to think. I scanned the room for John or Terry or Curtis. I saw a couple of familiar faces but couldn't place them.

If they were looking for me, let's say, they would be checking the bus station and the airport plus looking for hitch hikers etc. If I just stayed put and caused no attention maybe I could get out of this. I knew I couldn't go back to Emily's. Even if she talked she couldn't tell them much except what I looked like. I grabbed my razor out of my ruck sack and went into the bathroom and shaved off my mustache. I removed my glasses. Even though it was chilly outside I removed my coat. I removed the tie from my pony tail and let my hair down. I would have to find another coat and soon. I returned to my seat and waited.

I saw John walk in. I got his attention and called him over. He had heard the news. He knew Oliver. Everybody did.

After our greeting we sat down at my table.

I spoke first. "Did you hear about Oliver and the Smiths?"

"Yeah, sure did. What the fuck happened? Oliver wouldn't shoot anyone. Would he?"

"I don't think so. No, he wouldn't do anything like that unless he had to. I don't know. I've been in town for a short time and I was staying with him and Emily. A couple of days ago Oliver and I did some target practice with his new gun. You knew he was a sharpshooter. Right? He used to compete and stuff. Anyway. My prints are all over that gun and man, I'm in enough shit as it is. What I'm saying is can I crash with you guys until things cool down?"

"Of course. You handled the gun?"

"Yeah. We were shooting at bottles and cans. Harmless. You should see him shoot, he doesn't miss and he can quick draw like in cowboy movies. I couldn't hit the side of a barn. Like I said, he's a sharpshooter. I saw on TV just now that the cops went back to the Smith's apartment and that's when Oliver allegedly shot them. And the crazy Smiths got busted in the act of trying to burn some insurance company building. Fuck, I told Oliver to stay away from those idiots. Half the town knew about them and their dope and bombs and shit. They are so fucking uncool. Uh, fuck. Can you get me outta here?"

"Yup. I just got back from class and wanted a beer. You want one?"

"Yeah. Make it a double," I laughed.

We sipped our beers and finally walked out. John's car was two blocks away. I was very cold without my coat. We drove to his house.

"Did you guys work at the cannery this summer?"

"Yeah, we worked in the warehouse again. We missed you, man. Made some money. Hard work though."

"How 'bout you. What did you do this summer?" he asked.

"A little of this and a little of that."

"I can dig it."

Their house looked the same. In a state of constant disarray but comfy. Terry and Curtis had their rooms in the back of the house and John's was in front. I guess I could sleep in the living room. I'd known these guys for a couple of years by now and they knew about the draft business but not much else. They had been trusted by me and I felt it was time to tell them more. I don't know, I still waffled on that but I was leaning towards telling them.

John grabbed a couple of beers and we sat in the living room. The other guys were in class. We turned the TV on. Day time soaps were on. We'd have to wait a few hours to catch the news. Oh yeah, Nixon won in a landslide. Seemed trivial at the moment.

Terry and Curtis returned.

"Mark!"

We all hugged and the four of discussed Oliver and the Smiths and even Nixon.

A joint soon found itself being passed around and several more beers appeared.

"Guys, I have to tell you something."

I told them about the draft, which they already knew, and I lightly touched on the 'mailman' stuff and the latest troubles in the Cities. They didn't really look surprised but they were intrigued.

When I had finished I told them they just couldn't tell anyone because it could not only jeopardize me but themselves and others as well. They understood.

"So, can I crash here for awhile?"

"Fuck yes!" in unison.

The news came on. First the *CBS News*. All about the election results. It was a landslide. I don't even think McGovern's own mom voted for him.

Then the local news. After several annoying ads ... the report started. It led off with the Smiths and Oliver. It was pretty much the same story from this noon except that they mentioned that the three cops had all been shot in their right shoulders.

"I told you he was a sharpshooter. If he'd wanted to kill them they all would have been shot right between the eyes."

All were being held. A bond hearing would be forthcoming. The cops had found weapons, drugs, and bomb making materials in the house. I coulda' told you that.

I told the guys that I had been over there a few nights ago and the setting.

"You know. The cops were watching the place and they probably followed those idiots whenever they left the house. I told Oliver to stay away from them, but ..."

Terry chimed in, "I knew about those guys, too. They used to brag about how many chicks they balled and how they had the best dope. The whole town knew about them, you're right."

We spent the evening dropping out, turning on, and tuning out or however that went. I didn't want to think about anything. They had every album in the world. I had to hear *Anthem of the Sun* one more time.

Woke up on the living room floor. Had the nightmare again last night or just now. I don't know. I was in a sweat.

Somebody was up. I heard the toilet flush. I opened my eyes to a beer bottle full of cigarette butts. My mouth felt dry like concrete. I waited and then bolted to the bathroom to pee. Looked round and found a half cig and lit it.

"Morning."

"Ugh," I said.

It was John. He mercifully made some coffee and tossed me a whole cig. He already had the morning Milwaukee paper in his hands. The top half of the front page was about the election and the bottom half about Oliver and the Smiths. Couldn't wait to read it.

John summarized aloud. "Apparently the plainclothes men were wearing long haired wigs to look like hippies and Oliver stated that he thought they were breaking in to steal from the house. He claims he didn't know anything about the Smiths and their bombing plot. Oliver is quoted as saying that all he saw were three figures in the dark and when he said something to them they broke the door down and that's when he fired. And like it said on TV last night each guy was shot in the right shoulder. Here you read it. It goes on about the Smiths too."

The first thing I saw was a big picture of Oliver with a badly swollen face, a black eye, and no glasses. They must have beat the shit out of him. I carefully read the article. No mention of any other suspects but the police were inspecting the house and I'm sure asking a lot of questions to the neighbors and Emily and Oliver's mom.

"You know, I thought that when the police knocked on your door and you asked 'Who is it?,' that they had to answer, 'The police'. You know, if somebody comes barging into your home it's legal to shoot. Isn't it?"

"Yeah, I guess."

"Maybe that's what happened."

"It says here that all three are expected to recover from their injuries. Like I said last night, Oliver could have killed them if he had wanted to. But he's basically fucked. Shooting cops is hard core. There is supposed to be a bail and bond hearing next week. I wonder if they'll let him out. I don't care about the Smiths. Their daddy will bail them out anyway. And the girl who was driving. Do you know her?"

"No, I don't."

I waited a week around the house mostly but I did make a couple of calls; one to Mark to fill him in and the other to Jeff. Mark didn't seem surprised that much. Of course he had heard about it. It was in all the papers. He asked me, for once, what I wanted to do. I said I wanted to hang tight until the hearing and if Oliver was released to see if he wanted to go to Canada. I called Jeff and asked how things were there. He mentioned to me that trouble just seemed to follow me and I agreed. I asked him if he knew anybody that could get my friend to Canada and he said he did. He also mentioned that they weren't really too interested in me anymore because they couldn't prove anything and that I wasn't there anyway. That was a relief.

I spent the next few days cleaning up their house. The kitchen was pretty gross. Stacks of uncleaned dirty dishes and garbage. But these guys were just lovable slobs. I didn't mind in the least. Gave me something to do.

Finally. The day of the hearing. Oliver's mom had somehow managed to hire Bill Kunstler himself as Oliver's attorney. Kunstler got Oliver released on bail as were the Smiths and the other woman.

I had to get a hold of Oliver. Through a friend of a friend kinda deal I arranged for Oliver to call me. I was at a pay phone in the Union. I waited and waited. Again holding the receiver to my ear with my finger on the switch. Finally it rang.

"Mark?"

"Oliver?"

"How are you?" he asked like it was just another day.

"Are you on a pay phone?"

"Yeah," he said.

"Okay. Here's the deal. I can get you to Canada."

"Can't. My mom put her house up for bail. That's how I got out."

"So, you're going to fight this?" I asked incredulously.

"Yeah. They never said they were cops and Bill thinks he can get it reduced to like a self-defense thing. Maybe only serve a couple of years."

"Yeah, but ..."

He cut me off.

"My mom thinks you're FBI and that I shouldn't talk to you."

And he hung up.

I sat there looking at the phone. That statement hit me like a brick. My feelings were hurt. I was in disbelief. He didn't really just say that? How could this be? Tears welled up in my eyes as it sank in. No, no. How can you deny an accusation like that? You can't. What could I say. I wanted to call him back but had no idea of what number to call. Nobody had ever accused me of that. I hated the FBI. Everybody knew that. I felt sick to my stomach. I thought I might throw up. I tasted bile in the back of my throat. I was completely deflated. I wanted to give up. So this is how it ends, I thought. Like a scolded puppy I walked back to John's house. I had to think.

This had to be one of the lowest moments of my life. I contemplated killing myself. That'll show 'em. I didn't have the guts. I was a chicken shit wanna be. I wasn't worth spitting on.

I got back to John's and took some more speed. That always perked me up and made me feel positive. I'd been kicked in the balls and was down for the count. Fuck this! Fuck this shit. It's all shit. The whole fucking anti-war this and that. Let the crazy fuckers go on killing themselves. See if I care! Try to do good and help someone and I get kicked in the teeth. FBI informant. Kiss my fucking ass! AAAAAH!

Had to think.

I counted my money. I had $500. A fortune. I could go anywhere in the US. I thought of San Francisco. I know, I'll call Brian. I walked back to the Union and called Brian collect. He answered after two rings.

"Brian, it's Mark."

"Man, you won't believe this but Mark got busted yesterday. They found like 40 pounds of weed in his house."

"What? The guy wouldn't even let you smoke a cigarette in his house."

"I know. It's really fucked up out here. The fucking pigs are every-where. Don't come out here. I gotta go."

Could this day get any worse. Mark busted too. He didn't do drugs at all. I still remember his lectures on not doing drugs. Then, for a second, I thought maybe that's how he got his money. I don't know. I didn't know what to believe anymore.

I walked back to John's. They were all home. I told them I was leaving tomorrow. I had no idea where to.

"You look down Mark. Whats up?" Terry asked.

"It shows, huh. Yeah, rough day. Hey, listen, I'm leaving tomorrow for the West Coast. So let's party tonight!"

Chapter 20

Where to Next

Last night was a blast. I didn't really get that fucked up. Those guys were very supportive listening to my babbling. I couldn't have better friends.

I said my good byes and hugged each of them and thanked them for everything.

When I walked out the door I honestly didn't know where I was going. Mark in jail and Oliver in jail. I was determined not be next. I walked to the greyhound station in Madison, Wisconsin and looked up at the board of departures. There was a bus leaving for Chicago in less than an hour. Why not? I'll go to Chicago. Maybe I can crash with Paul.

I arrived downtown amidst the rush of Chicago. It had a good energy to it.

I called Paul from a pay phone. He seemed glad to hear my voice. I asked if I could crash there for a few days and he said sure.

"Did you hear about Mark?" he asked.

So he knew too. My paranoid mind wondered if the FEDS had put the network together yet. Fuck it, I'll take my chances.

Paul was the same. Generous and upbeat. We talked about Mark and we both wondered whether or not he had been 'set up' or was in fact deal-ing. We both wanted to believe the former that the cops had planted the pot in his place and set him up.

Paul said I was welcome to stay as long as I wanted but I felt that a few days would be long enough. Paul knew little about me so I filled him in. I told him about Oliver and the Smith Brothers. He had heard, of course, and said it was probably wise to leave Madison.

"Come on, let's get some food in you. You skinny son of a bitch."

He was right. I was hardly eating. Running on speed and adrenaline. We walked to a neighborhood restaurant and had burgers. I really liked the North Side.

"I don't know, Paul. I can't do this much longer. With Mark gone I don't know where to turn. I just may go back to California where it's warm and try to start a new life or something. Four more years of Nixon. I'm at the end of my rope. Besides, what am I going to do about money?"

"Yeah, see what you mean."

The subject changed to how this country had changed in the last couple of years. I told him about the Haight-Asbury days when the Flower Children arrived and how it had turned into a dangerous area with drug dealers and homeless people. About how you could just stick your thumb out and someone would give you a ride. I told him of one harrowing tale about a ride I got once in Indiana from some guy in a Camaro. "It was a really fast car and the guy didn't seem right. You know, kinda edgy, anyway he picks me up and the first words out of his mouth were that some 'niggers' were after him, so he shows me his gun, yeah, a great big pistol, a .45 or something, and tells me if I try any shit he's going to blow me away. I was near South Bend. You know, by Notre Dame. So I told him to drop me off there. And he did. I was on my way east. I decided to drop by the University to see my buddy, Jim. That was the craziest ride I ever got." I then told him of the gentle soul who picked me up in Utah and gave me a ride all the way to San Francisco.

"The days of hitching are over for me."

And we talked about the SDS Weathermen and their exploits. Rudd and the rest had gone underground. I admired their courage but not their actions. It just turned people off. We talked about RFK and JFK and Martin Luther King and Fred Hampton.

"Seems if you're a man of peace that they just put a bullet in your head," I said.

And we talked about the old days. The '68 Democratic Convention. And the Days of Rage. What did it all mean? Where did it get us? The fucking war still rages on. Every day more and more Americans and Vietnamese killed in this senseless slaughter. And here we sit in a Chicago restaurant sipping a beer.

What does it all mean?

We talked about pollution and how the water and air were poisoned. We talked about women who were still second-class citizens. We talked about the blacks who were third-class citizens. We talked about over population. We talked.

We walked back to Paul's. It was cold. Christmas was just around the corner. How I longed for those early days walking to Grandma's and counting the presents as they multiplied under her tree.

I slept in a bed for the first time in weeks. I never wanted to wake up again.

Paul was going home for Christmas. He said I could have the place for two weeks. Seemed like a good idea. He'd tell the neighbors I was just 'house sitting.' I liked this part of town. Mostly students and young people. Small neighborhood taverns. I agreed to stay here. At least until he returned. Besides, Paul had tons of books and a great record collection. I would be warm and safe. I had money for food. And he had a TV. I could watch all the Bull's games.

Paul was done with this semester so he planned to leave in two days. He was flying back to Connecticut to be with his family.

Paul handed me $200. "Dude, I can't take this," I protested, "Yes you can. Listen, my parents are rich. I'll get some money at Christmas anyway. You need it more than me. Buy some food and beer and a warm coat or something. My parents pay for everything and they're rich Liberals. If they knew you they'd give it to you personally. Don't worry about it. I wish I had more."

Paul insisted on going shopping and we could barely manage all the bags of groceries. Had enough beer for a frat party.

Paul told the apartment Super that I was staying there watching the place. He was cool. No problem there. He showed me where the garbage went and the laundry room. He gave me an extra set of keys and said if I had any problems to let him know. Wow! Fell into a bucket of shit and came out smelling like a rose!

Paul and I had a 'heart to heart' talk about Mark. He said that he'd met him at a party several years ago just before the Democratic Convention. They had spent a couple of days together and Mark had said at the time that he needed a Chicago connection. Mark had said that he was setting up an 'Underground Network' to pass information and letters and money for people who couldn't use conventional ways and means. Paul went on explaining how Mark had said that there might be people 'like you, Mark,' who would pass through from time to time and that they may just need a place to crash and some food and shelter. He said that this 'network' would extend over the entire country. He wanted to protect and hide as he called it, 'people of conscience' from prison because we had to end the war, and discrimination, and racism.

"So, he gave me a little test. You know, to see if I could be trusted. He gave me a package that was wrapped up but looked like a huge wad of money and he wanted me to fly to New York and give it to a guy at the airport and then fly right back. So, I did that. I guess I passed," he went on.

"He did the same thing to me!"

"No shit."

"Yup. Have you ever had another person, you know, like me, a messenger, or what have you, stay with you?" I asked.

"No. No I haven't. You're the only one."

"There must be other people. Has to be. Maybe not. Who knows. But this shit about him being busted with all this pot in his house ... what is that all about," I asked.

"I just don't know. I can't believe it, you know, after the lectures about dope and shit. I really don't know what to think."

"Maybe that's how he got his money, I mean, the guy always was slipping me $200. But then ... fuck, I don't know."

"Or maybe he just had money ..."

"This is what worries me, Paul, the FEDS are going to beat it out of him. You know, all the people like us in the network. They might find us out. You know. They have ways, you know, truth serum and brass knuckles really work."

"I don't want to think about that right now. Let's get high."

"Okie dokey."

Paul was up when I got up. I reheated some coffee. I looked outside and it was snowing. Not hard. At least I was warm. The apartment building was an old brick building. It was quiet. Didn't hear the neighbors.

"Had to run a couple of errands. Sleep okay?"

"My flight leaves at 10 so we should have an early night. If the phone rings answer it. Take a message. Oh yeah, and here's the key for the mail. Just leave it on the table. Thought we'd just hang out and go out and get pizza."

"Sounds great! Don't worry about this place. I'll take care of it. Leave me the number for your parents in case I have to call."

"Oh yeah."

I couldn't think of anything else. What luck, I thought. A place to stay for two more weeks. I'd make myself a Christmas dinner and watch a ton of football games.

Paul left the next morning and I had the place to my own. I found a copy of Henry Miller's *Tropic of Cancer* and was blown away by his descriptions of the streets of Paris. I wanted to go there. When I finished that I found a copy of William Blake's *Collected Poems* and was stunned by his imagery. They seemed contemporary. I reread Kerouac's *Satori in Paris* and *Mexico City Blues* and more. As the winter approached and cold windy Chicago became more foreboding, I was thoroughly entertained by Paul's magnificent library. The days passed into nights and into tomorrows. I was well fed and warm and kept the place neat. I only ventured out a few times to fetch a beer. I did watch a few games but they became background noise as I climbed into his books. I could only think that my English Literature major at St. Mary's had missed the mark. These were the authors I wanted to read. The two weeks passed by in a blur. The phone rang a few times and I took messages. Paul only called once to wish me a Merry Christmas and a Happy New Year. I went out New Year's Eve looking for fun but never made it to midnight. Too many drunks.

Chapter 21

1973

Paul returned this first week of 1973. He said he had a great time but was glad to be back home. He had a ton of new clothes and a pocket full of money from his folks.

He gave me a new coat and some pants and shirts. We were almost the same size so everything fit. I threw my holey jeans out and wore a new pair of Levi's.

"How's things here?" Paul asked.

"Well, I called Jeff and got caught up. Those guys from the Draft Board break-in are all out on bail and awaiting trial. Doesn't look too promising for them. I feel bad for my friend Gary. Oh yeah, and an old friend of mine, named Joe, I travelled to California with him a million years ago, well, he resisted the draft after I did but turned himself in and is now serving a five year sentence in Joliet Prison. That's pretty fucked up because that prison is for killers and shit. Jeff said the scene in Minneapolis is really bad. No more word on Mark. I called Brian but all he knew was that he was still in jail."

"I read some of your books. You have a great selection. I put your mail over there and here are some phone messages. Didn't see any other tenant, not even once. I think everybody left. Even the laundry room was empty."

"I read mostly and half watched a couple of football games. That's about it, I guess."

"How was your Christmas, Paul?"

"Oh just great. The whole family was there. My older brother and his wife and two kids and my sister. My mom goes nuts over Christmas. The biggest tree you ever saw and the whole house fixed up with lights all over the front and in the yard. It was nice. Dad's business is doing well so he gave each of us kids $2,000, can you believe it! Plus all the presents. We ate like gods. I feel a little guilty because of the way the world is, you know, people suffering and stuff, but get it while you can. So, here's your present."

He gave me another $200!

"Oh, Paul, I can't, man. I'm okay. Jesus, I didn't get you anything. I didn't even think of it."

"Write me a poem, then."

So I did. I wrote:

Going to War

> *used to worry*
> *about*
> *going to war*
>
> *now, I worry*
> *about*
> *war coming to me*

"Wow. Did you just make that up?"

"No, I wrote that some time back. Seems appropriate for what's been going on lately."

"Sure does. Thank you."

I'd had so much time and so much to think about. With all my friends in jail or tied up with the legal system, I felt useless. No more packages to deliver, no income, no more guys to take over the border etc. I was infertile. Unproductive. Sterile. I knew I had nothing left to prove. I'd passed that point long ago. Now I needed meaning again. Something to work for. The war was indeed winding down but there were still injustices to right. But, what could I do. The weather outside matched my disposition, dark and gloomy. Paul had done more than enough. People like him were the real strength behind the movement supporting us in real things like food, shelter, money, and moral support. Without them we wouldn't have lasted this long.

Paul slipped back into his routine at school. I was listless to say the least. I just had to go. Paul sensed this too, I think, and bless him for not saying that I was getting on his nerves. If the shoes had been reversed ...

"Hey, Paul. I gotta talk to you."

"'Bout what?"

"I'm going to be taking off. Maybe tomorrow. I honestly don't know where. Maybe LA. I've just gotta go, man. I'm driving you nuts ..."

"No, you're not ..."

"Then, I'm driving myself nuts. I need to get my purpose back. It looks like Mark is toast. Brian told me they're throwing the book at him. That was my main man, you know, I'm just in the way here ..."

"Mark, listen to me, you can stay here as long as you want, you know that ..."

"Paul, you've been a fucking savior, man, you really have. I's not you, I swear. It's me. It's way deep inside. Like, I can't control it. I just have to go."

With that, Paul resigned. He sighed deep and gave me a hug. I think he understood. I'm glad because I sure as hell didn't.

My last night in Chicago was special. Paul and I went to the South Side and listened to Blues. The real thing. It was beautiful being the only two white faces in the bar. Nobody paid any attention to us. We were all there for the same reason. The Blues. Chicago Style.

On the way back to Paul's I remarked, "Remember that movie *The Wild One* with Marlon Brando as the leader of a motorcycle gang and they invade this little town and a girl says to him, 'What are you rebelling against Johnny?' and he answers, 'Whaddaya got!' And that's how I feel right now. Whaddaya got. I need something right now and I just don't know what it is, you know. It's like there's just a big empty hole in front of me and I want to fill it up with something. So, whaddaya got?"

"You need to get laid."

"No, man, really. That ain't it. The music was great, you know, I escaped for awhile, but, I need something solid, man."

"I just gotta go Paul. I just gotta."

After a hardy farewell and much gratitude, I departed Paul's. It was too far to walk to the bus station downtown so I took a city bus. Chicagoans wrapped up in winter clothes looking stern and healthy. This was not a town for the meek. They pushed you around here and you had to push back. A tough town.

Where to go. The next bus was headed East for Detroit. There was also a bus headed to O'Hare. So I took it. Fate was my guide. I would follow her anywhere. I checked the departures. East or west. There was a plane headed to Logan in Boston. Why not. Bought the ticket and got on. It was just a ride anymore. Like a carnival ride. You buy a ticket. You grab a seat. You take a ride then get off.

I called Bruce. No answer. I called Allen. He picked up.

"Where are you?"

"Logan Airport."

"I'll pick you up."

He was there in a couple of hours. Luckily the roads were clear.

"Man, am I glad to see you!" I exclaimed.

"Like wise. Guess you heard about Mark, huh?"

"Yeah. What's the latest?"

"Just that they busted him with several pounds of weed. That's all I know."

"I can't believe it, you know. The guy didn't do drugs at all."

"I think he was set up myself. It was the only way they could bust him."

"I agree. Anyway, how are you?"

"Great. Got the place all fixed up for the winter. You'll like it. You know, it's weird, but I was kinda expecting you."

"Really!"

"Yeah, like a premonition or something."

"Yeah, like I left where I was this morning and just let Lady Fate take me here."

"I gotta tell ya," I continued, "I'm a little nervous about the network of people. I just hope Mark didn't write anything down. You know, names and phone numbers, shit like that. You haven't done anything wrong, except 'Aiding and Abetting' but they can't hold that up. My attorney friend told me that. Unless they catch you together it would never hold up in court. But, it's enough to make me wonder. How was you're Christmas? To change the subject."

"Just swell. Went to my folks and had a great time. Good to be back home though."

We got to Allen's place. Snow was on the ground. He had neatly shoveled a path to the front door.

"Here, grab a beer while I make a fire."

There was a slight chill in the cabin but within minutes the room was warm.

He made a couple of burgers. Really hit the spot because I hadn't eaten all day.

Allen and I chatted half the night. Talked about the election and Watergate. He had been closely following it and revealed some interesting things.

"These two journalists from the *Washington Post* have been writing some incredible stuff about the break-in and how there seems to be a cover-up by the White House. Which means Nixon. These two guys, Woodward and Bernstein, sounds like a law firm, are making some outrageous claims. This all might lead to some Senate hearings."

"Wow. Yeah, I've been following it too. But I'm totally confused. You mean that these thugs were being paid by the Republican Party? Why would they risk this.? They were so far ahead in the polls. I don't get it."

"Not only that but they think this is the same group that broke into

Ellsberg's Shrinks office."

"Really? Hadn't heard that. They don't call him 'Tricky Dick' for nothing."

"Hey, I was wondering, that package made it up to Canada okay? Right?" I went on.

"Yeah."

"I'd like to meet those guys sometime. You know that was a big one, right. I mean that package was important. Mark about shit until he was sure it made it."

"I know. Yeah, maybe we could do that. Depends on the weather. It hasn't snowed so much this year."

"I see that. You still driving the school bus?"

"Oh yeah. It's a great job."

"I can't tell you how crazy everything has been in the last few months. I'm worn out, man."

"You can take it easy here. Nobody ever comes out here unless they're lost. You can kick back."

"I've got some money to kick in too."

"Good, That'll help. Have another brew."

I slept by the fireplace. It was almost too hot. I let the fire burn down and fell asleep watching the embers vacillate.

Allen awoke early and headed out the door for his morning route. I stumbled around the kitchen and made a pot of coffee. He returned in a couple of hours. By then I had cleaned up and had a healthy fire going. The wood pile was stacked high. I carried some more wood in. I swept the place out.

"Allen, if I get in your hair just let me know."

"You won't. It's nice to have some company."

It was cold but not freezing so I went for a walk. I walked all the way back to his pond that I'd seen last summer. It was frozen solid. I wondered if Allen skated. The snow was only a few inches deep and it was pretty. The air clean and crisp.

When I got back to the cabin Allen wanted to run into town to get supplies.

"We need to get some groceries."

We made a list. I felt safe enough to go with him. He loaned me a stocking cap and some warmer boots. I looked like a lumber jack. The town looked the same except it was winter now and all the leaves had fallen.

I pushed the cart and Allen and I loaded it up with meat and potatoes and vegetables and ice cream and two cases of beer plus a carton of smokes.

"Anything else?"

"Coffee."

I darted to the aisle and grabbed a can of coffee.

We split the bill.

"That should hold us," I said.

"Allen, I appreciate you letting me stay here. I didn't know where else to go. And I'm still in a quandary about the future. I really don't know where I can go. I figure if I have enough time something will come up."

"You're welcome to stay here. It's a little tight for two guys but like I said, I enjoy the company."

"Let me know if there's any chores to be done. Be glad to help out."

"Okay. I will."

I came across a copy of *The Electric Kool-Aid Acid Test* by Tom Wolffe. A lively humorous romp about Ken Kesey and the Merry Pranksters. I discovered Hunter Thompson's *Fear and Loathing in Las Vegas* and the great *Sometimes a Great Notion* by Kesey. I loved to read. I spent many hours curled up by the fireplace catching up on current authors.

A couple of months passed. Several snow storms occurred and the temperatures constantly hovered in the teens. Allen continued working and I helped out when I could.

But, 'cabin fever' was getting me down. I'd been out of contact with everyone. The only interesting news concerned The Watergate and the unraveling tale of deceit from on high. But, I was bored silly. I talked to Allen again about meeting his friends from Canada. He finally called them and arranged a trip north. We had to wait for some clear weather. Allen said he could get a substitute for his bus driving if needed.

Chapter 22

Night of the Sun

The moment finally came. I had nowhere to go but up.

We packed up Allen's car and headed north. I was nervous as hell but Allen assured me that the Canadians would just pass us through. The timing was perfect because it was March and the schools were closed for a week because of a teacher's conference so all the kids were out any way. He wouldn't be needed for a week.

The weather was cooperating. Cold and sunny.

I had all my ID's in order. My Draft Card showed the student deferment just in case. Allen said that the trip back was different. The Americans usually wanted to see ID's for any American males under 25. We had planned to meet his friends and drive to Quebec. At first I thought we were going to Nova Scotia but Allen said they were all living in Quebec now.

We had a very long drive ahead so Allen and I brought plenty of food with us. We left on a Friday evening after Allen finished his shift. We planned on an all-nighter arriving the next afternoon.

We navigated Highway 95 and then hit 201 all the way to the Canadian border. Allen was so used to driving. It was second nature to him. My only regret was that it was night and the rugged vast land of Maine was lost to the darkness. Allen filled me in on the history of several small towns that we drove through. We kept the conversation going. I had a pit in my stomach though. But it beat sitting around the cabin waiting for spring.

We entered the town of Moose River, love that name. We were almost at the border. It was 2 a.m. There was no traffic. We came upon some flashing lights. We stopped at a gate. A man in a uniform came to the car.

"What is your business in Canada?"

Allen calmly stated, "seeing some friends in Quebec."

He flashed a flashlight into the car. He saw my rucksack. I had tucked my hair up under my stocking cap.

"How long will you be in Quebec?"

"A few days then we're coming back."

He waved us through.

Everything was in French! We were in Quebec Province. In Canada! "Parlez vous?"

"Nope."

The road signs were in English and French. Thank God for that.

We still had a few hours' drive ahead of us.

"See, I told you it was easy. We look like two nice college boys. They don't care anyway."

"I can breathe now," I exhaled.

"Oh, Mark, you worry too much."

"Yes, I do. It's a genetic thing."

It was midday when we drove into Sainte-Marie, several miles south of Quebec. This is where his friends Rene and Phillip lived. Allen made a phone call to get directions to their house. We were at a gas station and only a few blocks away.

We parked in the street. As we got out of the car I heard a voice, "Allen!"

We entered the house and I was introduced to Phillip and Rene.

"So, you're the famous Mark I've been hearing about," Phillip said.

"You must mean the other Mark."

"No, it's you the 'Mailman.' "

I felt embarrassed.

"You're the guys from Nova Scotia, right?"

"Oui. I mean yes."

"I just wanted to thank you. Everybody was kind of uptight over that one. And I don't want to know what was in it and who it was for," I laughed.

"We don't either," piped Rene.

"Is this your first time in Canada?"

"No, we used to visit friends near Windsor. I've been in Canada several times but never to this part of the country."

We unpacked our gear into the house. They had a two story house. We each had a bedroom on the ground floor. It would be nice to sleep in a real bed.

We converged to the living room.

"This is nice guys. Better than that dump in Nova Scotia," Allen stated.

"I'll say. Closer to civilization too."

"How far is it to Quebec?" I asked.

"30 miles or so. Takes about half an hour."

"I'd like to see the City."

"Oh, you will."

Allen hadn't been to Quebec either so we made plans to all drive there tomorrow. I couldn't wait.

In the meantime we decided we were hungry so we piled into Rene's car and drove to a bar. It was culture shock. Everyone spoke French. The TV had a hockey game on and everyone was screaming. As it turned out it was game one of the Stanley Cup between the Chicago Black Hawks and the Montreal Canadians. I didn't follow hockey much but it was obvious that these folks did.

We ordered rounds of beer and ate burgers. Just like in the States. You couldn't hear yourself talk so I was content to watch the show. The crowd was pulling for Montreal. Naturally.

Sainte-Marie seemed like a nice town. We left the bar and we drove around. Phillip and Rene pointed out several spots. I noticed the church. It was gorgeous.

"How old is that church?" I asked.

"It's actually a cathedral built a couple hundred years ago I think."

"It's beautiful."

"Especially at night with the lights on," cited Rene.

We got back to the house and drank beer and listened to music. These two guys were really curious about me and my escapades. I told them I couldn't talk about it much. They seemed disappointed but understood. I asked them, in turn, about the draft resisters up here. They were intimately involved in that movement and I wanted to learn everything about it.

Allen and I were tired from the drive and from being up all night. I fell into a cozy bed and slept.

We finally got going after lazing around in the morning. Phillip had made pancakes and eggs and bacon. Boy, did that hit the spot after several weeks of basically no breakfast.

We piled into Rene's car and drove to Quebec City. Entering Quebec City, crossing the St. Lawrence River, took my breath away. It seemed like going back in a time machine and entering another world. Every sign was printed in French and English but the 'official' language was French. I'd taken French in high school but remembered very little. Rene was driving and Phillip acted as our tour guide pointing out various points of interest. Speaking both the French and English names. I was agape. This was the most beautiful city I'd ever seen. I regretted leaving my camera back at the house. But, I figured there would be plenty of time for that later.

I asked them if they knew where or even if there was, an agency where the draft resisters went to get resettled. Rene drove me to the place.

"Come in. We know everybody in here," Phillip remarked.

It was basically an office in the middle of the city. There were several guys hanging out. A couple of them had their meager belongings with them.

Rene walked up to a receptionist.

"Rene! Comment allez-vous?"

Then they proceeded to rattle off their conversation in rapid French.

This agency processed American Draft Resisters. They really checked you out. They required you to complete long forms and then they checked out your record; to insure that indeed you were who you said you were and were not wanted for other crimes which the US could extradite you for. Canada would not send draft resisters home as long as they obeyed Canadian laws. They also provided housing and job placement. Many of the men were housed in private homes but most lived in one of several dormitories throughout the Province.

I found this place most interesting because I always wondered what happened to them once they got here.

I talked a bit with an American. He was from Denver and seemed scared out of his wits. It was obvious that he didn't want to talk much so I let it go.

"Take care, man."

"Thanks."

I asked Phillip if anyone knew how many guys were in Canada and no one really knew but I heard as many as 100,000. Many had married and made new lives up here becoming citizens never to return. One of the merits of living here besides not going to prison, was that you're family and friends could visit. Army deserters were also welcomed with open arms.

I had an epiphany! You know, one of those moments when the light goes on. I was going to stay here. I'm not going back to the States. I'd stay here, get a job, get my real name back, find a girl, get my fucking life back!

I asked the receptionist for the forms I would need. She handed me a thick packet. It would take half a day to fill out.

"What are you doing?" asked Allen.

"I'm staying."

"What? Where? Here?"

"Well, yeah, I'm staying in Canada."

"Are you sure?"

"Yeah."

I took the forms with me. We thanked everyone and walked out. Rene insisted that we take a walk around old, historic Quebec. What a place. It was like walking through a museum. Very European, although I'd never been there.

We walked into a bistro. It was an open bar with seating on the sidewalk. It was too cold to sit outside so we found a booth inside. Everyone was speaking French. I had thoughts about learning the language. We ordered beers and burgers.

"Mark, are you staying? Really?" Asked Phillip.

"I'm thinking about it, yes. All my friends and contacts are in jail and I don't really have anywhere else to go. Allen, you've been a saint. Letting me stay with you, but, you and I both know that it's a temporary arrangement. I always feel like I'm invading other people's space. It isn't right. I need to get my life back because right now I don't have one. I want a job and my own place to live. That's all."

They listened and nodded.

For the first time since I could remember, a ray of hope surged through me.

"I'll buy the first round," I boasted.

I was so excited by the prospect of beginning anew. Everything looked bright and shiny like opening a new toy at Christmas. I couldn't wait to play with it. I opened the pack and scanned through the pages. It looked complicated and thorough. They wanted to know everything about me. Maybe I was wanted for more than just draft resistance. Maybe I shouldn't fill these forms out. But, I'm staying here. That's enough.

We had four rounds, each of us buying one. Feeling a little tipsy, we walked around. Just a magnificent city!

We drove back to the house. It was dark and cold outside. We hung out in the living room and listened to tunes. Rene wanted us to hear a Canadian band called Rush. I'd never heard of them but they were great.

"Neil Young is Canadian, right?" I asked.

"And so is Joni Mitchel. Oh, and Gordon Lightfoot."

But, I was too caught up in thought to get into it much. I had some major decisions to make. I waffled a bit but thought that staying here would be best. I'd sleep on it.

I could smell coffee. Rene was making coffee 'French' style. After grinding fresh beans, he put the coffee into this contraption and then pushed a plunger forcing boiling water over the beans. He made one cup at a time. It was fantastic! C'est manifique! No more Folger's for me.

"Oh my God! This is the best coffee I've ever had!"

"I'll show you how."

He had a coffee grinder to grind the beans. They were fresher that way, he said. He boiled another cup of water. He put the fresh beans into a filter, poured the water in and then pushed a plunger down. None of the beans were in the water. The plunger separated them. Voila! Espresso!

"Let me try."

I made the next cup and the next.

We were all seated at the kitchen table.

"Hey, guys, I need to talk to you about something."

I'm sure they could all guess what it was.

"I had to sleep on this; I've decided that I want to stay in Canada. That much is certain. But, I haven't decided whether to fill out these forms or not. There could be incriminating offenses that I've been accused of that might lead to my being extradited. And I don't want that. So, I need to find what would and could happen if that was the case. I guess there's always Amsterdam! But, seriously, I'm in a pickle about that. In the meantime, and here's the deal, where can I stay?"

Like identical Twins, Phillip and Rene both chimed, "you can stay with us."

"Before you say that though, I want to make sure it's okay. Because I don't want to think that I'm pressuring you ..."

"Quiet! We said you can stay here. We talked about it last night and we were going to offer anyway," said Rene as Phillip nodded.

"Allen, you've been like a brother to me. How can I ever thank you."

"You just did!"

Tears welled in my eyes. I was so grateful.

One of the tenets of all religions is helping those less fortunate. And one point I picked up from Merton was that when someone gives to you, you give to someone else in an unending chain. I liked that. I promised in my heart to give as much of myself as I could. Or at least be conscious and mindful.

"Well, you just picked up a butler," I joked, "and, I know how to make coffee!"

It was bitter cold out. We stoked up the fireplace, rolled a few, drank beer and listened to music. I helped Rene fix up a room for me. They had an extra room with all their junk in there. We just cleared an area and dropped a mattress on the floor. That was all I needed.

Allen stayed a few more days. It was very emotional for me.

"Sorry, man that I'm not going back with you. I just can't."

"Oh, Mark. I'm fine. It was a pleasure knowing you."

"Likewise."

We hugged and he was gone. It felt like the last chapter of a book. Like a death almost. Permanent. I had just severed all ties with my country. It was unsettling.

These guys were party animals. Every night turned into a drunken stoned daze. I was doing massive amounts of hash, beer, and speed. It was so fucking cold out that there seemed to be nothing else to do. I wasn't eating much. The times we did go out were to bars.

Each night I stared at that packet of papers and each night I put it off until tomorrow.

Both of these guys drove delivery trucks, part time, for a liquor distributor so we always had plenty of beer and I found out that they also dealt hash and speed. Money and drugs were no problem. They also had various girl friends who would visit from time to time and I sampled some of their wares as well. They told me not to worry about money for right now. They promised they'd find me a job and place to live in the summer.

My crystal ball of speed was licked gone but I had a few whites left. They generously resupplied me. I really had everything I needed.

These two fun loving guys lived in the moment without a care in the world.

Finally, the weather began to warm and the first sprouts appeared on the trees. The snow began melting and the grass was again visible. There was that distinct smell of spring in the air.

But, somehow I felt trapped. I was ravaged by guilt and speed. I was troubled because all my friends were in jail and I wasn't. I'd run away from my country and myself. I was dropping so many whites I'd lost count. I couldn't sleep. I was very thin. I couldn't eat. I was getting sick.

I was vomiting a lot. I had chills at night, sweating. My hands trembled. I drank constantly.

I told the guys I had the flu. I spent a week in bed shivering with a fever. I'd never been this sick before. I lost track of time. Whether it was night or day. Morning or afternoon. I could barely make it to the bathroom to throw up.

Rene would come in with chicken soup. I couldn't keep it down. I coughed constantly. My chest hurt. I had difficulty breathing.

Boy, was I sick.

After, I guess, ten days or so, I felt strong enough to get out of bed for short stretches. Occasionally, the sun would peek out and I'd sit outside.

Another month passed. Rene and Phillip had been so patient with me.

One day in June. Was it June already? Still sick and weak, Phillip came into my room and stated that we were going up north to a lake where his friends had a cabin and maybe some fresh air would make me feel better.

The next day we packed the car and the three of us rode north. I had no idea where we were headed. I sat in the back seat and enjoyed the scenery. They both had a two week vacation from work.

I was back to my usual ways of taking speed and drinking. We drank and smoked the entire trip. We passed through several very small towns. I couldn't imagine living way up here. I slept some. We drove all day. I'd never been this far north before. The woods were beautiful. The highway a thin two lane forlorn stretch. An occasional farm but mostly trees and more trees. Mountain passes. Patches of snow. Trees budding. Wildflowers. Wilderness.

At last we came into some flatter land and we got the first glimpse of Lac Saint-Jean. It looked like an ocean.

We drove into a town called Metabetchouan. I was pretty sure no one spoke English. Rene and Phillip spoke to each other in French. I wasn't offended, it was their natural language. I was too sick to care anyway.

We drove along the lake for several miles until Rene turned left and we drove down a long driveway. There sat the most beautiful cabin I've ever seen. Cabin doesn't do it justice. It was a mansion. I call it a cabin because it was by a lake. It was two stories high perched on a slight incline not 100 feet from the water's edge.

We're staying here? I thought. These people must be rich.

A woman came running out of the house. A gorgeous woman, I should say. Then a man appeared. I was introduced to Monique and Charles. Everyone was hugging and kissing each other and speaking French. It was early evening and the sun still shined brightly. We entered the house and Charles showed us around. Apparently, Phillip had been here before so he unloaded the car. The living room was huge, opening up to both stories. An eight foot high fireplace, all stone, graced one side of the room. The entire house was made of pine. It was sensational. Charles took us upstairs and showed us to our bedrooms. There was a railing around the second floor offering a view of the entire living room below.

"Mark, this will be your room."

It was huge. It had a bathroom in it. A huge bed. Windows from floor to ceiling that looked out onto the lake.

We continued our tour. Phillip and Rene's rooms were equally as large. He showed us the master bedroom which was twice as large and dominated half the upstairs. Their view was stupendous!

This would be my home for the next two weeks. I couldn't believe it.

The look of disbelief on my face must have shown because Charles looked at me as if to say, 'What can you do.'

We walked back downstairs and Charles showed us the rest of the house. An immense kitchen. We could smell something delicious being prepared, and a large dining area. He then showed us the doctor's study.

"The doctor?" I asked.

"Yes, the house belongs to Monique's parents. He is a surgeon in Quebec. This house has been in their family for generations. It has been added on over the years."

He then led us outside. A narrow rock path led to the lake. There must have been a thousand steps. It zig-zagged with two open areas that had benches to sit on. At the end of the path was a large dock and a power boat.

The lake took my breath away. There must be 100 foot walleyes in here, I thought. You couldn't see the other side and they had no close neighbors.

"We've been coming up here every summer for years," Charles explained. He appeared to be about 35. He was a Professor in Quebec and Monique a nurse.

We walked back up to the house. Monique handed me a beer. "Merci."

I noticed another woman in the kitchen helping Monique. That was Brigitte, the maid. An elderly lady who had worked for the family for years. She only spoke French, I later found out. They 'borrowed' her for the next two weeks.

The five of us congregated to the living room. Fifty people could have fit comfortably. I sat by the fire place. They spoke mostly in French. Monique looked at me and walked over. Her long blonde hair and big blue eyes. She was lovely. Her expression showed concern.

"Rene was just telling me that you've been sick."

"Yes, that's right."

She put her hand on my fore head.

"I think you have a temperature. Can I take your temperature?"

"Sure."

She returned in a moment with a thermometer.

"Hold this under your tongue."

"Mm k."

After a few minutes she read it.

"You have a slight fever."

She brought me two aspirin and a glass of water.

"That should do the trick," she said.

Guess I'd felt lousy for so long that I didn't notice anymore.

It was time for dinner. We ate steak and potatoes and salad and soup served with a red wine. Candle lit. The days of living on dog food were a long ago memory.

Brigitte ate in the kitchen.

I really couldn't eat that much. I felt nauseous. I excused myself and went to the bathroom and puked. I cleaned myself up as best as I could. I was sweating and felt lousy.

I didn't understand. If it was the flu the others would be sick too. But, they were feeling fine.

I returned several minutes later.

"Are you okay, Mark?"

"Yeah, fine."

Monique felt my forehead again. "Now you feel cool."

"Come with me."

We walked into the study and she took out a stethoscope and checked my chest. Then she took my blood pressure.

"Your heart is racing. Have you been taking amphetamines."

"Yes. I've been taking whites and meth crystal for a long time."

"I think that's why you're sick. Your body can't take anymore. My God, you're as skinny as a rail. You have to stop."

"How?" I pleaded, "every time I've tried to stop I break out in cold sweats and it feels like my heart is going to explode. I get really depressed like I can't move. I can't eat or sleep. I've tried."

"How many whites to you normally take in a day?"

"I don't know. Some days 5 or 6, I guess, and other days more."

"Okay. Here's what you do. Stop right now. You're going to feel bad for a week or so and feel depressed. That's normal. Don't worry. I'm right here. I can help you get through this. After a week or so your appetite will return and you will feel much better. Alcohol will only increase the depression so cut back on that too. I'll nurse you back to health. If you'll let me. Deal?"

"Deal. Thank you."

I'd started taking No-Doz in college to stay up and study and I soon moved to the harder stuff. My crystal ball of meth and the bags of whites helped me through so many tough times when I needed to be alert. I didn't realize how dependent I was on this stuff.

I wasn't ready to surrender my stash yet. Just in case.

We joined the others. I was embarrassed. I felt a little better. I vowed to nurse myself back to health.

We sat out on the back deck and watched the sun slowly setting. It was ten o'clock at night and the sun was still up. Phenomenal.

A slight breeze and cigarette smoke kept the bugs away.

At last, we bid each other 'Bonne Nuit.'

I climbed into the largest bed I'd ever slept in. It was still light with a twilight sky overhead. The lake glistened. Peace.

Awoke to another sunny day. Walked right into the shower. Walked downstairs. Brigitte had French waffles and cheese and bread spread out on the table. There were scrambled eggs and bacon too. Help yourself. I poured a heaping cup of coffee and ate a waffle. Washed it down with orange juice and coffee. The others were half up and about. I guess I was the first one down stairs. I walked to the deck and smoked a cig. I saw several boats out on the water. That would be fun!

I walked down to the dock. I tested the water. It was ice cold!

So, of course, I dove in!

Wow. It shocked my body. I came out immediately and sat on the dock. The sun was warm but I shivered none the less. I didn't notice any other swimmers.

I figured I'd just shock my body back into health.

I went for a long walk along the beach. I hadn't walked on a beach for I don't know when. I was intrigued by the driftwood that found its way to the beach. Strange human and animal shapes. Bleached-out wood. Some of the shapes even had eyes. Should have brought my camera.

I walked back to the house.

"Where were you, I was worried," said Monique.

"I jumped in the lake and then took a walk. God, that water is cold."

"You went swimming? Mark, you should be resting and taking it easy. Did you eat breakfast?"

"Yeah. Had a waffle and some juice."

"Here, eat some more."

"Okay."

She felt my forehead. No temperature. I hadn't taken any speed today. I felt edgy but figured I could handle it as long as Monique was around.

I walked onto the deck and talked with Charles.

"Feeling better?"

"Yeah, I guess. Hey, I was wondering, does the lake freeze over in the winter?"

"Some years, yes. It's such a large lake that some years you can look out and see patches of open water."

"Wow. I jumped in this morning. It was freezing."

"You're braver than me."

"And I got right out, too."

"Maybe we'll take the boat out this afternoon. Take a ride around. Can't show you the whole lake because we'd run out of gas," he laughed.

And after lunch and a nap we all piled into the boat. It was a beautiful wooden inboard craft. Charles captained, of course, and the rest of us just sat back and enjoyed the ride sipping red wine and letting the wind blow through our hair. We saw several other cabins, well hidden amongst the trees. A few docks and some other boaters out. Mostly fishing. Charles insisted that we wear life preservers just in case. I could attest to the temperature of the water. One wouldn't last long out here.

He showed us the Marina where they stored the boat for the winter. In fact, this was their first time out since recently getting it out of storage. You couldn't leave a boat in the water here, the ice would crush it.

Monique had also insisted that we all wear hats to protect us from the sun. I was as white as a ghost. The sun and the spray from the water felt so good. I wanted to water ski.

The water got choppier as we headed out. This was more than a lake, it was a Sea! Why would anyone want to war when there was this beauty. I just couldn't understand. This was peace. Riding around a lake with friends.

We docked and moored the boat. That was so much fun. We were cold though. It was warm on the shore. We walked back to the house and something was cooking. Brigitte was humming in the kitchen. Monique shouted something to her in French.

"Oui, Madame," and laughed.

Brigitte was hard of hearing so Monique always shouted at her. It was comical.

Monique wanted to check my temperature again so I patiently sat while she also checked my blood pressure. "A little high but okay. How are you feeling?"

"Like I can't sit still."

Coming down from this shit was not going to be easy but easier than quitting smoking. In fact, I'd noticed I was smoking a lot. Maybe I should stop that too. Nah. One thing at a time.

Allen and Phillip were just two happy guys. They were smoking a joint on the deck. Laughing and rattling in French. Everyone just seemed to have their own space. It was very comfortable.

"Can you see the Northern Lights up here," I asked Charles.

"Sometimes. Need a dark sky and no moon. Then you can. They're amazing," answered Charles overhearing me walking between rooms.

"Will we see them tonight?" No answer, he was gone.

Guess I'd find out. Of course not, the sun never sets in the summer. It would have to be in the winter. Duh.

I asked Monique if I could look at the Library and select a book to read. She lead me to the study. It was like a real library with a sliding ladder and everything. Most of the books were in French but I did find several titles in English. I found a collection of poems by William Blake.

I took it back to my room for later.

Tonight's meal consisted of chicken and potatoes and soup. With a cream pie for desert. Hadn't eaten this well in eons. I still didn't have a great appetite but at least I didn't get sick tonight. Monique said it would take a week or more before I felt better. This was only day two.

The food did make me feel better. Didn't feel like drinking tonight. Just a couple of glasses of wine. There was no TV so we were forced into conversation. Somebody said that they should speak English but I said that was okay. I liked hearing French. I was just starting to pick up some words here and there. I was fine with that.

They spoke mostly English anyway. They were all old friends, it seemed, so they spoke about people whom I did not know. I just snuggled up in a huge chair and listened. There was a night chill even though the sun was up so Charles made a fire in the fireplace. I could have slept right here.

I went to my room and reveled in Blake. His pastoral poems were true but I was more interested in his cynical views of society and government. The irony didn't escape me; being in this awesome natural setting and being critical of my government.

I had to think of all the kindness in the world. Starting with these people of whom I was after all a guest. These last few years and maybe my whole life up to now was negative. I was very depressed and still wasn't feeling all that well. I had to get out of this funk.

I couldn't sleep. I silently walked out to the deck. I didn't want to wake anyone. The sun had just dipped below the horizon. A twilight night. The night of the sun. I walked down the path but didn't go all the way to the water. I could see just fine in this half-light. I walked off the path and hiked to a spot where I sat by a tree and stared at the water. A crescent moon reflected and danced on the water. I sat there for a peaceful time. I looked back and reflected on everything. My childhood, my turbulent childhood, one doesn't realize reality sometimes until you achieve a perspective. I saw everything clearly now. The 'Masters of War' manufacturing wars for their own profit. Machiavellian Governments dividing people against one another through propaganda and lies. The illusion that money and religion create. The masses being herded like sheep. The fallacy of history.

The sun gradually re-rose. Long deep shadows. A warming air. Just a touch of a breeze. The gentle hiss of wind blowing through the trees.

I recalled the first moments on Haight Street with all these gentle people and then that was soured by drugs and hustlers. The music I'd heard when for an instant I felt free. All the girl's and how my heart still hurt over Carol.

Canada was not for me. It wasn't my country. America was my country. I was a patriot. I truly was. I was sick. I was tired. I'd had enough. Enough of running and hiding. Enough of my aliases. I'd lost me. I wanted me back again. I was going insane. I missed my family. I hadn't seen them or heard from them in a long time. I'd sent them letters from time to time just to let them know I was alive. I don't even know if they received them. It was the end for me. I couldn't do this any longer. I knew I'd go to prison but I resigned myself to that. I'd do my time and get out. I'd only be 30. Young enough to start over. I'd been deceiving myself long enough. I hadn't shortened the war, I hadn't affected anyone in the ways I'd wanted.

I'd probably alienated more people than converted.

I sat there until the sun was again high in the sky. I hiked back to the cabin.

It was the night of the sun.

"Good morning Mark."

"Morning Phillip. I didn't sleep last night. I'm going to lay down for a while. Could you tell the others?"

I managed to sleep. For how long I have no idea. Can't tell the time because the sun is always out. Slipping in and out. I'm so tired.

Monique checked my temperature again. I'm burning up. She made me get up and drink some water. I have a bad headache. She gives me a pill. I slept for sixteen hours.

I awoke and walked into the shower. It could be the middle of the night for all I knew. I felt much better. A bit groggy though.

I walked downstairs to join the others. No one around. It was 5. Must have been a.m.

Made some coffee. Hope Brigitte won't mind. I walked to the dock and stared at the lake. Glass like calm. Some birds skimming across the surface. Lovely.

What day was it? What did Monique give me? Must have been a sleeping pill. I did feel rested somewhat. That anxious feeling wasn't there. By the time I finished my coffee and a cig the others were up.

"Are you feeling better?"

"Yeah. I think I am."

Monique felt my forehead again and seemed satisfied. I was suddenly ravishing hungry. I could smell Brigitte's cooking a mile away.

I stuffed myself with eggs, toast, and bacon. Several glasses of orange juice and copious amounts of coffee. Most I'd eaten in one sitting in a long, long time. Maybe I'm getting better.

The others wanted to go into town tonight to a tavern. That would be fun. In the meantime I grabbed Blake and headed for the tree to read and take a nap. I felt like that little kid who sat high atop his tree and read Twain. I'd found this neat spot. 50 feet or so above the beach. The sound of the waves just knocked me out. I was woozy from the huge breakfast and dozed off again.

A speedboat woke me up. Ha. Look at that. A water skier. He must be freezing. I watched until he disappeared in the distance.

Walked back to the house. Late afternoon.

Back at the cabin. Everyone seemed to be hungry so we drove into Metabetchouan to a restaurant/bar. We walked inside and the place was bustling with mostly fisherman. They all spoke French. We were seated in a booth by the window. This so much reminded me of the resort towns in Northern Wisconsin. I felt right at home except I couldn't understand a word anyone said. Just as well. Phillip helped me order. I ordered trout with potatoes and a salad. The waitress knew Charles and Monique and treated them like royalty. The place was decorated with dead animal heads and fish. There appeared to be a bar in a back room. It was filled with smoke and I could hear music coming from there.

The fish was delicious. It was fresh all right. Chased everything down with a Canadian beer. Very strong. We chatted. The other four switching from English to French and back again. I was amazed. I was having second thoughts of returning to the States but then again. No, I'd made my mind up. That was that! I was returning. I passed on desert. Just wanted more beer. Charles had said it was on him. I'd been so fortunate to run into generous people. I had a life time of giving ahead of me.

It seemed that Charles and Monique knew just about everyone in here. I could sense the respect they demanded.

We walked into the bar. A huge moose head hung in the center of the bar. I couldn't take my eyes off it. There was an assortment of wolves and fox and other animals on display as well. It was like being in a zoo except all the animals were dead. We had to sit in a booth. There was no room at the bar. These Canadians were a different breed, that's for sure. They were a hardy bunch. Charles said most of these guys lived here year round.

"What are the winter's like?"

"Long and cold, exactly the opposite of this."

Charles left us for a while and talked to a guy at the bar. They seemed like long lost pals, joking with one another. This was what I was missing. Friends!

We drank several pitchers of beer. We were pretty happy by the time we drove home.

We got back smoked some dope, drank more beer and watched the sun dip below the horizon.

The days ran into days. My body clock was off because of the constant sun.

After another week of slumming around the cabin it did become a bit boring, Rene and Phillip and myself drove back to Sainte-Marie. We thanked our guests for their hospitality, great food, and generosity. My God, we hadn't spent a cent except for cigarettes.

The first thing I did when we got in the car was to drop a couple of whites. Within minutes I was feeling human again.

Rene had mentioned a couple of times that they had to get back to work. Since I'd known them they hadn't worked much.

I just had to ask.

"I know you guys work. What do you do?"

"We work for a liquor distributorship. We drive delivery trucks mostly. We both took a month off for vacation. I guess we just hadn't mentioned it."

"Oh, and now you have to get back to work?"

"Yeah," said Phillip.

"The business actually closes down for two weeks each summer. The boss loves to fish and camp. So he just shuts it down. We're going to be busy when we reopen," added Rene.

"You don't suppose they'd have something for me, do ya?"

"Hey, you know what, I'll ask him. He's a great guy."

We got back to their house. I walked into my room and dropped my stuff. The Immigration Papers sitting on a desk.

The boys still had another day before returning to work so we partied heavy. It wasn't long before I was back to my old ways.

We sat around. I spoke briefly of my desire to return to the States. They seemed hurt. But, I explained, it wasn't about them at all. I just needed to get my life back. I'm not sure if I convinced them or not.

The boys went back to work that following Monday. I'd asked them to speak to their boss if there was any work. It would have to be cash though. Under the table.

I had the house to myself so I straightened the place up. The boys came home from work with two cases of beer and a bottle of whiskey. Here we go again.

"My boss said you could help out two or three days a week filling orders. We have three trucks that deliver all over Quebec. Each truck makes a morning run and an afternoon run to bars and liquor stores. And then twice a month or so one of the big trucks runs to Bangor, Maine. That's an overnight trip. But, yeah, you can come with us tomorrow, Mark."

I was so happy I could cry.

"Thank you. I need some money so I can chip in. I've been feeling useless lately. Thanks."

Bingo! I wanted to be on that truck going to Maine. I didn't say anything out loud.

Life was good. We had endless Molson's, whiskey, pot, and music. We partied for a while but I cut it short. I had to work tomorrow.

We drove to the warehouse. It was rather a large brick building by some railroad tracks. Rene introduced me to the boss who spoke broken English. He said he'd pay me $5 Canadian an hour, cash. I didn't know how much that was American. Rene took me out into the warehouse where I met the foreman. Seemed like a nice chap. My job was to fill the orders and load them onto a pallet while another guy would pick it up with a fork lift. He gave me an order sheet which was in French but I could read the numbers and the Brand Names. This place was huge. I've never seen so much booze in one place. They had several varieties of Canadian beers and other spirits. I was slow at first because I didn't know where anything was. I'd haul down a case of beer and use a hand truck to put it on a pallet. It was easy but hard work because some of the product was stacked up pretty high requiring a ladder to reach it. They also had barrels of beer which required some strength to move. By lunch break I was exhausted. There was a break room and I was the only guy who didn't speak the language. Rene and Phillip were both out in trucks making deliveries. I'd say there were ten people who worked here. Three fork lift guys and four or five of us pulling orders. During lunch a semi backed up to the dock with a delivery. It was full of Whiskey. Jeez. So, two of the guys swore in French and went out to empty the truck.

We got off work. I had to wait for Rene and Phillip. Because of being closed for two weeks they were really busy trying to catch up. No problem. Half an hour later or so they both showed up.

"We both spent the whole day in Quebec driving around. Tomorrow will be the same. How was your day, Mark?"

"I'm pretty sore," I laughed, "haven't used those muscles in a long time. But, I'm great. Felt good to work."

"Let's grab a 'cold one', as you Yanks say, on the way home."

"Good idea, Ollie."

We stopped by their favorite watering hole and ordered some burgers and fries to go. Had a couple while we waited.

I was so stiff and sore I told the guys I wanted to take a shower and crash.

Up the next morning. Coffee and speed to wake me up. No breakfast. Today was the same as yesterday and the next. Finished the week and the boss called me in. Four days of pay. $160! In cash! Had to be $120 or so American. Rene said he could exchange the Canadian money for American. No problem. They didn't work weekends so we headed home, cleaned up, ate and ventured to a bar in downtown Saint-Marie. Pretty scary place on a Friday night. Loud and filled with just-paid lumber jacks and other assorted French Canadians. The men looked rough and the women even rougher. Was content on staying in the booth for protection and as an ideal spot to witness the carnage.

The jukebox was so loud you couldn't hear yourself talk which was fine because I didn't understand a word anyway. Except the lyrics to the songs. It was like 1959 in here. More dead animal heads all over the walls. Mostly short haired men. A few gals clinging to their men. Haight-Asbury never reached here. Rene and Phillip seemed right at home. They knew everybody in here so there were no problems but I did catch a couple of lingering stares from guys ogling the fucking Yank. Oh well. Who can blame them.

I went to work for the next two weeks. One day the boss called me into his office and informed me that they had caught up and my services wouldn't be needed any longer. I was devastated. He paid me and said I could work the rest of the day. At first I was angry and hurt but as the day wore on I realized it had been a blessing to work at all.

Rene and Phillip were kind of bummed out too. I asked when one of them was driving to Bangor again. Rene thought he had a trip in a couple of weeks. I asked if I could tag along.

"No you can't go with me. You don't work for us."

"What if you let me borrow one of your shirts and a cap. They'd think I was your helper."

"Well, I don't know."

"Do they check you out at the border?"

"No, they just look at the invoice and wave me through. They all know me."

"Well?"

"Let me think about it."

"What about the return trip? Do they check you out. No, no ... they just wave me through."

"Listen, you guys, I want to return to the States. I can't live here. It isn't you, honest. I just have to go home. I'm burned out. I've had enough."

I started to cry. It wasn't an act. I was strung out on speed again and felt sick all the time. I started to shake when I didn't take my speed and I'd lost my appetite ... again. I couldn't take any more of the sickness, of the isolation.

Impressed with my theatrics, Rene conceded.

"Okay, Mark. I'll drive you to Bangor in a couple of weeks."

"Merci, bon ami."

Chapter 23

The Long Way Home

The next two weeks were a blur. I was very anxious. I just had to move. I called Brian in San Francisco and he told me that Mark was still incarcerated. That was bad news. Oliver was out on bail and his trial was pending. I was next. I thought of turning myself in. Of going to prison and just get it over with. I was obsessed with death. The same trike nightmare visited every night. I couldn't sleep. I'd get up and pace. I was losing my mind. I needed resolution!

"Mark, we'll leave first thing tomorrow morning. Here's a shirt with the company name on it and a hat. They'll have the truck loaded and ready to go. All I have to do is go to the warehouse and pick it up. I'll drive back here and pick you up. If they find out I'll get fired so don't tell anybody."

"Okay. I won't. Just wake me up and I'll be ready to go."

Another sleepless night. What if they ask to see my 'papers?' But Rene said they won't check. I hope he's right.

The next morning the boys woke me up. I hugged Phillip and thanked him for everything. Rene said he'd be back in an hour or less. I put the shirt on, packed my things. I was ready.

Rene pulled up in a semi-truck packed full of booze. This was it.

"If they ask you anything about me just tell them that I'm a new guy and am in training or something."

"You worry too much. They just want to know what's in the truck. They won't even check. Besides, I know all those guys. Don't worry."

It was pretty cool riding shot gun in this rig. We could see down on the passing cars from the opposite direction. Every truck driver had stories about topless women on hot days or giving blow jobs. No such luck on this ride though.

It was a long haul just to get to the border. We wouldn't be at his destination for hours.

"We'll get to Bangor after the warehouse has closed so we'll stay in a motel and then unload in the morning."

As we neared to border I became more and more anxious. I had knots in my stomach. If I was captured I told Rene I wouldn't implicate him in any way. He just nodded and smiled with the look of 'don't worry.'

The border was less than ten miles away. But, at least, I had no doubts I was doing the right thing. I figured I'd take a bus from Bangor to ... I paused. I hadn't decided yet. Maybe Boston or New York. Rene assumed I was going back to Portland but I decided against that. It would be winter in a few months and there was no way I was spending a winter there. I had a few hundred dollars on me so I was fine. Just need to get across the border.

Rene slowed the rig down and we pulled over to the far right to a lane marked for trucks. A gate blocked our path. A border patrol agent approached the truck. I was calm on the outside and petrified on the inside.

"Hey, Rene, long time no see. Whatcha got?"

Rene handed him a set of papers with a list of the inventory.

"Be right back."

In a few minutes he returned. The papers had been stamped.

"Got your helper with you today, huh?"

"Yeah, breaking him in. See ya, Sal."

The gate lifted and we drove into the States.

"Mark, you can breathe again. See I told you ... piece of cake."

"I never doubted you for a minute Rene."

Jesus H. Christ, that was hairy!

And yeah, I could breathe again.

We still had a few hours' drive until we reached Bangor. I finally start-ed to notice my surroundings. Some of the trees were already turning. We passed through a very hilly almost mountainous part of Maine. God, it was beautiful.

It was good to be back home again.

It was early evening when Rene pulled the rig into a motel on the outskirts of town. I'd get to the bus station tomorrow morning. Rene ran in and checked in. It was a nothing small motel with maybe twenty rooms. We couldn't drive anywhere but there was a tavern just two blocks away. After cleaning up some we walked the two blocks and had burgers and of course, beer. I was finally relaxed. The tension had worn me out so we called it an early night.

Brought some more beer with us and I watched the late news. Boy, this Watergate thing had really taken off. They're going to impeach that prick! I hadn't watched any TV or seen a newspaper in a few months. Man, what was I missing.

I slipped into bed and got a good night's sleep. We had to rise early. Rene said he could drop me off by the bus station in the morning.

6 a.m. is an awful cruel hour. We each showered and made some fake coffee in the room with one of those things that you plug in and it gets hot. They had instant coffee in the room. Awful stuff but better than nothing.

I thanked and hugged Rene with all my might. We both knew we'd never see each other again.

"It was a blast, my friend, thank you ... I mean, merci!"

"Once I drop this off I switch trailers and I'll 'dead head' back to Sainte-Marie. Piece of cake. I'll drop you off near downtown. I don't know where the bus station is but it's got to be down there somewhere."

"That's fine. I'll find it."

We got into the rig and not two miles down the highway I spotted the Greyhound Station. It wasn't downtown. Wow. What luck. Rene pulled into the parking lot.

"Au revoir. Oh, here's your shirt."

"Keep it. Bye, Mark."

And off he drove.

Royal Canadian Distributing. Nice.

I walked into the station and looked at departures. A bus for New York left in two hours. I bought the ticket.

I had to transfer in Boston. No big deal. I'd just stare out the window and smoke.

I found my favorite seat in the back. The last seat. I got the window seat. I was in for a long haul.

It took about five hours to get to Boston. I had to wait an hour to catch the next bus to New York. I'd be in New York tonight.

It was late when we arrived in Manhattan. I got off the bus intending to spent the night in a hotel. I looked at the departures. It was fate. That's all there is to it. A bus left for Pittsburgh in an hour. I purchased the ticket for Pittsburgh. I had to see my family!

If there hadn't been a bus leaving for Pittsburgh at that moment ... I just don't know.

It was an all-night ride. I didn't get my 'lucky' seat but I had a window seat in the back. I managed to half doze off. Not real sleep.

We pulled into Pittsburgh. It was early morning. I searched through my wallet and found their phone number.

It rang three times.

"Dad. It's Mike."

"Where are you? Pat, it's Mike!"

I sat on a bench and waited. I knew it would take them a couple of hours to drive in.

I saw them first. They walked right past me. My little sister, Becky, recognized me first.

"Mike!"

She jumped into my arms and gave me a hundred kisses. I looked up and saw the rest of them staring at me. They didn't even recognize me for a moment and then I was surrounded and hugged. My mom, who is very unemotional, had tears in her eyes.

"What did they do to you?" were her first words.

I hadn't seen them in three years.

John carried my ruck sack for me. I put my arms around Casey, and Mary, John, and Paul, and Becky, too. I was overcome with emotion when we piled into the car.

My dad looked kindly on me. I think he was too choked up to talk. Luckily, Dad was still driving a huge station wagon so we all fit in.

"Where's Tim I asked?"

He was the only one missing.

Mom said he was in Winona but was coming out next week for a visit.

I looked at these faces. The kids had grown up so much. John was tall, Mary wore lip stick, Becky was still the tom boy, Paul had grown some too, and Casey, the baby, was still a kid but no longer a baby. Mom and Dad looked a little older, but not much. I'm sure I looked like hell. My hair almost to my waist, skinny as a rail, hollow cheeks, unshaven and raggedy clothes. Yeah, get a load of your 'Prodigal Son.' Fucking burned out from speed and fear.

They had recently moved to the side of a hill into a mobile home. The front lawn was a pile of rocks and dirt. They lived in a burb called Harrison City. We drove down a long winding dirt driveway. Home! I was fucking home!

The kids couldn't wait to show me around. The property was edged by a 'slag heap.' Many acres of discarded coal from the mines.

Walked into the trailer. It was pretty big. There was an extra room added onto the back of it, so there was plenty of room. Two baths.

I put my gear down in the back room. I walked into the kitchen.

"Everybody ... in here," I shouted.

"Listen, you can't tell anyone I'm here or I'll be arrested and you won't see me for another five years ... at least. You can't tell anyone. Don't tell your friends, don't tell the neighbors, don't tell anyone. Now I want to hear you say it out loud."

A chorus of 'we won't tell anyone' rang out.

"I mean it you guys. Now go out and play, I need to talk to Mom and Dad."

The kids cleared out.

Mom gave me a cup of coffee. Neither had spoken much but I could tell they were overwhelmed on seeing me.

"I wanted to spend some time with you before I surrender. I'm going back to Minneapolis to give myself up. I can't do this any longer. I have to tell you that I'm strung out on speed. You know, those little white pills that truckers take. I'm really sick."

"How much do you weigh?" asked my dad.

"I don't know."

I walked into the bathroom and weighed myself. 115 pounds. I'd lost 50 pounds since high school.

"Please don't tell anyone I'm here. I missed you so much it hurt."

"You put us through Hell. Never knowing if you were even alive."

Mom's anger was still alive. I conceded the point.

Dad told Mom to shut up. "Look at him. He's a fucking mess. He needs food not your crap."

"Don't fight. Please. I can't take any more."

Mom simmered.

"Pat, I'm going to the market."

Dad drove off.

Mom filled me in on the news. There was a flood at the other house and all the books and the piano were lost. John was a star basketball player in high school and Mary was getting good grades. Becky was still into her own world. She had a horse in a stable at the neighbors, Paul couldn't attend school because of his disability, and Casey was the darling of every girl in the county. Grandma and Grandpa were still going strong. Emil was still playing in the band.

Dad returned with enough food for an army. He put a steak on the stove and heated up some potatoes. Handed me a beer.

"We're going to put some weight on you. Christ, you'd blow away if you weren't nailed down."

As I ate Mom told me about the FBI agent who came once a month. "I won't let him in the house. We sit on the stoop and drink coffee. He's an older man and a decent man. All the kids have been taken out of class a couple of times and they were asked where you were. Once, Agents boarded the school bus that Mary and Becky were on. Of course, we didn't know where you were. They even bothered your grandparents. They scared Grandma something terrible. You know how she is."

"What's his name?"

"Agent Riley."

"You know, I was thinking it might be best if the kids didn't have any of their friends over for awhile. Can I take a nap?"

I was so worn out I walked into the back room and laid down on my sleeping bag. I dozed off immediately. I didn't wake up until 5 a.m. the next morning.

Mom was always an early riser.

She had coffee made. Dad got up grumpy. He told me about all the work that needed to be done in the yard. Nothing's changed, I thought. Always with the chores. Dad made me eat some eggs and toast. When I went to the bathroom this morning I flushed all my whites down the toilet. That was that. I knew I was going to have a rough week but I had to stop.

Dad showed me the yard. It was mostly rocks and stones. He showed me a wheel barrow and told me to get busy.

"You can earn your keep around here, just like everybody else. No free rides. Besides, the work will do you good."

"Yes, sir."

Yep, nothing's changed. He treated me like I'd been gone for a day and then had come back. There was no pleasing him.

I got busy picking up the larger stones by hand and putting them in a wheel barrow and depositing the stones on a large pile by the edge of the yard. I saw no end in sight. The ground was saturated with rocks. Finally, I started throwing them at the pile. Soon, the other kids were up and we were all throwing stones. I had arrived on a Saturday morning so everyone was home today. My siblings and I grumbled and laughed at the same time over the absurdity of removing these billions of stones.

The next morning was a different story. All the kids except Paul went to school and Dad, dressed in a suit and tie took off for the rest of the week. He was still working for Essex Wire and he was driving to Philadelphia and New Jersey for the week. He gruffly said goodbye and drove off. The kids had all walked to the bus stop. I reminded them again not to tell anyone I was here.

Emil was supposed to fly in on Wednesday. I was really excited about that because we were nearer to the same age and I'd have someone to talk to.

After everyone was gone, Mom and I sat in the kitchen, drank coffee and smoked. Poor Mom, I thought. She wasn't looking too good. She told me all the stories about living in the other home and she completed her story how the flood had ruined almost every book and they had lost the piano as well. Their old house was at the bottom of a hill and it had rained so hard that a river of water had broken through the basement windows and before anyone could do anything about it four feet of water filled the base-ment. It only took ten minutes to fill the basement, she said. They hadn't gotten along with the neighbors anyway, so they decided to move out here. It was pastoral. The property brushed against Bushy Run, a small National Park commemorating a Civil War Battle just days before Gettysburg.

She caught me up on the cousins and their families. The latest news from Rice Lake.

She made me feel like the 'Black Sheep' of the family.

By early afternoon I told Mom I wanted to take a nap. I felt sick and shaky. Lack of speed no doubt.

Later on, the kids came home from school. I asked each of them if they'd told anyone I was here. None of them had.

Casey had a bike he wanted to show me. He rode it out on the slag heap. They were like giant sand dunes except the material was discarded coal. He rode up and down the hills with grace sometimes coming over the top of the hill and catching air. Never seen anyone ride a bike like that. He was amazing. He also showed me a few spots where if you scraped the sur-face with your shoes a flame of fire would appear. Christ, this whole area was burning underground. A frightening thought.

We were supposed to throw rocks but no one did. Mom didn't care one way or the other.

Becky took me down to the neighbor's stable to see her horse, Jake. He was huge. An Arabian, I think she said. She saddled him up and took off. She let me ride him too. That was pretty neat. I wanted to hike up to Bushy Run and check that out. She said maybe tomorrow as it was getting dark already.

Mom showed me her pottery collection. She'd taken interest in pottery the last couple of years. Under wraps was a kiln Dad had bought for her. She had some tables and chairs set up in the back. She said once a week some of her friends would come over and do pottery. I mentioned it might be best if I got lost for a few hours when they came over. "Oh, yeah, hadn't thought of that."

Emil was coming tomorrow or the next day, depending on whether he flew or took a bus. I told the others not to tell him I was here in case he called. I wanted to surprise him. I told Mom I wanted to ride with her when we picked him up.

That night I watched the news. They were talking about Senate Hearings on the Watergate debacle. A lot of people speculated that Nixon was behind a 'cover-up' as they were calling it. In the meantime, Nixon had gone to China to everyone's approval.

Dad called from somewhere and talked to Mom.

"He's ordered a bull dozer to finish the yard. Supposed to be here in a few days," Mom said.

He'd finally come to his senses. A bull dozer could do in an hour what would take me a week.

I joined the rest of the kids watching TV. It was so great to be with them.

Got up early. Was starting to feel a little better. I was eating a lot and had managed to put a few pounds on. After the kids left for school, Mom and I heard a rumble. It was the bull dozer! He was leveling the driveway. He worked himself up to the trailer and knocked on the door. He said that he wanted to work on the yard next. If you could even call it that. Mom walked out with him and talked to him for a few minutes. She came back in laughing.

"I told him to shape the yard in three tiers. To level it off around the trailer, make a small incline to another area and level that off and then gradually even the slope down to the tree line. And he said, what's a tier?"

"Oh, that's what you were doing with your hands."

"And after he does that, Dad ordered a truck full of dirt to cover everything. They'll pack that down and then we'll seed it. By next spring we should have a real yard. He said it would take him two or three days."

"Better than throwing rocks forever."

The phone rang. It was Emil. I motioned to Mom not to tell him I was here. Emil was just leaving on the bus. It would take him about twenty hours to get to Pittsburgh, I reckoned.

After hanging up I told Mom I'd go with her to pick him up. Boy, will he be surprised.

I watched the guy push and shape the yard. The bulldozer rumbled and shook the trailer. At least the driveway was even. No ruts. All it needed now was a load of gravel. The guy was a real master with that machine.

After several hours it was starting to look like something.

The kids came home from school. Casey couldn't resist riding his bike up and down the tiers until Mom made him stop because he was leaving deep ruts in the smooth ground. Becky wanted to go ride Jake so I hung out with John and Paul. Mary was at her friend's house. John showed me some of his sketches. He drew faces. They were amazing. Life like. He was really good at eyes. He said he wanted to go to college to an Art School. He also mentioned he liked to play the piano but of course that was lost in the flood. Paul just stayed in his room most of the time and listened to his music.

Mom called the bus station in Pittsburgh and got the arrival time for Emil's bus. It was about an hour and a half drive. His bus arrived at 8 a.m. So we'd leave at 6.

Watched some TV and went to sleep early.

Mom got me up at 5. Brutal. She had told John to get the kids off to school. Paul would be okay alone for a couple of hours.

It was a hard drive into Pittsburgh with the morning commute. We were running late because of the traffic. It was great chatting with Mom. She talked mostly of her pottery. The girls were coming over on Saturday afternoon so I told her I'd take a hike.

Mom knew downtown Pittsburgh really well and we drove right to the station. There was a spot in front of the station where people could park for a couple of minutes to drop people off or to pick them up.

"Wait here, Mom, I'll go in and find him."

I saw him immediately. He wasn't expecting me to pick him up. I sat down next to him and he looked at me and it took him several seconds before he blurted out. "Mike! Where'd you come from?"

"Come on, Mom is outside in the car."

Emil looked as shocked as I've ever seen him.

"Oh, yeah, ... yeah."

He grabbed his stuff and within five minutes we were headed back to the trailer. He caught me up on all the news in Winona and he mentioned that the FBI had hassled him several times on my whereabouts. Emil still looked like a wild man. His long thick hair growing shoulder length.

"What are you doing coming home, man?"

"I wanted to see everyone and then I was going back to Minneapolis to turn myself in. I can't do this anymore."

"No shit."

"Yeah, no shit."

"I can hide you out in Winona. They'd never think to ..."

I cut him off. "Nope."

Mom had a half smile on her face. I think she was actually happy. Tim,

Emil, was always her favorite. Who could blame her. Emil was the show. Easily the funniest person I've ever met and outside of Dad the best musician I ever knew. Yep. Mom was happy all right!

And that was just dandy with me.

I was two years older than Emil so I at last had someone to talk to. We had a lot of catching up to do.

This was Emil's first visit to the trailer as well. He just laughed when he saw it. We looked like 'poor white trash.' He said.

We saw the bulldozer. There a large truck leaving as we pulled in. There were several mounds of fresh black dirt.

"That's our yard," Mom stated pointing to the mounds.

Emil and I laughed.

"Dad wants the yard finished by the time he gets home," I said.

"Where's Dad?" Emil asked.

"Out making sales calls."

Emil came in and Paul was waiting in the kitchen.

"Hi, Tim," Emil hugged Paul. I thought he'd break him in half he hugged him so tight and he lifted Paul right up off the floor. Paul just giggled.

"I'm sleeping in the back room. You should see it. Mom's got a kiln back there for doing pottery."

"Pottery?"

"Yeah, it's pretty cool. Check it out."

Emil said he was tired from travelling all night and he needed to lay down. He dropped his stuff and rolled out a sleeping bag and tried to sleep.

"You better sleep fast 'cause the kids will be home from school in a few hours."

Meanwhile, the bulldozer guy was leveling the fresh dirt out in the yard followed by a road roller which compacted the soil. It was looking great. All we had to do next was plant the grass seed. We'd have to rent a seeder for that and we needed sprinklers and miles of hose to water it. I think Dad would be pleased.

Emil managed to sleep a few hours before the kids tore him apart. It was a real family reunion! Dad was coming home in a couple of days to complete the reunion.

Mom wanted to plant a garden around the house and to make a patio. Winter was around the corner and at least we could dig it out. Mom marked the area and I grabbed a shovel and started turning the dirt. It was good hard work. My body was coming back to life. Even Emil remarked on how thin I was. He also remarked on the length of my hair. I could almost sit on it.

The kids came home and Emil didn't have a chance. John jumped on him and woke him up. It was one big happy McAndrew pile! Mom and

Mary made a bunch of hamburgers and we had a nice dinner. I hadn't felt such joy in years. Mom and her brood. Seven kids. I was the oldest to Casey the youngest. As diverse a bunch as you'd ever seen. We filled the trailer with music from Paul's stereo.

The kids left for school the next morning so Emil and I walked around the acreage. I showed him the abandoned mine buildings down below and walked across the slag heap and walked into Bushy Run and back to the house. He caught me up on some more Winona news and specifically about how he had left the 'Ferrais' and formed a new band named 'The North Country Band,' which sounded like a Dylan song to me. I told him how I was going back with him to Winona to turn myself in. Again, he didn't like that idea. I would probably go to Joliet to join Joe who was already there.

We got back to the trailer and grabbed a couple of beers and watched the road roller finishing up the yard. Mom wanted us to seed the yard but there was only one seeder so Emil began that daunting task as I continued digging around the house. It was hard work so I took a break and walked inside to have a cig and a cup of coffee. Mom was at the kitchen sink. The phone rang and she answered.

"Yeah, he's right here."

She handed me the phone. It took an instant before she realized what she'd done.

Without uttering a word, I took the phone, giving her a look of dismay.
"Hello."

"Well, well, well. At last, we meet."

"Who's this?"

"I'm FBI Agent Riley. I've been looking for you for three years. Where have you been?"

"Here and there."

"Yes, you have. You've been busy. Haven't you."

I didn't answer. I wanted to run but was paralyzed. A neighbor must have spotted me. Fuck! I should have been more cautious.

"This is what we're going to do. I assume your mother has told you about me. We've actually become friends over the years. I know how hard this has been on both your parents and your brothers and sisters. This country has been torn apart. But, I digress. I'm about to retire from the agency in a few months. I chase bad guys. You're not a bad guy. I have to tell you, even my own son ran up to Canada to avoid the draft. So, this is the deal, Michael, may I call you Michael instead of Mark. Oh yeah, we know about that too. You stay out of Berkeley, Madison, Ann Arbor, Chicago, Minneapolis, and the Bay Area. Go get lost someplace. Use your real name and Social Security number because you're free as long as you stay away from and don't associate with your political pals. You'll be okay. You have my word on that"

I was shocked.

"Let me get this straight. If I stay out of these places and away from my people you'll let me walk? Is this on the level? Do I have your word on this Agent Riley?"

"You have my word. May I speak with your mother?"

"Agent Riley?" I said.

"Yes."

"Thank you."

I handed the phone to Mom and he repeated everything to her. And, that was that.

The End

Epilogue

Agent Riley said I could stay home as long as I wanted but I didn't want to stay here. Winter was coming and the trailer was already too full. Emil and I hung out until after Thanksgiving. Dad booked a flight for us to Chicago with a connection to Winona. I wanted to see everybody there one more time. I had looked at a road atlas one night and chose Santa Cruz, California for my final destination. Didn't know one person there but I'd been through there before. I'd once stayed on a farm near Watsonville, just down the road.

Agent Riley was good to his word so far. Not one agent or phone call or any cops ever came to the trailer.

I'd been home for almost two months. No speed at all. I managed to put 15 pounds on. I was feeling strong again.

The big day came. Dad drove Emil and me to the airport and on the way he said, "You really stuck it up the ass of the FBI."

That is the one and only time I can remember my dad validating me.

It was a long drive to the Pittsburgh airport. Dad talked about how hard things were for him being away from home so much. He was making good money though. He said he didn't want to have to relocate the family anymore so he was looking to work for another company. Emil and I listened.

We crossed the Three Rivers Bridge where the Allegheny, Monongahela, and Ohio Rivers converge. An awesome sight.

The Pittsburgh airport loomed ahead. Dad pulled up to the entrance for 'Departures' and gave each of a hundred dollar bill. Our tickets were at the gate. Dad got out and shook our hands and wished us luck. I never saw my dad again.

Emil and I checked in, got our tickets and just had minutes to spare as we ran through the terminal to the gate.

We were the last two to board. As we were walking down the aisle I noticed the shocked and critical stares from the other passengers at two long haired hippies getting on their plane. I made a ticking sound as we walked down the aisle sounding like a bomb. Emil and I were both laughing. We took off within minutes. I noticed that Emil was terrified! He hated flying. I had no idea.

The 'No Smoking' sign went off and you could hear all the lighters clicking. Emil and I lit up. Soon we were over Ohio looking down on Lake Erie probably flying right over Tiffin. It wasn't a long flight. Couple hours or less and we landed at O'Hare. We had to catch a puddle jumper to La Crosse and then onto Winona. We waited for a few hours and finally got on a 4 engine prop job. We took off and Emil was really nervous. It didn't take long to land in La Crosse and Emil said he was getting off and would rather walk to Winona. I said okay can you call anyone? So he called a friend of his. In an hour we were headed to Winona.

I stayed with Emil in an old building down the street from the notorious 3rd Street apartment. The place was a zoo. People coming and going. The strong odor of pot wafting and swirling in the living room. I knew just about everyone in the room and I received quite a greeting. There were amps and mics and a drum set in the living room.

There was really no place to sleep. The party never ended. So I didn't plan on staying very long. One of my good buddies, Lenny, dropped by and he offered to drive me out to San Jose. He was going to visit his friends Jim and Mary.

"When are you leaving?"

"Day after tomorrow. I need someone to share gas expenses."

"Well, sure."

As we were hanging out, still in the back of my head, I feared that at any moment the FEDS would come crashing in and pick me up. But they didn't.

Lenny and I left on a brisk Minnesota morning. Emil looked sad that I wasn't staying but I just couldn't. I needed a new life where I knew no one. I would never speak to anyone about these past years. Never.

Lenny had an old Chevy but it ran like a top. The winter snows hadn't arrived yet so we had clear sailing all the way to Denver where we stopped for a couple of days at his friend's house. Then it was on to California.

San Jose is like a smaller version of LA. Huge and sprawling. We had some trouble finding Jim and Mary's house but we did. They had moved to Winona after I left so I didn't know them. Jim worked for his dad's business and Mary was attending San Jose State. Lenny had never been to California before so he was in for a treat. Jim and Mary's neighborhood skirted vast fruit tree orchards. Lenny had never seen an orange tree before.

Lenny only stayed for a day or so and was headed to LA to see some other friends but said he'd come back in a week or so.

I didn't know Jim and Mary so it was somewhat awkward at first but they were fine people. I said I wanted to go to Santa Cruz so Jim drove me there. I said goodbye and thank you. He left me downtown and I walked into the first hotel I saw. The St. George Hotel. They had monthly rates and I got a seedy room above the Catalyst, the local rock and roll club. No way to sleep before 2 a.m. I unloaded my things and walked down Pacific Avenue. Down the street by the JC Penney's was a restaurant called the Downtowner. There was a help wanted poster in the window. I walked in and asked for an application. I filled it in and walked back to the hotel. It was full of hippies. I checked out the Catalyst that night and listened to music and had a couple of beers. I still had enough money for a few months. The room was cheap. The bathroom was in the hall. No kitchen. Just a room with a bed, dresser, and a chair with a busted table. I didn't get to sleep until the bar closed. Fuck. It was loud. No wonder it was cheap!

The next morning I cleaned myself up as best I could and returned to the restaurant with my application. The job position had stated 'Dishwasher Wanted.'

The place was packed. It was a diner that served breakfast, lunch, and dinner. I met Al the owner. You know, sometimes fate smiles on you and gives you a break. The man hired me on the spot. He asked me when I could start and I said right now. He grabbed an apron for me and trained me how to wash the dishes and how the dish washer machine worked. I never even asked what he paid. He was really a nice man and I thank him to this day.

I worked at the Downtowner, nicknamed the Towndowner, for about a year until Al sold the place and some new owners took over. I didn't like them so I quit. In the meantime I found a 'grandmother' apartment on Peyton Street. Hung out at the greatest bar ever, The United Bar making some good friends. I even played on their softball team and became one of the better pool players in Santa Cruz.

But, I needed another job so I applied at an auto parts store named Sweet's Service. The manager required me to cut my hair and I reluctantly did. I was hired to clean the store and the rest rooms each day and eventually was hired to help in the adjacent warehouse. I would work in the auto parts business for the next fifteen years.

In the meantime, Nixon had left office and was replaced by Gerald Ford who quickly pardoned him.

A few years later ...

I quickly learned the auto parts business. How to read the catalogues. Which manufacturers produced which parts etc. The economy was slow so some of us were laid off. While on unemployment insurance I had a lot of time on my hands and I met a wonderful woman who I later married. Julie and I rented a great duplex in town. Life was good. One of the best clients from the warehouse called me one day and asked me if I wanted a job at he and his father's parts store in Scotts Valley. Dick and Wes Stipes turned out to be the best bosses I've ever had. We were family. Working for Coral Auto Parts has to be the highlight of my life. I blossomed there.

Wes and I shared season tickets for the Warriors basketball team in Oakland making countless runs to the games. They even won the NBA Championship one year. Great times.

I was at work one day. I had taken the garbage out and walked in through the back of the shop. Two suits were waiting for me.

"Michael McAndrew?"

"Yes."

"You're under arrest. You have the right to remain silent ... blah, blah, blah."

"What's this for!" I protested as they cuffed me.

"Draft resistance."

"What?"

They led me out to their car passed shocked customers and Dick and Wes. Once in the car they uncuffed me and took my pocket knife away. I sat in the back seat with one of the agents. The younger one apologized to me saying that they had better things to do than waste their time arresting draft resisters. I asked if I could smoke and he asked if he could bum one.

"Where are you taking me," I demanded.

"To the Magistrate in Monterey and then to Salinas to get printed and booked."

I guess Agent Riley had finally retired.

"Shouldn't you guys be out chasing bad guys? I thought we had a deal."

The agent with me just glared at me a moment. He remained silent.

We arrived at the Magistrates office. It was in the court house in Monterey. We had to wait in the hallway for an hour or so. The one agent kept smoking my cigarettes. What could I do. They cuffed me to a bench as I waited. The handcuffs hurt my wrists.

Finally, I was led into an office to meet the Magistrate. He was this large jovial gentleman.

"Mr. McAndrew please have a seat."

The cuffs were off. The phone rang. It was my wife, Julie. He calmed her down by consoling her with, "He'll be fine," and, "Oh, Don't worry Mrs. McAndrew, we'll take good care of him."

I could hear Julie's voice coming through the receiver. I couldn't hear the words but she was very upset.

"Mr. McAndrew, you have an impressive list of offenses here. The Agents are now going to take you to Salinas where you will be booked and printed. Are there any questions?"

I had a million questions but I couldn't think of any.

Re-handcuffed, I was lead out to the car. Un-handcuffed, we drove to Salinas. Twenty miles away.

Cuffed again I was led into the jail. The Agents handed me over to the jailer. The Agent took two more cigarettes, handed the jailer a pile of papers, told me to have a 'nice day,' and left.

They took my mug shot and printed me. I was led to a holding cell. There were about 10 other guys in there. They all spoke Spanish. The first thing they did was take my smokes. I was terrified! Menacing glares, I heard the word 'gringo' spoken several times. I isolated myself by sitting in a corner with my knees up against my body. I would be in this cell for many hours, most of the night. I had to piss and there was a single toilet for all these guys. No privacy. I peed and I heard snickers. Glad I didn't have to poop.

It was late at night. I don't know what time it was. Some of the guys were sleeping.

A bailiff came down the hall. He came to the cell door and called my name. Fuck. Now what?

He led me back to a desk after opening a series of locked doors. He gave me back my stuff. Wallet, the pocket knife, and opened the door. There sat my wife and her friend Sheila. I've never been so happy to see anyone in my life.

We fucking ran out of there and got into Sheila's car.

"Give me a smoke, would'ya. They took mine away."

I inhaled deeply.

Julie told me that my boss, Dick, had put his house up for bail. I had no intention to run anyway but this cinched it. I couldn't believe he would do that for me. He was a saint.

We eventually arrived back home in Santa Cruz. Sheila dropped us off. Julie said she was too upset to drive. That was nice of Sheila. We were both so wired that we couldn't sleep. Now what?

Julie told me she had called several attorneys in town and most referred her to Ray Gruenich, who had represented draft cases in the past.

I called Ray's office at ten. I told him about my predicament. He said he'd get back to me. I called Dick and he said I could take a few days off. It was 2 p.m. and I passed out. I was so tired.

The next morning Julie and I met with Ray. By this time he had a copy of the indictments in front of him. He was a tall gangly guy with a long red pony tail. I liked him immediately and hired him as my attorney after he told me that he had gone to the Supreme Court on two occasions representing draft cases. One case involved a client deprived of a CO (Conscientious Objector) hearing and the other case involved a client who was called ahead of the order. In other words, was drafted ahead of others. Exactly what had occurred with me!

He had a copy of the indictments and charges in front of him. 42 in all. One by one we went through them.

"Did you do this?"

"Yes."

"Did you do this"

"No."

And so forth.

We even found that I was in two places at once. The indictments were very specific with times and dates. This document was bogus. They were fishing.

We met several times over the next weeks. I returned to work. The word got out. Most people were very supportive. Some not. I was proud of what I'd done but had never spoke of it except to Julie. She knew. But it wasn't a big deal. It was like, 'oh you resisted the draft, cool.' And that was about it. No biggy.

Ray was a good lawyer. He found out that Minneapolis had a new federal prosecutor and he wanted to clean out all the 'old' files. He was unrelenting and agreed to none of our demands, including dropping the dual accusation.

Meanwhile, Jimmy Carter looked like a sure thing to be our next President. One of his campaign promises was to pardon the draft resisters, now numbering in six figures. That was great but what about the other 41 indictments. They had me for crossing State lines with weapons to dealing drugs to conspiracy charges to planning and participating in destroying Government property to aiding and abetting felons to crossing State lines to incite riot ... on and on. Ray told me they couldn't prove a thing.

Besides being in two places at once, my favorite was they claimed to have my footprint in the Draft Board in Wabasha. I never go barefoot. Never. And besides, I was never there.

Ray told me what to expect. A couple of months went by. I was scheduled for a hearing at the Federal Court House in St. Paul. It was late September.

The Presidential election was held in November. I had registered to vote and for the first time in my life I voted. I cast my vote and as I exited the polling booth I noticed a camera crew and a reporter from the Monterey TV station. She asked my if she could interview me. I said sure.

I had to fill in a form stating my name and address and stuff. The light went on and she asked who I voted for and I answered, "Carter", then she asked me why I voted for him instead of Ford and I answered by stating that Carter had promised to pardon all the draft resisters and that because of Watergate and Vietnam I felt the country needed a new direction blah, blah, blah.

I returned to work and finished my shift.

When I got home I told Julie that the Monterey TV station interviewed me after I voted and that I wanted to watch the news. The whole day was about the election results and lo and behold if I wasn't on TV for ten seconds. Pretty cool. The phone rang and some friends of ours had seen it too.

Walter and the *CBS News* followed and I had planned to stay glued to the TV all night. My very future hinged on this election. I believed Carter would do what he had promised.

About ten minutes into the evening news *CBS* had several people who had been interviewed this day and I was on that too. I couldn't believe it. I was on *CBS News* with Walter. The phone rang, it was my mom. "I saw you on TV." Then another phone call. Several before the night was over. They announced that Jimmy Carter won before our election polls in California were closed.

It was a great day!

I had to be in St. Paul next week. In the meantime, I called Jeff and he offered to represent me in St. Paul pro bono. I hadn't seen him in a few years so it would be nice to see him.

Ray was doing everything he could to keep me out of jail, but the Federal DA was holding firm. No deal!

I resigned myself to the fact that I was going to jail for awhile until my trial. I was pleading not guilty to all charges. The ones that I actually committed I knew they couldn't possibly prove. No evidence, just hearsay. Anyway, Julie drove me to the airport in San Jose for the flight to Minneapolis. I had $50, no change of clothes, not even a warm coat. I was going to jail for at least a few months. Julie and I kissed and hugged each other. She was crying.

I got on the plane by myself,

Arrived in Minneapolis. Late November 1976. Took a cab to my friend Kathy's house. An old Winona friend who offered me a place to stay for the night. My hearing was 9 a.m. tomorrow. Kathy and I walked down the street to a bar and had a few beers. I slept on the couch that night. Don't think I really slept at all. I was so scared.

I called a cab at 7:30 and got to the court house with time to spare. A huge foreboding place. With statues and inscriptions reminding us of justice. Yeah, right.

I had called Jeff last night and he told me where to wait for him. There he was. We hugged and quickly got up to speed on my case. I was basically fucked. I had the worst judge you could have. He had sentenced dozens of draft resisters to the maximum five year sentence. But, this was a pre-trial hearing. This judge was expected to put me in jail until a bail hearing. Could take two or three months.

As we were talking the DA walked up.

"Ah, Mr. McAndrew. So nice you could make it."

"Fuck you," I said refusing to shake his hand or stand up.

Jeff tried to apologize for his clients behavior. It didn't fly.

I really didn't care at this point. The pompous ass was way out of line. Getting votes was more important to him than seeking justice.

Jeff led me into the courtroom itself. There was a sentencing case going on as we waited. The judge looked like a mean Jimmy Stewart who sat way up high behind this huge panel of wood. He was really scary looking. Before him stood an Indian boy who had been found guilty of murdering and raping a girl on the Reservation. He was just a boy. People were crying. He slammed his mallet down like thunder from God and pronounced, 'Life without parole.'

A pause.

Sobbing people walked out of the court room as the shackled prisoner was led out.

Next case.

Jeff and I walked to a podium.

"The United States of America vs. Michael Patrick McAndrew."

My knees were shaking so hard I had to hold on to the podium. I really thought I was going to fall down.

The bailiff read all of the counts on the indictment.

When he finished the judge looked at me and said,'How do you plead?"

Before I could answer the DA spoke citing that since Jimmy Carter was President-elect and that he was going to pardon the draft resisters that it might be best to wait until after the Inauguration. We expected that but then the bomb. The DA was willing to drop the rest of the charges based on no or little evidence. At first I didn't get it. The judge looked at me with pure hatred. He reluctantly dismissed 41 counts and delayed any action on the draft issues. I was free to go!

"Thank you, your Honor."

I walked over to the DA and apologized for telling him to go fuck himself. He just nodded.

'Fuck you, anyway, man,' I said to myself. Julie and I had spent every dime we had on legal fees and on the flight. But I was free to go. One problem. I had almost no money, no clothes. Jeff said I could stay with him and that he would book a flight and I could pay him back.

We started walking out of the court house and there appeared to be a TV crew and a bunch of reporters out on the steps.

'Must be a big trial going on,' I thought.

We opened the doors and I felt like I was being attacked. A mic popped in front of me and flashbulbs were going off.

Jeff nudged me aside and did the talking. He told them what had happened inside but added that the draft case was still pending. He said that they didn't have a case because the Draft Board in Winona had called my name out of order, they called me ahead of others, and that I had not had a CO hearing which violated their own rules.

As Jeff was talking a reporter asked me 'How it felt to be the last active draft case.' "Really?" I guess I mumbled some other stuff because it appeared in the paper the next day. The tone of the article seemed to favor me and put a hard light on the DA for wasting tax payers money. He really was a dick.

Jeff and I finally broke free. All I wanted to do was call Julie. We got to his office and I called her. She was ecstatic. "I'll call you later when I get the flight schedule." Jeff called Ray in Santa Cruz on another phone and gave him the news. I called Emil and told him to call Mom and Dad. I kept the phone calls short because I had so many calls to make. I even called friends in San Francisco. Everyone was thrilled!

A reporter for the *Star-Tribune* called and Jeff talked to him. I didn't want to talk to the press. I wanted to shrink back into a corner.

I was in shock. One minute, I'm going to jail and the next ...

I recall when I saw Julie at the airport that both of us had tears in our eyes.

I got quite a reception when I returned to Santa Cruz. Julie and I invited several of our friends over for a party.

The *Santa Cruz Sentinel* did a small story on me. I had shunned publicity all these years and now it fucking rained attention. I really didn't like it. I went back to work. I had to pay Ray for his attorney fees. He didn't charge me hardly, only about $800 as I recall. A mere pittance of what he could have billed.

I guess all we could do was wait for Carter to make his move. January 20, 1977 in the second paragraph of his Inaugural Speech, Jimmy Carter pardoned the draft resisters.

And that was that!

Several weeks later I received a letter from the White House.

It was a letter giving me a pardon signed by Jimmy Carter. I turned the letter over and the paper was dented on his signature. He had hand-signed it!

This called for a party. Julie and I gathered the tribe and we had a big bash. Everybody in Santa Cruz was there. I called attention to the letter and passed it around. Everyone had a chance to hold and read it.

I asked for the letter. Held it up for everyone to see, took out a lighter, and burned it.

A symbolic act completing the cycle. I had burned my draft card way back when. Seemed only fitting.

Addendum

Several months later I received a package in the mail. It was a ring made by Mark in prison. I remembered once when he measured my ring finger. At the time I thought it odd but ...

It was an Egyptian Blood Stone set in a silver setting. I wear it to this day.

I eventually found out that three FBI Agents had set him up with the pot. Mark was later released from prison.

Acknowledgements

Anyone who has known me for thirty years or less is aware that I've been threatening to write this book for a long time. My excuses were; working too much, raising a son, no time, etc.

Sometime around December in 2012 a friend of mine, after listening to me rant and rave about one of these escapades, said, "You should write a book!"

So I did. Writing every day for eight months. Crawling along with this tale. I didn't know where to start so I started at the beginning. I realized early on that I couldn't accurately recall every day from forty years ago. Robin Williams was right: "If you remember the 60's you weren't there."

Well, I was there and I do remember a few things.

As I mentioned in the Prologue, several of these characters are a combination of people. Many of the people I dealt with didn't use their real names anyway.

But, I digress. I want to thank the following for their encouragement, support, tips and ideas, and patience. I couldn't have written this without them.

Cody McAndrew, my son and biggest fan.

Charlie Letterhos, my 8th grade teacher, wherever you are, who opened me up and allowed me to blossom.

My grandparents, Florence and Emil Mally (both deceased), the two most loving people I've ever known.

My parents, both deceased, who (somehow) nourished a liberal and learning environment.

For Emil, deceased, my younger brother, who always supported me.

The rest of my siblings, John, Mary, Becky, Paul, and Patrick (Casey) who will always have a place in my heart.

Michael Hale for the magnificent cover art and encouragement.

Mary Bradley (a real writer) who urged me on and did a magnificent job editing the book.

John Baker who inspired me with his book, 'The Green and The Blonde.'

The Internet. It saved countless hours of research.

To the people who read excerpts and offered suggestions:
John Baker, Mary Bradley, Maz Hale, Brian Koser, and Cody McAndrew.

Thank you!

Peace!

self-portrait

Mike McAndrew is a retired photo journalist
living in Port Townsend, Washington.